# THE CHISHOLM TRAIL

*Public Lands History*

GENERAL EDITORS

Ruth Alexander
Mark Fiege
Adrian Howkins
Janet Ore
Jared Orsi
Sarah Payne

# The Chisholm Trail
*Joseph McCoy's Great Gamble*

JAMES E. SHEROW

*Foreword by* JAMES P. RONDA

UNIVERSITY OF OKLAHOMA PRESS : NORMAN

This book is published with the generous assistance of the Wallace C. Thompson Endowment Fund, University of Oklahoma Foundation.

LIBRARY OF CONGRESS CATALOGING-IN-PUBLICATION DATA

Names: Sherow, James Earl, author. | Ronda, James P., 1943– writer of foreword.
Title: The Chisholm Trail : Joseph McCoy's great gamble / James E. Sherow ; foreword by James P. Ronda.
Other titles: Public lands history ; v. 3.
Description: Norman, OK : University of Oklahoma Press, [2018] | Series: Public lands history ; volume 3 | Includes bibliographical references and index.
Identifiers: LCCN 2018005483 | ISBN 978-0-8061-6053-5 (hardcover)
ISBN 978-0-8061-9555-4 (paper)
Subjects: LCSH: McCoy, Joseph G. (Joseph Geiting), 1837-1915. | Cattle trade—United States—History. | Cattle trails—United States—History. | Chisholm Trail—History.
Classification: LCC HD9433.U52 S54 2018 | DDC 381/.413620097809034—dc23
LC record available at https://lccn.loc.gov/2018005483

*The Chisholm Trail: Joseph McCoy's Great Gamble* is Volume 3 in the Public Lands History series.

The paper in this book meets the guidelines for permanence and durability of the Committee on Production Guidelines for Book Longevity of the Council on Library Resources, Inc. ∞

Copyright © 2018 by the University of Oklahoma Press, Norman, Publishing Division of the University. Paperback published 2024. Manufactured in the U.S.A.

All rights reserved. No part of this publication may be reproduced, stored in a retrieval system, or transmitted, in any form or by any means, electronic, mechanical, photocopying, recording, or otherwise—except as permitted under Section 107 or 108 of the United States Copyright Act—without the prior written permission of the University of Oklahoma Press. To request permission to reproduce selections from this book, write to Permissions, University of Oklahoma Press, 2800 Venture Drive, Norman OK 73069, or email rights.oupress@ou.edu.

*To the memory of my mentors*
William Unrau
*and*
H. Lee Scamahorn

# Contents

List of Illustrations  **ix**

Foreword, by James P. Ronda  **xiii**

Preface: *Putting Your String on Her*  **xvii**

Acknowledgments  **xix**

Introduction: Joseph McCoy's Great Gamble  **3**
1. The Smell of Money: Texas Cattle down Fifth Avenue, New York City, in 1866  **13**
2. Trails' Ends  **30**
3. Why Abilene, Kansas?  **46**
4. A Trail Is Formed  **84**
5. The Seasonal Round  **112**
6. Tick, Tick, Tick  **141**
7. Confronting Fire and Ice  **191**
8. Indian Cattle Travails  **212**
9. The End of the Trail  **250**

    Conclusion: Shifting Trails  **278**

Appendix: Explanation of Weather Statistics  **287**

Notes  **293**

Selected Sources  **317**

Index  **329**

# Illustrations

*Figures*

1. Joseph McCoy  66
2. Sarah McCoy  67
3. Washington Market, New York City, 1866  68
4. "Cattle Driving in the Streets—Who Cares for Old Women and Small Children?"  69
5. Joseph and James McCoy  70
6. Front cover of menu-cookbook *The Epicurean*  71
7. Freight train of livestock  72
8. Henry Bergh  72
9. View of Communipaw Abattoirs  73
10. Chicago Union Stockyards, 1868  73
11. John Tracey Alexander  74
12. Timothy and Eliza Hersey  75
13. Drovers Cottage, Abilene, Kansas, 1867  76
14. Lou Gore  77
15. Great Western Stock Yards, 1867  78
16. The Steamship *Victoria*  78
17. James Daugherty flogging  79
18. Black Beaver  80
19. Jesse Chisholm  81
20. Territorial survey map, Sumner County, Kansas, 1871  82
21. Loading cattle at Abilene  83

22. "Abilene in Its Glory"  **83**

23. "The Texas Cattle Trade"  **172**

24. Fort Hays, Kansas, 1873  **173**

25. "The Cattle Plague"  **174**

26. Loading bison  **175**

27. Loading cattle onto a Mississippi riverboat  **176**

28. Theobald Smith  **177**

29. Cowboys fight a prairie fire  **178**

30. "Wintering on Hay in Central Kansas"  **179**

31. "Stampede of a Herd of Cattle"  **180**

32. Cattle fording the Arkansas River, 1869  **181**

33. Amanda Burks  **182**

34. Dennis Bushyhead  **183**

35. David Payne  **184**

36. Surveying Sedgwick County, Kansas, 1867  **185**

37. First Santa Fe depot, Wichita, Kansas, 1877  **186**

38. Cattle on a boat  **187**

39. "American Beef for Old England"  **188**

40. "First National Convention of Cattlemen at St. Louis," 1884  **189**

41. "The Cattle Industry of Chicago," 1889  **190**

42. Meteorological register, Fort Richardson, Texas, July 1875  **288**

*Maps* (Cartography by Erin Greb)

Trail System of the Eastern Continental Cattle Trade  **21**

Trail System of the Trans-Mississippi Cattle Trade  **116**

Cattle Trade Network in Indian Territory  **215**

## Charts

1. Cattle Driven North out of Texas Compared to Cattle Received into New York City, 1866–1884   **22**
2. Beeves Sold at Allerton's, Week Ending November 18, 1867   **22**
3. Beeves Received into the New York City Market, Week Ending August 18, 1868   **24**
4. Beeves Received at Jersey City, January 5–6, 1885   **24**
5. Temperature Range, Fort Hays and Fort Riley, Kansas, November 1871   **205**
6. Temperature Range, Fort Hays and Fort Riley, Kansas, December 1871   **205**
7. Temperature Range, Fort Hays and Fort Riley, Kansas, January 1872   **205**
8. Range of Average Monthly Temperatures, Fort Richardson, Texas, March 1868–May 1878   **291**

## Tables

1. Estimated Profits in the Texas Cattle Trade, 1870   **136**
2. Sample and Averages from Meteorological Register, Fort Richardson, Texas   **289**
3. Wind Speed Scale   **289**
4. Cloudiness Scale   **289**
5. July Temperatures, Fort Richardson, 1868–1877   **289**

# Foreword

The foreword to a book does not usually carry a title. This one should. The title ought to be "Connections and Consequences." James Sherow's book is really all about the widespread and varied connections between the cattle trade as represented by the Chisholm Trail, the life of Joseph McCoy, and the wider world. These were connections that had consequences for the land itself and for people far from the trail. In a sense I see this book as a response to a single line from E. M. Forster's classic novel *Howards End*. The line is: "Only connect."

To appreciate the magnitude of what Sherow has accomplished, it is worth recalling a map that can be found in virtually every American history textbook. This is the map usually titled "Western Cattle Trails." It shows a series of thin lines running north from Texas, crossing the Red River, heading to such Kansas cattle towns and railheads as Caldwell, Newton, Ellsworth, and Abilene, and perhaps ending at Ogallala on the Platte River. In this map—and in text that sometimes accompanies it—trails are depicted as narrow passageways. The trail narrative is confined by the edges of the route. What is important in that vision of trail and cattle trade history is the "drive" itself. This is a story with a small cast of characters acting parts brief in time and limited in meaning and influence. Perhaps that version got its earliest and most compelling expressions in print with Andy Adams's *Log of a Cowboy* (1903), Emerson Hough's *The Story of the Cowboy* (1908), and J. Marvin Hunter's *The Trail Drivers of Texas* (1925). Hough's subsequent novel *North of 36* (1923) was the basis for one of the earliest cattle drive movies. The long-drive story remains alive and well in its many print and visual expressions. The image of the trail as tunnel can also be seen in writing about American rivers, exploration routes, railroads, and highways. The Rivers of America series is a good example. The Potomac, the Ohio, and the Missouri were portrayed as passages whose life is bounded by riverbanks. The shelves groan with railroad company histories that never get beyond miles of track laid and freight carried. This conceptual framework has had an iron grip on writing about cattle trails for a long time. That Sherow has broken that grip—or at the very least demonstrated how it can be considerably weakened by expanding the view nationally or even internationally—is a measure of his accomplishment.

This is a daring book. Any book with a title that includes Chisholm Trail and Joseph McCoy, yet begins at the New York City cattle markets and pays close attention to matters of health and sanitation in that city before moving on to the life cycle of a particular tick and the development of refrigeration, is a daring approach. A book that treats federal Indian policy, arguments about grassland fires, and changes in the national diet is daring as well. Sherow has done all this. He has taken the trail and Joseph McCoy as vantage points—jumping off places—from which to explore a set of landscapes far beyond the confines of the trail itself. I use the word "landscape" intentionally here because I mean—and I think Sherow means—that the trail both exemplified and promoted change of all sorts. "Landscape" is about change as a result of human agency. We are misled by the static views inherent in so-called "landscape" painting. Some might call this "contextualization." I'd call what Sherow has done an expansion of the historical imagination. Think again about that textbook map. Sherow has moved from line to region, from region to continent, and from continent to something very nearly global. To put it another way, the trail line has become a complex, multilayered narrative of connections and consequences, an ecological drama played out on a large stage with an expanded cast of characters.

To fully grasp what Sherow has done, it is worth pausing for a moment to place this book in company with others that emphasize connections rather than boundaries, expansive areas rather than small spaces. These are books that make the land itself both a document and an actor in the play. John Stilgoe's *Metropolitan Corridor: Railroads and the American Scene* is a good example of just that. Stilgoe's book begins with rail lines and then expands the story beyond the roadbed to grain elevators, small town depots, and big-city electric generators. D. W. Meinig's *The Great Columbia Plain* does that for the Columbia, the River of the West. Meinig's story quickly moves beyond the river's banks to the wheat fields of the Palouse country and irrigation projects in the Yakima Valley. Once again line becomes area; connections are what counts. I think it is important to recognize that both Stilgoe and Meinig are historical geographers who have thought carefully about relationships between time, space, and the built environment. The expansion of area and the reach of connections is plain in Alan

Taylor's *American Colonies*. That book begins long before the arrival of Europeans and concludes not with the American Revolution but in the Pacific Northwest in the first years of the nineteenth century. Taylor changes the narrative, expands the chronology, and breaks the geographic determinism that has long dominated the writing of Early American history. I see that same expansion of narrative in William Cronon's *Nature's Metropolis: Chicago and the Great West*. What Sherow's book has in common with these books is this: a broad vision of the past set in a sure sense of place and informed by a remarkable command of the sources. And it certainly helps to tell the kind of good story Sherow has to offer. One of the best ways to see this is to look at chapter 4 under "Knitting the Elements Together," Sherow's remarkably synoptic treatment of climate, grass, water, geography, and technology. That portion of the book alone is worth the price of admission.

The sense of enlargement pervades Sherow's work, both here and elsewhere. He makes that clear in his cast of characters. There are trail drivers, of course, including my favorite—G. O. Burrows, a cowboy from Del Rio, Texas. Burrows knew there was no romance in the hard work on the long drive. As he recalled: "I put in eighteen or twenty years on the trail, and all I had in the final outcome was the high-heeled boots, the striped pants, and about $4.80 worth of other clothes, so there you are." But Sherow's book is also filled with hotel owners, real estate developers, Indian chiefs and tribal councils, state and local politicians, railroaders of all sorts, and whole grange halls of farmers. McCoy is always in the story but he is not *the* story. Again, Sherow has a keen sense of place and he makes clear the difference between nature and landscape. His discussion of the natural world is enlivened by such insights as describing grass as "stored solar energy." In all of this, what Sherow is getting at is landscape transformation. Writers like J. B. Jackson and John Stilgoe describe landscape as "the surface of the earth people shaped and shape deliberately for permanent purposes." Sherow's trail as "a transitional ecosystem" changed not just the lay of the land and texture of the terrain but what human beings did on and with that land. What Sherow reveals is a built environment that spreads out from the trail. Here are town sites, general stores, stockyards, farmsteads, railroad structures, plowed fields, fenced pastures, and crowded city streets. Sherow then traces the connections between places like San Antonio and London, Abilene, and Paris (France, not Texas). These connections link together the lives of cowboys, bankers, locomotive engineers, slaughterhouse workers, and waiters at Delmonico's. Black Beaver's remarkable life as a Delaware

Indian scout and rancher is connected to Jackson Schultz trying to deal with the consequences of large-scale animal slaughtering in an urban setting. What might seem at first glance to be the story of one famous trail and one remarkable, even emblematic character becomes something far larger and far more consequential. We all try to find ways to enter and explore a deeper, richer past. James Sherow has found that path into the past with a trail and one life that leads to many places and many lives.

James P. Ronda

# Preface
*Putting Your String on Her*

When a ranch hand roped a cow, they often called it "putting your string on her." For some time now I have been trying to "put my own string" on the history of the Texas cattle trade. The story of the famous Chisholm Trail has been told many times before in history, fiction, and film. Doing a new version of this larger-than-life American tale runs the risk of taking "a dolly welter"—that is, throwing my lasso around this cow story without fixing the rope to my saddle, flying off my horse, and falling flat on the ground.[1]

I've been wooing this story for some time now. In the spring of 1995, Professor William Unrau of Wichita State University invited me to give a presentation on some aspect of the Chisholm Trail. I titled the piece that I gave during the Old Cowtown Chisholm Trail Symposium "The Chisholm Trail as Historical Environment." This started me on the trail.

I "took a little more hair off the dog" in 1998. The "big boss," Char Miller, invited a group of us "waddies" to San Antonio for a conference on water.[2] This gave me a chance to float my ideas about the Chisholm Trail to a group of first-class scholars. The big boss decided that I knew "dung from wild honey" and offered to publish my piece in a collection of book chapters authored by other notable participants. The chapter appeared as "Water, Sun, and Cattle: The Chisholm Trail as an Ephemeral Ecosystem," in *Fluid Arguments: Five Centuries of Western Water Conflict* (2001).

Maybe in some places it might seem that "I ain't got any medicine."[3] I'm not an ecologist or a rancher by training or profession, but I have taken steps to ensure that the ecological material in this work is as accurate as I can make it. It helps to have experts in grassland ecology right on your doorstep, as I do here at Kansas State University.

In 2001, Jeffrey Stine, Curator of the Division of Medicine and Science in the National Museum of American History in Washington, D.C., made it possible for me to pursue additional research on the cattle industry through a short-term

Smithsonian Institute Fellowship. The fellowship opened additional avenues to explore, especially the vast urban beef market that emerged in the post–Civil War era. As I plodded along with this project, former K-State President Jon Wefald introduced me to a Chisholm Trail enthusiast in 2008. That was when I met Ken Selzer, who provided research funding to further my work. Ken, who currently serves as the Kansas Insurance Commissioner, has been, and continues to be, a strong supporter of my work.

From 2007 to 2013, I got sidetracked while serving as a city commissioner and mayor and then doing something Bonnie, my wife, regarded as "as dangerous as walkin' quicksand over hell":[4] I ran for Congress, with the results one should expect when traipsing over quicksand. Once I got politicking out of my system, which is like finally having enough sense to let go of the hot end of a branding iron,[5] I returned to my university office to find this story of the Chisholm Trail waiting to be finished.

In the spring of 2016, I met Mark Fiege, an environmental historian who, as a Texas cowboy might describe him, is "wise as a tree full of owls." Mark took a keen interest in this work and, as a general editor of the Public Lands History series, thought my work on Joseph McCoy and the Chisholm Trail would make a good contribution. He met with the Editor in Chief of the press, Chuck Rankin, who has "gotten more wrinkles on his horns."[6] Soon I found myself with a book contract and two fine editors who were always quick to ask me to "cut the deck a little deeper" when they wanted a better explanation or warned me to "cinch up a little, yo' saddle's slippin'" when I was making a careless mistake.[7]

Now I have come to the end of the trail for telling this story. I must point out that I am responsible for any of the whoppers in this book, anywhere it is apparent that I know as much about my subject as "a hog does about a side saddle."[8] Still, I have "cut a rusty" in telling this story.[9] So, dear readers, "tie your hats to the saddle and let's ride"; we're going up the Chisholm Trail in a new way.

# Acknowledgments

It nearly sounds clichéd, too commonplace, for an author to write that his or her work is more than a sole endeavor, that it is a team effort. Yet that's the case; a work like this one represents far more than my thoughts or research. I am fortunate to have had the invaluable research assistance and critical reading of this work by a number of people.

Like a good herder leads cattle to water, Professor William Unrau led me to this topic in 1995. Unrau was known as one of the foremost historians of Indians, Kansas, and the American West. As an undergraduate and master's student at Wichita State University, I was fortunate to have Unrau as a mentor. He followed my career as it led me to my current position at Kansas State University, where I have worked since 1992. I just regret that Unrau is not alive today to see what he had put into motion.

I owe a great debt to Char Miller, one of the most gifted environmental historians around, who encouraged my first publishing on this topic. Char introduced me to Jeffrey Stine, curator of the Division of Medicine and Science in the National Museum of American History in Washington, D.C., who took an interest in my work, and furthered it along by supporting a summer fellowship for me at the Smithsonian Museum of American History in 2001. Stine has read every page of this work, and his insights have been invaluable. Ken Selzer has enthusiastically supported my research and writing that has led to this book. Selzer, like Stine, has read every page of this work in manuscript, and his comments have helped me make this a more readable work.

Two other people, Professor Derek Hoff and Connie Oehring, have read this work completely while in draft. Their critical abilities, acute sense of clear writing, and keen editorial eyes have strengthened this work beyond measure. Joshua Specht, a rising star among young environmental historians, has also read the manuscript in its entirety and has helped me chart new paths toward understanding the Texas cattle trade. James Ronda, a dean among historians of the American West, provided insightful, constructive criticism that immensely improved my work.

Michael Hook, the director of the Convention and Visitors Bureau in Abilene, Kansas, has also read this work page by page. He has assisted me considerably in crafting readable, storytelling prose. In the same vein, Fergus Bordewich and Thom Marshall both read early versions of this work and pointed out how I could cast the story more vibrantly. Virgil Dean, the leading authority on Kansas history, has also read, and helped me improve, portions of this work. Professors John Briggs and David Hartnett, nationally recognized ecologists who work on Konza Biological Research Station, a tallgrass prairie preserve (one of the Long Term Ecological Research sites funded by the National Science Foundation) have read portions of this work and have helped guide my understanding of the amazing ecology of the grasslands. Briggs currently is the director of Konza Prairie.

Over the years, I have been assisted by a number of gifted graduate and undergraduate research assistants. Early on, Micah Lewis and Whitney Grande combed historic Kansas newspapers. More recently, Brittany Tanner diligently compiled large amounts of weather data reflected in this work. Kenneth Smith located many of the illustrations found in the pages of this book.

The staffs at several archives made researching this book much easier. Patricia Michaelis, who has just recently retired, made my research easy in the Kansas Historical Society's archives. Mary Nelson was invaluable in helping me navigate Special Collections and University Archives at Wichita State University. Maryjo McAndrew, the Senior Archive Assistant at Knox College, Galesburg, Illinois, made copies of Joseph McCoy's academic record for me. James R. Akerman ably helped me with finding maps in the Newberry Library in Chicago, Illinois. The staffs at the Center for American History at the University of Texas, Austin, and the Oklahoma Historical Society Research Center in Oklahoma City aided me in researching their holdings on the Chisholm Trail.

Katie Dziminski and Terre Heydari at the DeGolyer Library at Southern Methodist University, Kathy Lafferty at the Spencer Research Library at the University of Kansas, Thomas Lisanti at the New York City Public Library, Rachel Mosman at the Oklahoma Historical Society, Hillary Peppers at the Jacksonville Library in Illinois, and Nancy Sherbert at the Kansas Historical Society were exceptional in helping me locate and acquire many of the illustrations. I was also fortunate to have Erin Greb produce the illuminating maps that grace this work.

Any work over twenty years in the making will have snippets and portions of it showing up in previous publications. My first attempt to make sense of the cattle trade appeared as a chapter, "Water, Sun, and Cattle: The Chisholm Trail as an Ephemeral Ecosystem," in Char Miller's edited anthology, *Fluid Arguments: Five Centuries of Western Water Conflict* (2001). A second article, "Why Abilene," appeared in a special sesquicentennial celebration of the Chisholm Trail in the summer 2017 issue of *Kansas History: A Journal of the Central Plains*. Earlier versions of my work on grassland ecology appeared in my *Grasslands of the United States: An Environmental History* (2007), and an earlier depiction of Alexander Gardner appeared in my and John Charlton's *Railroad Empire Across the Heartland: Rephotographing Alexander Gardner's Westward Journey* (2014).

A special thanks go to both my series editor and my University of Oklahoma Press editor. Mark Fiege and Charles Rankin have been a source of encouragement, inspiration, and constructive criticism. It has been an immense pleasure to work with both of them. Also, I want to recognize several folks at the press who helped me avoid having my writing sound as if it had been done by an elephant using a keyboard. For possessing this exceptional ability, I want to thank Steven Baker, managing editor; Bethany Mowry, editorial assistant; and especially my press copy editor, Kerin Tate.

In many ways, Bonnie Lynn-Sherow should appear first and foremost in this acknowledgment. I have probably wearied her more with tales of Joseph McCoy and Texas cattle than she ever expected to hear in one lifetime. I hope she is none the worse for the ordeal. I am the most fortunate man alive to have her as my colleague, my champion, my sharpest and most insightful critic, my soulmate, the love of my life.

# THE CHISHOLM TRAIL

INTRODUCTION
# Joseph McCoy's Great Gamble

In January 1899, delegates representing nearly every aspect of the livestock industry in the United States and its territories took their seats in the auditorium of the magnificent Tabor Grand Opera House in Denver, Colorado, to attend the second annual convention of the National Live Stock Association. On the first day of the gathering, January 24, during the Tuesday afternoon session, sixty-one-year-old Joseph Geiting McCoy took the stage to report on the condition of the livestock industry in Kansas. Everyone in attendance knew Joseph McCoy as the man who had blazed the Chisholm Trail for the great cattle markets of the United States,[1] the man who had seeded "cattle to replace the buffalo on the vast plains." When McCoy spoke, people paid attention.[2]

McCoy proudly touted the Kansas livestock market, valued at $116 million in 1898, as ranked second in the world. Eliciting uproarious laughter from the audience, McCoy quipped that this was "actually more money than I have in my pocket." This market, McCoy bragged, gave Texas cattle and ranges a value worth $40 to $50 million. It supplied ranchers in Colorado, Wyoming, and Montana with the cattle to stock their ranges. It provided the working classes in the great industrial cities of the Northeast with affordable beef. It offered ambitious people the means to become "cattle kings, and their wives and daughters queens." The end result? As McCoy saw it, Kansas originated the "grandest live stock market in the world . . . gave it a corporate existence, and sent to that market sufficient live stock to make it, as a corporation, exceedingly prosperous." McCoy, who always thought of himself as a stockman, took absolute pride in his accomplishments in creating the conditions and markets of Kansas that had given rise to the vast cattle

3

trade that flourished throughout the United States in 1899.³

McCoy was not oblivious to the role women played in developing the cattle trade. Kansas, he claimed, had "the most magnificent womanhood . . . of any other state in the Union." Perhaps he had in mind Sarah, his devoted wife, who shared in several of their economic ventures. Maybe he had in mind his two highly accomplished daughters. Mamie had been an acclaimed public school teacher in Wichita, Kansas, and later, after attending Worcester College of Domestic Science in Massachusetts, she became a domestic science professor. Or maybe it was his youngest daughter, Florence, an osteopathic physician who had her practice in Wichita. Whatever motivated McCoy's appreciation for women in their own right, he clearly celebrated women's abilities beyond those prescribed by the prevailing cult of domesticity.⁴

His sensibility probably explains why he took the opportunity to promote Lillian Gregory's illustrated magazine, *The Kings and Queens of the Range*. Gregory had been married to John F. Gregory, a stockman operating out of Kansas City. By one account, he "was unfortunate in his speculations," and when he died, he left Lillian "compelled to earn her living." In debt, she began publishing the magazine, in which she touted women, the "co- or silent partner of the great cattle industry." McCoy, to prove that Kansas indeed had the "most magnificent womanhood" of any state in the nation, offered as proof Gregory's magazine. Hers was "a literary production," he declared, "not exceeded either in taste or in art, by anything published in New York." Later, when Gregory addressed the delegates, she emphasized that women not only kept the "hearts and souls [of their husbands], but of your herds and larder; when you are away, she tends to your herds . . . [and] were she to leave, you would follow after, thus reversing the old saying, that 'Man came first and woman after.'" And not solely with McCoy, the delegates held Gregory in high regard, and demonstrated their admiration by awarding her with an honorary and lifetime membership in the organization.⁵

Still, McCoy made it clear, regardless of the importance of women to the trade, that it was *stockmen* who "always have led." He asked his receptive audience, Did God "go into the ranks of the bankers and their sons? Did he go into the ranks of merchants; into the ranks of the ship owners? Oh no!" McCoy especially added young men of leisure to this list of the unworthy. Did God "go out and hunt up any of those boys with a foot-ball head, a base-ball brain and a croquet muscle?" At this point, McCoy had the attendees in the palm of his hand. "Oh no!" an ebullient McCoy continued. "Did he go to look among those youths, those dudes, that dawdle on our street corners, ogling beauty when she walks forth to air herself and see the sunshine?"[6]

Just as McCoy was hitting his stride, his voice faltered, and he reached for a glass of water. As his Cuban cigar–smoking, Kentucky bourbon–drinking audience knew, Kansas had embraced prohibition in 1880. And this crowd also knew that the Democratic Party in Kansas was no friend to the temperance movement. So after McCoy took a swig, he jested, "Gentlemen. It is hard on a Kansas Democrat to make him drink water," which the audience greeted with applause and laughter.[7]

Now revived, McCoy declared "stockmen have been, from the beginning of early history, nature's uncrowned Knights of Navarro. They are the noblest of fathers, the most affectionate husbands, the most ardent of lovers, the best men. They are God's noblemen and God's chosen." McCoy was on a roll, but the chairman indicated that his time was up. Given the signal, McCoy asked the attendees, "And, gentlemen, are you not all glad of it?" Again, his jest was met with laughter and applause. The reason that the membership embraced McCoy so enthusiastically was that they, too, thoroughly valued the high social standing of the stockmen. McCoy, and the delegates, knew stockmen were not cowboys. Stockmen owned ranches teeming with massive herds of cattle, controlled the open range, raised and bred livestock, and sold and bought cattle, seeking to make a fortune in the trade. Cowboys worked for stockmen. Cowboys were hired labor, the herders.[8]

On the third day of the convention, during the afternoon session, M. A. Daugherty, a stockman and the leading delegate from Nebraska, took the stage to deliver a paper on railroads and stockmen. Before doing so, he asked for a special privilege to make a motion, which the president allowed. Daugherty followed by nominating Colonel Alexander Majors and Colonel Joseph McCoy as the first "honorary and life members" of the association, and his motion was quickly seconded. McCoy was deserving of this honor of a lifetime for his work and toil as a stockman, and for blazing the way so that others might follow and prosper in the cattle business, might "find ranges," as the president said, "might find homes, might find happiness in this great and boundless western country." Association president John W. Springer continued, saying of both McCoy and Majors that they "made the wilderness to bloom and blossom as the rose." He then called for a vote of the delegates signified by standing: seeing the vote, the president declared the proposition "unanimously carried."[9]

Of course, McCoy was asked to give a few remarks, which he was never at a loss to do. He cast his work as more than an "effort," defining it as "one mission." "I have," he asserted, "given myself to a service; 90 per cent of it contemplating benefits to mankind at large, and 10 per cent, possibly, to myself. Generally, the 10 per cent escaped and the 90 per cent the other fellow got." He hoped it would be said of him after death, "Old fellow, like the upper part of that horn, you poured out your energy and your capital, and your best thought, like the horn of Cornucopia, abundantly, although you are at the little end of the horn yourself." He asked that it might be said of him, "He was faithful." The delegates, moved by his humility, paid him tribute with prolonged applause.[10]

Everyone in attendance at the convention knew how Joseph McCoy and his older brothers, James and William, of Springfield, Illinois, had bet their collective fortunes on a little, shoddy way station known as Abilene, Kansas, in 1867. Instead of an endless horizon of prairie grasses, the trio saw a bustling outlet for hundreds of thousands of Texas cattle coming up the Chisholm Trail. The true terminus of the Chisholm Trail, however, was Fifth Avenue, New York City. Wealth awaited anyone who could corner the middleman role in this trade, and Joseph McCoy, the youngest of the brothers, took the gamble.

Like many investors in the cattle trade, McCoy banked on lady luck as he ignored or remained oblivious to the risks. The lure of wealth drew him toward supplying the burgeoning urban demands for beef despite the many forces roiling the cattle trade between 1867 and 1885. Texas cattle fever decimated domesticated herds, drawing fierce opposition from northern cattlemen to the presence of longhorns. Prairie fires, thunderstorms, blizzards, droughts, and floods lay beyond McCoy's control. He encountered unscrupulous railroad managers, stiff competition from other brokers, Indians who resented the appearance of longhorns consuming their grasslands, and farmers who preferred growing wheat to raising cattle. Despite the difficulties, McCoy's efforts spurred the growth of the modern beef economy.

Joseph McCoy referred to the cattle trade as a faro game. Faro was a favorite card game played by cattlemen and cowboys. A dealer, the banker, places one suit, usually spades, all thirteen cards, face up on a tabletop. The gamers gather around to place their bets by placing their chips on any of the faceup cards. Once these wagers are made, the banker takes a regular fifty-two-card deck, shuffles it, places it facedown, and begins the game by turning over the first card on the top. This card, called the "soda," has no bearing on the bets. The banker then turns over a second card, places it to his right, and then turns over a third card and places it to his left. The second card is called the "loser," and the third is called the "winner."

The way the game works is fairly simple. For example, let us imagine that a Texas cowboy places his chips on the jack of spades. When the banker shows the three of hearts as the soda, nothing happens. If the soda had been a jack, then the cowboy would have neither won nor lost on his gamble. The next card, the loser, turns up as the six of spades, and the cowboy's bet is still safe. The next card, the winner, is the ten of hearts, which means that the cowboy has neither won nor lost yet.

The banker again draws three cards, the soda, the loser, and the winner. Remember, the Texan still has chips worth $30, a month's worth of his salary from driving cattle to Abilene, on the jack of spades. Well, the soda is the ace of hearts. The cowboy breathes a sigh of relief. The loser, an ace of diamonds, causes a flourish of profanity from one of the other players, who had his chips on the ace of spades. It is the rank of the card that matters, not the suit. When the winner is shown, it is the jack of diamonds, and the cowboy gives out a yelp, as he has just doubled his earnings. At this point, the banker settles accounts with the winner and loser.

A faro player who could remember the cards played, and was good at counting, might have been able to tip the odds a bit in his favor. But the owners of the cattle-town saloons could also count on a little, or a lot, of alcohol befuddling the thinking of the players, which of course favored the banker! For those in the cattle faro game, like McCoy, no matter how well they counted the cards, when the bets were placed on cards showing mild temperatures and gentle rains, control of Texas fever, steady beef demands in rapidly growing cities, little loss of beef in transit, and free access to bountiful grasslands in the public domain, rather than turning up as *winners*, they could turn up as *losers*.

McCoy always thought the odds of playing the cattle faro game favored him. He understood that during the Civil War years, the Union Army had blocked Texans' access to northern and New Orleans cattle markets. As a result, the numbers of their free-ranging cattle herds multiplied on the vast mesquite rangelands. By the end of the war, as one prominent Texan put it, "a man was poorer in proportion to the number of cattle bearing his brand." This was not the case in

New York City, where butchers paid fifteen cents per pound for an animal that returned a mere five cents in Texas.

Between 1860 and 1865, the northern cities swelled, with New York becoming the largest by far. This urban population growth created a strong demand for beef. McCoy wagered on owning an outlet where Texas cattle could be bought for pennies per pound and then sold for dollars on the hoof in New York City. All that was needed was a safe outlet where milled cattle could be sold and bought and then transported eastward by rail. Like many investors in the cattle trade, however, he either ignored the risks, or obliviously discounted them too readily. McCoy never calculated the odds correctly because he could not control the forces that affected the trade between 1867 and 1885. A great many of these forces were ecological and beyond McCoy's control. Yet, despite several reversals, he set in motion the modern American beef economy.

McCoy understood one thing clearly: it was pointless to drive cattle to Abilene without the growth of urban markets. By 1866, the population of New York City had reached nearly one million. Along with this growth emerged a rising middle class that had a taste for high-quality beef and the means to buy it. The London market also became a powerful magnet attracting Texas cattle. But reaching these ultimate destinations, as McCoy would find, proved anything but a simple matter of shipping cattle in stock cars destined for the big cities.

The Texas cattle trade and drives depended on free and abundant natural resources found throughout the public domain. The sine qua non of the trade, water and grass, abounded throughout the region. It was essential that prairie grass, the stored solar energy fueling the trade, be free and unregulated. As McCoy fully realized, sustaining these natural resources made the cattle drives possible despite the risks, especially those posed by the spread of Texas fever.

The cultural values held by McCoy and fellow stockmen, and the physical forces they used in their environment to sustain these tenets, made humans as a species, *Homo sapiens*, a *keystone species* that shaped the ecosystems in which they lived. Not only did cattlemen extract the resources of the grasslands—the stored solar energy collected in the grasses, and the water from living streams—in the pursuit of certain well-defined economic goals, they simultaneously transformed the animal and plant compositions of the grassland biome. In short, the cultural values of stockmen worked as powerful ecological forces shaping the lay of the land.

McCoy, and like-minded stockmen who depended upon open-range cattle grazing and trail driving, however, found they had to adapt to, or overcome, other competing or destructive ecological forces in order to survive. Take for example, *Rhipicephalus annulatus*, a tick native to the warm climate of Texas that harbored a deadly protozoan. When the tick fed on a bovine host, this protozoan was released into the cow's bloodstream. Over generations of exposure, native Texas cattle had developed immunity to the protozoa, but northern cattle lacked this trait. Texas cattle carried the tick with them as they entered midwestern and East Coast markets, where the ticks found their way onto the hides of northern cattle. Once a protozoan found itself in its host's blood system, it invaded the red blood cells and multiplied to the point of rupturing the cell membranes, which in turn, released numerous "daughter parasites." The newly freed parasites sought other red blood cells to attack, and their spores multiplied again. This feeding frenzy resulted in internal bleeding and the rapid death of the infected animal.

Kansas farmers held vastly different cultural values than stockmen. The farmers set into motion forces creating ecosystems different from the ones that sustained cattle driving. In this light, growers had ample reason to fear the spread of Texas fever to their small domestic herds of shorthorn cattle. In 1860, while Kansas farm families struggled with searing drought, longhorns spread the fever to Kansas herds anywhere near where Texas cattle had been driven. Farmers demanded laws to prohibit the importation of Texas cattle into the state, and the legislature complied in 1861. The Civil War suspended the threat of Texas fever in Kansas, but it reappeared in 1866 as Texans, desperate to sell cattle into eastern markets, attempted cattle drives through portions of Kansas and Missouri. This time Kansans and Missourians responded with violence.

The Chisholm Trail traversed sparsely inhabited areas in 1866, and consequently McCoy's outlet at Abilene could sidestep furious farmers. So McCoy's gamble paid off for a while until Texas fever began striking down domestic herds in Illinois, Iowa, Pennsylvania, New Jersey, and New York. The pall of Texas fever hung over the trade, leading to quarantines and bans throughout the Midwest and East. In 1868, the Texas cattle markets plummeted in Chicago, Pittsburgh, St. Louis, and New York City. By the mid-1870s, London merchants were boycotting American hay, believing that Texas fever had its origins in the grass. McCoy spent a fortune on public relations to quell fears among East Coast consumers. He lobbied the Kansas and Illinois legislatures to modify their bans, and thereby prevented a total collapse of the trade. Yet the fever continued to shape the entire industry until Theobald Smith, a veterinarian working for the US Department of Agriculture, finally identified the cause of the disease and a cure for it in 1889, long past the end of the great cattle drives.

Ticks were not McCoy's only worry. Prairie fires also posed great risk to cattlemen. Recent ecological studies have shown how prairie fires are responsible for creating and sustaining the grasslands. Indians clearly understood this and used fire as a tool to create lush grasslands. In 1870, one observer called Indian fire practices "heroic farming. . . . The wild game of the country is his crop. Autumnal fires were his reapers, to aid in collecting and harvesting." In short, those prairie fires had created the grasslands that made the great cattle drives possible in the first place. Yet, understandably from their viewpoint, Texas drovers saw little if any good in prairie fires and worked to suppress them. Suppression, however, worked against their interests by creating a pathway for farmers to sow the region with domesticated grasses, which put an end to open-range grazing practices throughout much of the plains.

Moreover, had McCoy understood the global climatic forces arrayed against him, he might never have gambled on Abilene. Scholars have not fully explored the variability of the grassland climate's effect on shaping the great cattle drives despite abundant evidence. For example, McCoy encouraged cattlemen to *overwinter* cattle herds before placing them into eastern markets. Northern winters killed the ticks carrying Texas fever, and the cattle fattened quickly on spring prairie grasses. As a result, these fat longhorns stood first in line bound for eastern markets and fetched the highest prices of the season.

For McCoy and others, the practice of overwintering cattle worked if mild weather prevailed on the open rangeland. But the blizzards of 1871–72 proved just how risky this practice could be when perhaps as high as 90 percent of the cattle in some herds succumbed to cold and dehydration. Harsh winters also killed horses and cowboys working the herds and bankrupted buyers, drovers, and ranchers. Reconstructing the climate of the central grasslands from 1866 through 1885 puts the memories of men and women in the cattle trade into a more meaningful context—that of historical weather patterns. This analysis provides a better understanding of the conditions under which the cattle trade operated at any given time.

Scholars have also paid too little attention to the role Indians played in the trade. As McCoy downplayed the risks of overwintering cattle, he also advertised to Texas drovers that Indians posed little risk to cattle driving. He assumed that the Chisholm Trail cut an unimpeded path between reservation-bound tribes to the west and the "Five Civilized Nations" to the east. Tribes near the Chisholm Trail, however, understood the threat that longhorns posed to their ways of life, and the ecosystems that sustained it.

But there was no unified Indian response to the cattle business. The Osages, for example, established a toll structure for Texas drovers driving herds across their lands because Texas cattle, in essence, were consuming the fuel sources that powered Osage herds and that sustained the wildlife that the Osage people hunted. The tolls compensated for the loss of valuable grazing grounds. In some cases, Indians reacted with force to protect their grazing grounds. In 1870, Fort Sill post commander, Brevet Major General Benjamin H. Grierson, noted that the Kiowas were angry about the Texas cattle arriving "to eat up their grass." As a consequence, the Kiowa warrior Satanta and his followers exacted retribution by killing the Texas cattle being driven to Fort Sill.

The Five Civilized Nations had their own cattle herds that competed with Texas herds. In 1866, Cherokee drovers, for example, took a herd of two hundred beef cattle to supply Fort Larned, Kansas. Cattle buyers and sellers commonly referred to these beeves as "Cherokee cattle" regardless of which nation they came from. Because of the fear of Texas fever, however, the owners of these herds experienced the same difficulties in selling their cattle as did Texans.

Federal Indian agents were working to turn the western reservation tribes—the Kiowas, Comanches, Cheyennes, and Arapahos—into pastoral peoples. Complicating the agents' efforts, Indians killed Texas cattle, while Texans stole cattle from the reservations. The agents often found themselves asking the US Army to keep the peace or to retrieve stolen Indian cattle in Texas. At the same time, the need to feed reservation Indians created a huge market for Texas cattle. In short, Indian peoples played a major role creating and shaping cattle markets and the cattle trade, but the role they played was multifaceted.

By 1885, ecological, cultural, and technological factors pushed the trade from town to town until forces coalesced with enough combined power to put an end to it. By 1880, McCoy was working for the Census Bureau, enumerating the livestock industry that he had played such a prominent role in launching. The Chisholm Trail no longer served any need whatsoever, and large packing firms such as Swift and Armour had come to control and dominate the cattle trade.

McCoy, and his appreciative audience of stockmen in Denver, had transformed the American diet. At the same time, McCoy's outlet in Abilene had led to a revolution in cattle markets and unleashed ecological forces that transformed the sweeping grasslands of North America into the breadbasket of the world. In a way, this book is the story of cattle drives, gambling cattlemen, and prime rib served at Delmonico's. But it is also a story of connections that bound McCoy's adventures in the cattle trade to the ecological, technological, and economic linkages wrought by the trade he initiated in 1867.

CHAPTER I

# The Smell of Money
*Texas Cattle down Fifth Avenue, New York City, in 1866*

WASHINGTON MARKET RAISES A STINK — THE SAMUEL ALLERTON PROTOTYPE —
THE ILLINOIS CONNECTION — CATTLE HEALTH AND MARKETS

In 1866, thousands of pedestrians crowding Lower Manhattan in New York City considered the smell of cattle manure wafting off the streets nothing less than a wretched stench. But cattle buyers and sellers like William McCoy breathed it in as a sweet fragrance, one that filled the air with the "smell of money." He and his brothers, James and Joseph, operated a profitable cattle buying-and-selling business in Springfield, Illinois—by some accounts, one of the largest such businesses in the country. New York, with its nearly one million people, offered aggressive and ambitious businessmen like the McCoy brothers an opportunity to play the nation's largest and best cattle market. William, the eldest of the three, conducted the Chicago and New York City side of the family business while his brothers stayed in Illinois.

McCoy smelled more than money as he made his way to Washington Market, the public outlet where vendors sold vegetables, fruits, and meat. On the way he could have passed some 180 slaughter-butcher shops clustered within a one-mile radius of Canal Street. Crowded into the same area, people lived in some of the worst tenement housing in the nation. The Seventeenth Ward held 95,000 people with about 64,000 of them crammed into 1,890 tenement houses. Over 150 of these rickety three- to five-story dwellings lacked any kind of toilets or sewer connections, and about 2,500 people lived in their dank, dark cellars. Altogether, at least half the population of New York City lived in tenement houses in 1866.[1] These same impoverished men and women made up the majority of the consumers to whom W. K. McCoy and Brothers hoped to sell the meat cut from Texas longhorns.

## Washington Market Raises a Stink

Cuts of beef from the cattle that McCoy sold reached four public city markets—Catharine, Fulton, Franklin, and Washington.[2] In 1813, New Jersey farmers had built the first, Washington Market, a large red brick pavilion where they could sell dairy and eggs to the growing population of New York City. The streets of Barclay, Vesey, and Fulton all led to Washington Market on the waterfront of the North River (now Hudson River). Every day, throngs of buyers stood nearly shoulder to shoulder buying most of the food eaten in the city.[3]

Washington Market failed utterly to merit a seal of approval from the Metropolitan Board of Health. As bemoaned in the *New York Tribune* in January 1867, the place had "within a few years been twice indicted by the Grand Jury as a public nuisance," and the reporter believed the other three markets deserved the same denunciation. From the time it was built, few improvements had been made to the Washington Market structure aside from wooden stalls extended from its brick core. As one writer would describe it later in 1877, the structure was not "worthy of the extent of business done or deserving of praise on economic or sanitarian grounds." Yet inside hung "avenues with crimson drapery—the best of beef in prodigious quarters," all made possible by cattle dealers like McCoy.[4]

While William McCoy might have smelled the money, he also contributed to one of the rankest urban environments in North America. For most New Yorkers the streets did an excellent job of covering the scent of the money. The city thoroughfares stank and posed dangers to anyone near or on them. No one had to remind residents of that fact in 1866. The odors of horse, sheep, and hog dung filled the nostrils of pedestrians, coach passengers, and teamsters alike. Hogs ran free, feeding on whatever garbage residents threw onto the streets. Pedestrians often forgot that under the tons of manure deposited on the streets each day, the streets were paved with cobblestones.

Travel by any means had become increasingly difficult anywhere in the city. New York's population had swollen beyond the capacity of its streets, and its downtown areas groaned under the daily additions of people. Overcrowded "street railways" failed to transport their customers comfortably. In 1866, the legislature, in an attempt to relieve the congestion, approved funding for a subway system.[5]

The butchering and consumption of meat in these crowded, smelly urban confines only compounded pollution and street-congestion problems. Swine provided a ready source of meat for their owners who often butchered their animals at home. The poor often dined on captured "wild" hogs found running at large. Each week butchers slaughtered thousands of sheep and prepared cuts for sale in 180 shops located in the heart of downtown Manhattan. Then the butchers discarded the offal in back alleys, where hogs fed on it.

While hogs and sheep provided most of the meat eaten in the city, New York consumers also developed a healthy taste for beef. Between 1855 and 1865, the annual consumption of pork grew from over 250,000 to over 650,000 animals, and during the same period, mutton consumption increased from over 550,000 to over 1,000,000 animals. Beef consumption also rose dramatically, increasing from nearly 160,000 animals in 1855 to over 270,000 in 1865.[6]

Eating certain cuts of beef became a symbol of class status. In 1830, John and Peter Delmonico opened one of the first restaurants in the city, and soon competitors followed. The brothers dominated the business by specializing in a menu offering French-styled cuisine. In 1837, they opened a distinctly upscale, opulent restaurant at the intersection of Beaver and William Streets that catered explicitly to the elites of the world. In 1850, the chefs added to the menu the "Delmonico steak," a twenty-ounce cut of sirloin, a favorite of Abraham Lincoln. In 1862, Charles Delmonico opened an exclusive restaurant next to Union Square on 14th Street and 5th Avenue, and hired Charles Ranhofer, one of the earliest examples of a celebrity chef. On August 29, 1866, his banquet menu for the dinner given to President Andrew Johnson included as part of one course a tenderloin called Filet de boeuf à la Pocahontas.[7]

By 1866, meeting the demand for beef in the rapidly growing city approaching one million people required the massive importation of animals. During one week in March 1866, for example, 4,100 steers still fell short of supplying consumer demand in the city.[8] Buying cuts of meat and other foodstuffs created a daily rush to Washington Market, where during the forenoon it became "almost impossible for merchants to deliver their goods to the various forwarding lines in the vicinity, and pedestrians experience[d] great difficulty in passing through the crowd of wagons and carts in that section of the city." By the end of 1868, the entire cattle market for New York and its vicinity consumed 7,000 beeves weekly, or more than 350,000 animals served on dinner plates for the year, and amounted to over $35 million in total annual sales.[9]

The sheer volume of animals slaughtered exacerbated the pollution problem from butcher shops and spurred public health concerns. While Mayor John Hoffman thought the city Board of Commissioners of Health possessed adequate authority to regulate the butcher shops, Governor Reuben Fenton, responding to public outcries from New Yorkers, differed decidedly with the mayor. Fenton preferred an independent professional board, one with authority vested in it by the state and free from city control. The governor's goal, as reported in *Harper's Weekly*, was a board free of "politicians or speculators" and served by "men of the highest practical science."[10] Initially created to contain cholera, this state-sanctioned board also possessed the authority to regulate the cattle trade and butcher shops in the city.

By early March 1866, the governor had appointed Jackson Schultz the president of the health board. No stranger to the city's cattle trade, the fifty-one-year-old Schultz owned and operated the nation's largest leather-working business. A reformer at heart, he dearly wanted to see a healthier, cleaner environment in the city. He found complete and professional support from the three physicians whom he had appointed to the sanitary committee.

Under Schultz's energetic leadership, the board took immediate action to abate the horrid conditions of the slaughterhouses in the heart of the city. The butchers found themselves summoned to report to the board to answer a series of questions. On Monday, March 12, at 3 P.M., when the butchers arrived at the trial room in the Metropolitan Police Building, they had to address the question first and foremost in the minds of the board members: Was there any justification for operating their establishments among the tenements and commercial buildings? Second, if the butchers kept doing their work in Lower Manhattan, how could they protect the public from the thousands of cattle daily driven along the main streets of the city, "maddened by fever, hunger, thirst and fright?" And how would nearby residents or passersby be shielded from "fat-trying, bone-boiling and hog-feeding on the offal of slaughtered beasts?"[11]

The butchers gathered as a group determined to show themselves as an aggrieved profession. Prior to their meeting with the board, they had convened at the Butchers' Hide and Melting Association's offices at Fifth Street and First Avenue to agree on their rationale for retaining their locations. The butchers elected George Starr to chair their meeting and to represent them along with a committee of five other butchers. At the end of the session, after the airing of differing points of view, all that Starr promised the butchers was that he would do his best to protect them "from unlawful abuse." The meeting adjourned, and all headed to the Metropolitan Police Building for the three o'clock meeting.[12]

Once the health board and butchers had assembled, health board president Jackson Schultz made one thing perfectly clear to all attendees. "It is useless," he pointedly warned the butchers, "to disguise the fact that very soon your occupation must leave the populous part of the city." He further informed them that although the public demanded their removal, he preferred that the butchers themselves take the lead in relocating. The ultimate goal, Schultz said, was to have a publicly owned and managed "abattoir," located well to the north of the city, where the slaughtering would be conducted, and then the quarter sections could be transported to the city's butcher shops.

The butchers came prepared with a number of arguments to counter Schultz's relocation plan. Identifying themselves as skilled members of a profession, they recoiled at having their shops declared both unhealthy and offensive. Mr. Lalor, one of the butchers present, asked why blacksmith shops or tenement houses were not to be banished. He further asserted that the squalor of the tenement houses created a worse nuisance than either butcher or blacksmith shops. Christopher Wier, another member of the association, alleged that slaughterhouses were less grievous than either coal yards or private stables.[13] One butcher identified as Captain Phillips conceded that some slaughterhouses were so "utterly filthy that it is impossible for a man to pass them some mornings without the loss of his breakfast." Despite this, he also made the fantastic claim that slaughterhouses possessed a peculiar health benefit. "I have had sick persons often come into the slaughter house and sit over the beef while it was drawn that they might inhale the steam and so be cured."[14]

Although this steam treatment might seem an unusual treatment today, it was apparently a common practice at the time. A few years later, Thomas F. De Voe, the superintendent of the Washington Market and a butcher by trade, besides being a member of the New York Historical Society, also described the healing effects of a slaughterhouse. De Voe recalled that, as a child, he had suffered from "weak and shriveled" lower limbs. Three times a week, his mother had taken him to a slaughterhouse for physical therapy. The treatment followed a peculiar procedure: "As the warm entrails were taken from the animals and placed in a tub, the mother thrust [De Voe's] puny legs into them, and had the satisfaction of seeing vitality imparted to the limbs." In following similar curative regimens, others reported the return of strength to a formerly paralyzed individual and how, in a separate case, a "confirmed invalid" became "an active, muscular man."[15]

Other butchers tried to make a case for the healthful nature of their business by pointing to their "own portly bodies." However, not everyone agreed with the butchers' self-analysis of their trade. A reporter covering the meeting for the *New York Times* took great exception to the butchers' claims. He allowed that perhaps the butchers' trade might be "imminently health-giving, but *their* bodies" (emphasis included) did not prove it. The reporter also pointed out that the butchers and their families did not live near their establishments, while the poor living in tenements did, and that the health of those dwelling in the area suffered. The reporter went on to castigate the butchers for "parading" cattle down Fifth Avenue while the people using the streets encountered the drives as "abominations and nuisances, intolerable to any other people under the sun."[16]

This cattle parade on the streets of New York began as a number of railroad companies delivered cattle straight to the Jersey City and Hoboken stockyards lining the docks along the North River shoreline directly across from Lower Manhattan. At the piers, workers reloaded the animals onto the ferryboats that transported the cattle to the holding pens in the Third, Fifth, and Ninth Wards of New York City. From there, drovers headed the cattle along the downtown streets to the various butcher shops. Often this work was done in the evening to avoid the greater congestion of the streets during the daytime. As George Starr, the spokesman for the butchers, judged the practice, driving cattle through the streets caused fewer accidents than "horses and cars."[17]

The reality, however, was that cattle driving made the streets a hazardous place for people. At the same time that Starr pleaded his case, not more than a mile away, eight-year-old Matilda Kregan and eleven-year-old Matthew Meyer were playing in the vicinity of Avenue B between Third and Fourth Streets. Along Avenue B, drovers were also driving a herd of cattle toward downtown slaughterhouses. Suddenly, one of the steers broke loose and made a "furious rush down the avenue." In its flight, the steer knocked Matilda and Matthew down, "severely bruising both children." Police from the Seventeenth Precinct were called. After a "long and exciting chase," the police captured the steer and led it to Elias Kutz's slaughterhouse at 55 First Avenue, who promptly butchered the animal. Abraham Loch, who operated a butcher shop in the third block of East Tenth Street, had actually bought the animal and had a claim to it. When he found out the location of the carcass, he quickly rushed to Kutz's shop and retrieved it. Meanwhile, as the parents of Matilda and Matthew found out, the downtown streets were not safe from panicked cattle, as Mr. Starr averred.[18]

Besides addressing concerns over the safety of street traffic, the sanitary committee had identified nearly twenty-five streets in "filthy condition" and classified five "fat and offal-boiling" facilities as nuisances, which resulted in suspending their businesses.[19] The employees of the department had cleaned nearly 200 water closets, removed over 960 cartloads of "night soil," (each cart with a capacity of about one square yard), removed over 80 dead horses from the streets, and removed an additional 360 dead calves along with more than 1,700 barrels of offal from the butcher shops located in the city.[20] As the public outcry mounted over the poor sanitary condition of the city, Jackson Schultz and the Metropolitan Board of Health saw a remediation plan coming into view.

## *The Samuel Allerton Prototype*

Potential profit and improved public safety were to be gained by opening a new kind of trail for cattle into New York City.[21] By the end of 1866, Samuel Allerton, steeped in his family's long-standing leading role in supplying New York City with cattle, had exerted control over vast segments of the cattle business. In the 1850s, he traveled between New York City and the Illinois farms where cattle herds flourished. The ever-increasing demand for beef in the city had outstripped the ability of upstate cattlemen to supply it, so Allerton ventured even farther westward to seek access to abundant supplies of cattle. By the outbreak of the Civil War, rail connections linked Chicago, New York City, and Philadelphia, and Allerton took up residence in Chicago where he could direct the flow of cattle from the fields of central Illinois to the butcher shops of New York City.

His first major effort to consolidate the business occurred with the building of the East Liberty stockyards just a few miles outside Pittsburgh, Pennsylvania. Prior to the direct rail connections to Chicago, drovers placed their herds in any number of small holding pens where buyers and sellers met. Allerton knew that the business of shipping cattle could be made much more efficient if one large facility were built that could accommodate a number of railroads bearing stock cars loaded with cattle. Add to such a stockyard an office building for conducting the trade and a hotel where drovers, buyers, and sellers might lodge comfortably, and the whole business might be rationalized in one centralized location—a union stockyard.

Small stockyards simply could not handle the influx of cattle made possible by the direct rail connections tying Chicago to Pittsburgh. Cattle shipments began pouring into Pittsburgh on the Pennsylvania Railroad (PRR) tracks in 1859. In that year, the rail company transported more tonnage in livestock than in any other commodity, and by 1863, the company had quadrupled that amount. The East Liberty stockyards, once completed in 1864, had a capacity of thirty-five thousand hogs and ten thousand cattle. In addition, the yards provided a hotel and an office space for cattle drovers, brokers, and sellers. The East Liberty facilities connected to several railroad lines, all headed to the East Coast's burgeoning urban markets. Shortly after the yards opened for business in February, Samuel Allerton and fellow Chicagoan Joseph McPherson were hired to manage it.

After the success of East Liberty, Allerton turned his attention to consolidating the small stockyards in Chicago, which resulted in the building of the Chicago Union Stockyards that opened on Christmas Day 1865. Through his influence, Allerton kept the operation of the Chicago yard in the family with the hiring of his cousin John Brill Sherman as its manager. All of Allerton's work in Chicago, Pittsburgh, and later Philadelphia still had one goal in mind: to corner the cattle trade flowing into New York City.

The managers of several railroad companies recognized the need to consolidate livestock facilities in Jersey City. Their effort resulted in the building and opening of the Communipaw Abattoirs in October 1866, which seemed to solve many of the problems identified by Jackson Schultz and the Metropolitan Board of Health. The success of *union* stockyards quickly made obsolete the small slaughterhouses in Lower Manhattan, and abetted the cleanliness and safety of the city streets. The New Jersey Stock Yard and Market Company, including Chicago investors Samuel Allerton and Joseph McPherson, owned the operation. While the company considerably advanced the goals of the New York City Metropolitan Board of Health, the owners saved a lot of money by not ferrying live cattle across the Hudson River and then driving them through the streets of New York City.[22]

Following the East Liberty union stockyard model pioneered by Samuel Allerton, the New Jersey Stock Yard and Market Company built pens capable of holding 30,000 sheep and hogs and additional pens with the capacity of 20,000

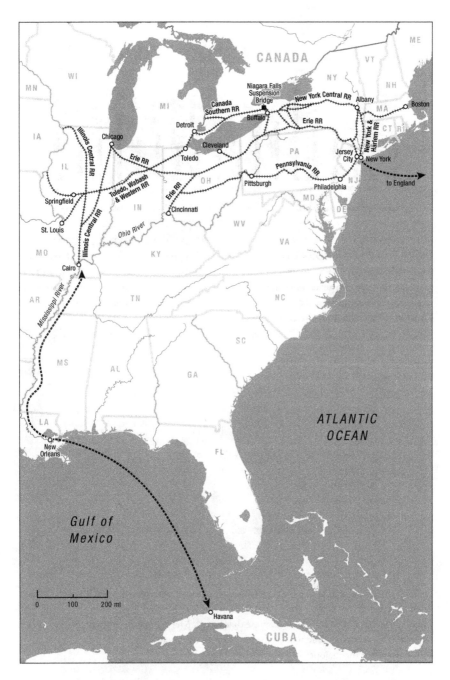

TRAIL SYSTEM OF THE EASTERN CONTINENTAL CATTLE TRADE

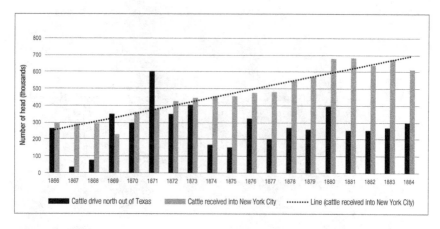

CHART 1. CATTLE DRIVEN NORTH OUT OF TEXAS COMPARED TO CATTLE RECEIVED INTO NEW YORK CITY, 1866–1884. This graph shows that even if all the Texas cattle driven north had been applied to satisfying the New York City markets between 1866 and 1884, in only two years, 1869 and 1871, would those drives have met the market demands of the city. In short, the urban beef markets in the United States were vastly larger than what Texas stockmen could fill alone.

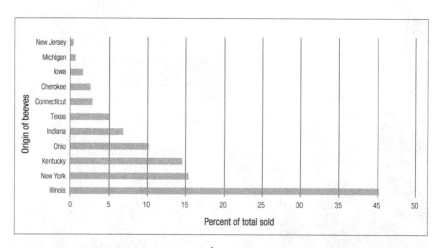

CHART 2. BEEVES SOLD AT ALLERTON'S, WEEK ENDING NOVEMBER 18, 1867. Total sold during the week = 6,584 head. This graph is a snapshot of the sources of cattle that supplied the New York market at the time that Joseph McCoy opened Abilene, Kansas, as an outlet for Texas cattle. As remained the case during the great Texas cattle drives, the state of Illinois supplied the majority of beeves that fed New Yorkers.

beeves. Workers in the abattoir could daily slaughter up to 1,500 hogs, 3,000 sheep, and 700 beeves, which many times came close to supplying an entire day's demand in the city. The New Jersey cattle company also built an office building where drovers, sellers, and buyers could conduct their business. And for the drovers, the company built a fifty-room hotel. The drovers enjoyed cushy accommodations as the rooms were "comfortably furnished" besides being "spacious and airy."[23]

Samuel Allerton had established the prototype for consolidating railroad lines into a single stockyard-slaughterhouse operation. Undoubtedly, William McCoy witnessed the advantages of this type of operation as he conducted the family business in Chicago and New York City. Certainly, he related Allerton's innovative approach to his brothers. Joseph, the youngest of the three, took inspiration from Allerton and began planning a similar stockyard facility in Kansas, where no one else saw the prospects.

## *The Illinois Connection*

By the end of the Civil War, Illinois cattlemen, like the McCoy brothers, played a dominant role in the New York market. The cattle trade in 1865 bears this out quite clearly. Of the 273,274 beef steers that were sold in the city that year, 100,978 came from the state of Illinois. The next-largest supply came from New York with a mere 21,878 head of cattle placed into the city markets. But not one head of cattle reportedly came from Texas.[24] In 1866, similar trends held sway with Illinois providing 165,287 of the 298,882 head of cattle that entered the city markets. But subtle changes were also taking place. Though amounting to a tiny percentage of the cattle delivered to the city, for the first time, Texas and Cherokee Nation cattle directly entered the city markets.[25]

In just one week in March 1866, as Jackson Schultz's sanitation workers labored to keep the city streets clean, Illinois stockmen sold over 1,762 of the 3,829 cattle sold to buyers at the Allerton yards, the largest facility in the city, located at Forty-Fifth Street. The cattle arrived via several railroad companies and their attendant ferry lines: the New York and Erie Railroad (Erie), the Hudson River Railroad (HR), the New York and Harlem Railroad (NY&H), the New York and New Haven Railroad (NY&NH), the Camden and Amboy Railroad (C&A), and the Central Railroad of New Jersey (CNJ). In total for the week, 5,341 steers, 14,822 lambs, and 7,023 hogs were imported into the city to feed its rapidly growing population.[26]

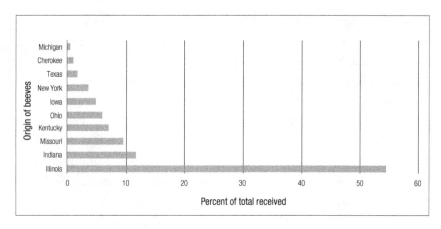

CHART 3. BEEVES RECEIVED INTO THE NEW YORK CITY MARKET, WEEK ENDING AUGUST 18, 1868. Total received during the week = 6,693 head. This graph shows the sources of cattle for the New York City market at the height of the cattle plague of 1868. Although some Texas and Cherokee were sold, their numbers were a miniscule percentage of the total for the week.

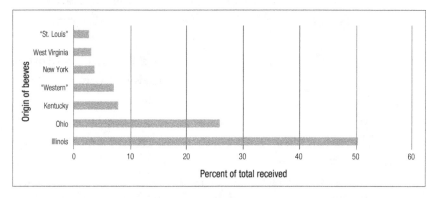

CHART 4. BEEVES RECEIVED AT JERSEY CITY, JANUARY 5–6, 1885. Total received during week ending January 6, 1885 = 9,025. Although this graph shows that Illinois stockmen still dominated the New York City beef market, this was one of the first indications that cattle raised on the western grasslands of Colorado, Wyoming, and Montana were beginning to become an important part of the East Coast beef markets. But those ranges had been overstocked by Texas cattle driven north to build up herds on the open range. Their numbers flooded urban markets, and stockmen decided to keep their herds on the open range over the winter in hopes of creating a shortage and driving up prices. The blizzards in Kansas during the winter of 1885–86 and the "great die-up" blizzard of 1886–87 effectively ended open-range grazing.

John T. Alexander of Morgan County, Illinois, stood out as the most successful and prominent stockman in the state. Alexander ran a feed and fattening operation on 80,000 acres of prime farmland. In 1865, he had raised 18,000 acres of corn to supplement his pasture feeding of 15,000 hogs and 32,000 head of cattle. He bought his stock in the fall and overwintered and fattened his herds on his vast holdings. In the spring he shipped them into the urban markets of Chicago and East Coast cities as soon as the animals had put on weight. He amassed a fortune in this trade with profits reportedly topping $175,000 in 1865.[27]

The McCoy brothers and Alexander were good friends, and though not operating at the same level as Alexander, the McCoys also made handsome returns on their Illinois operations. In Chicago and New York City, William McCoy marketed the cattle that his brothers bought. James focused most of his attention on their operation near Springfield, Illinois. In 1867, he would accompany his younger brother, Joseph, to Abilene, Kansas, where together they would convert the lonely outpost beside the tracks of the Union Pacific Railway Company, Eastern Division (UPED) into a huge outlet for Texas longhorns. In pursuing his vision of building a cattle outlet in Abilene, Kansas, Joseph would demonstrate an abundance of entrepreneurial energy. He could smell the money where no one had gone before.

By some accounts, the three brothers ran the largest cattle dealing operation in Illinois. Whether or not this was actually true, they certainly were well set in the business. A look at their references reflects how well they were received among some of the most prominent politicians and businessmen of their time.[28] Their list included the governor of Illinois, R. J. Oglesby; the Illinois secretary of state, Simon Tyndale; the president of the Ninth National Bank in New York City, Joseph U. Orvis; and a prominent attorney in Chicago and personal friend of Abraham Lincoln, J. G. Scammon. The McCoys reportedly had a well-established personal friendship with Lincoln before he became president.

In New York City, William conducted a brisk business for his brothers. Some indication of it is given in the cattle market reports regularly published in the *New York Tribune*. For example, on June 19, 1866, William McCoy sold 234 head of cattle. Only one other dealer sold more cattle that week than McCoy, and he was also an Illinoisan. Of the 3,171 beef cattle sold to the Allerton Stockyard, 2,826 head were from Illinois, and William McCoy had supplied nearly one-tenth of that lot. On September 4, William McCoy employed other brokers to sell 168 head of cattle for him.[29]

While the meat markets of other rapidly growing cities paled in comparison to the demands of New York City, they contributed to an ever-growing demand for beef cattle. In March 1866, the cattle trade in Boston amounted to one-third of that in New York City. Philadelphia's cattle trade in the same week was less than 20 percent of that in New York City. But when added together, it is clear that the urban demand for beef rapidly grew immediately following the Civil War. The demand outpaced supply, and therein lay the great opportunity for opening an outlet for Texas longhorns at Abilene, Kansas.

## Cattle Health and Markets

In 1866, Joseph scarcely could have predicted how bovine health and disease would cast a pall over every aspect of the Texas cattle trade. After the Civil War, New Yorkers focused an increasing amount of attention on creating a healthy urban environment. One of the most pressing concerns was abating the spread of cholera. By September 1866, it was apparent to the reporters of the *Tribune* that, slowly but surely, the work of the Metropolitan Board of Health was paying dividends.

As the board labored to stem the outbreak of contagious human diseases, other reformers saw human health tied directly to the condition of beef cattle arriving in the city, stressing the connection between healthy beeves and a wholesome diet. Reports in New York papers associated public outbreaks of diarrhea with the arrival of scrawny bullocks. Besides affecting the health of New Yorkers, "thin, inferior cattle" inflicted ruinous prices on cattle sellers, as was the case in October.[30]

In March 1866, New Yorker Henry Bergh organized and led the filing of incorporation papers for the Society for the Prevention of Cruelty to Animals. His inheritance from his wealthy shipyard-owning father allowed Bergh to live a rather carefree life. During his travels in Europe during the Civil War, he had acquired a heightened awareness about cruelty to animals. Once he returned to New York City, he, along with the backing of other well-established businessmen and city reformers, focused his attention on addressing the problem in the city as he saw it.[31]

The *New York Tribune* fully supported his efforts. In conjunction with the formation of the health board, the paper noted that the creation of the Society for the Prevention of Cruelty to Animals marked "a cooperative public spirit of reform." The *Tribune* especially hoped that the creation of the society would lead to abating "the every-day notorious cruelty practiced" on animals in the city, and also the "even more baneful, character . . . of the drove-yards, and butcheries of the metropolitan district."[32] In April, the legislature voted to incorporate the SPCA, and a few weeks later, the assembly enacted the nation's first legislation preventing cruelty to animals.

Bergh found support beyond those people whose sole interest lay in how animals were treated. Consumers' concerns over the quality of food led enforcement of the law preventing cruelty to cattle. In November, an article by Bergh in the *New York Times* clearly revealed a lack of enforcement of the act for the "protection of the health of animals designed for human food." From August to October, the society, under Bergh's direction, sent three agents to Chicago to observe and record cattle distribution from the Union Stockyards to the markets in New York City. The investigators reported that the Chicago yards were thick with "poor, dwarfed, nearly-starved cattle, which have just arrived from Texas by the Illinois Central Railroad." The investigators followed these beeves from the time they were loaded onto trains until the stock cars arrived at the stockyards in Buffalo, New York. The cattle were neither fed nor watered for the duration of their time in transport: 538 miles in fifty hours.

New York state law required that cattle could not be contained in stock cars for longer than twenty-eight consecutive hours without being fed or watered. The legislation, however, exempted two railroad companies: the Buffalo State and Line and the Atlantic and Great Western. Although Bergh deemed these two exceptions wholly unacceptable, he also reported that other lines shipped cattle into the state without paying any heed to the provision of the law's demands for the humane transportation of cattle.

Bergh next traced the route of cattle from the Buffalo stockyards to the holding pens at Bergen, New Jersey. Cattle bound for New York City markets were not fed or watered but ferried directly from New Jersey into the city and then led to the slaughterhouses. After the steers were unloaded at the docks, Bergh followed them as they were driven through the streets to where they were "confined in rocky yards fronting on the fashionable Fifth-avenue." There the poor creatures waited, as Bergh phrased it, until "the tender-hearted butcher" arrived to "drag them to execution."[33]

Of course, there was more to Bergh's concerns than just the well-being of the cattle. He also astutely framed his argument in how humanely treated cattle equated to better health for people. One of the agents following the cattle to the butcher shop related that he had "visited many slaughter-houses, and examined the meat"; he said that when he pressed the carcass with his finger, a "yellow corruption spurt[ed] out from beneath the surface."[34]

In citing this case, Bergh made the obvious point that no consumer would knowingly purchase such unwholesome meat. His solution was not to have live cattle transported to the city at all. Rather, he believed that "justice, mercy and profit are on the side of swift slaughtering of animals designed for human food, at or near the pasturages." Transporting "fresh" beef from the grazing grounds in Illinois, Kansas, or Texas into the city, as opposed to hauling "live" cattle to New Jersey, however, was going to require new type of freight car, one that could keep meat fresh for long stretches of distance and time. The railroad and slaughter-houses had yet to perfect this form of meat transportation, but Bergh understood its potential. As the *New York Times* summed up the situation, Bergh's position would find ample public support "not only on grounds of humanity to animals, but from a selfish interest in the character of the flesh which we devour."[35]

Besides mounting public concerns over the ill effects of harshly treated cattle transported to New York City, health reformers and consumers targeted the importation of cattle showing the effects of disease. At the time, London was the largest city in the world, and keeping its population fed was a huge concern for the authorities wishing to keep social order. In Great Britain the deadly cattle disease rinderpest (German for "cattle plague") had made its unwelcome appearance throughout the countryside and in cities. At the beginning of January 1866, over five thousand head of cattle were succumbing to the plague each week. The mortality rate for infected cattle reached nearly 100 percent, which, according to the *London Times,* equated to the loss of meat production for a population of ten million people per day.[36] The health authorities worried above all that cattle affected by rinderpest posed a serious threat to the humans who ate them. By the middle of February, the number of afflicted cattle in Great Britain had topped ten thousand.[37] In response to the spread of rinderpest, the New York health board implemented a total ban on any and all importation of cattle from England. But the door remained open for the eventual exports of cattle from the United States to Great Britain.[38]

The McCoy brothers knew that an outbreak like rinderpest in American herds would devastate their bottom line. But rinderpest seemed confined to the

European continent and Great Britain, and if kept there, posed no direct threat to beef supplies in the United States. When North American cattlemen imported English cattle, it was to crossbreed with their own herds in the pursuit of creating beeves with higher fat content and more tender meat. If rinderpest broke out in a midwestern herd, the deadly results would have far-reaching effects. But rinderpest was fairly well understood, and somewhat effective treatments for the disease existed.

Such was not the case with another cattle disease that no one seemed to understand. Stockmen referred to this malady interchangeably as "Spanish fever" or "Texas fever." This disease first became apparent with the importation of Texas longhorns into midwestern and northern cattle herds. Perplexing everyone engaged in the cattle business was the fact that Texas cattle never seemed to die from it. However, scores of cattle in midwestern or northern shorthorn herds died from it after they had been in close proximity to Texas cattle.

The *New York Times* first took note of this malady in August 1866, when it reprinted an article that had appeared in the *Leavenworth* (Kansas) *Times*. "Disease among the Cattle in Kansas," read the headline. If it were not enough that reformers like Bergh worried about the effects of transporting debilitated Texas cattle, now they also agonized over whether or not those same cattle might be carrying a deadly disease affecting both humans and their domestic meat supply.[39] This disease would cast a pall over Joseph McCoy's and his brothers' efforts to create a great cattle-shipping nexus in Kansas. But in 1866, Joseph had no understanding of how a protozoan parasite less than three microns in size would create misfortune and travail for him and his brothers.

CHAPTER 2

# Trails' Ends

ALEXANDER GARDNER'S PHOTOGRAPHS — GARDNER AND THE UNION PACIFIC
RAILWAY COMPANY, EASTERN DIVISION — WHAT'S IN A PHOTOGRAPH — GARDNER'S
PHOTOGRAPHS OF ABILENE ON THE CUSP — RAILROAD TRAILS TO ST. LOUIS,
CHICAGO, AND NEW YORK — STEAMBOAT TRAILS TO LONDON AND HAVANA

In 1867, Texas cowboys headed their herds north to Abilene, Kansas. Joseph McCoy, in his *Historic Sketches of the Cattle Trade of the West and Southwest* (1874), gave the American public its first colorful insights into cowboy culture, cattle driving, the Chisholm Trail, and the infamous end-of-the-trail cow town, Abilene. Gamblers and women gathered there in the saloons and dance halls to fleece trail-worn, naive Texas cowboys of their scant earnings. As McCoy succinctly put it, "After a few days of frolic and debauchery, the cow-boy is ready . . . to start back to Texas, often not having a dollar left of his summer's wages." So it was that Abilene became known as the end of the trail for both the cowboy's money and his cattle.

In this context, McCoy's Abilene certainly can be considered the end of the trail. Yet it was an outlet to other trails that led cattle to far-flung destinations. Some of these trails crossed open prairies leading to army forts and Indian reservation headquarters. Some led to the west, crossing the Rocky Mountains and ending in Salt Lake City, or eventually West Coast cities such as Los Angeles or San Francisco.

But trails could, and did, take other forms. One of the most well-known newspaper reporters of his day understood this quite clearly. An exceptionally well educated New Yorker, A. C. Wheeler found initial fame writing and reporting for the *New York Times*. He left the *Times* before the Civil War to spend a few years in the "wild West" of Kansas, Iowa, and Colorado. During the war he worked as correspondent contributing stories to several newspapers, and afterward returned to New York to work for the *World* and later the *Sun*.

In the mid-1870s, Andrew Carpenter Wheeler traveled the Atchison, Topeka, and Santa Fe Railroad (AT&SF) from Kansas City to Pueblo, Colorado. By this time Joseph McCoy had helped promoters in Wichita, Kansas, corner the cattle trade arriving along the Chisholm Trail. One result was that the AT&SF rather than the Kansas Pacific Railway (KP) had become the primary cattle shipper in the country. As Wheeler rode the same rails on his way to Colorado, he reflected on his course across the grasslands, one that followed the old Santa Fe wagon trail. "Commerce," he wrote, "which upon the ocean or in the wilderness follows its own laws and lines, still travels the Santa Fé trail—but it is now an iron trail." Wheeler hailed the tracks as "one of the finest and fastest *trails* in the country" (emphasis added).[1]

Wheeler was one of many who began to see "trails" as something more than dusty paths crisscrossing open prairies and cutting through forests. A successful Texas stockman who had ridden the Chisholm Trail as a young man, William J. Bennett was a thoughtful, if not somewhat imaginative, thinker on this score. In 1920, he marveled at the rapid advances in aviation and other forms of transportation, and he understood trails as something more than a route traversing a wild or rough landscape. He predicted "that in another sixty years somebody will have established a *trail* to Mars or other planets, and our descendants may be signaling the latest market quotations to the cowmen of those parts" (emphasis added).[2] Obviously, humans have yet to fulfill his prediction despite Matt Damon's attempt to colonize Mars in the 2015 movie *The Martian*. Yet, as Bennett did, we should envision cattle trails in a broad context.

Iron formed cattle trails just as assuredly as did wagon wheels, and horse and bovine hooves. Instead of cowboys, freighters and train engineers conducted cattle to stockyards in Kansas City, St. Louis, Chicago, and New York City. Steamboats followed other trails along the great rivers of the continent. At the ports, dockworkers loaded cattle onto steamboats that riverboat captains piloted on the great river trails connecting cities such as New Orleans and St. Louis. Trails' ends also led Texas cattle to the transoceanic ports of England or Cuba.

Moreover, whether longhorns traveled a trail on the hoof, or whether rail or boat carried them, all forms of transport shared an important commonality: they relied on the same fundamental resources—stored solar energy and water. All locomotion, biological or mechanical, required the consumption of stored energy provided by the sun, whether in the form of grass or coal. Cattle and horses needed lush grasslands if they were to flourish. The furnaces that powered steam engines consumed coal, a resource that was little more than grass compressed over eons. All earthborn lifeforms, to a lesser or greater degree, require water. Cattle and horses failed quickly if not able to quench their thirst daily. Mechanical steam-powered locomotion also required a regular supply of water. Joseph McCoy could never have linked the Chisholm Trail to the tracks of the Union Pacific Railroad Company, Eastern Division (UPED) without the ability to draw upon abundant stored solar energy and water resources.

In one sense it is fine to think of Abilene as the trail's end for the great post–Civil War cattle drives, though this small cattle shipping point on the UPED tracks was simply one stopping point of just one trail, and the beginning of several others. It was through visionary work of the "Illinoisan," as McCoy referred to himself in his *Historic Sketches of the Cattle Trade*, that Abilene became that central outlet that connected with other trails. In the fall of 1867 workers loaded Texas cattle into stock cars to be hauled along the iron trails that led ultimately to the kitchens and restaurants of great cities.

### *Alexander Gardner's Photographs*

Given its appearance in 1867, few people could have imagined that Abilene, Kansas, would become a crucial link in the cattle trade. In the fall of that year, Alexander Gardner, a nationally renowned photographer, visited this small, nondescript town. There he took several photographs that showed the bonds of technology and ecology that McCoy relied upon to create his cattle-shipping empire. At first blush, Gardner's photographs show little more than a creek, a prairie-dog town, a newly built three-story building, and a stockyard with stock cars sitting on a rail siding.

On the surface Gardner's photographs show few signs of the impending greatness of this lonely site on the UPED tracks. Yet for a brief moment in time, from 1867 to 1872, it would become the hub of cattle trade in the United States, all because of the foresight and ambitious aspirations of a young Illinoisan cattle trader from Springfield. Only twenty-nine years old, Joseph G. McCoy understood that Abilene offered the sine qua non for linking together into one gigantic system the rapidly growing national and international beef markets, millions of cattle in Texas, the ecology of the open grasslands in the public domain, and the technological advances in railroads and shipping.

Prior to 1867, Abilene had little going for it. The origin of the town dates back to the fall of 1856, when twenty-nine-year-old Timothy F. Hersey left Illinois and became the first American citizen to arrive on the scene. He decided to build a log cabin beside Mud Creek where the Smoky Hill Trail intersected with the stream.

He chose an austere place. The bleakness of his environment is evident in the territorial survey maps of 1857. Federal surveyors Frederick Hawn, John A. Goodlet, and Lot Coffman located the Smoky Hill Trail (labeled the "Ft. Riley and Santa Fe Trail" on their plat map) near the northern bluff of the Smoky Hill River and showed where it intersected with Mud Creek in section twenty-one. Their map also showed a scattering of trees hugging the bends in the Smoky Hill River and a few trees where they clustered at the confluence of Mud Creek and the Smoky Hill River. Apart from this, their survey map of the township revealed a boundless range of prairie grass.[3]

Another four years would pass before anything resembling town development would begin. In 1857, Hersey brought his twenty-two-year-old wife, Eliza, and their two-year-old daughter, Mariah, to his log cabin. There the small family established a household, a farm, and a stop for travelers along the Smoky Hill Trail. In the following years, Timothy and Eliza improved their farm and added Sylvia to their family in 1859. A year later Charles Thompson came to the area and took up a claim just to the east of the Hersey's. He intended to lay out a town site on forty acres of his land, and one story has it that he implored Eliza to name this new venture.[4]

According to this tale, Eliza decided to call the place Abilene. Apparently, she knew her Bible well. There is only one reference to the word "Abilene" in the Bible in Luke 3:1, as the realm where John the Baptist began his proselytizing. Some scholars believe that the region acquired its name as a derivative of "Abila," the name of the capital where the governor Lysanias ruled. The word "Abila" is derived from the Hebrew *'abel*, which might refer to a stream or brook. Other scholars think the word is derived from the Hebrew word meaning "land of meadows." Eliza may have taken inspiration from either meaning, given the location of the Hersey's farm on Mud Creek and the open prairie that surrounded her home. Here, of all places, Alexander Gardner stopped to take several photographs where Joseph McCoy had launched his plans for cornering and funneling the immense potential cattle trade of Texas.

## *Gardner and the Union Pacific Railway Company, Eastern Division*

The rail connections that made McCoy's venture possible in the first place almost did not happen. The extraordinary struggle of building the railroad placed Gardner at this critical juncture where McCoy had built his outlet for Texas cattle. Gardner arrived at Abilene because John D. Perry, the president of the UPED, faced a serious problem with the president and Congress. The Transcontinental Railway Act promised support for his undertaking by providing treasury bonds and public lands for each mile constructed according to federal guidelines, but Perry faced financial disaster given the very real possibility that federal capital and political support might be delayed, or even pulled, for his bold ambition to span the North American continent by rail from Kansas City, Kansas, to the West Coast port cities of San Diego and San Francisco. He badly needed to reassure Congress that subsidizing his railway line with bonds and land grants still made sense.

Perry's problem became urgent when President Andrew Johnson received reports indicating that the UPED line from Kansas City to Lawrence had been poorly constructed and therefore failed to merit federal support. In 1866 the president authorized a special commission to investigate the situation and make a formal report as to the quality of the construction. The commissioners' report pointed out several deficiencies in the line, such as a poor location of the route, cuts and embankments that were far too narrow, grades that were too steep in several locales, too few crossties under the rails per mile, not enough ballasting to sustain the weight of trains, underbuilt culverts and bridges, and too few support buildings such as depots. The report raised serious alarms among investors in the railroad, given the prospect that the Johnson administration might not release federal bonds and public lands to the company.[5]

Perry responded quickly on several fronts to avoid disaster. To demonstrate just how well done the construction and operation of the line were, he gave tours of the route to important congressmen, their wives, and newspaper reporters. Perry also sought to impress important politicians not in attendance by having the route photographed and then publishing the prints in albums for congressional consumption. Perry anticipated an additional benefit of reaching a wider audience through lithographic reproductions of the prints or through books that chronicled and illustrated expeditions along the route. He also wrote a formal refutation of the commission's findings to the secretary of the interior.[6] Perry's effort to bolster the construction of the UPED line is how Alexander Gardner entered the picture.

Perry recognized in Gardner an artistic genius that Walt Whitman and Abraham Lincoln also highly esteemed. Gardner was nothing less than a master of his art. As Walt Whitman observed, "Gardner was a real artist—had the feel of his work—the inner feel, if I may say it so . . . he was also beyond his craft—saw farther than his camera—saw more: his pictures are an evidence of his endowment."[7]

Gardner's personal history offers a fascinating story by itself. Inspired by American utopian reform movements, he immigrated to the United States from his native Scotland in 1850. He and his brother James soon were in the thick of the abolitionist movement, but nonetheless he became enthralled by photography and quickly perfected his craft. For a while during the Civil War he worked as a photographer for Mathew Brady, famous for his Civil War photographs. But Gardner clashed with Brady, and so he began his own firm and subsequently took many famous photographs of battlefields and Union Army life.[8]

Gardner was more than a war photographer, he photographed Indian delegations and took portraits of the rich and famous as well as young soldiers off to war. Some writers justifiably consider Gardner the first photojournalist. His shots of the hanging of the Lincoln assassination conspirators and of Henry Wirz, the notorious commander of the Confederate prison at Andersonville, are just two examples of his remarkable journalistic work. By 1867, Gardner's fame as a photographer had spread far and wide, which was why Perry employed him.[9]

The owners of the UPED knew that Gardner could meet their expectations to show the progress and accomplishments of their company. They assumed that photographs of the landscapes, inhabitants, prominent geological formations, and general botany along the route would dramatically illustrate the potential riches to be derived from building this railroad. Perry's instructions were also why Gardner took a keen interest in photographing Abilene. McCoy's undertaking at Abilene demonstrated unmistakably one of the most valuable assets made possible by the railroad: the creation of an outlet for Texas cattle. Gardner knew photographs of Abilene would figure as a potent resource for Perry's company.

## What's in a Photograph

Alexander Gardner produced more than just high-quality visual advertising for the UPED line. His photographs richly detail the economic, social, and ecological consequences of railroad building. Above all, his prints show one form of cultural grassland management yielding to another, the remnants of a receding landscape once manipulated by American Indians and the emergence of a landscape shaped primarily by African Americans and European Americans. No one had yet rendered the startling path of "American civilization" the way Gardner did through the lens of his cameras in 1867. While American painters and illustrators such as John Gast and Fanny Frances Palmer provided allegorical renderings of the march of progress, Gardner offered framed views tracing the *actual* unfolding of the American empire.

Gardner's photographs revealed a tragic reality: American Indians with their horse-borne hunting cultures, open-range ranchers, American farmers, city dwellers, and industrialists could not all occupy the grasslands simultaneously because of the different ways in which their respective cultures employed plant, mineral, energy, and water resources. For Indians, European Americans consistently and inevitably held the balance of power because of their ability to draw on remote, abundant sources of fuel, fiber, and food to power their occupation of the region. In time this capacity overwhelmed Indians and, later, open-range cattlemen, who failed to disengage from an increasingly weakened grassland ecosystem and trade networks that had once sustained them.[10]

## *Gardner's Photographs of Abilene on the Cusp*

Alexander Gardner's photographs of Abilene in the fall of 1867 capture a place on the cusp of becoming the hub of the American cattle trade. At first glance, Gardner's photographs lent credence to Joseph McCoy's depiction of the town as a "dead place." Before McCoy selected this crude burg as the destination for a cattle-shipping point, the town had little going for it. McCoy described it as nothing more than a "dozen log huts, low, small rude affairs, four-fifths of which were covered with dirt for roofing." A saloon, in one of the log huts, was the most prosperous business in the town. Still, Abilene had something going for it as the Dickinson County seat.[11]

McCoy had a grand vision for the future of Abilene regardless of how he initially found the place. A few days before his company loaded the first stock cars with Texas cattle, he explained to some reporters the purpose of his undertakings in Abilene. As summarized in the newspaper, the McCoy brothers' "purpose is not only to purchase cattle themselves, but to provide for the purchase and sale by stock raisers and cattle dealers, and to open up the way for furnishing a market for the immense herds of the Western plains, which shall give cheap beef to the laborers of the East."[12] This was a bold enterprise, one made possible only by tying the bounty of the grassland biome in the public domain and urban markets together with the threads of railroad technology. Remarkably, Gardner's photographs captured McCoy's facilities shortly after they had begun operating.

By the time Gardner arrived on the scene, McCoy had already built the infrastructure of his cattle-shipping operation. Undoubtedly McCoy's venture captured Gardner's interests. More than this, Gardner's photographs also illustrate the features that had led McCoy to build at this spot in the first place. Setting up his camera on the west bank of Mud Creek looking east, Gardner took a photograph with McCoy's operation appearing in the far distance. The view centers on the trestle bridge across Mud Creek that carried the UPED tracks. Obviously the UPED tracks conveyed trains headed both east and west, yet Gardner chose an eastward view as though that were the primary direction in which the company's trains would be bound. If this was his intention, then he had an accurate understanding of which direction Texas cattle were headed.

In the same print, to the north side of the tracks are wagon-wheel ruts that cut both the east and west banks of the creek. Perhaps this was the location of the Smoky Hill Trail crossing. Just beyond the creek to the east stand some farm buildings. Dominating the center of Gardner's frame are the railroad tracks and the telegraph poles along the north side of the rails. It is as if Gardner was showing how railroads and telegraph were overtaking ox-drawn wagons, and it was the advance of these technologies that had made McCoy's aspirations possible in the first place.

Gardner framed another of his photographs on the prairie-dog town with a view to the south. On the horizon is the scattering of trees lining the banks of the Smoky Hill River, a major source of reliable water that would quench the thirsts of the large herds of Texas cattle. Besides the prairie-dog town on the north side of the tracks, all else to the south is the unencumbered prairie that Texas cattlemen would rely upon to graze their herds.

Another photograph displays the wide-open prairie-grass realm and one of its most prominent inhabitants, the prairie dog. These sweeping grasslands stretching across the public domain, free to the drovers, were essential for the success of McCoy's operation. Texas cattlemen required access to unimpeded grazing grounds to feed their massive herds as they awaited loading into stock cars destined for eastern markets. This photograph, taken looking north, shows—most likely—Josiah Jones mingling with the residents of the dog town. The fellow certainly meets McCoy's description of a man known as "Old Man Jones": "a corpulent, jolly, good-souled, congenial old man of the backwoods pattern." McCoy observed him frequently "feeding his pets," the prairie dogs that lived on his land. Many others besides McCoy knew Jones as the proprietor of a store in one of the log buildings, where he stocked an ample supply of spirits for travelers—and for Texas cattlemen, who, McCoy realized, greatly appreciated the availability of whiskey.[13]

McCoy clearly understood that Texas cattlemen and cattle buyers all needed a comfortable place where they could drink liquor, eat well, and have a good night's sleep. One of Gardner's photographs shows the very building that McCoy built to serve cattlemen in style. McCoy had invested about $18,000 in building this guesthouse, the Drovers Cottage. The hotel was designed as a first-rate, comfortable accommodation. It had fifty rooms that could lodge one hundred guests at a time. The hotel also featured amenities such as a billiard room, saloon, and dining hall. When Gardner took his photograph, the hotel had yet to open and apparently was still in a state of construction, given the materials strewn about the grounds surrounding the building. In the following year, however, cattlemen, cattle brokers, and travelers alike would bask in the hospitality of this establishment.

Nearly all the future success of the Drovers Cottage would rest on the superb management skills of Louise and James W. Gore. McCoy was a keen judge of ability, and he was on the lookout for someone who could manage the hotel. On one of his business trips to St. Louis, he took a room in the St. Nicholas Hotel. McCoy understood that the steward, James Gore, was anxious to manage his own place. A quick interview between Gore and McCoy resulted in both Louise and James packing their bags and heading for the greener pastures of Abilene and the Drovers Cottage.

Like James, Louise, known as Lou, was well acquainted with the hotel business, and McCoy had the highest regards for her. He recalled that in no time whatsoever, Texas drovers came to regard her with the "kindest respect and tenderest memory, and feelings near akin to the holy passion that binds earth to Heaven."[14] She had been raised in a hotel at Niagara Falls owned and operated by her father. Both the Gores were well known for their "genial manners, and rare social qualities." Their fame spread, given the "good table" they set, and how they maintained an establishment of "neat and cozy appearance, well calculated to entice the weary traveler."[15] In building their business, by 1870 the Gores employed fourteen waiters, six women and eight men, nearly all of whom were in their twenties. Also employed were four cooks, including Charles and Janet Stover, a married couple from Canada.[16]

In addition to the photograph of the Drovers Cottage, two other photographs depict the heart of McCoy's cattle-shipping venture at Abilene. Both show the stockyards that Joseph and James McCoy had built. The brothers began building their stockyard, along with the barn and hotel, shortly after Independence Day in 1867. Altogether, McCoy recalled investing somewhere between $25,000 and $30,000 in constructing the yards and buildings. Once they completed their work, the stockyards could accommodate 1,500 head of cattle, and the UPED had the capacity of loading and transporting forty stock cars each day.[17] By the end of the 1868 season, after the first two years of its operation, the "Great Western Stock Yards" at Abilene had loaded over 100,000 cattle into UPED stock cars headed east.[18]

By the end of December 1869, the McCoy brothers had loaded cattle into 2,051 stock cars, which would have amounted to between 38,900 and 41,500 cattle bought and sold exclusively by the brothers in that year alone. At the same time, the Kansas Pacific Railway Company (as the UPED was known by then) increased its rolling stock to about 100 stock cars on a daily basis. McCoy accurately estimated that over 120,000 head of cattle total would change hands at Abilene during the 1869 season.

Gardner's photographs of the stockyards show the facility shortly after it had opened for business. In one photograph Gardner shows seven stock cars, with a capacity of twenty head of cattle in each, or a total of 140. The stock pens are in view to the right of the stock cars. The McCoy brothers imported a substantial quantity of timber to build the pens, given the solid nature of their construction.

Gardner labeled the other photo of the stockyards "Shipping Point for Texas Cattle, Abilene, Kansas." In this one, only four stock cars are shown. The unidentified man standing on top of a stock car bears a striking resemblance to Joseph McCoy. The loading ramp is clearly shown, as are several employees. The photograph also captures a man standing by a fence and handling a load of hay obviously meant for feeding the livestock. From this locale, the "Great Western Stock Yards" captured in Gardner's photographs, Texas cattle would be transported to other remote destinations along different kinds of trails.

## Railroad Trails to St. Louis, Chicago, and New York

Railroads should be considered a type of cattle trail. Consider the similarities, which may or may not be obvious. Trains hauled cattle in stock cars as opposed to cowboys driving them through the public domain grasslands. With steam locomotives, either wood or coal generated the energy that powered the engines. Cattle fueled themselves with the stored solar energy found in the grasses that they ate. Either way, stored solar energy, whether bound in wood, coal, or grass, fueled the transportation of animals to a trail's end, whether it was Abilene or Chicago.

Geography determined the route of the trail, whether through the central grasslands or the surveyed routes of train tracks. Often, the tracks of a railroad company followed trails formerly plied by Indian peoples, American wagons, or herds of wild or domesticated animals. Like all trails, they had destinations. The cattle trail to Abilene was an obvious destination but not an end point. The town and McCoy's cattle-loading facilities simply served as a transfer site where cattle arriving from one trail were redirected onto another trail leading to other destinations.

From the beginning, McCoy had no intention of making Abilene anything more than a transfer site. However, it was one thing to create a trail that funneled Texas cattle to Abilene and quite another to blaze the trails that would ultimately lead cattle primarily to burgeoning urban markets. He needed the support of railroad companies to provide the rolling stock and facilities that would eventually make it possible for a longhorn steak to land on a dinner plate in Delmonico's Restaurant in New York City. Perry considered McCoy's plans "wild, chimerical, visionary." However, Perry understood the need to haul freight east if he ever wanted his company to turn a profit. After some hard bargaining, he relented to a degree and told McCoy that he would provide "such switches, cars, etc., as would be needed, and if it proved a success the projector should be liberally paid, but they having no faith in it were not willing to risk a dollar in the enterprise."[19] With Perry's tepid commitment, McCoy had in place the means to transport cattle as far east as Leavenworth, Kansas.

McCoy's next step was to find the trail leading to either Chicago or St. Louis. The UPED tracks stopped near the ferry landing at Third Street in Leavenworth. There the McCoy brothers built stockyards where the cattle could be unloaded from the stock cars and then, as one reporter wrote, "be transferred immediately across [the Missouri River] with very little delay."[20] After the ferry landed at East Leavenworth, the cattle could be reloaded onto stock cars bound for either Chicago or St. Louis.

Knowing that he had everything in place for landing cattle on the east bank of the Missouri River, McCoy proceeded to forge the next links in the chain of trails leading to urban markets. Unloading cattle at Leavenworth and ferrying the herds across the river made sense, as ready transportation connections existed to either Chicago or St. Louis via the loading stockyards of the Missouri Pacific Railroad Company (MoPac), or to the yards operated by the Hannibal and St. Joseph Railroad Company (H&StJ).

McCoy traveled to St. Louis hoping to persuade George Tyler, the president of the MoPac, to provide the means to transport cattle directly to that city. However, negotiations proved fruitless. McCoy utterly failed to reach an agreement with Tyler, who brusquely rebuffed his ideas. Tyler's response to his proposal, as McCoy recorded it, was: "It occurs to me that you havn't [sic] any cattle to ship, and never did have any, and I, sir, have no evidence that you ever will have any, and I think you are talking about rates of freight for speculative purposes, therefore, you get out of this office, and let me not be troubled with any more of your style." Given his poor reception, McCoy turned around, left Tyler's office, and shut the door that could have opened to a great cattle market in St. Louis.[21]

The following day McCoy headed to the offices of the H&StJ. He knew he needed to negotiate a good freight rate in order for there to be any possibility of making money, so it made sense that he would seek out H. H. Courtright, the general freight agent of the company. Apparently, McCoy and Courtright hit it off, as McCoy left feeling buoyed and with a contract in hand setting "satisfactory rates of freight from the Missouri River to Quincy, thence to Chicago." One factor that may have played a part in McCoy's satisfaction with this arrangement was the formation of the Chicago Union Stockyards.

Prior to 1867, Joseph McCoy and his brothers, James and William, had created one of the most flourishing cattle-trading companies in all of Illinois. The Civil War demolished the cattle trade in the South, and had the opposite effect on the trade conducted at Chicago. In 1860 Chicago packinghouses processed over 51,000 beeves, and the various stockyards received more than 117,000 cattle. In 1865 over 95,000 beeves were processed, and the yards handled more than 330,000 animals. This massive increase in the cattle trade conducted in Chicago allowed stock buyers such as the McCoy brothers to reap handsome profits.[22]

However, the numerous stockyards operating in Chicago created hazards for drovers, buyers, and city residents alike. Drovers had to drive cattle through several city streets to reach any of the stockyards. Often cattle suffered hoof injuries that led to illnesses and serious infections. All who participated in the cattle trade advocated for a more centralized stockyard facility. John Sherman, who owned and operated the Sherman Yards, led the effort to consolidate the various yards into one entity. He convinced the managers of nine railroad companies to provide over $925,000 in capital to build a facility on the outskirts of Chicago. Once completed, the Union Stock Yard and Transit Company provided railroad links to nearly all the major lines leading to East Coast cities. The McCoy brothers were well aware of the advantages this yard provided in shipping cattle.[23]

McCoy had little to do with transporting cattle from Chicago to the East Coast. That lot fell to other dealers and railroad companies. Cattle often fared poorly on several of these trails leading to cities like New York. After being hauled to New York City by the Atlantic and Great Western Railway Company (A&GW), the cattle arrived in such terrible shape, "wasted by disease consequent upon confinement," that they fetched twenty dollars less per head than what they sold for in Chicago.[24]

Often, transporting beeves from Chicago to the East Coast resulted in more than a loss in investments. Professor Eban Norton Horsford of Harvard University investigated the consequential losses to the army in the shipment of cattle from Chicago to Boston. His report to the Medical and Subsistence Department of the army detailed how cattle purchased in Chicago weighing 1,500 pounds could lose as much as 200 pounds of "dress beef" by the time they reached Boston stockyards. This situation resulted in poor meat quality as well as great economic losses for any shipper purchasing cattle in Chicago, whether the federal government or an independent buyer. Of course it also speaks to immense cruelties endured by cattle traveling the iron trails leading from Chicago to the East Coast.[25]

Two other trails commenced once cattle arrived at the stockyards outside New York City or Boston. One trail led through the city streets to the slaughterhouses in lower downtown Manhattan. The Board of Health identified at least 180 slaughterhouses killing on average four thousand animals a week, and disposing of about four hundred tons of blood and offal via the sewer system that led to the slips along the western wharfs.[26]

These packinghouses were located in the heart of the city. A small one was located at 218 Mott Street, and others stood nearby at 185, 189, and 193 Elizabeth Street. There the houses of Haw, Hanlin, and Quimby not only slaughtered animals but also operated a "fat boiling establishment and hide curing vats." Eisner, Kutz, Harrington, and Westheimer operated slaughterhouses occupying nearly the entire block of First Avenue between Houston and First Street. There nearly one-fourth of all the meat consumed by New Yorkers was slaughtered and dressed. At all these shops the refuse associated with slaughtering and dressing the animals was simply disposed of on site. As reported in the *New York Times*:

> All of these establishments are located in the most densely populated portions of the City, are surrounded by long rows of tenement houses, which are filled to overflowing with men, women and particularly children. These latter congregate in swarms around the slaughter pens and revel in the filth there accumulated. To describe in detail what we saw would be to sicken our readers, and make them foreswear the use of meat forever.[27]

Eventually the Board of Health succeeded in relocating the slaughterhouses to 106th Street along the East River and removing one set of well-trodden cattle trails in the city.[28] Close by on 100th Street were the National Stockyards, where Texas cattle were unloaded and driven to the "New Abattoirs."

## Steamboat Trails to London and Havana

The other trail led to the wharfs, where longshoremen loaded cattle into steamboats headed to English ports. Not until 1868 did enough cattle follow the trails into New York City to warrant being shipped abroad. And even then, Texas cattle were largely shunned by English importers. The earliest recorded attempt to ship live cattle and dressed beef from Chicago to London occurred in 1868. One report indicated that $733,395 worth of cattle was exported to Europe in 1868, and fully 62 percent of that trade transpired with England.[29] The "live" transatlantic Texas cattle languished until English importers became confident in the health of the animals. By 1884 their confidence had grown to the point that 95 percent of the cattle exported to England originated west of Chicago.[30]

By 1875, the Anchor Line steamship company had dramatically improved its methods for hauling cattle across the Atlantic Ocean trails leading to the ports of Glasgow and London. The improvement was the result of advances in refrigerated technology in its steamboats. This opened a flourishing transatlantic "dead meat" trade. By 1877, the company had outfitted six of its mail steamers with this technology, and each of the vessels could haul between 360 and 450 carcasses.[31]

Besides the trails' ends in the rapidly growing urban markets of the United States and London, other trails' ends existed. One was Havana, Cuba, reached by drovers who headed their longhorns to Galveston, where the cattle were loaded onto steamboats bound for Cuba. In 1866, the export trade of Texas cattle in Galveston, Texas, had begun to resume its prewar activity. Again it became commonplace to watch shippers like Captain Ricker oversee the loading of three hundred longhorns onto his steamboat, the *Mexico*. In May 1866 the captain began hauling cattle regularly between Havana and Galveston.[32] By 1884 Cuba had become the second largest importer of American cattle.[33]

McCoy fully understood how Abilene was to function as a way station for cattle to be driven to other destinations. Besides supplying urban markets, McCoy intended to tap the vast "territorial" markets. These arenas, as McCoy put it, "greatly aided [Abilene] in becoming a complete market—one in which any kind, sort, or sized cattle could either be bought or sold; and the driving of herds purchased at Abilene, to the Territories," as he called the public domain, "became quite as common as driving from Texas to Abilene." Indian reservations more often than not formed the trail's end for cattle entering this market. Northern cattle buyers acquired most of the contracts for supplying reservations with their beef rations. This became a lucrative market for both southern drovers who sold their herds to northern buyers, and for the northern buyers who supplied the reservations.[34]

McCoy's and the UPED directors' development of the Texas cattle trade created more than trails' ends for cattle; it also created another type of trail leading to the end of the wild grassland ecosystem. The full-blown economics of the cattle trade coupled with European American cultural values created domesticated grassland. In essence, the Chisholm Trail, a region encompassing the grasslands from central Texas north to central Kansas and directed by North American and British economic forces, should be more readily understood as a transitional ecosystem than simply as a pathway for Texas cattle herds. As an ecosystem, or a dynamic community of life forms and physical forces, the Chisholm Trail was ephemeral, bridging a previous ecosystem that had been largely shaped by the presence of Indians and a later one formed when farmers dominated the landscape.

From 1860 to 1885 Texas drovers endeavored to control the water and solar-energy resources of the Chisholm Trail in culturally and economically shaped pursuits. In doing so they altered the dynamic properties of the trail's environment. These changes remade not only the plants, animals, and water resources but also the culture and lives of the people who occupied the region.

As farmers took hold of the Chisholm Trail environment by the early 1870s, they constructed an entirely new biome, one conducive neither to open-range cattle operations nor to American Indian hunting practices. The long-standing biomes of American Indians, prairie grasses, and animals disappeared. The public domain grassland biome, necessary for Texas cattle drives, also gave way to agricultural biomes that displaced the wild grasslands altogether. For both American Indians and Texas drovers, the results were the same: they could not maintain their material cultures.[35] In 1867, at the small hamlet of Abilene, Kansas, Alexander Gardner had captured in his photographs the beginning of this ecological drama.

CHAPTER 3

# Why Abilene, Kansas?

PRE–CIVIL WAR CATTLE TRADE — NEW ORLEANS AND GALVESTON CATTLE SHIPPING — THE WATERLOO OF SIXTY-SIX — THE KANSAS QUARANTINE LINE, AND GOVERNOR CRAWFORD WINKS AN EYE — JOSEPH MCCOY AND THE UNION PACIFIC RAILWAY, EASTERN DIVISION

There is little indication in Alexander Gardner's photographs that Abilene would become the hub around which would spin the Texas cattle trade. But there would be the hub—all through the efforts of a young twenty-nine-year-old Illinoisan with unbounded ambition and foresight. Joseph McCoy intuitively understood many of the forces that would allow Abilene to become the major outlet for the Texas cattle trade. But he could not see all the risks involved as he placed his bets on Abilene. Some risks were infinitesimal organisms powerful enough to wipe his table clean. Others were vast market and ecological forces that lay beyond his comprehension. Yet McCoy paid little heed to the risks. As the man who owned the house, he thought that he had fixed the odds in his favor as he placed his bets on the cards laid on the great cattle faro table.

During the day on September 4, 1867, workers at Abilene busily erected large tents beside the tracks of the Union Pacific Railway Company, Eastern Division (UPED). Under canvas shade, one special table was set with bottles of wine, serving plates, and glasses, while cooks prepared a "substantial repast . . . devoured with a relish peculiar to camp life." McCoy, the host of this "auspicious event," as he would later call it, anxiously anticipated the arrival of his guests, including his buddies in the Illinois cattle business "and others," including UPED railroad managers, politicians, and businesspeople and their spouses. By evening, the guests had arrived and found everything ready for a night of drinking wine, making toasts and speeches, eating, singing, and most likely drinking more wine. They came prepared to witness on the following day the first loading of four hundred Texas cattle into twenty stock cars bound on the first leg of a trip to the

Chicago stockyards. On the following day, September 5, 1867, before the sun had set, the celebrants watched as the locomotive steamed out from Abilene with its first load of Texas longhorns.[1]

In the great game of cattle wheeling and dealing, McCoy believed his bet on Abilene would turn up a winner. He knew the recent history of the Texas cattle trade well enough to have confidence in the potential success of his "Great Western Stock Yards." But as in any game of chance, the Texas cattle game involved numerous risks, and sometimes the odds failed to work in McCoy's favor.

## *Pre–Civil War Cattle Trade*

Before 1867, Joseph McCoy was well acquainted with how the spread of Texas fever had shaped the Texas cattle trade. Midwestern cattlemen's and farmers' shorthorn herds never encountered this disease unless they were near a drive of Texas longhorns. Perplexing all ranchers, however, was the fact that longhorn cattle seemed unscathed by the disease. But midwestern cattlemen knew that whenever Texas cattle were close, their own herds rapidly succumbed to the disease in distressingly large numbers. So it was in Kansas in 1860.

Even under the best conditions, establishing a farmstead in a territorial state was hard work and often led to failure. Given the conditions endured by Kansans in 1860—high temperatures compounded by a severe lack of rain—it is a wonder that any of them remained in the territory a year later. Major Surgeon Thomas C. Madison kept the daily weather reports at Fort Riley, located at the junction of the Republican and Smoky Hill Rivers that formed the head of the Kansas River, and his records indicated harsh, dry conditions during the spring of 1860. In March, Madison recorded zero rainfall at the post. In April, he recorded only a mere 0.13 of an inch of rain. In May only 1.16 inches of rain fell on four separate days—the 5th, 7th, 22nd, and 31st. Temperatures soared at the same time, with highs of 89 degrees in April, 95 in May, 97 in June, 113 in July, and 108 in August. Altogether, during what should have been the prime planting and harvesting seasons, farming in Kansas had turned into a dusty disaster.[2]

By September, only the lucky grower eked out a miserable existence in the territory. At best, farm families endured a desperate situation and looming destitution. In Lyon County, the people of Fremont Township reported a corn crop that might produce 2 bushels to the acre. In Pike Township, people reported a similar situation, whereas the year before they had harvested 70 bushels of corn per acre. In Auburn Township in Shawnee County, farmers had raised a mere 95 bushels of corn, whereas the year before, they had harvested over 30,000. Of the sixty-four families living in the township, thirty-three were flat broke. Judge Graham of Center Township in Madison County noted that three-fourths of the residents there were on the verge of leaving. Making matters worse, Texas fever appeared and decimated the small cattle holdings, leaving families without dairy or meat animals.

In fact, Texas fever had made its presence known throughout the counties from the eastern boundary of the territory to the westernmost organized ones, a little west of Fort Riley. Territorial Kansans correctly associated the presence of the disease with the arrival of Texas cattle being driven near their own herds. Texas drovers favored a few routes through Kansas as they headed their herds north toward Illinois. One route extended along the Neosho River, to the Verdigris River, then to Eagle Creek and along the Cottonwood River to Dow Creek and the Kansas River Valley. From there, most drovers took their herds east to the Missouri River where a ferry took them to St. Joseph, Missouri. By 1860, the tracks of the Hannibal and St. Joseph Railroad (H&StJ) had reached the city, and the railroad company provided a direct access to the Chicago market. The other cattle route led along the eastern border of the state and followed the military road connecting Fort Leavenworth to Fort Towson to the south. This trail also led to Missouri River ferry crossings that provided connections to the H&StJ line.

Texas cattlemen also drove their stock north along what they called the Shawnee Trail. From central Texas, the trail led through Indian Territory below the southeastern border of Kansas. Once in Kansas, the trail crossed the southeastern portion of the state and beyond into Missouri until reaching either the city of Sedalia or St. Joseph, both of which had rail connections leading east.

Along all these routes, Texas fever struck native cattle herds with a vengeance. In six weeks, Texas longhorns left a trail of dead animals from the Neosho River to the Kansas Valley. During this time span, one estimate put the Kansas losses at over three hundred head of cattle. Although this overall loss may appear small, it created an intolerable situation for farm families. Most of the residents owned small herds that supplied their immediate meat and dairy needs. If fortunate, they might have possessed a few steers for market. In one township in Lyon County, William Shockly lost four cows, one bull, and two calves. S. F. Graham and his family lost four cows and two steers. G. R. Harper's family suffered the loss of four steers, one cow, and two yearlings. In total, this one township lost over forty cattle in the space of a week.³

Angry farmers gathered in Emporia to seek restitution. At the very least, they resolved to keep Texas longhorns out of Lyon County. Failing to achieve this goal meant that anyone pursuing stock raising in Kansas "may as well abandon that branch of the . . . business at once." They were not ready to forsake cattle raising, so they resolved to use force "sufficient to secure the end aimed at."⁴

Earlier in the year, the residents of Bourbon County had devised a recommendation for preventing the spread of Texas fever, which the Kansas legislature would eventually embrace. A mass meeting of angry county residents living in Osage Township took place on account of the "severe losses" that they had endured as a result of Texas cattle drives through their range. The farmers wanted formal legislation that would "prohibit droves of Spanish cattle from passing through [their] township after the first of April each year, and until the last day of October." They, like many others, believed that longhorns posed no imminent danger to their native herds during the cold months from November through March. Experience seemed to support their thinking, even if they failed to understand the reason why this was largely the case.⁵

Without hesitation, the members of the first legislature of the state of Kansas acted to protect their livestock raisers from Spanish fever, now called Texas fever. In section 4 of "An Act to Provide for the Protection of Stock from Contagious Diseases," the legislature placed strict restrictions on the movement of Texas cattle into Kansas. The law prohibited anyone from driving "any drove or droves of cattle from the States of Texas, Arkansas or the Indian territory lying south of the State of Kansas, between the first day of April and November in each year." Governor Charles Robinson signed the legislation into law on May 1, 1861.⁶

## *New Orleans and Galveston Cattle Shipping*

During the Civil War, Kansas farmers' fears of Texas fever receded as ranchers in Indian Territory and Texas lost all access to cattle outlets to the north. About the only markets that Texans could reach were at Mississippi River towns, and once those cities fell to Union forces, no other safe outlets remained. By May 1862, the port city of New Orleans had fallen to Union naval forces commanded by David Farragut. The Union occupation of the city cut off all river traffic that could have delivered Texas beef to Confederate forces. By mid-June, fewer than half of the meat stalls in the city market had anything to offer, and what was offered was of inferior quality, hardly suitable for sale. A reporter for the *New Orleans Picayune* simply called the beef "wretched." Even this meat commanded exceptionally high prices. A beef steak cut from this inferior grade commanded over a dollar a pound, whereas prior to the war, a "vastly superior steak" had seldom realized more than forty cents a pound.[7]

The editor of the *Picayune* anxiously longed for a return to prosperity. The Civil War had wrecked the trade that had once flowed into his city. The cost of food had dramatically risen, and as a result, many people vacated the city to look elsewhere for work and sustenance. One factor could alleviate the situation and bring down food costs, and that was the importation of beef and mutton from the "great grazing State," Texas.[8]

The editor took heart from the example of driving sheep to New Orleans. In 1862, Texans with large flocks of sheep in the Rio Grande Valley had driven their animals to New Orleans and received a nice return on their efforts. As reported, the sheep had crossed rich meadowlands dotted with numerous fresh water ponds. The care given by the drovers resulted in animals reaching the city in better shape than animals "imprisoned" and crowded onto steamboats and flatboats without anything to eat but dry hay. The reporter thought the same result would come to postwar Texas ranchers who raised "fat and deliciously flavored beeves" on their mesquite grass (*Hilaria belangeri*) pastures.[9]

Yet more often than not, driving cattle from Texas to New Orleans resulted in emaciated animals on arrival. First, the drovers had a difficult path to travel before reaching New Orleans, given the Union forces' readiness to intercept them. Second, Confederate forces often seized the herds and gave the drovers a difficult time if the animals were not intended to feed soldiers. In October 1862, Confederate forces still controlled the port of Mobile, Alabama. This meant that Texas drovers had the prospect, if not a difficult one, of delivering a herd to Mobile and disposing of it there. This meant swimming a herd across the Mississippi River.

At Goliad, Texas, W. D. Saunders launched a drive of eight hundred head of cattle with the goal of Mobile in mind. Twice, Confederate forces, thinking Saunders's herd bound for Yankee forces, arrested him and his fellow cowhands. Each time, Saunders and his crew demonstrated their rebel loyalty and were released. After swimming his herd across the Mississippi River, but without ever reaching Mobile, Saunders eventually sold his longhorns to buyers in Woodville,

Mississippi. Saunders found this a hard way to make cattle driving pay.[10]

Only fifteen years old at the time, E. M. Daggett helped drive a herd of steers rounded up north of Fort Worth, Texas, with the goal of reaching Shreveport, Louisiana. He tied sacks of biscuits, dried beef, and coffee to his horse and rode across a rough route. As he recalled the ordeal, the herd "stampeded pretty nearly every night from the time we left the prairies . . . until we got them loaded on boats for shipment to New Orleans." The proceeds from the drive were hardly worth the effort. The price per head amounted to little more than six dollars. On the ride home, Daggett had to hide continuously from African American Union troops stationed between Marshall, Texas, and Fort Worth. During the Civil War, driving cattle out of Texas proved difficult at best and rendered poor returns on investments.[11]

The editor of the *Picayune* correctly realized that New Orleans was cut off from the immense herds of Texas cattle that languished without any prospect of reaching the markets of his city. Even the scant number of herds that reached New Orleans arrived showing "very bad usage on the long route from Texas." The editor attributed their condition to either a scant supply of forage or a "rebellious spirit" that produced "a very lean and unwholesome condition of flesh and blood, in man or beast."[12]

Not until the very end of the Civil War did Texas cattle start returning to the New Orleans markets. A slight change began in July 1865 when a Yankee steamboat, appropriately named the *New York*, transported the first Texas cattle to travel the river since the fall of New Orleans to Union forces in May. The 106 head of cattle launched the editor into poetic joy: "Hard times come no more, Better times come of yore." This gave hope to the editor that Texas cattle would now arrive via steamboats rather than driven over land, which would result in longhorns only "somewhat reduced" before reaching the city. Of course, this trade relied on Union forces and Yankee ships which was not an ideal situation for rebel cattlemen.[13]

If Union control of the Mississippi River made it almost impossible for Texans to deliver cattle into the New Orleans market, transportation costs made such drives unprofitable regardless of whether or not Texas cattle could reach the city market. Drovers from eastern Texas who headed their herds due east to Shreveport, Louisiana, hoped to load the animals onto steamboats headed downriver to New Orleans. What they did not foresee was the high riverboat transportation costs that surpassed the initial purchase price of each head. As a result, numbers of cattle piled up at Shreveport as drovers waited for either the cost of transportation to fall or cattle prices to rise. Anticipating an increase in cattle prices proved hopeless as the numbers of cattle increased at the port. This created a dismal state of affairs for cattlemen—after having driven herds three hundred miles to Shreveport—when they had to sell their stock for less than it had cost to buy it in the first place.[14]

Also, drovers had to confront the fact that some shippers dominated the trade out of Texas to New Orleans. Sam L. Allen was one such individual who had his company office in Houston and shipped out of Powder Horn, Texas. Powder Horn was a port town on Matagorda Bay that by 1857 had a semiweekly line of steamers sailing to New Orleans.[15] After the end of the Civil War, William J. Bennett recalled that Allen regularly sent runners advertising his connections to the New Orleans market. Soon thereafter Allen held a monopoly on shipping cattle out of Powder Horn to New Orleans. But Allen's line could handle only so many cattle, and this still left millions of longhorns bunched on the central rangelands of Texas, waiting for other outlets.[16]

## *The Waterloo of Sixty-Six*

With the end of the Civil War, Texas ranchers saw outlets opening other than just New Orleans for placing their herds into rapidly growing urban markets. Texans possessed enormous herds that were essentially worthless without markets commensurate with the size of their holdings. As one rancher summarized his plight:

> Any man in [Texas] who does not own 400 head of cattle and 70 or 100 horses and mules is worse than worthless. Beef sells here at five cents per pound, horses and mules from $15 to $30 for round lots; and are within 250 miles of a good market. As far as the eye can reach in every direction, and as far as you may go, the country is alive with stock. The whole market of the United States might be supplied here, and there would not be any apparent decrease.[17]

Judge Quinlan of San Antonio, Texas, succinctly described the situation this way: "A man was poorer in proportion to the number of cattle bearing his brand."[18]

By June 1866, many drovers had attempted to drive their herds east to the Mississippi River docks. In a letter from Travis County, the writer noted how "a large amount of all kinds of stock has been driven to Missouri, Tennessee, Louisiana, and other States." However, the drovers faced some deadly obstacles going east to Tennessee and Louisiana. Unusually high rainfall in May had flooded many rivers and made swimming cattle across them exceptionally dangerous. In one report, large numbers of horses and cattle drowned while crossing these swollen streams. As a result, one writer predicted that "Texas stock speculators" would sustain serious losses. For Texas ranchers, it was simply a matter of too many cattle with too few places to go.[19]

Trailing north to railroad connections in Missouri would prove no easier than heading east. With the plight of 1860 still fresh in their memory, Kansas farmers knew that they had good reason to fear the spread of Texas fever with the return of Texas cattle drivers. While farmers displayed remarkable ignorance about the nature of this disease, they understood that their own domestic shorthorn cattle often suffered immensely whenever Texas cattle herds were nearby. They also realized that legislation passed in 1861 still allowed Texas cattle to enter the state. Understandably, they took every action within their power to prevent any losses to their own herds. And they wanted their legislators to craft restrictive measures to keep Texas cattle completely out of the state.

In January 1865, it was clear to nearly every observer, whether in the South or the North, that it was just a matter of time before the Confederacy would fall. For those serving in the Kansas legislature, the end of the war raised the frightening prospects of the return of Texas cattle into the state. These lawmakers understood just how unpopular Texas cattle were among their constituents. In February 1865, they enacted a more stringent law prohibiting any drive of cattle from "the state of Texas, or from the territory south of the south line" of the state from entering.

Governor Samuel J. Crawford signed this legislation into law on February 11, 1865. On the face of it, one would think that this act would have thoroughly discouraged Texas drovers. However, the 1865 act had little real effect on Texas cattle drives into Kansas toward the end of the Civil War. Even if Texas ranchers wanted to drive a herd into Kansas, the chaotic postwar situation in Texas precluded them from putting one together. In the first place, in the spring, Confederate forces were still resisting the Union Army. Not until June did Texas commanders finally capitulate, which meant the season was far too advanced for anyone to organize a herd for a drive to the north.

By the early spring of 1866, order and conditions had improved enough for

Texas drovers to organize herds intended for northern markets. Realizing this, and understanding the potential economic gains to be realized in the Texas cattle trade, Kansas legislators softened their position on allowing Texas cattle drives through the state. Governor Crawford signed into law an act repealing the 1865 legislation that had prohibited Texas cattle from entering the state.

Few Kansans favored this act of the legislature, and many feared the "destruction of thousands of dollars worth of stock, and the ruin of now prosperous farmers." However, there was a motivating factor in the legislature's change of heart. Apparently, several prominent Kansas stock buyers saw a great opportunity in traveling to Texas, buying cattle cheaply, and reaping fantastic returns when unloading them into northern markets. Obviously, their ambitions would be thwarted at the outset without a repeal of the 1865 legislation.[20]

When the legislature passed its 1866 act regulating Texas cattle drives, it left intact the provisions of the 1861 act. Consequently, the door into Kansas remained shut to Texas drovers and their herds until November 1. By the end of April 1866, reports flowed back into Kansas newspapers informing readers that thousands of cattle had been gathered and were bound for Kansas. This set off alarms throughout the state. An article from the *Wyandotte* (Kansas) *Gazette* encouraged "farmers in this and adjoining counties" to combine to "make a crusade against any persons who shall dare attempt to bring Texas cattle" anywhere near the city and its environs.[21]

For Texas drovers, it was simply that if they could get their longhorn herds to St. Joseph, Missouri, then they could load the cattle into the stock cars of the H&StJ, which led directly to the Chicago market. Some northeastern Kansas cattlemen raising shorthorn herds were doing very well for themselves doing just that. In August, they were loading thousands of cattle on the St. Joseph and Hannibal line. William Ellsworth, who owned the St. Joseph and Elwood ferry, did a booming business hauling Kansas cattle across the Missouri River to his landing at St. Joseph. One day at the end of July, during one early morning between two o'clock and nine o'clock, he transported 1,048 cattle across the river. In the month of July, he crossed over 7,000 head of cattle, all raised in northeastern Kansas.[22]

The conflicting aspirations of Texas ranchers and Kansas farmers resulted in making the cattle-driving season of 1866 one of the worst ever encountered by Texas drovers. Their problems did not include a lack of animals to drive north; they had plenty. They did not lack rail connections that would transport their herds north; there was one at Sedalia, Missouri, and another at St. Joseph, Missouri. Their problems lay in where the cattle trails led.

The routes to either city passed through the southeastern portion of Kansas and the southwestern portion of Missouri. The farmers in those areas were aware of the thousands of longhorns being assembled into herds south of the Kansas and Missouri borders and they were ready to mount massive resistance to the intrusion of Texas longhorn herds. For the Texas drovers, their efforts proved "disastrous in the extreme." By one estimate, Texans managed to save "only a few thousand" of the over 240,000 cattle that they attempted to drive to the railheads in Missouri. For the stockmen involved in this season, it became known as the "Waterloo of sixty-six."[23]

Not all Kansans opposed the transit of Texas cattle through the state. Some enterprising individuals anticipated making remarkable gains from this pent-up cattle trade. As reported in the papers at the time, some Kansans left for Texas to purchase cattle at rock-bottom prices with the intention of driving them north to fetch higher returns.[24]

More often than not, they found themselves in discouraging situations as they neared or crossed the southern border of the state. For example, the sheriff of Douglas County, a Mr. Knowles, acquired two hundred head of cattle, and the Leavenworth firm of Repine, Eves, and Company purchased one thousand longhorns. In May 1866, Knowles had his herd grazing on the upper reaches of Rock Creek in the Cherokee Neutral Lands (today the lower southeastern counties of Kansas), where he thought he was outside the area where Kansas law applied. About fifteen men "called on" him and ordered him to take his cattle back south of the border immediately. Repine and Eves met a harsher reception. They were keeping their cattle south of the border when about fifty head of their herd stampeded and crossed into Kansas at Turkey Creek (in present-day Chautauqua County). Some "citizens" quickly organized a vigilante posse, overtook the cattle, and slaughtered all of them.[25]

Their brutal and illegal activity aside, Kansas farmers reacted fiercely given their good reasons to fear the spread of Texas fever, and they never hesitated to prevent the passage of longhorns anywhere near their own herds. In May, in Johnson County, men met in several townships and formed committees charged with informing Texas drovers that they must avoid bringing herds into the state. A. Arrasmith chaired a meeting in Oxford Township in which a resolution was drafted notifying "the owners of Texas cattle that they will be resisted by law and all other means." In Shawnee Township, Samuel Pitt conducted a meeting that made it clear that its members had "suffered greatly heretofore, and we well know that Texas cattle and our cattle cannot range and live on the same lands."[26]

Throughout the late spring and early summer, any Texas drover attempting to pass through Kansas met with concerted opposition. In May, men turned out near Owl Creek (Linn County) and stopped a herd of six hundred Texas cattle being driven north. As reported, the Kansans residing there were "wide awake and determined to keep the Spanish fever" from destroying their own herds.[27] In June, the sheriff of Greenwood County arrested a drover, made him pay a seventy-five-dollar fine, and then forced him to drive his herd south of the border.[28] In July, again in the Neutral Lands near Fort Scott, an armed group attacked a Texas herd and "shot down" a number of the cattle.[29] In late July, the folks residing near Pleasant Hill struck down a herd, killing 150 cattle intended for the St. Louis market.[30] Understandably, these farmers willingly took every conceivable action to prevent any losses to their own herds.

Besides losing their herds, Texas drovers themselves risked bodily harm if not, on a rare occasion, death, once they entered Kansas. J. Hargus recalled helping his stepfather drive a herd north starting out in Martindale, Texas, in March 1866. When they crossed over the southern borders of Kansas and Missouri, they claim to have encountered a James M. Daugherty tied to a tree.

Daugherty, merely twenty years old, had led a crew driving a herd of one thousand longhorns toward Sedalia, Missouri. From there, he intended to load the cattle into Missouri Pacific Railroad stock cars bound for St. Louis. As he recalled what followed, somewhere near the Kansas-Missouri border, horse-mounted vigilantes stopped him, and the leader told Daugherty "them thar steers couln't go an inch fudder." Daugherty tried to negotiate a safe passage, but the vigilantes would hear nothing of it given their fear of Texas fever. To emphasize that they meant business, the border men dragged the young Texan from his horse, tied him to a tree, took a hickory switch, and whipped his back until it was lacerated and bleeding.[31]

Next the vigilantes stampeded his herd, but luckily, the cowboys in the rear of the herd understood the danger and raced ahead of the rampaging animals until they found a meadow to the west where they milled the herd until it had calmed down. Once in control of the cattle, they drove the longhorns several miles westward where they hoped to be out of harm's way. In the meantime, Daugherty's tormentors untied him and told him to leave and not come back. Instead, the young Texan adroitly followed the path left by his stampeding herd and eventually found the rest of his outfit.

With considerable resolve, Daugherty eventually disposed of his herd. He held his cattle near Baxter Springs, Kansas, for a couple of weeks while he recovered from his beating. Then he took one hundred head and under the cover of night, drove them to Fort Scott, where he was able to sell them. Next, he worked out an arrangement with a buyer in Baxter Springs and sold the remaining herd to him.

Hargus may or may not have met Daugherty while working his own herd north. He simply may have heard of Daugherty's plight as it was a well-known tale. Regardless, Hargus's experience was less harmful. His stepfather, Reverend W. H. Farmer, managed to deliver the herd to the outskirts of Joplin, Missouri, where he grazed the cattle all summer long. Unlike Daugherty, Farmer had friendly connections in Missouri, and through these he arranged to pay ten dollars for each head of cattle that any farmer lost within a ten-mile radius of Farmer's herd. This gave local farmers insurance coverage and Farmer time enough to fatten his longhorns before loading them into stock cars bound for St. Louis.[32]

The majority of drovers, however, obeyed Kansas law, and began waiting until November before entering the state on their way to take their herds to either Sedalia or Saint Joseph. By September, drovers had gathered large herds to the south of the state border, and some attempted to drive them north a good month before Kansas law allowed it. A few others ran the risk of driving herds through western Missouri, then circling back into Kansas to reach the St. Joseph ferry crossing. Toward the end of September, despite being harassed by armed farmers, a few Texas drovers reached Ellsworth's ferry operation with over 1,500 head of cattle.[33] But these intrepid drovers represented just a few of the ones who remained in Cherokee Nation with their herds. By the end of September, drovers had an estimated 100,000 longhorns readied for drives to Saint Joseph, as this city had become favored over Sedalia for its better rail connections.[34]

Even with November 1 looming—marking the time when Kansas law allowed Texas cattle to be driven through the state—Kansans still organized to prohibit drives anywhere near their homes and farms. Josiah Kinnaman, who lived near Eureka, Kansas, helped organize a meeting with the express purpose of stopping any drives through Greenwood County. The attendees drafted a clearly stated resolution that stated, "We hereby give notice to owners, dealers, herdsmen, and contractors in [the Texas cattle trade] of our determination" to prevent any drives. The resolution continued, "We will not hesitate to take the lives of men or beasts, if it should become necessary, in order to protect our property."[35]

In November this backlash created a dire situation for Texas cattlemen on the southern border of Kansas. What struck Joseph McCoy, as he later summed up the situation, was that very few Texas cattle "found their way to a profitable market." While drovers waited for the first "very cold" weather of November to appear, McCoy described how the grass had "long become dead and unnutritious" resulting in cattle losing so much weight that they often sold for less than the drover had paid for them in Texas. Making matters worse, after the first frost had dried out the grass, the "whole country" was set on fire. This could have been the work of Cherokees who had grown impatient with Texas cattle eating up their rangelands. Setting the grass on fire destroyed the stored solar fuel supply for the Texas herds, and this lack of fuel forced drovers out of the area. In summing up the 1866 season, McCoy called it "one of great disaster to Southern drovers."[36]

The debacle of 1866 gave the young Illinoisan a vision for creating a safe cattle and profitable outlet for Texas longhorns. The idea gelled in his brain when he met W. W. Suggs. Suggs was thirty-one years old when he met McCoy, and had, like many other young men of his day, wandered about the West looking to make good prior to the Civil War. After the war, he returned to his native Texas and in 1866 drove a herd of longhorns, hoping to unload them in Illinois. Like Daugherty's his back showed the scars left by a well-laid-on hickory branch. Despite his ordeal, somehow he managed to bring his herd to Christian County, Illinois, where he overwintered his cattle. In the early spring, he looked for a buyer, who turned out to be Joseph McCoy.

As the two sealed the deal, Suggs told McCoy of "Texas' great supply of cattle and the insurmountable barrier in Southwestern Missouri and Southeastern Kansas" to any passing of longhorns. This chance meeting launched the twenty-nine-year-old McCoy on a mission to find a suitable location where he might build a cattle-loading depot on the UPED where drovers like Suggs might conduct their business unimpeded and unmolested. From that moment on, Suggs and McCoy became fast friends and business accomplices.[37]

One other cattleman provided Joseph McCoy with the impetus to build an outlet for Texas drovers. In 1866, while some drovers like Suggs headed toward

Illinois, others pushed on for Sedalia, Missouri. Those who finally did make it to the rail connections and stockyards in Sedalia lost heavily in terms of animals and money. Colonel John Jacob Myers was one such unfortunate fellow. By 1867, he had tucked quite a bit of life's experiences under his belt. He was born in 1821 and raised in Missouri. As a young man, he traveled extensively through the western portions of North America, served in the US Army during the War with Mexico, married, and had taken his family to Texas by 1851. With the outbreak of the Civil War, he joined the Texas cavalry, and rose to the rank of lieutenant colonel before the end of the war. After the war, he resumed his farming and ranching and, like many other Texas cattlemen, desired a means to place his cattle into northern markets. Much older than the youngsters James Daugherty and W. W. Suggs, he too bore signs of abuse received for his effort to drive a cattle herd through Kansas in 1866.

In the spring of 1867, John Myers, who was assessing the prospects of driving cattle into the state, stopped to rest at the Hale House in Junction City, Kansas. This hotel offered some the finest accommodations west of the Missouri River. Myers probably understood that an improved climate existed for the importation of Texas cattle into Kansas. By the middle of October 1866, the tracks of the UPED had reached Junction City. Many living there had great aspirations for making Junction City a major point of commerce, especially for ranching and farming. This was a good place for a Texas cattleman to get a read on the future possibilities of driving cattle to that portion of the state. The hotel parlor, known for its elegant furniture and tasteful decor, also provided a good setting for a successful Illinois stock buyer to assess the possibilities of cornering the transportation of Texas cattle onto railroad lines headed east.

Following up on his meeting with Suggs, Joseph McCoy arrived in Junction City in June 1867. One day, while staying in Hale House, he saw a man whom he described as "a small sized, quiet gentleman, who was evidently entering that class upon whose head Time had begun to sprinkle her silver frosts." McCoy was introduced to this Texan from Lockhart, the fifty-six-year-old Colonel J. J. Myers. McCoy viewed this as an opportune moment to discuss with Myers his vision for opening a stockyard where Texas drovers could safely ship or sell their herds. Myers agreed to hear McCoy out, so the two of them left the hotel and walked a few blocks until they found a lumber pile. There they sat for the next two hours, discussing the potential future of cattle driving into Kansas.

As McCoy recalled their conversation, Myers advised the young stock buyer "that such a depot, for cattle sale and shipment, was the greatest need of Texan stock men, and that whoever would establish and conduct such an enterprise, upon legitimate business principles, would be a benefactor to the entire Texan live stock interest, and would undoubtedly receive all the patronage that could reasonably be desired."[38] Together they discussed how to avoid trouble with Kansas farmers and find another route for placing Texas cattle into the burgeoning urban markets to the east. From that moment on, McCoy fixed his attention on building a loading dock, which in time would be at Abilene, Kansas.

## The Kansas Quarantine Line, and Governor Crawford Winks an Eye

Joseph McCoy and his brothers were ever on the lookout for new lucrative opportunities in the cattle trade. Together they managed a highly successful cattle buying-and-selling operation centered in Springfield, Illinois. Joseph, the youngest of the three, had the most to prove. The older two brothers, James and William, had already established themselves in the rapidly growing cattle markets of Illinois and New York. In 1866, it was not unusual for them to buy and ship a thousand head of cattle selling for $80 to $140 each. At least, that was what Joseph would have had one believe at the time. By the time James and William added Joseph to their endeavors, the three brothers did so much buying and selling that they amassed enough capital to invest elsewhere.

Standing out among the three, Joseph exuded an aggressive entrepreneurial bent. People who encountered him observed a nearly irrepressible spirit. Reporting for the *New York Tribune* in 1867, Samuel Wilkison described Joseph as a "young cattle-dealer, with Scotch blood in his veins, and the shrewdness, courage, and enterprise of his race in his head."[39] While Wilkison captured one aspect of McCoy's personality, he missed how prickly he could be and how intensely he could lash out in response to affront, real or imagined. Undoubtedly, McCoy could harbor a grudge for a long time—years, in fact.

In 1874, McCoy complained about Wilkison's article and berated the reporter as possessing "more stupid incredulity than brains." Somehow McCoy had read the *Tribune* piece as characterizing the opening of his Texas outlet at Abilene "a visionary farce."[40] McCoy, by 1874, smarting with his own run-in with the UPED, probably thought Wilkison had given far too much credit to the management of the railroad company for advancing the Texas cattle trade. In the 1867 write-up,

Wilkison had lauded the company as *the* "cheapener of beef to the people of the United States." McCoy found himself nowhere in the reporter's admiration, and he let Wilkison know it—seven years later.

As Wilkison pointed out, however, the McCoys foresaw vast potential gains in moving Texas beeves into eastern markets or into the territories by controlling the selling and buying at some spot accessible to Texas drovers. The demand was evident, and the means were beginning to come into focus. Railroad links to growing urban markets or open trails leading into the territories to the west were coming into view. The geography had to be just right because Texas drovers were understandably gun-shy, literally, about mixing with Kansas farmers and ranchers in the eastern half of the state. McCoy, after some intensive investigation, thought he had found the perfect location to connect Texas cattle with domestic and international urban markets.

In 1867, two events opened the door for the McCoy brothers. First, the Kansas legislature passed new legislation making it a little easier, under strict conditions, to bring Texas cattle into the state. Representative William Brown, a lawyer from Emporia, certainly had no intention of allowing Texas cattle anywhere near the farmers and ranchers in his district. He knew their fierce opposition to the presence of Texas cattle. However, Brown also realized, as did other businessmen in the state, the promise of buying cattle for pennies on the dollar in Texas or Indian Territory, and then reaping handsome profits by selling the stock at prevailing market prices in the Midwest.[41]

Brown's legislation mirrored the former 1861 act in that it allowed Texas cattle into the state during certain cold months of the year. The act permitted Texas drovers to drive cattle freely into Kansas during December, January, and February. But that was where the similarity with the 1861 act ended. Brown devised a quarantine line protecting the northern tier of counties and the eastern half of the state from cattle entering anytime other than during the winter months. The line, however, allowed drovers to drive cattle west of it at any time of year provided the herds were kept at least five miles away from any settlement or ranch unless the residents gave permission to do otherwise.

The quarantine also cleverly kept Texas cattle herds from being driven through the state to the Union Pacific Railroad (UP), which was being built across the state of Nebraska. This aspect protected the corporate interests of the UPED by ensuring the convenience of shipping cattle on its line. Even if the officers of the

UP tried to undercut the freight rates of the UPED, Texas drovers still lacked direct access to UP stockyards in Nebraska during the prime shipping months of the fall. Brown's legislation met with nearly unanimous approval in the House, passed in the Senate, and was signed into law on February 26, 1867.

Second, the UPED was making rapid progress in laying its tracks. On March 14, workers had completed laying track just to the west of Mud Creek. Abilene then had a rail connection. By early April, the company's rails were within a few miles of Salina, Kansas, the midway point across the state. By April 29, the company's trains began running regular schedules from Salina east to Wyandotte, Kansas (today Kansas City, Kansas). Although Salina and Abilene both remained well within the quarantine line, from Joseph McCoy's standpoint, they rested well west of where troubles had erupted between Texas drovers and Kansas farmers the year before.

Encouraged by his conversation with Colonel Myers, McCoy thought first to convince the folks of Junction City of the fine prospects in establishing a shipping facility. McCoy approached the "leading business men" in the city in an effort to acquire his lots next to the tracks of the UPED. The owner, according to McCoy, in an act of "donkey stupidity and avarice" asked for an exorbitant amount of money for his property. This unsatisfactory attempt to effect a deal shifted McCoy's focus to the west.[42]

McCoy's next stop was Solomon City because he was aware of the bountiful grasslands and ample water sources surrounding the settlement. Despite McCoy's view that the city had the potential to be a "fine site for stockyards," the residents, he asserted, greeted his proposition with "stupid horror." After failing there, he gave it another try with the folks of Salina to convince them that a stockyard there would be of great benefit to the city. Given their fears of Texas fever, the citizens of Salina deemed McCoy, as he recalled, little more than "a monster threatening calamity and pestilence." At this point, McCoy turned his attention to "a very small, dead place" called Abilene, Kansas. After some tedious negotiations, he managed to buy a small parcel of land from Charles Thompson, the farmer who owned the town site.[43]

McCoy knew Abilene had all the traits that made for a good cattle-shipping point, but he mischaracterized the country surrounding Abilene when he described it as "entirely" unsettled. Calling it unsettled implied that there was no one nearby who would get up in arms about the presence of longhorns and Texas fever. "Sparsely settled" might have been a more appropriate description, and those residents would need pacifying. McCoy also understood that the ample water sources and "excellent grass" made the area "adapted to holding cattle." After sealing the deal with Thompson, McCoy went straight to work building his operation beginning on July 5, 1867.

Despite having negotiated a successful contract with Thompson, McCoy expressed a low opinion of him. Thompson served as a representative in the Kansas legislature, which led McCoy to say, "alas! for his virtue" for being a politician. But McCoy probably kept on good terms with Thompson for sound reasons. For the two men to make good on their agreement, there had to be a way for McCoy to build his stockyard and shipping facility despite the fact that Abilene lay within the quarantine line imposed by the legislature.

The key lay, as McCoy saw it, in convincing the governor of the lucrative potential of his enterprise. Certainly it would not hurt for McCoy to have Thompson on his side working a deal in Topeka. As McCoy remembered it, Governor Crawford, who sensed "the magnitude and importance" of McCoy's undertaking, "freely gave a letter commending" McCoy's Abilene venture and the integrity of the McCoy brothers. The fact that Texas drovers combined to provide a $50,000 bond to cover any stock losses incurred by Kansas farmers as a result of Texas fever might also have played a role in the governor's disposition.[44]

Of course, critics opposed making an exception for Abilene. By 1865, William Lamb had built up a small herd of about twenty cattle in Dickinson County. In August 1867, he wrote to the governor regarding his concerns about the impending approach of Texas cattle. He referenced the 1867 legislation and asked, "If there is such a law why not enforce it, for there is now, or will be still coming, several thousand head of Texas Cattle." The settlers, Lamb claimed, were against McCoy's operation. He explained how there were "some very fine herds of cattle in this part of Kansas, and now to have the Texas cattle fever break out among them, would indeed be to [sic] bad. We are all afraid."[45]

By October 1867, the situation had turned dire for some in the county. Newton Blair, in a letter to the governor, accused all the locally elected officials of being "bought up." He failed to find any justice of the peace who would take up his charge that Texas cattlemen had broken state law. He also believed that local farmers had lost cattle due to "Spanish fever" and that Texas drovers had refused to reimburse the farmers for their losses. Blair was at a loss for what to do next when "civil courts refuse to act."[46]

According to McCoy, the governor retorted, "I regard the opening of that cattle trail into and across Western Kansas, of as much value to the State as is the Missouri river." With the governor's blessing in hand, the McCoy brothers still had several other tasks to complete before they could count on shipping cattle east on the UPED trains.

## *Joseph McCoy and the Union Pacific Railway, Eastern Division*

McCoy had to finalize details with the officers of the UPED before he could make Abilene the loading center for Texas cattle herds. At the corner of Fifth and Clark Street in downtown St. Louis, Missouri, stood the office building housing the railroad company offices. The president of the firm, John D. Perry, had his office on the second floor of this colonial red brick building. In the spring of 1867, when Joseph and James entered the president's office, they greeted a man little prepared to accommodate their proposal. The McCoy brothers intended to ship tens of thousands of Texas cattle in UPED stock cars, however Perry thought the brothers' proposition little more than a pipe dream.

Perhaps Perry understood something the McCoys did not. At the time, his company lacked the rolling stock that could facilitate the loading of tens of thousands of longhorns. In the fall of 1866, the *Junction City Weekly Union* reported that the company had yet to receive its order of a mere twenty cattle stock cars. In other words, in October 1866 the UPED lacked the resources to haul one single steer. In the near future, the twenty cars, if one car could haul 20 to 25 head of cattle, could transport only 400 to 500 head at a time. Consequently, an untold number of beeves would be left awaiting the next available loading, with the McCoys anticipating the arrival of individual herds numbering 1,000 animals or more. Perry knew he would have to invest heavily in stock cars if he were to meet the demand for the number of cattle estimated to arrive at the McCoys' stockyard. A lack of the necessary rolling stock would obviously blemish the company's reputation. So maybe there was more to Perry's initial hesitation other than thinking the McCoys foolish dreamers.

Perhaps in an attempt to mask his company's lack of rolling stock, Perry's bluster astonished both McCoy brothers. He knew he could order more stock cars, which he did soon by adding seven more cars by the middle of August, but he did not have them when he met with the McCoys.[47] So he responded aggressively: "I do not believe that you can, to any extent, establish or build up a cattle trade on our road. It looks too visionary, too chimerical, too speculative and it would be altogether too good a thing to ever happen to us, or our road." While Perry downplayed McCoy's vision, he was savvy enough to realize that his company could make a haul if the risk were left entirely with the brothers.[48]

After a brief moment of what appeared to be reconsideration, Perry told Joseph, "If you think you can get cattle freighted over our road (it is just the thing we want) and are willing to [use] your money in a stock and other necessary appendages, we will put in a switch and, if you succeed, *I will pledge that you shall have full and fair recompense.*" McCoy would later come to realize just what "fair recompense" was to mean, but when he and James left the office, they believed that they had nearly all the pieces put together that would allow them to harness the vast potential of the Texas cattle trade.[49]

Joseph McCoy must have felt elated, and perhaps some trepidation, too, while celebrating the building of his stockyards at Abilene on that cool night of September 4, 1867. As the celebrants ate the food he had prepared and drank his wine, his mind raced in anticipation of his prospects. He knew he was undertaking a huge gamble with his and his brothers' fortunes. But all the pieces seemed to be coming together. Longhorns had arrived, the stock cars stood ready to be loaded the next day, and cattle prices in Chicago and New York seemed strong. Above the eastern horizon of an unbroken grassland, a waxing moon rose, casting a soft glow on the festivities. Many had stood and had given rousing toasts to the young McCoy's achievement. Then it was Joseph's turn: "Whether this enterprise ultimately proves to be to our financial weal or woe, as individuals, it has been begun and will be prosecuted to the end, with the confident hope that it will be of great benefit to the people of the Southwest and the Northwest, as well as to the laboring millions of the Northeast."[50]

JOSEPH McCOY (b. December 21, 1837, d. October 19, 1915)
McCoy's life work was instrumental in transforming the American diet by creating a Texas cattle outlet in Abilene that led to a revolution in beef markets. More than this, his labors resulted in an ecological transition that transformed the sweeping grasslands of North America into the breadbasket of the world. As McCoy understood his work, he had cleared the wilderness and paved a path for American civilization to follow. As noted in one short biography of McCoy, he was conceded to be the "'Founder of the Southwestern Cattle Trade,' and by the federal and state governments has been recognized as an expert in matters pertaining to the livestock industry in the grazing regions." Courtesy of the Kansas Historical Society, Topeka, Kansas.

SARAH (Epler) MCCOY, THE WIFE OF JOSEPH MCCOY
(b. January 16, 1838, d. November 10, 1911)

Sarah came from a well-to-do farming family in Illinois. She married Joseph on October 22, 1861. Sarah and Joseph had seven children, only three of whom lived to adulthood. She stuck by Joseph through thick and thin, poverty and wealth. She followed him to Abilene, later to Springfield, Illinois, in 1868, and to Wichita in the early 1870s when it was nothing more than a boom town. She remained in Wichita for the rest of her married life, and was well known and respected in the city. Courtesy of the Dickinson County History Museum, Abilene, Kansas.

**WASHINGTON MARKET, NEW YORK CITY, 1866**
This engraving by Stanley Fox shows the crowded nature of buying and selling produce and meats in New York City. The view looks to the west, and the east bank of the Hudson River appears in the background. That is the location of Jersey City, where cattle arrived, were unloaded into stockyards, and later were transported across the river in barges to Lower Manhattan, New York City. From there they were driven to the slaughterhouses, butchered, and delivered for sale in city markets, the largest of which was Washington Market. From "Washington Market, New York City," *Harper's Weekly*, May 26, 1866, p. 332.

"CATTLE DRIVING IN THE STREETS—WHO CARES FOR OLD WOMEN AND SMALL CHILDREN?"

This engraving shows the public concern over, and hazards of, driving cattle through New York City streets. The accompanying article read that the illustration was "an example of what can be done to outrage a million of people living in a great city, by a few wealthy men engaged in the business of buying and selling cattle." The practice of driving cattle through the busiest part of the city resulted in "stopping businesses, frightening horses, ailing eyes, mounts and clothes with dust, stopping travel, getting even into Broadway." The disregard for public safety was acute, as killing "a few old women and small children are not of consequence." From *Frank Leslie's Illustrated Newspaper*, April 28, 1866, p. 1.

**JOSEPH AND JAMES McCOY**

This photograph of Joseph, who is sitting, and James, who is standing, shows two young men on the cusp of making a name for themselves in the great cattle trade of the United States. In this staged photograph, the two appear a little unsure of their embarkation. It is as if James is reassuring Joseph, his younger brother, that all will turn out well. To date, a photo of William, the oldest of the three, has yet to be located. Courtesy of the Kansas Historical Society, Topeka, Kansas.

*THE EPICUREAN*
This is the cover to one of the more famous menu-cookbooks ever. This work was authored by Charles Ranhofer, the French-born, Paris-trained, famous chef of Delmonico's. The cover illustrates not only the building that housed the restaurant, but all the components that went into making it work. The sources of its food, domestic crops, animals, wildlife, and plants, are all shown along with a proper table setting on the lower left and the restaurant's massive kitchen on the lower right. Prominently, a very fat, domestic shorthorn steer is depicted along the left hand side of the cover, the obvious source of the renowned Delmonico steak. From Feeding America: The Historic American Cookbook Project, Michigan State University Digital Collections, http://digital.lib.msu.edu/projects/cookbooks/images/books/400w/book47_frontis.jpg.

**FREIGHT TRAIN OF LIVESTOCK**

A locomotive hauls a long train of livestock cars in this revealing photograph. Daily, scores of stock cars loaded with hundreds of cattle arrived daily at Jersey City and New York City stockyards. Courtesy of Miriam and Ira D. Wallach Division of Art, Prints and Photographs, Photography Collection, New York Public Library Digital Collections.

**HENRY BERGH**

Henry Bergh founded the American Society for the Prevention of Cruelty to Animals in New York City in 1866. Motivated by the poor treatment of draft animals in the city, the arrival of diseased and terribly injured cattle prompted Bergh to wage a campaign to improve the safe transport of cattle by stock car or ship. Courtesy of Miriam and Ira D. Wallach Division of Art, Prints and Photographs, Photography Collection, New York Public Library Digital Collections.

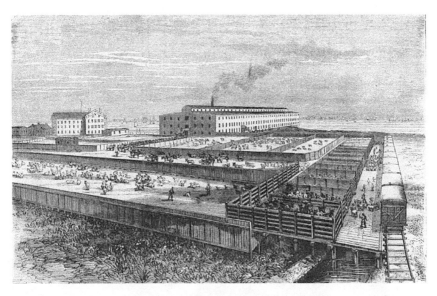

**VIEW OF THE COMMUNIPAW ABATTOIRS**

This shows Allerton's operation on the New Jersey shore across from Lower Manhattan. It was this facility that would put an end to the small-scale slaughter-butcher shops in Lower Manhattan. From "The Great Abattoirs at Communipaw," *Frank Leslie's Illustrated Newspaper*, November 17, 1866, p. 137.

**CHICAGO UNION STOCKYARDS, 1868**

A view of the cattle pens, hotel, and business office of the stockyards just a few years after they were built in 1865. From "Chicago, Illinois—Cattle Market," *Harper's Weekly*, October 31, 1868, p. 701.

**JOHN TRACEY ALEXANDER**

After the Civil War, John T. Alexander became the most prominent Illinois cattle shipper to the New York City markets. He and the McCoys were personal friends. The 1873 panic destroyed his cattle shipping empire, but Alexander recovered his losses and made good his debts of over $1.3 million by the time of his death at age fifty-six in 1876. Courtesy of the Jacksonville Public Library, Jacksonville, Illinois.

**TIMOTHY AND ELIZA HERSEY**

In 1857, Hersey brought his twenty-two-year-old wife, Eliza, and their two-year-old daughter, Mariah, to his log cabin, where the city of Abilene would eventually be built. Apparently, Eliza knew her Bible well. There is only one reference to the word *Abilene* in the Bible in the Gospel of Luke, 3:1, as the realm where John the Baptist began his proselytizing. Some scholars believe that the region acquired its name as a derivative of *Abila,* the name of the capital where the governor Lysanias ruled. The word *Abila* is derived from the Hebrew *'abel*, which might refer to a stream or brook. Other scholars think the word is derived from the Hebrew word meaning "land of meadows." Courtesy of the Dickinson County Historical Society, Abilene, Kansas.

DROVERS COTTAGE, ABILENE, KANSAS, 1867

McCoy clearly understood that Texas cattlemen and cattle buyers all needed a comfortable place where they could drink liquor, eat well, and have a good night's sleep. McCoy's Drovers Cottage was designed as a first-rate, comfortable accommodation. It had fifty rooms that could lodge one hundred guests at a time. The hotel also featured amenities such as a billiard room, saloon, and dining hall. When Gardner took his photograph, the hotel had yet to open and apparently was still in a state of construction, given the materials strewn about the grounds surrounding the building. Nearly all the future success of the Drovers Cottage would rest on the superb management skills of Louise and James W. Gore. Courtesy of the Spencer Library, University of Kansas, Lawrence.

LOU GORE

Lou Gore and her husband operated the Drovers Cottage, the hotel McCoy built in Abilene. Joseph McCoy said of her that Texas drovers "had a true sympathizing friend, and in their sickness a true guardian and nurse, one whose kind motherly heart was ever ready to provide for their every proper want—be they hungry, tired, thirsty or sick, it mattered not; she was the Florence Nightingale to relieve them." From Joseph G. McCoy, *Historic Sketches of the Cattle Trade of the West and Southwest* (Kansas City, Mo.: Ramsey, Millett & Hudson, 1874), 120–21.

### GREAT WESTERN STOCK YARDS, 1867

This 1867 Gardner photograph shows the McCoy brothers' operation shortly after it was put into high gear. Gardner labeled this photograph the "Shipping Point for Texas Cattle, Abilene, Kansas." In this view, four stock cars are shown with an unidentified man standing on top of one of them. That man bears a striking resemblance to Joseph McCoy, and the man standing near the tracks to the left bears a resemblance to James. The loading ramp is clearly shown, as are several employees. Four signs appear above the stock cars. They read, from left to right, "Great," "Western," "Stock," "Yards." Gardner's photograph captured the point where Texas cattle would be transported to remote markets along different kinds of trails. Courtesy of the DeGolyer Library, Southern Methodist University, Dallas, Texas.

### THE STEAMSHIP *VICTORIA*

The Anchor Line steamship company, Glasgow, Scotland, dominated the transatlantic transport of live cattle and sides of refrigerated beef during the 1870s and 1880s. The steamship *Victoria* was one of the company's vessels configured to accommodate cattle and beef. Courtesy of Protected Art Archive, Alamy Stock Photo, Alamy, Inc., Brooklyn, N.Y.

JAMES DAUGHERTY FLOGGING

Daugherty became one of the most successful cattle drovers in all of Texas. However, in 1866, as a young drover, he got off to a rough start. He was tied to a tree and whipped with a hickory branch during the 1866 cattle driving debacle. In his book, McCoy misspelled Daugherty in the caption to this engraving. From Joseph G. McCoy, *Historic Sketches of the Cattle Trade of the West and Southwest* (Kansas City, Mo.: Ramsey, Millett & Hudson, 1874), 25.

**BLACK BEAVER**

A wealthy Delaware leader, Black Beaver was as responsible for blazing the Chisholm Trail as Jesse Chisholm. This is one of the few photographs of this amazing entrepreneur. Portraits of Tribal Delegations to the Federal Government, 1872, Records of the Bureau of Indian Affairs, photo by Alexander Gardner, courtesy of National Archives and Records Administration, Washington, D.C. (no. 75-ID-118A).

**JESSE CHISHOLM**

This is the only known photograph of Chisholm, who was a highly successful trader with Indians and Americans both. After the Civil War, he opened a route from his trading cabin in present-day Wichita, Kansas, which led south well into Indian Territory and terminated near the Canadian River in present-day Oklahoma. Courtesy of the Kansas Historical Society, Topeka.

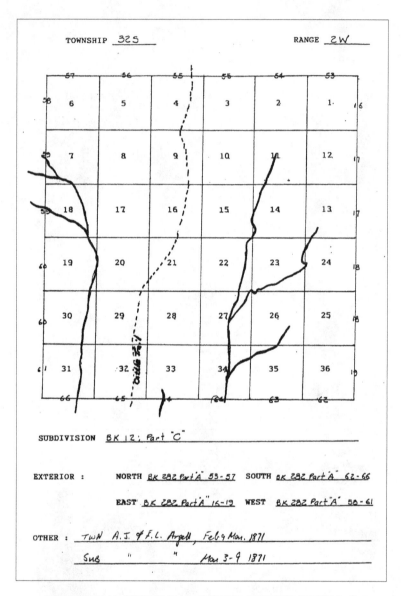

**TERRITORIAL SURVEY MAP, SUMNER COUNTY, KANSAS, 1871**
Sumner County is located along the southern boundary of Kansas. This redrawn map of the original by the author shows the route of the Chisholm Trail through one of the townships in the southern portion of the state. The trail took the high ground between two water courses, and not a single tree appears anywhere. All these features made the trail good for cattle driving—abundant grass, water, and no trees. Territorial Survey Map, Township 32 South, Range 2 West, February and March 1871, courtesy of Archives Division, Kansas Historical Society, Topeka.

**LOADING CATTLE AT ABILENE**
Illustration by Henry Worrall, courtesy of the Kansas Historical Society, Topeka.

**ABILENE IN ITS GLORY**
This Henry Worrall illustration depicts the Drovers Cottage in its completed state. Two locomotives are shown hitched to eight stock cars each capable of carrying twenty head of cattle. Given the smoke pouring from the stacks of both locomotives, Worrall has depicted them powered and ready to haul. One train is stopped at the loading gate, and the other is ready to take its place after the first is loaded. Worrall was a popular illustrator and did the illustrations for McCoy's *Historic Sketches of the Cattle Trade of the West and Southwest* (1874). From Joseph G. McCoy, *Historic Sketches of the Cattle Trade of the West and Southwest* (Kansas City, Mo.: Ramsey, Millett & Hudson, 1874), 205.

CHAPTER 4

# A Trail Is Formed

**BLACK BEAVER SOLVES COLONEL EMORY'S DILEMMA — JESSE CHISHOLM TRAVERSES BLACK BEAVER'S TRAIL — KNITTING THE ELEMENTS TOGETHER — JOSEPH MCCOY MEETS SUCCESS AND FAILURE IN 1867 — PROSPEROUS PROSPECTS FOR 1868**

October weather turned cool and pleasant as Joseph and James McCoy shipped cattle from their newly built stockyards at Abilene. By the middle of the month, prairie fires danced across the grasslands to the east and turned the rising moon red. At the same time, over 150 miles to the southwest, Captain Black Beaver, born into the Delaware nation, and his good friend Jesse Chisholm, of Cherokee and Scots-Irish parentage, set up camp at Medicine Lodge Creek. In the shady groves of trees lining the creek, thousands of Plains Indians met with US negotiators in an attempt to quell the warfare raging across the central grasslands.

Black Beaver and Chisholm had gained a reputation as some of the best guides in the American West. Army explorers crossing the southern plains often relied on both of these men. Now, at Medicine Lodge Creek, Black Beaver and Jesse Chisholm served as official translators for the Comanche and Kiowa representatives during the negotiations that would conclude with signed treaties by the end of the month.

Indians, the US Army, and railroad builders all had something to gain if conditions for peace could be agreed upon. Texas drovers also had much to gain from an effective peace accord if they ever hoped to drive cattle safely through Indian Territory. Black Beaver and Chisholm had ranching and trade ventures, just like the McCoy brothers, and they all stood to profit from peace on the plains.

Paradoxically, Black Beaver and Chisholm, firm champions of Indian peoples, opened an ecological pathway that loosened the Indian peoples' grip on the central grasslands. Before 1867 Black Beaver and Chisholm had plied a trace slicing the central grasslands in a north-south direction. This pathway had every resource necessary for horsemen to drive cattle from Texas to Abilene, and to arrive no worse for the wear. As far as McCoy and Texas drovers were concerned, the water and grass along the way existed free for the taking. It was as if today one could drive from coast to coast on interstate highways without ever paying for fuel. This well-supplied route through the grasslands on the public domain formed the initial crucial link making McCoy's Abilene venture possible. At the same time, the pathway transformed a grassland ecosystem once managed and shaped by Indians.

## *Black Beaver Solves Colonel Emory's Dilemma*

When Black Beaver was born in Illinois in 1806, American pioneers were pushing his Delaware family farther and farther to the west. By the mid-1820s, when a portion of the Delawares had taken up residence in Indian Territory, Black Beaver had little interest in remaining with them. For the next ten years he worked for the American Fur Company and in so doing traversed the West as far north as the Columbia River; as far west as the Pacific Ocean and throughout the Southwest in the valleys of the Gila, Rio Grande, and Pecos Rivers. In the course of his travels, besides learning English, French, and Spanish, he mastered the languages of several Indian nations.

During this time Black Beaver became a well-known and reliable friend of Americans. In 1834 he served as an exceptional guide and interpreter for General Henry Leavenworth's expedition across the grasslands of present-day Oklahoma. In 1846 a small company of Delaware and Shawnee Indians joined the US forces during the War with Mexico. Black Beaver numbered among them and became captain of the unit.

After the war, he served as a guide and interpreter for Captain Randolph Marcy as he led five hundred overlanders on their way to California. Black Beaver understood the importance and locations of water sources when traveling across the plains. More importantly, he knew how to keep stock animals alive when encountering dwindling water sources. By the later 1850s, Black Beaver had largely foregone guiding and had taken up ranching and farming near Fort Arbuckle, Indian Territory, where from time to time he worked as a translator.[1]

Before the Civil War broke out, Black Beaver maintained a prosperous farm and ranch. He owned a herd of six hundred cattle, over three hundred hogs, four horses, a mule, farm equipment, and a well-furnished four-room log house as well as ninety acres of fenced, improved farmland on which he raised corn. Black Beaver, then in his midfifties, and his wife anticipated a comfortable life into their waning years. Yet as for so many other people, the American Civil War brought them hardship and loss.

By early spring of 1861, Colonel William Emory found himself in a dangerous bind. General D. E. Twiggs, of the US Army, had already surrendered the US Arsenal and Barracks at San Antonio, Texas, to Colonel Henry E. McCulloch of the Confederate Army in February. By the end of the same month, Lieutenant Colonel G. Morris had surrendered Fort Chadbourne, and Captain Edmund Kirby Smith had vacated Camp Colorado in early March. Commanders at other Union outposts in the state were quickly following suit, and by the end of March the Union presence in Texas was nearly nonexistent.

Isolated at Fort Washita, less than twenty miles north of the Red River in Indian Territory, Emory was ordered to vacate before Texas Confederate troops arrived. Despite his own Southern sympathies and heritage, he followed orders and he left on April 16, just one day before Texans entered and occupied the fort. Emory combined his forces with the retreating soldiers from Fort Arbuckle and Fort Cobb, and continued north with the goal of reaching Fort Leavenworth. The colonel's plan had only one problem: he completely lacked knowledge of the area between Fort Cobb and Leavenworth. He needed to find a guide as fast as he could.

His small command of 750 uniformed Union Soldiers (accompanied by "150 women, children, teamsters and other non-combatants"), who had manned frontier forts, could not march east through hostile Confederate lands. With only enough forage and supplies to see him and his command through the end of May, Emory had to ride north quickly to fulfill his orders if he wanted to reach friendly Union territory. He feared the hazards of following the more well-traveled military road along the western borders of Arkansas and Missouri, so heading due north made the most sense if he only knew the locations of good grazing and water sources for his horses and draft animals.[2]

In desperation, he prevailed upon Captain Black Beaver, who convinced a few other "faithful Delaware guides" to accompany him, in leading his troops north. Most of the Delawares who knew the countryside had already refused to help Emory even before being asked. Emory was well acquainted with Black Beaver, who had ties to the federal government. As Emory put it, "of all the Indians upon whom the Government had lavished its bounty, Black Beaver was the only one that would consent to the column."

Black Beaver knew an unimpeded way into Kansas, a route plentiful in grass and water. His vast knowledge of the region proved a godsend for Emory's command, which Black Beaver led north out of Texas to an intersection with the Santa Fe Trail in present-day Kansas. As Emory later reported, his command took the "most direct course . . . that the nature of the ground would permit," in other words, a route that provided good grazing and water resources for his animals.[3]

They reached the north side of the Arkansas River in Kansas by May 19th. Then on the Santa Fe Trail, Emory headed his command safely toward Fort Leavenworth. At this point Black Beaver and the other Delaware guides parted company with the colonel and headed back south toward their homes. Black Beaver had just traced a route through the central grasslands that would later be followed by Texas cowboys driving hundreds of thousands of cattle along.[4]

Little fame would come to Captain Black Beaver for establishing this route. In fact, he paid a heavy price for leading Emory to safety. When the Texas Confederate forces reached Fort Cobb, it took them little time to find out who had assisted Emory's escape. In short order, Confederate soldiers confiscated all of Black Beaver's property that they could and destroyed the rest. Black Beaver realized that he was no longer welcome anywhere near Fort Arbuckle. Following the same route over which he had led Emory's command, he fled north until he reached a trading post that had been built by another man who knew his way through the grasslands. Jesse Chisholm's trading operation was located at the junction of the Big and Little Arkansas Rivers, the location of present-day Wichita, Kansas. Black Beaver knew Chisholm well, and together they and their families waited out the Civil War.

After the war ended, James Wortham, superintendent of Indian Affairs, hired Black Beaver as an interpreter. By midsummer 1867, as Joseph McCoy was building his shipping facility at Abilene, Black Beaver was living in Lawrence, Kansas, and working for the Bureau of Indian Affairs. In October, as an interpreter for the bureau, Black Beaver went to the treaty grounds at Medicine Lodge to translate for the Comanches and Kiowas. Certainly, Black Beaver was aware of the Texas cattle being driven north along the same route that he had followed to lead Colonel Emory's command to safety in 1861. Perhaps he wished that under different circumstances he could have driven his own cattle to Abilene. Or maybe he was much too busy translating for the federal government to give it much thought at all.

## Jesse Chisholm Traverses Black Beaver's Trail

Only a year older than his friend Black Beaver, Jesse Chisholm had also worked in the fur trade. Chisholm thrived under the tutelage of A. P. Chouteau, who had located near Fort Gibson and managed his family's fur-trading empire with the Osages. Chisholm possessed a natural knack for diplomacy and eventually built his own flourishing trade connections with scores of competing and warring tribes. In the course of his dealing, by some accounts, he mastered fifteen or more languages. Like Black Beaver, through his travels he acquired a vast storehouse of geographical knowledge about the grasslands.

Chisholm understood water to be the most important resource in the grasslands, and at times it was difficult to find. But the environment provided him with enough clues that he could find a source even when in an unfamiliar place. Bison cut straight trails toward water and left meandering paths after drinking. Sparrows and wrens were headed toward water if they were flying with their beaks open. At dusk doves flew in small flocks toward a water source. Chisholm understood how these signs kept one alive while traveling through an unmarked sea of grass.

Like Black Beaver's, his skills as a translator and guide were in sharp demand by the army. In 1853, as Lieutenant A. W. Whipple passed through Shawnee country with his railroad survey expedition, he and his men encountered difficulties in crossing small streams, ascending hills, and passing through woods. Within a few days the lieutenant was leading his command through the open grasslands, and his Shawnee guide refused to go any farther because of his fear of Comanches and Kiowas to the west. Whipple had only the vaguest idea where he was going and knew he would be well advised to hire a guide if he wanted to survive his adventure. He was provided with three names: Jesse Chisholm, Black Beaver, and John Bushman. Black Beaver left word that he was too ill, and Bushman told Whipple, "Maybe you find no water; maybe you all die."[5]

This left Chisholm, who refused government pay because it was less than half of what he was making in his trading business. By this time, Chisholm's enterprise had made him a wealthy man. He supported a sizable family, possessed a healthy herd of cattle, and owned several "Spanish boys and girls," Mexican slaves whom

Chisholm had purchased from Comanches. Despite refusing to guide Whipple, Chisholm did supply him with beef cattle, and hired out one of his seven Mexican captives, a young man named Vincente, as a guide. Vincente spoke English, Spanish, and Comanche fluently. He was also proficient in sign language, and he knew his way around the grasslands. Vincente proved his worth as a guide when he led Whipple's mounted command to ample water and grass sources, and as a translator when Whipple parlayed with Kiowa and Comanche leaders.

Less than ten years later, the Civil War proved too dangerous for Chisholm to remain where Confederate soldiers or Texans could reach him. He had much to lose, so he moved his entire operation and family to a location along an east-west Osage trade route. The junction of the Little and Big Arkansas Rivers was a well-known resting and trading location for numbers of Indians and traders such as James R. Mead. By the early 1860s James and Agnes Mead, with their two children, lived in a cabin at a tiny outpost called Towanda, some twenty miles east of Chisholm's trading post on the Arkansas River. Mead conducted a flourishing Indian trade that he stocked by buying goods from wholesalers located in Leavenworth, Kansas.

Chisholm struck up a friendship and trading relationship with Mead. By 1865 Chisholm had built an Indian trading post in the shady grove of trees just above where the Little Arkansas met the Big Arkansas River. Like Black Beaver, many Wichitas, Caddos, and Delawares had fled Confederate forces to the south, and settled there as well. By the end of the Civil War, Chisholm, working with Mead, was using this location for his freighting and trading business with the Indian peoples living in present-day Oklahoma. His first trek due south followed the still-visible trace left by Emory's escape. Chisholm traveled during a rainy season, and his wagons left deep, easily followed ruts over the traces left earlier by Emory's wagons and draft animals. By the time Chisholm's mule skinners had driven their lumbering wagons to his reestablished trading post near present-day El Reno, Oklahoma, an obvious pathway cut north and south through the mixed-grass prairies.[6]

Chisholm and Black Beaver both traveled this route because they knew its resources provided the water and solar energy, or grass, needed for their draft and pack animals. The route also crossed nearly level terrain with generally safe fords across eastward-flowing creeks and rivers, free of nettlesome woods. Most importantly, the grass was free for the taking given that the federal government considered this vast grassland part of the public domain. In a short time, these same features attracted the attention of Joseph McCoy.

McCoy clearly understood the positive features of the trail for supporting massive cattle drives. As he put it, the Chisholm Trail "is more direct, has more prairie, less timber, more small streams and less large ones, and altogether better grass and fewer flies—no civilized Indian tax or wild Indian disturbances—than any other route yet driven over, and is also much shorter in distance because [it is] direct from Red river to Kansas." As McCoy recognized, all of these energy-rich resources and geographic features of the public domain could sustain great drives of Texas cattle drives on the Chisholm Trail that led directly to his Great Western Stock Yards in Abilene, Kansas.

## *Knitting the Elements Together*

McCoy knew it was senseless to undertake a cattle drive unless ecology, technology, and markets could all be knitted together. As McCoy and everyone involved in the cattle trade would soon understand, they stood at the mercy of the variables shaping the vast grassland ecosystems. Indisputably, the variability of climate reigned over the Chisholm Trail biome. Although this observation might seem self-evident, let us take a moment to see how climate shaped the region. As any good-hearted Texas cowboy might phrase it, what could make one day "hot as the underside of a saddle blanket after a hard ride," and another day "colder than a well-chain in December"? What forces could make a land "drier'n jerked buffalo with an empty water barrel"? What could make "ever'body wished they'd growed fins instead of feet"?[7]

### CLIMATE

One good definition of climate is the "composite weather of a region."[8] McCoy, and cattlemen in general, had little, if any, real understanding of the many interlacing forces shaping the climate of the Central Grasslands. Still, they intuitively recognized that the sun played a leading role in creating weather patterns. Cattlemen understood less well the physics of solar energy and how changes in it affected their own lives and those of their animals.

For example, a good decade after trail driving became more mythic than actual, Edward Walter Maunder, an astronomer at the Royal Greenwich Observatory, noticed a related pattern of sunspot numbers and global climate conditions. In short, a lower number of sunspots often correlated with cooler global surface temperatures. Although cowboys and their herds experienced some years cooler and some warmer than others, they did not make the same connections to sunspots and temperatures that Maunder did.

Maunder reviewed sunspot records from the fifteenth, sixteenth, and seventeenth centuries. He knew that typically somewhere between forty thousand and fifty thousand sunspots might normally be recorded in any given thirty-year period. Yet something odd had occurred during those three centuries, as in one given thirty-year time frame, 1672 to 1699, fewer than fifty sunspots had been sighted. He verified these numbers and, after long analyses, announced his findings in 1893, the same year that Frederick Jackson Turner proclaimed the end of the American frontier.

Maunder and Turner shared something in common: their work was shaped by the effects of a period of global cooling often referred to as the "Little Ice Age." The American frontier, and chilly terrestrial temperatures, may have been shaped by the waning of sunspots over a 450-year span. From 1861 through 1890, observers recorded around fifteen thousand sunspots, or less than half the number that might be recorded during any given thirty-year time span from 1749 through 2011. The great Chisholm Trail saga spanned the waning years of the Little Ice Age, when an unbroken sea of grass covered the broad central region of the United States.

While on the Chisholm Trail, most likely cowboys' conversations around a campfire seldom, if ever, treated the orbit of the earth around the sun, and how that affected climate. Yet, the distance of the earth from the sun sustained their lives. Recently, one group of scientists reported how the fluctuating distance of the earth's orbit around the sun in conjunction with its tilt helps to explain the appearance and disappearance of terrestrial species. Unbeknownst to Chisholm Trail cowboys, they had been enjoying life at a time when the earth's tilt and orbit around the sun maintained a climate conducive for their existence.

The solar energy produced by the sun also powers global air currents, which are an essential element in shaping all climates on the face of the earth. The continental United States has always experienced three mighty, shifting air masses that intersect over the grasslands, acting as a mighty force in shaping the ever-shifting boundaries of plant communities. These alternating air currents have varied the climates of these intermontane regions, and grassland species have alternatively perished, struggled, or thrived as they have adapted, or failed to adapt, to shifting winds.

The first air mass is formed by a large continental air conditioner of snow and ice covering the arctic that chills the atmosphere above. This heavy air drifts south, and the greater the volume, the farther south it travels. The second air mass is formed by the Pacific Ocean warming the atmosphere above it. This accumulation flows to the east as a result of the rotation of the Earth. As it does, the West Coast mountains capture most of its moisture, which results in dry zephyrs caressing the grasslands to the east. The solar heating of the Gulf of Mexico generates the third mass, a moisture-laden, energized air mass that flows northward.

The shifting intersections of these major air masses have created generally defined, seasonal patterns. For example, in winter a diagonal line of cold polar air masses can stretch from the southern tip of Lake Michigan to the Big Bend of the Rio Grande. In the late spring, the farthest reach of the warm gulf air masses forms a line from the middle of the Front Range of the Rocky Mountains in Colorado to the southern half of Minnesota and, with a gentle curve, swings eastward along the southern tips of the Great Lakes. A frontal boundary that angles eastward from around Denver, Colorado, to the southern tip of Lake Michigan forms a demarcation separating the northern flow of the gulf masses from the southern flow of the polar masses in winter.

What is exceptionally interesting about these lines is the way in which the boundaries of plant communities seem to follow these same shifting margins. Plant communities associated with the mixed-grass and short-grass regions flourish northwest of the southernmost reach of the winter polar air masses. To the west of this same line, the short-grass and xeric grasslands have dominated where these desert grasslands remain below the boundary of where northern gulf and southern polar air masses meet in winter. The tallgrass prairies emerged westward from the eastern woodlands and have generally flourished along the winter line, dividing the reaches of the northern polar and southern gulf air masses. Certainly, a relationship exists between these frontal patterns and the location of plant communities.[9]

Also beyond drovers' comprehension while they headed their herds north was how Pacific Ocean currents were affecting all of their lives. On a cycle of about every seven years, the easterly trade winds flowing across the equatorial waters of the Pacific Ocean tend to slow. Essentially, there are two levels of water in the Pacific Ocean. The upper level is warm, and the bottom layer is cold. The trade winds shape how these two interact. When the winds are strong, the cold layer near the western coastlines of South America rises to mix with the upper layer and creates a nutrient-rich, fish-abundant environment. During the span of months when the winds decrease, or reverse, the upper layer deepens and forms a thicker, less penetrable barrier for the colder water to enter.

Fisherman off the coast of Peru noticed that every few years the temperature of the ocean seemed to increase, their fishing hauls collapsed, and an increase in flooding occurred along the Andes Mountain range. This event always fell around Christmas, and the fishermen began referring to it as the *El Niño*, the boy child. To a lesser degree, a similar effect occurs at the same time along the Pacific Coast of North America, and it can have comparable results inland. Rainfall records indicate that the Southwest receives higher than average rainfalls during strong El Niños.

When analyzed, the rainfall in Kansas averaged 36 to 76 percent above the average of the past century during the months of December through March whenever an El Niño occurred. For Texas the averages increased between 16 to 96 percent above the average for the past one hundred years. When El Niños occur, the eastward-flowing Pacific winds weaken across the grasslands, allowing now feebly contested, warm, moist, gulf air currents to flow northward. As a consequence, more rainfall descends upon most of the grasslands.

An opposite effect to El Niño also occurs, and it is called La Niña. Although these Pacific Ocean warming and cooling cycles occur periodically, they have not been regularly spaced. However, they seem to come in roughly alternating periods of three to seven years with some spacing of years in between each event.

Without ever realizing it, cowboys and their herds experienced a grassland environment shaped by El Niños and La Niñas. During an 1877 strong El Niño, the meteorologist at Manhattan, Kansas, recorded the highest rainfall during the growing season that had occurred between 1861 and 1890. During the years between 1861 and 1890, there is a slight positive correlation between the strength of an El Niño and the rainfall at Manhattan: the stronger the El Niño, the higher the average rainfall.

The reverse of an El Niño, the La Niña, has opposite effects. Generally, the stronger the La Niña, the weaker the rainfall during a growing season. This situation was particularly true during 1870. In reverse to El Niño trends between 1861 and 1890, there is a more pronounced negative correlation between the strength of a La Niña and the rainfall at Manhattan: the stronger the La Niña, the lower the average rainfall.

When the occurrences of El Niños and La Niñas are compared to the frequency of sunspots, an effect on the growing seasons in the grasslands appears. In 1870, a large number of sunspots were counted during a very strong La Niña. At the same time, the rainfall during the Manhattan, Kansas, growing season was the lowest in the thirty years between 1861 and 1890. Such conditions certainly affected grazing conditions throughout the southern and central grasslands. Conversely, in 1877 one of the lowest numbers of sunspots was recorded during a strong El Niño. In Manhattan, the heaviest recorded rainfall in the thirty years between 1861 and 1890 fell during that particular growing season.

## WATER

When Joseph McCoy plotted his trail for Texas drovers, he made note of each and every watering hole along the entire route. Water—you can't get up the trail without it. If anything made the trails to the rail points possible, it was reliable sources of water between central Texas and the Union Pacific line to the north. Experienced cowmen such as Jasper Lauderdale could recite by memory all the important watering stops, nearly eighty in all, from San Antonio to Chugwater, Wyoming. Lauderdale had also carefully calculated the mileage between each of these locations. If a drover were to miss any one of these, he would surely encounter great difficulties in keeping his herd healthy, if not alive.[10]

On the mixed-grass prairies, water, the solvent of life, was always limited, localized, and varied in quality. Stream courses flowed intermittently and in variable volumes depending on chaotic weather patterns. Moreover, great stretches of the prairies had little surface water, and the life thriving on free-flowing water naturally congregated in or near those sources. Indian peoples, cattlemen, and farmers always sought reliable sources of water to sustain their respective material cultures.

Whenever possible, drovers avoided going more than a day without watering their stock. Richard Withers, an experienced cowboy, knew the great difficulty in herding thirsty cattle. He likened driving a water-deprived herd that had caught the scent of alkali springs to handling "a bunch of mixed turkeys."[11] The best any cowboy could hope for in such a situation was to catch up with the herd and mill the animals once they quenched their thirst.

Sometimes, drovers lacked even the option of catching up with a thirst-crazed herd. The cowboys, who were working a herd of one thousand cattle for the firm of Hart and Hazlewood Brothers, learned this the hard way. They had been driving the herd west toward the Double Mountain Ford of the Brazos River in search of better grazing conditions. As the herd approached the river, the cattle sensed water and broke into a stampede. Instead of reaching the river, the herd had turned into a canyon that ended with a perpendicular cliff, "over which they crowded each other until about 175 head were piled up dead at the foot of the bluff."[12]

Summer herding in the proximity of railroads always meant that a drover had to locate a "living" water source in order to sustain the cattle. In the summer of 1873, San Antonian C. W. Ackermann kept his father's herd on the Ninnescah (an Osage word meaning "clear water") River for more than three months before loading his cattle some thirty miles to the north in Wichita, Kansas. Of course, no one else could use the same water and grass to nourish their herds while someone like Ackermann and his longhorns were there.[13]

Cattle cannot live on grass alone. It did not matter how good grass resources were if water sources were scanty or unavailable along the trail. Early rangeland ecologists recognized this fact many years ago. As K. A. Valentine observed in 1947, "Range lying so far from water that domestic livestock cannot reach it has little or no effective or usable grazing capacity even though it may consist of an excellent stand of good forage plants." He added a corollary: "Accessibility of range, and hence its grazing capacity progressively decreases as distance from water increases." For trail drivers, this meant a rather compressed route through the grasslands, one that had ample, easily accessed grass and water sources.[14]

Valentine had one additional insight about the distance of water from good grazing ground that drovers undoubtedly had to consider. He defined what he called the *sacrifice zone*. Pastures adjacent to a water source that were frequently and heavily grazed failed to produce well after a couple of years. Not surprisingly, cattle try to keep close to both grass and water. The closer to both, the less energy required of the animal to feed and water itself. Over time, regular, intense grazing near water sources reduces the capabilities of grasses to reproduce themselves. The ground becomes compacted, and weeds rapidly take over. A few years of this, and cattle have to range farther away from the water source each passing year in order to find good grazing ground while the land surrounding the water remains unfit for supporting range grasses. In a fenced-in pasture, Valentine concluded that the sacrifice zone determined the maximum stocking ratio; that is, the number of cattle that could prosper on a given acreage of grass without destroying the grass itself. This zone ranged between a quarter to a half mile in extent around the water source. A sacrifice zone larger than this would mean that cattle would expend more energy than they gained from grazing on more distant pastures, regardless of how abundant and rich the grasses were.[15]

Of course, trail drivers operated in open-range conditions, not fenced ones. Still, nearly all herds traveled the trail north at nearly the same time of year, when grass resources were most abundant. The first herd that headed north got to graze the closest to any water source along the trail. The following herds had to graze a little farther from the water source in order to reach a grazing ground that had not been cropped short by the preceding herd. And each succeeding herd stopping at the same watering holes had to graze farther out from the water source than the preceding one.

## GRASS

As Joseph McCoy fully realized, as did any cattleman worth his salt, grass, which in essence collects and stores solar energy, fueled the cattle trade. At some point in the course of their evolution, humans learned how to harness and consume both wild and domestic grasses. In brief, humans domesticated some species such as wheat, oats, and corn and transformed them into a food source. Some species, such as tall and short bluestem, buffalo grass, and mesquite grass, lacked the properties that allowed humans to transform them into agricultural crops. Rather, through fire management, humans learned to nurture their growth, and in so doing, created the richest grazing grounds found on the planet for both domesticated and wild herbivores.

Grasses, which number some ten thousand species, along with humans, made a late appearance on Earth. For illustrative purposes, let us round off the age of Earth at 4.5 billion years. If the age of Earth is made the equivalent of one solar year, then one day represents 12.3 million years. According to reputable scholars, the ancestors of contemporary grasses made their first appearance on the planet around sixty to seventy million years ago, or during the last five to six days of our Earth year. The first human ancestors, on the other hand, began appearing around six million years ago, or in about the last twelve hours of our Earth year. Beginning in the last seventy seconds of this Earth year, humans and grasses began emerging as dominant species in what would become the grasslands of North America. Although arriving late on the scene, human societies and grasses certainly complemented each other's expansion. Grasses have nourished human civilizations, such as they have been, and human beings, in returning the favor, have aided and abetted the spread of grassland ecosystems in a few select places on the planet, such as the central and intermontane regions of the North American continent.[16]

The word "grass" has an interesting history. It may be a derivative of an old Aryan word, *ghra-*, which means "to grow," and some English words such as "grain," "green," and of course, "grow" could trace their ancient origins to *ghra-*. The Romans probably used it to form their word *gramen*, or grass.[17] Within this word lies the health, and perhaps sum, of human life. While McCoy's cattle trade flourished on rich wild grasslands, Kansas senator John James Ingalls observed a fundamental connection between humans and grasses. In *Kansas Magazine* (1872), he wrote: "Grass feeds the ox: the ox nourishes man: man dies and goes to grass again; and so the tide of life, with everlasting repetition, in continuous circles, moves endlessly on and upward, and in more senses than one, all flesh is grass."[18] Although the senator understood, even if in a somewhat simplified manner, the importance of the grasslands to humanity, much of the grassland biome remained a mystery to him, McCoy, and the people of their times.

Joseph McCoy, and most cattlemen, grouped grasses throughout North America into two categories: "warm-season" and "cool-season" grasses. Not surprisingly, warm-season grasses were observed growing late in the spring, thriving throughout mostly dry summers, maturing in the fall, and going dormant throughout the winter. Cool-season grasses flourished well in wetter, cooler environments. Such places often encompass the northern prairies early in the spring or later in the fall, or the more southeasterly grasslands throughout the winter.

In 1968 two biologists, W. J. Downton and E. Tregunna, figured out the different ways in which warm-season and cool-season grasses combined visible light and carbon dioxide to form carbohydrates, the basic fuels of all biological life. A simple, but crucial, problem confronts grasses: they must take in carbon dioxide, and at the same time, retain the water necessary for their lives. Plant leaves regulate the absorption of carbon dioxide, which is indispensable for photosynthesis, through microscopic holes in their leaves called "stomata."

When a climate is wet there is little need for a leaf to close its stomata to prevent water loss, so it can easily capture as much carbon dioxide as its stomata can inhale. But if the climate is hot and dry, then keeping the stomata open can prove exceptionally costly for a plant. Water loss through open stomata will result in dehydration, and plants easily die as a result. Shutting off the stomata for a long period results in another problem: the plant has no means to absorb carbon dioxide for photosynthesis. This would be like a human stopping breathing in order to avoid dehydration in a desert. Such a decision would have only brief beneficial results.[19]

So how did grasses fix the problem of inhalation without dehydration? Downton and Tregunna observed that warm-season and cool-season grasses differ in how they deliver carbon dioxide to where photosynthesis occurs. Cool-season grasses, which they labeled "C3 grasses," absorb and distribute carbon dioxide differently than do the warm-season grasses, which they labeled "C4 grasses." In short, C4 grasses are more efficient at grabbing carbon dioxide from the atmosphere when they open their stomata. This capacity allows these plants to shut their stomata more often and for longer periods of time than C3 plants and allows C4 grasses to thrive in much drier climes. There is a cost involved to C4 grasses, however, as they are less efficient at grabbing carbon dioxide out of the air and applying it to their growth metabolism than are the cool-season grasses when water or temperature are not controlling factors.[20]

Cattlemen like McCoy relied upon C4 grasses to power their herds. These grasses once thoroughly dominated the landscape of the central grasslands. Throughout the eastern extent, or the tallgrass prairies, big bluestem (*Andropogon gerardi*) flourished; in the mixed-grass prairies to the west; little bluestem (*Andropogon scoparius*) was the main species; everyone knew the short-grass plains and desert grasslands by the carpet-like appearance of the prevalent buffalo grass (*Buchloe dactyloides*), and across the southern plains mesquite grass (*Hilaria belangeri*) prevailed. Of course other plants lived alongside these mainstays, but any half-observant traveler knew when he or she had entered one plant association or the other by simply detecting which of these grasses was most abundant.

Unbeknownst to McCoy, and cattlemen in general, the well-being of grasses, and their nutritional value for herbivores, depended upon a symbiotic relationship between grasses and a microorganism. One group of organisms had an extremely important effect on many other life forms in the grasslands, yet it was certainly one of the smallest to inhabit the region. Today ecologists call these organisms mycorrhizae.[21] "Mycorrhiza" is a word derived from the Greek *myco*, meaning fungus, and *rhiza*, meaning root—fungus-root. These fungi resemble tiny round balls covered with branched web growths called "arbuscular" or "little tree"; hence the term "arbuscular mycorrhiza." These organisms average in width five microns, a micron (symbolized by µ) being one-millionth of a meter.

Among tallgrasses as many as twenty species of arbuscular mycorrhizae live in symbiosis with grasses. The out root cells of healthy $C_4$ grasses will be thoroughly colonized with these fungi. In fact, bluestem or buffalo grass will fail to grow without a healthy bond with the fungi. Phosphorus is a crucial element to the well-being of any $C_4$ grass, and these fungi effectively transfer this essential element to the root system of the adjacent plant through the hyphae, or web extensions of the fungi. Prairie fires have the effect of increasing mycorrhizal populations by stimulating a greater production of spores. Heavy grazing will reduce the diversity of the mycorrhizal species in the soil, and diminish the colonization of grass roots. However, the webs of the fungi will respond by spreading their strands throughout the soil.

Although McCoy lacked any understanding about the symbiotic relationship shared by arbuscular mycorrhizae and $C_4$ grasses, he knew when this relationship had gone astray. The fungi live within a prescribed range of soil moisture. Their populations fall off when too much rainfall saturates the ground, and as a result the grass loses its access to minerals, especially phosphorous, which is crucial to carbon uptake. Grasses in this condition thrive less well.

In any growing season, rainfall could also affect how nitrogen-rich grasses might become. As McCoy observed grass conditions in the summer and fall of 1867, he referred to grass as "washy" because of the high water content in the stems and leaves. Grasses in this condition also possessed poor nitrogen value for grazing livestock. When heavy rains occur in the spring or early summer, $C_4$ tallgrasses grow quickly, but the nitrogen uptake does not keep pace. So cattle had abundant bulk that was more filling but less nourishing. The first cattle to arrive in Abilene were in poor shape and possessed low market values. Attempting to fatten them up on the surrounding grasslands before selling a herd or loading into stock cars proved fruitless. On the surface the prairie grasses seemed lush, but the cattle put on little fat even though they ate their fill. McCoy astutely blamed the "washy" condition of the grass on high rainfall.[22]

McCoy had identified the cause. During the growing season of April through September, higher than average rain fell on the central grasslands. For example, during the growing season, twenty-three inches made the average rainfall for

Manhattan, Kansas, from 1858 through 1940. In 1867, at nearby Fort Riley, nearly twenty-seven inches fell. At Fort Arbuckle, near where Texas drovers crossed into Indian Territory, heavy rains fell in June and July, or just at the time drovers would be moving their herds through Indian Territory. These cattle herds experienced rain nearly every third day while on the trail. McCoy also realized that these heavy rains swelled rivers, and the thunderstorms spooked the cattle into stampedes. Simply, the weather made cowboys, horses, and cattle miserable and weak.

McCoy understood well the relative values of wild grasses as a food source for Texas cattle. He had traveled the open-range country from Texas to Nebraska, and like any good Texas drover, he knew where he wanted to see his cattle grazing. He touted the virtues of two grass species, above all the others, as providing the best nutritional value for cattle. Buffalo grass prevailed in the northern range and other, curly mesquite dominated in the southern realm.[23]

Buffalo grass, along with blue grama, once had an amazing range. In the central grasslands they carpeted over 90 percent of the land failing to cover only its sandy soils. On more than 190,000 square miles of open rangeland on the public domain, cattlemen could find rich pastures of buffalo grass. This area covered nearly the western half of Nebraska, Kansas, and Oklahoma, along with the Texas panhandle and the eastern plains of Colorado. Buffalo grass stands up well under heavy grazing, and where heavy grazing by bison or cattle occurred, there buffalo grass prevailed and spread, while its usual partner, blue grama, failed under the pressure.

There had to be more than a good relationship between plants, microbes, and soils for grasses to flourish in areas between the eastern woodlands and the Rocky Mountains, and throughout many parts of the intermontane regions between the Front Range of Colorado and the Sierra Nevada Range to the west. Three other significant variables contributed to the success of grass biomes in these areas. The first has already been noted: the plants had evolved by adjusting to the aridity of these lands. The second variable precedes the former. It would be very difficult for grasses to adapt to aridity if the lands were not sub-humid to arid in the first place. The third, and perhaps most important, variable was human behavior.

Humans learned to wield one of the most effective agents ever to modify a landscape, fire. Without reoccurring fires throughout the subhumid to arid regions of North America, plant compositions would have been much different five hundred years ago. There is an odd place in south-central Kansas called

Flowerpot Mound. It is surrounded by grassland, yet prairie and sand sages blanket the top. What accounts for this lonely outpost of sage in a sea of grass? The likely answer: fire and grazing animals could never reach the top of the formation. A slight overhang of sandstone caps the top of Flowerpot, and consequently the tableland atop has seldom if ever been visited by fire or herbivores. For several thousands of years fire and grazers, on the other hand, shaped the grasslands around it. How different the grasslands would look today if not for the effects of fire and ungulates.[24]

J. M. Hankins, like all good cowhands, understood the importance of good grass conditions for the well-being of his horses and cattle. Personal experiences could and did indelibly mark his memory. In 1868 scant rainfall in central Texas had resulted in poor grazing conditions throughout the entire region. Hankins owned three corn-fed horses that his employers, the Smith Brothers at Prairie Lea, promised to feed while he and a few others rode south to round up cattle for the drive north. He had ridden his horse long and hard without benefit of corn. He also grimly faced poor grass conditions and rivers with skimpy flows. These streams, which formed the main traveled routes throughout the region, normally had ample flows for horses and cattle and the valleys usually teemed with lush stands of grass.

In the spring of 1868, Hankins could not find suitable grazing for his horse or cattle within three miles of any of those depleted rivers. Before Hankins arrived with his herd, other cattle herds and horses had grazed bare these well-traveled corridors, creating in effect a "sacrifice zone." Soon the strength of his horse gave out and Hankins traveled as much on foot as he did mounted. Finally, his horse became so weakened that he traded it for another; finding that one weak as well, he traded it for another in the same day. His last trade turn out to be a "scag," (in this case, slang for an unattractive, unkempt, broken-down female horse) and when he lifted the saddle a "foot of hide" came off with it. The equation was a simple one for those fellows—no grass equaled horses without energy.[25]

## GEOGRAPHY

The territorial survey of Kansas illustrates the geographical advantages of cattle driving along McCoy's route. In 1871, A. J. and E. L. Argell mapped Downs Township, Sumner County in south-central Kansas. Their map shows geographical features common to the entire length of the route. The surveyors traced the main route on a rise between two creeks in a treeless grassland. As McCoy said, no trees hindered the movement of cattle; pasture and water were on either side of the route; and traversing the rise gave drovers a clear view of the countryside for miles around. For the Argells, driving their herds ten to fifteen miles a day through such resource-rich grasslands allowed them to keep their stock fit, if not fattened while on the trail.[26]

The ecosystem of the Chisholm Trail encompassed vastly more territory than a narrow cattle path leading from central Texas to the railheads in Kansas. The southern realm included a huge expanse of rangeland in central Texas that nourished millions of cattle and horses. In the middle portion lush grasslands and ample water sources abounded throughout Indian Territory, or present-day Oklahoma. Both were essential for fueling the vast herds driven north.

In several places, the north-south corridor itself embraced a swath more than fifty miles across. In some spots millions of cattle and horse hooves beat the trail bare and as hard as a modern paved highway. To graze cattle meant leading herds well away from the route where it had become barren rangelands. Under such conditions, prairies, once luxuriant with nutritious little bluestem, the mainstay fuel for cattle and horses in the region of the trail system, quickly became sparse pastures of buffalo grass. Although buffalo grass possessed great nutritional value, it did not produce the same pound per plant, per acre as little bluestem.[27] Of course, drovers felt the pressure to keep their herds well within range of bountiful pastures when tens of thousands of cattle relied on the same sources of grass during any one cattle-driving season.

Joseph McCoy, in a diary that he kept in the summer of 1880, reflected on how thirteen years of cattle driving had created a broad and extensive trail system. He noted that drovers in Indian Territory, while awaiting orders from their Texas bosses, routinely routed their herds far away from the trails in order to secure adequate grass and water to sustain them. The valleys and flats near the main line of the trail showed the effects of overgrazing, which forced drovers to search the uplands away from the trail for locations where their herds could graze on untouched "sagegrass," or little-bluestem pastures.[28] On these grounds, however, cattlemen ran the risk of relying upon skimpy water sources in the same area. But their options were few, as there was simply not enough grass and water to supply simultaneously all the herds moving through the same vicinity at nearly the same time.

At the northern end, the Chisholm Trail system embraced the grasslands and watercourses near and west of the major cattle towns in Kansas. These open rangelands sustained herds until the cattle could be loaded onto the transportation systems leading to eastern markets or packing plants. The way in which drovers used the broad prairie flats near the Great Bend of the Arkansas River to graze and fatten their herds before taking them to Wichita, Kansas, illustrates the point. In 1874, drovers wintered more than forty thousand cattle between Great Bend and Wichita in anticipation of spring markets.[29] By 1880, however, before this type of concentrated grazing could alter the composition of the prairie grass rangeland, farmers would occupy the same land and convert it into cropland.

**TECHNOLOGY**

When Alexander Gardner photographed McCoy's stockyards at Abilene, he captured the "March of Empire" propelled by the railroad, the "new agent of civilization." McCoy always compared his work to a publicly minded undertaking much in the same way that promoters viewed railroads as the harbinger of civilization. Any technology initially begins as a human-produced tool, but it becomes more than human-crafted aid as it reshapes the culture that created it and transforms ecosystems. Even though McCoy thought the UPED provided little more than a means to transport cattle, he completely missed how this technology was reshaping American social, economic, and ecological relationships wherever it was built. Hence, theorist Kevin Kelly referred to the "essential self-propelling momentum" of technology.[30]

More specifically, railroads worked as an ecological force reordering the grassland ecosystems of Kansas. Gardner's photography of the UPED route through Kansas in 1867 displays this transformation. In fact, Gardner's contemporaries expected that the UPED would make over the prairies, and Gardner's photographs caught the realities of this ecological transformation. The humorist Charles Leland summed up the views of many when he proclaimed, without tongue in cheek, that the "prairies were made by Providence for railroads." He viewed the land grants held by the company as giving title to "the richest lands in America," which were capable of producing an "infinitely prosperous" population—assuming that railroad connections to eastern markets converted these lands from "wilderness" into a European American styled civilization.[31]

This notion that railroads possessed the technological prowess to render a "wilderness" into "civilization" was a nearly universally accepted axiom in western thinking. Kate Brown illustrates this nicely in her comparative study of railroad building in Karaganda, Kazakhstan, by Soviet planners in the 1930s and in

Billings, Montana, by the Northern Pacific Railway Company (NP) in the 1880s. Both were created, as Brown wrote, "for commerce and the quick extraction of resources at railheads and responded not to ecological limits but to the surveyor's rational grid." Similarly, if UPED president Perry understood anything in building the UPED rail across a trackless, city-less, farm-less landscape, he realized that the landscape and its extractable resources had to be rationalized in order to be quickly loaded into his boxcars, because empty boxcars would produce only economic woe for him and the investors. Building railroads also meant, as in the cases of Karaganda, Billings, and Abilene, eliminating the presence of the people who occupied the land prior to the arrival of the railroad. The Kazakhs in Kazakhstan, the Sioux and Crow in Montana, the emigrant tribes in eastern Kansas, and the Southern Cheyennes and Arapahos in western Kansas would be removed by state force. Their respective uses and management of the resources of the grasslands in Kazakhstan, Montana, and Kansas all conflicted with the *needs* of railroaders and cattlemen to have those resources employed and shaped in an entirely different manner.[32]

Cultural and state power drove railroad building. Consequently, a set of American cultural values streamed into the grasslands in the wake of advancing railroad lines. Both the UPED line and the cultural values that propelled it acted as ecological forces: technology and culture became new elements added to the mix of physical and biotic entities shaping the grasslands and thereby forcibly creating a *domesticated* grassland.

This transformation, as ecologist Robert O'Neill has written, shows that human beings should be seen as a "keystone species," one that has a "disproportionate effect on the persistence of other species to the extent that their removal may lead indirectly to the loss of such other species in the community."[33] Human beings act as more than an external force "deriving goods and services" from any particular biome. Rather, humans and their various cultures and technologies participate directly in shaping ecosystems, and when one culture and its technologies displace others in a landscape, a different set of ecological relationships emerges.

In O'Neill's ecological terms, the UPED line created an "invasion pathway" for "populations that would not otherwise occur."[34] Railroad builders such as Perry, who sought to tap the resources of the grasslands, converted them into capital and fixed the pathways that transported those resources to meet the demands created by urban markets. These pathways allowed cattle to replace bison, wheat to replace little bluestem, and gridded cities and farmscapes to replace the open grasslands surrounding Indian villages. With this transformation, an American empire, one that McCoy fully embraced, became literally fixed in the soil, and it created its own set of demands and constraints upon the very culture that spawned it.

Emphasizing the place of humans in a living ecosystem demands that we consider the technology of railroads as something more than machinery and steel tracks. As Kelly would argue, the railroad was a force possessing its own power to shape an ecosystem just as thoroughly as the humans who built the locomotives. The effects of this force rolling across and transforming the grasslands becomes apparent in Gardner's photographs of Abilene.[35] Railroad building followed its own logic as it molded workers' lives, displaced American Indians, established the placement and design of towns and farms, harnessed the national economy, and created new industries and markets. All of this occurred beyond the free choices of American Indians, town developers, organized laborers, and capitalists. Railroads were more than a tool for transportation; they embodied cultural, social, economic, and ecological forces sweeping through the grasslands and altered everything in and around their paths.

According to Kelly, three important characteristics shaped railroad building in the grasslands, and made Abilene work for McCoy. First, there was the *inevitability* of railroad technologies; that is, the physics of steam locomotion, steel manufacturing, and construction techniques, which led inevitably to the forms and structures of railroad systems, no matter where on earth they were built. Second, the development of railroad lines was *contingent* on what happened in the past. An example that Kelly gives is that ancient Roman war chariots accommodated two large war horses, and the ruts left by the chariot wheels had an average width of four feet and eight and one-half inches. Carriages through the ages were built to fit these ruts, and when English engineers first built tramways, they kept the rails spaced four feet and eight and one-half inches apart for horse-drawn carriages. The rail distance was kept intact once steam-powered locomotives replaced horses.[36] The third characteristic is *human free will*, which flourishes within the confines of inevitability and contingency.

McCoy eagerly employed the railroad to usher onto the prairies of Kansas new cultural and economic forces, which in turn altered the ecology of the grasslands. Again, railroads carried more than freight and passengers. They transported people's views about religion, gender, and education into the region. The UPED line provided the means by which McCoy could place his limitless ambitions into the large market forces radiating out from the large urban areas of the Midwest and eastern seaboard cities. The locomotive also made it possible for these same economic forces to reach out into the grasslands and mark the landscape with urban outposts. Railroads made possible shipping points such as McCoy's Abilene, an economic magnet that attracted cattle to it.

As railroads channeled the economic and cultural power of cities by tapping and reshaping the natural resources of the grasslands, they transformed American Indian–managed landscapes into ones dominated by Euro-American cultural and economic values—the values of American empire as touted by McCoy and Texas cattlemen. Perry and his fellow railroad financiers and supporters at the time heralded this empire as ordained, as right and proper. As one of the main chroniclers of the 1867 UPED-sponsored tour, the journalist Joseph Copley heralded how railroad building across the grasslands created a new order of Euro-American settlement. "The old process must be inverted," he wrote. "The locomotive must precede the plough, and the town the farm. Even Kansas, with all its fertility . . . could not be occupied in any other way."[37] In June 1867, the UPED entourage held a great banquet at Fort Harker, Kansas, and there Senator Richard Yates of Illinois proclaimed "the *new* fashion" of railroad building: to push railroads far into the "wilderness" well in advance of populating the land. "The locomotive is the new agent of civilization," Yates exclaimed. "The railroad," he assured his companions, "is carrying our institutions far into the centre of the West. We need nobody to fight the Indians, when the whistle of the locomotive shall frighten the wolf and the antelope before it."[38]

Like Senator Yates, Copley informed his eastern readers that the land was well suited for "the habitation of civilized people." He also asserted that "population will *follow*" the UPED line. Copley was certain that Euro-Americans could not precede the railroad because the "log-cabin can never be an institution" on the plains, and "the ranch is no place for women and children."[39] The Englishman William Bell chimed in with the same refrain: "In the great West, where continuous settlement is impossible, where . . . spots of great fertility and the richest prizes of the mineral kingdom tempt men onward into those vast regions . . . the locomotive has to lead instead of follow the tide of population."[40] The correct means for advancing the American Empire had been found.

## Joseph McCoy Meets Success and Failure in 1867

On September 5, 1867, a chuffed Joseph McCoy watched the first load of cattle headed east on the tracks of the UPED. He had overcome great obstacles to make his outlet for Texas cattle work. He had shown Texas drovers a safe route to drive cattle, a route abounding in grass and water. He had convinced important Texas cattlemen that he could place longhorns into the burgeoning urban markets along the East Coast. Most importantly, he showed Texas cattlemen that they actually could make money by working with him to market what otherwise would have been worthless stock. McCoy also had persuaded the residents of Dickinson County that they had little to fear from the presence of Texas cattle, because even if by some chance Kansas stockmen lost animals to the mysterious and deadly Texas fever, he would make good their losses. And then there was simply the money that the people of Abilene, and the farmers in the area, stood to make by entertaining, supplying, and fleecing the Texans. McCoy even envisioned building a packinghouse operation at Abilene, even though he probably had no idea how to transport "fresh beef" over 1,800 miles to the urban markets back east.[41] As McCoy watched the locomotive pull the stock cars away from his stockyard, he must have thought he was surely on his way to riches and fame.

By the end of the shipping season in December, an undertaking full of promise and profits had left few unscathed by loss and ruin, including the McCoy brothers. By September 20, over 20,000 head of cattle grazed in the vicinity of Abilene. Outlandish predictions had been made about the numbers to arrive such as a report from Lawrence estimating that 100,000 longhorns would reach Kansas before the end of the trail driving season. The number actually reaching Abilene totaled around 35,000 beeves.

At the end of shipping season, McCoy realized paltry returns at best. Altogether, the workers at the Great Western Stock Yards loaded 1,000 stock cars. This amounted to around 25,000 longhorns. Of the over 24,000 sent to Chicago and beyond, the owners of the Chicago stockyards bought a mere 3,000.

McCoy watched as the first shipment of cattle to Chicago resulted in a "small profit to the shipper." A second shipment of around forty-five car loads found no buyers in Chicago. The cattle were forwarded to Albany in the hopes of finding at least a buyer. There a buyer emerged, but the shipper received $300 less than he had paid for the herd ($17,500) plus transportation costs.

McCoy understood the unsound logic of shipping longhorns directly into eastern markets. Once on the grazing grounds near Abilene, the cattle had little time to fatten before being placed into stock cars. As McCoy described them, "The cattle were thin in flesh and made only the lower grades of beef, for which there was but little demand, at ruinously low figures." The seller in the case just mentioned needed to make at least three cents per pound gross on his Texas longhorns to break even in the Chicago market where "fair to good steers" were returning four to nearly five cents per pound gross. Not able to sell a herd for even three and four cents a pound gross implies that Chicago buyers considered such longhorns far too thin for butchering.

The next step for the seller was to try the market at Albany, New York. Transportation costs to Albany probably raised the break-even price for the herd to five cents per pound gross weight. Yet, as McCoy observed, eastern buyers and consumers considered Texan cattle uneatable and "as unsalable in the Eastern markets as would have been a shipment of prairie wolves." As the season progressed, McCoy watched as other sellers who sold cattle at market prices fared poorly, as did those who sold directly to packing companies. Some other sellers did a little better by unloading their herds in the Indian agencies in Nebraska.

Several thousand head of cattle were slaughtered in a packinghouse built in Junction City, Kansas. A Mr. Patterson, a cattleman from Indianapolis, Indiana, built and opened a packing plant in Junction City capable of handling two hundred head of cattle per day. His intended markets were in the cities of Baltimore, Philadelphia, and New York. He and his investors anticipated enlarging the capacity to three hundred a day.[42] The venture, however, crashed from the beginning. As McCoy explained it, "The cattle were not as good or fat as both parties had anticipated, and it proved a disastrous loss to all concerned."[43]

Several factors combined to create an exceptionally weak market for those lean Texas cattle. By the fall, corn crops in Indiana, Illinois, and Ohio had failed. Without enough feed for their herds, cattlemen from the Midwest flooded Chicago and eastern markets with their own beeves. Predictably, the return on cattle plummeted, and this was especially so for the bottled-up longhorns awaiting loading in Abilene. By November, newspapers in Kansas reported the countryside "covered with cattle" and herds sold for as low as five and six dollars a head given their "lean kine" appearance.[44] Such returns ran parallel to the common purchase prices per head in Texas, so it made little sense for a Texas drover to sell his herd to a potential buyer.

Compounding Joseph McCoy's embarrassment and problems, poor grazing conditions existed for Texas longhorns awaiting shipment. Heavy summer rains around Abilene had produced a "rank and heavy" growth of grass. This was the grass that cattlemen called "washy" because of its high water content. Their cattle could graze all they wanted but prairie grass in this condition lacked the protein and minerals that put fat and weight on them. Shippers and buyers took one look at these beeves and lost all interest in buying them.

The thick, yet low-nutrition grasses produced another difficult situation for McCoy. A warm "Indian summer" had quickly dried out the prairie grasses and once dormant they became susceptible to fire. That was exactly what happened in the fall of 1867. Fires raced throughout the tallgrass prairie of the Flint Hills to the east of Abilene. To the west, prairie fires swept the buffalo grass plains "all around the country from Hays to the head of Saline and the Smoky creeks." By early November, no further cattle could be driven to Abilene. Texas drovers reported that from Abilene "to Texas the whole country was black, having been burned off by Indians and settlers."[45]

As already shown, settlers had reason to fear the spread of Texas fever to their own herds. They knew one sure way to put a stop to the appearance of longhorns: make sure there was not a blade of grass left for grazing by burning off the rangeland. Indians usually burned grasslands in the fall as a management practice. Also, by setting the prairies afire the settlers and Indians put a halt to any intrusion of Texas cattle through their lands. An additional benefit for Indians was by setting fires at key locations they could also keep Texas cattle away from their own grazing grounds that sustained their horses and the wildlife that they hunted.

McCoy summed up the first season this way: "Shipping cattle at the rate of one thousand each shipment, costing nearly a score of thousands of dollars, and having them sold for considerable sum less than the freight bill, is a lively way to do business, but a poor way to get rich quick."[46] Upon reflection, he wished that the drovers had placed their herds into "winter quarters and kept their stock until the following season." Had they done so, McCoy reasoned, they would have realized "a fine profit." The herds could have grazed freely on the public domain and would have fattened quickly in the spring. Common experience among cattlemen seemed to show that stock overwintered posed no disease threats to midwestern shorthorn breeds. Consequently, buyers had little fear of purchasing these fattened longhorns, which made for profitable returns.

## *Prosperous Prospects for 1868*

Not everything had turned dire for the McCoys. Some signs pointed toward the possibility of a profitable 1868 season. By December 1867 several drovers had started making arrangements to have local farmers and ranchers overwinter their herds. Kansas farmers knew a good deal when they saw one, and those who could began buying up unshipped longhorns in November. Their goal was simple: graze and fatten the herds on harvested prairie hay through the winter. This was exactly what several farmers did in the rich river and creek bottoms of places like Eureka Valley, just to the west of Manhattan, but over forty miles east of Abilene. The silver lining to this practice was that Chicago and East Coast buyers considered overwintered longhorns free of Texas fever and safe to mingle or ship with midwestern Durham herds. Moreover, a Kansas farmer stood to profit with each pound a longhorn gained during the winter and early spring. As predicted in the *Kansas State Record* (Topeka), "To a man who is prepared to winter them, an investment in these cattle will by spring prove the most profitable in the country."[47]

Given the weak market prices in the late fall, other drovers decided not to sell their herds. Rather, some paid local farmers for a grazing right through the winter. For the going rate of one dollar a head, farmers were quick to make terms with a drover. Other drovers took the risk of driving their herds westward beyond any settlements and allowing their stock to range freely on the public domain during the winter. The idea was to round up the herd in the spring after the cattle had fattened on the rich buffalo grass prairie. Even if a drover lost a few head to cold and starvation, the returns on selling spring-fattened cattle more than compensated for those losses and for the weak prices offered for their scrawny beeves in the fall.

Despite his critics, McCoy had demonstrated the potential of his Abilene outlet. The directors of the UPED recognized how profitable shipping cattle could be, and geared up for hauling greater numbers in 1868. Writing for *New York Tribune* readers in November 1867, Samuel Wilkison predicted that 200,000 longhorns would arrive in Abilene in the next year. He lavished praise on Joseph McCoy for potentially creating a venture profitable beyond anyone's expectations—except, apparently, for Joseph and his brothers.[48]

Joseph and James had spent money recruiting Texas drovers as well as personnel to operate their livery stable and the Drovers Cottage. They made cash settlements with local farmers who had lost stock to Texas fever. They had employed runners to persuade drovers not to drive their cattle north to the Union Pacific tracks in Nebraska. The UP directors had taken note of the rich potential of shipping Texas cattle, and were taking steps to undercut the UPED's hold on the trade.

In 1868 Joseph had other reasons to feel more confident about the approaching season. In the 1867 season he and his brothers had offset some of their losses by taking a cut of the per-head shipping rate charged by the UPED for each head of cattle hauled by the company. The McCoys received $13,000 for "yarding and loading" at their Great Western Stock Yards facility in Abilene. For the 1868 shipping season, the agreement obligated the railroad company to pay out three dollars per car loaded.

In 1868, herds began arriving in April, and McCoy watched the first cattle shipment of twenty-eight stock cars leave the Great Western Stock Yards on Wednesday, June 10. Louise and James Gore had the Drovers Cottage completely ready to host cattlemen and stock buyers. The town of Abilene had more recreational venues ready to take the Texans' money. And urban markets looked strong for beef imports. In fact, everything looked so promising that Joseph McCoy decided to invest in a sure thing.

Early in the spring, one fine herd of 800 longhorns arrived, and the drover placed it on rich grazing grounds a few miles from the Great Western Stock Yards. McCoy frequently rode out to the herd and carefully observed the cattle. He took note of each animal and made a selection of 224 of the finest and fattest in the herd. When he felt that the time was right, he approached the drover and negotiated a price of $7,468 for the lot. McCoy then drove the herd back to his stockyards and weighed them; to his delight, the beeves averaged 1,238 pounds each. With prices for "fair to good" beeves prevailing at fourteen cents per pound net weight in the New York City market, Joseph could have calculated the herd going for over $18,000. After deducting transportation costs that could easily have reached $7,500, Joseph still could envision a return of over $3,200 on the entire deal, or more than a 40 percent return on his initial investment. Joseph had calculated the odds, placed his bets on the great cattle faro gaming table and waited to see what cards the dealer would turn up.

CHAPTER 5

# The Seasonal Round

THE SOUTHERN REALM OF THE CATTLE EMPIRE — THE MIDDLE REALM —
THE NORTHERN REALM — THE URBAN REALM — SUNNY PROSPECTS — PERILS AND
PITFALLS IN THE ROUND

Joseph McCoy and Texas cattlemen understood that placing their stock into the burgeoning national and international meat markets rested upon navigating the ebb and flow of a seasonal round. The seasonal round of cattle driving up the Chisholm Trail occurred in three distinct phases. Beginning in early spring, the first phase was marked by the roundup of Texas cattle and organizing them into herds for the drive north. The second phase included driving the herds across the Red River and through Indian Territory before the end of September, which generally marked the conclusion of the growing season of prairie grasses. The third phase, usually between June and the end of November, was when Texas drovers held their herds in the rich grasslands of central Kansas beyond where farmers had already begun to transform wild prairies into domesticated fields of corn and wheat. Longhorns often arrived far too thin to merit immediate purchase, and drovers needed to locate a grazing ground for their herds on the wide open, bountiful public bluestem rangeland to fatten their cattle in an effort to entice buyers.

In 1874, at the same time that Joseph McCoy completed his description of this great Southwest cattle trade, T. F. Oakes, the freight agent for the Kansas Pacific Railway, published his *Guide Map of the Great Texas Cattle Trail from Red River Crossing to the Old Reliable Kansas Pacific Railway*. Oakes probably drew upon McCoy's vast knowledge of the industry, given that he asked for permission to reproduce the illustrations that were to accompany McCoy's work on the Texas cattle trade.[1]

Oakes's guide detailed a web of cattle trails throughout southern and central Texas that all converged at the Red River Station. One of the more common routes through the southern realm of the Chisholm Trail system began in the vicinity of San Antonio. From there, drovers headed north, passing New Braunfels on the banks of the Guadalupe River, and then to San Marcos, and then crossing a spring-fed river of the same name some four miles below the city. The next major crossing occurred on the Colorado River about three miles below the city of Austin. After that, drovers led their herds north past the small cities of Round Rock, Georgetown, Salado, Belton, and Cleburne, where the herds were driven over the Brazos River. At Fort Worth, which in its early days C. H. Rust remembered as a "little burg on the bluff where the panther lay down and died," herds were forded across the Trinity River.

From this staging area, the drovers followed a well-traveled trail generally due north to a crossing of the Red River named, fittingly enough, the Red River Station.[2] From the crossing to the border with Kansas, Oakes showed a nearly straight path north through Indian Territory. Several Indian nations laid claim to portions of the territory through which cattle were driven, but the federal government held a different perspective on the region, considering the Chisholm Trail well within the confines of the public domain. The trail led through lush grasslands and ample water sources, and the area teemed with wildlife that Indian tribes hunted.

The trail's northern portion traversed a sparsely populated region of Kansas, a place with grasslands and water sources every bit as abundant as those in Indian Territory. When Oakes published his map in 1874, a couple of years after Abilene had faded as the Texas cattle outlet on the Kansas Pacific Railway, the route through Kansas veered west of the quarantine line, passed by Wichita, and terminated at Ellsworth, also on the Kansas Pacific line.

The McCoys and cattle dealers reckoned with a factor that made trail driving worthwhile: free cattle fuel abounded in the public domain. No one paid for the grass eaten by the cattle and horses headed north along the Chisholm Trail, nor did cattlemen pay for any of the grass grazed by their herds on the rich prairie pastures surrounding any of the Kansas cattle outlets. Place cattle on a ship or in a railroad stock car, and the cattle buyer had to pay for the stored solar energy in the hay eaten during transit, and the stored solar fuel in the coal or wood that powered the steam engines. Besides, cattle often lost weight, and sometimes died, as they endured or succumbed to overcrowded confinement.

An obvious, but important fact: cattle in transit had to drink water and eat to stay alive, and it was better yet if they could retain or gain weight until slaughtered for their meat, tallow, and hides. It did no good to the buyer if cattle died in transit. While most shippers figured a 20 percent loss on any shipment of cattle, any greater loss meant losing money on the deal. But Texas drovers bore no such expense or peril while driving their herds north along the Chisholm Trail. Their cattle and horses had nearly unrestrained access to free fuel: the stored solar energy in the grasses and water sources that abounded along the Chisholm Trail and throughout the public domain.

Each section of the trail responded to seasonal and annual climatic variations. Ranchers, drovers, herders, and cattle all were dependent upon an ecosystem conducive to their well-being. Seasonal temperatures had to be mild enough not to kill animals and the humans who tended them. Precipitation had to fall within certain parameters in order to nourish the grasses and watercourses that sustained the cattle herds. Too much rain caused all sorts of problems, ranging from flooding streams and less nourishing grasses to lightning storms that caused herds to stampede. Too little rain meant the cattle starved and became parched during the drive and arrived in a horribly weakened condition, completely unfit for sale.

Drovers had good reasons to start their herds on the trail during the spring and to try to have their herds loaded into stock cars no later than the end of November. Ideally, if a cattle herd owner could load animals in Kansas in June, so much the better for his chances of making greater profits on his sale into northern markets than if he waited until late summer. Texas cattleman John Burkhart outlined the benefits of following this calendar. "Start as early in the spring," he wrote, "as the grass will permit . . . [and follow the Chisholm Trail] as the grass is better; water plenty; herding grounds good. Abilene is by far the best market, and the herding grounds are decidedly the best in the State." Burkhart encouraged drovers to "take your cattle as near town as possible, as buyers do not like to go far to examine stock." He warned drovers to reach Abilene by the first of August, otherwise "come prepared to winter." Overwintering a herd had a distinct benefit to it, however, in that "wintered stock sells for about twice as much as those just in from Texas." It also helped to have marketable beeves in the first place.[3]

At outlets like the McCoy brothers' Great Western Stock Yards, sellers and buyers met, judged the quality of the herds, made deals, and set into motion a second seasonal round, one marked by different means of transport, labor, and ecological conditions. Workers at stockyards loaded cattle into stock cars that locomotives hauled to other urban stockyards and packinghouses such as those found in Kansas City and Chicago. Some herds were bought and then driven again to territories farther north to feed Indians on reservations or to build herds on the open rangelands of Colorado, Wyoming, and Montana. Most of the herds were loaded into stock cars, hauled to the Midwest, and unloaded. There, they overwintered on the great corn and hay fields owned by prominent stockmen in Illinois, or on similar ranches in Iowa, Indiana, Ohio, and Kentucky. The experience of midwestern stockmen taught them that Texas cattle overwintered and fattened on their pastures were safe to mix with local herds because they evidently posed little, if any, danger of spreading the dreaded and deadly Texas fever associated with the presence of longhorns.

With these enhanced feeding operations, imported cattle quickly gained the muscle and the fat that made their meat tasty to urban consumers. Indeed, each pound gained was money in the bank. As soon as cattle had thoroughly fattened, midwestern cattlemen made new deals with urban brokers and placed beeves in stock cars headed daily to Philadelphia, Boston, New York, and other major midwestern and East Coast cities. By 1874, international markets had opened, particularly those in England, and American beef began lining the butcher shelves in London. While it might take two years before the meat from a Texas longhorn reached London markets, in the intervening years, each spring, a new round of cattle drives had begun in Texas.

The seasonal round, however, did not always operate this smoothly. In fact, it was more typically erratic. No one involved in the trade had the clairvoyance to discern its variable climate, grassland ecology, animal biology, and urban demographics and economies. Because everyone involved in the trade had to make constant adjustments to their practices to have any hope of success, the cattle business was not for the faint of heart. But for some, like Joseph McCoy and his brothers, who were gamblers by nature, it promised enough success to offset any foreseeable losses. But the gods of the cattle trade were not always kind to the lowly humans who placed their wagers on it.

## *The Southern Realm of the Cattle Empire*

Joseph McCoy recognized two distinct classes of cattle arriving at his stockyards, and they originated in two distinct regions of Texas: northern and southern. He considered the southern realm to be a harsh, arid clime where predominantly

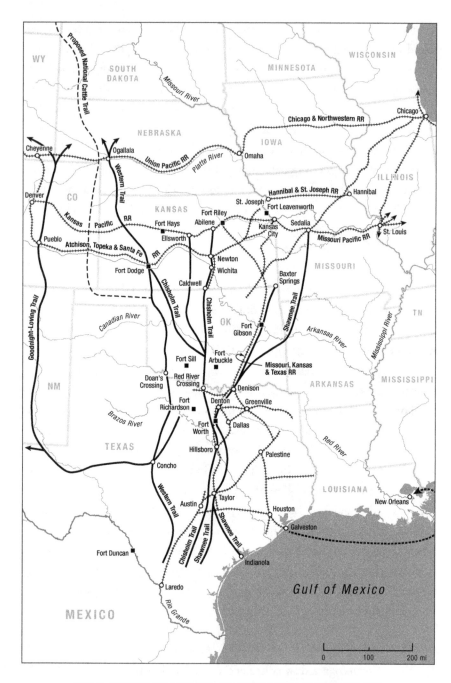

TRAIL SYSTEM OF THE TRANS-MISSISSIPPI CATTLE TRADE

longhorn herds grazed a mesquite grassland. McCoy viewed the grasslands of the northern half of Texas as the more hospitable grazing environment.

A report in the *Daily Herald* of Dallas, Texas, in 1882 highlights how Frio County represented the rangeland in the southern, arid portion of the state. It was described as a "stock-raising" county where cattlemen had twenty-one thousand head grazing on the "abundant" native-grass pastures. Water was abundant only in the "water holes" dotting the county. The summers were "very hot" and the winters "mild and pleasant." This climate, the article stated, produced a "natural range [that supported] stock all winter without extra cost or trouble."[4]

McCoy intuitively understood the climatic differences between the two regions of the state and how the dissimilarities created distinct grazing environments. The weather records from two army posts highlight those regional distinctions. Fort Richardson stood some seventy miles south of the Red River, the southern border of Indian Territory. The extant weather records from this post, collected by the post surgeon from March 1868 through May 1878, are a good representation of the climate in the northern portions of Texas.

The other post, Fort Duncan, was located on the east bank of the Rio Grande near the small border-crossing town of Eagle Pass, Texas. The arid grasslands to the east encompassed the vast southern open range. Uvalde, Texas, the main town where cowboys gathered and sorted herds and started drives headed north, was about sixty miles slightly northeast of the fort. The extant weather records from this post, recorded from June 1873 through October 1879, are a good representation of the climate marking the southern cattle range in Texas during this decade.

A comparison of the two record sets reveals that median temperatures around Fort Richardson were considerably cooler than those recorded each month at Fort Duncan. From 1868 through 1877, July stood out as the hottest month of the year at Fort Richardson. When analyzed, the post weather records during this time period reveal that the median of the monthly average temperatures in July was 83.92 degrees. Altogether, between 1868 and 1878, the recorded monthly average temperatures for July ranged between 82.05 and 86.96.[5]

Applying the same analytical techniques to Fort Duncan reveals that between 1873 and 1879, August was the hottest month of the year. During this time period, the extant records from the post reveal that the median of the monthly averages of August was 87.44 degrees Fahrenheit, nearly 4 degrees warmer than the median recorded at Fort Richardson. The range of August average monthly temperatures at Fort Duncan was 80.33 to 90.14 degrees, also a distinctly larger range of highs and lows than those recorded at Fort Richardson.[6]

Similar trends mark the winter months at Fort Richardson compared to those at Fort Duncan. In December 1874 and January 1875, Captain William Forwood, who served as the post surgeon at Fort Richardson, recorded a number of very cold days. On four days in December, he logged below-freezing daily average temperature readings. In January, he recorded thirteen days with below-freezing daily average temperatures. January 9 was exceptionally cold, with a morning reading of 3 degrees below zero and a daytime high of 10 degrees at 7 P.M. The daily average temperature for the month barely topped freezing at 33.35 degrees Fahrenheit.

Stockmen regarded cattle overwintered under these conditions free of transmitting Texas fever to native herds in the Midwest anytime thereafter. If given adequate nutrition, cattle easily survived under winter conditions such as those recorded at Fort Richardson in northern Texas. Moderately cold weather like this seemed to eliminate the Texas fever vector that cattle raised in the southern part of the state seemed to carry with them. Given the purifying effects of overwintering, anyone involved in the cattle trade willingly purchased cattle raised under these conditions, and confidently mixed Texas cattle and native in the same herd.

In January 1869, John Wentworth, an Illinoisan cattle buyer and rancher, touted the virtue of overwintering Texas cattle in his home state. "My experience," he informed Texas cattlemen, "confirms this statement. The first frost of this season arrested [Texas fever] not only in my herd, but throughout the neighborhood. I mean to say there were no new cases after the frosts." He did point out, however, that any cattle manifesting the disease prior to the frost died.[7]

Cattle raised in the warmer, southern portions of Texas, however, seemed to carry the vector that caused Texas fever. No one at the time understood that warmer temperatures in the southern portion of the state failed to kill the tick that harbored the protozoan that caused the disease. A great many stockmen knew enough, however, to view Texas cattle raised in the southern portion of the state with suspicion and dread.

An analysis of the winter temperatures recorded at Fort Duncan reveals the extent to which the southern portion of the state was much warmer than the northern areas in December 1874 and January 1875. The post surgeon took weather readings three times a day—at 7 A.M., again at 2 P.M., and the last at 9 P.M. The temperature fell below freezing at Fort Duncan only once in December, and in January, temperatures fell below freezing on only five days. In the weather records, post surgeon C. C. Gray's record of only one daily average temperature below freezing, that of January 9, is a clear reflection of warm temperatures in the southern portion of the Texas cattle range. A further indication of temperate winter temperatures is that Gray computed a daily average temperature for the month of 46.3 degrees Fahrenheit; at the same time, post surgeon Forwood at Fort Richardson farther north calculated the daily average temperature for the month at 33.4 degrees Fahrenheit.

In any event, stock cattle seemed to flourish better in the northern half of the state than they did in the south. Stock cattle differed from longhorn beeves in an important respect: most stock cattle were the offspring of longhorn cows that had been interbred with shorthorn bulls, initially Durhams.[8] As interbreeding advanced in northern Texas and the ranges of Kansas, Colorado, and Wyoming, stockmen experimented with other shorthorn breeds such as Hereford, Angus, and Galloway.[9] The offspring of interbreeding were referred to as "native" stock, whereas longhorns were always referred to as "range" cattle.

Raising stock cattle became a passion in Texas. Colonel Dillard R. Fant, one of the most successful stockmen in the state, had taken up stock raising seriously by 1874. He had his main ranch in Goliad County, where he had enclosed his rangeland and introduced Durham and Hereford bulls into his herd. At the height of his operations, he controlled over 700,000 acres of pasture in several counties. His reach stretched from the far southern part of the state, where he owned the 225,000-acre Santa Rosa Ranch in Hidalgo County, to his operation in Tarrant County in the north, where the city of Fort Worth was established.[10]

By 1882, the more than 130 registered members of the Texas Livestock Association were actively working to improve their breeds with stock animals. Even in the southernmost regions of the state, stockmen made extraordinary efforts to improve their breeds. C. M. Rogers of Corpus Christi interbred his herd with Durhams as well as Devon and Brahmin bulls. T. H. Mathis of Rockport, Texas, in Aransas County, interbred his herd with Durhams and Herefords. James F. Miller of Gonzales, Texas, interbred his herd with Holstein cattle.[11]

Stockmen understood that the reproductive rate of longhorn cows, with a calf "dropped" nearly every year, outpaced shorthorn reproductive rates by 40 to

60 percent. Stockmen also had observed that Durhams fattened better on corn than longhorns did, or could. The goal of interbreeding, then, was to advance the reproductive rate of cattle better suited for fattening on corn in Illinois. Buyers found these animals more readily saleable than pure longhorns in the eastern beef markets. Earlier attempts at interbreeding had occurred in 1860, but the Civil War had put a stop to those efforts. With the war at an end, Texas stockmen resumed their efforts to breed beeves with higher market potential than purebred longhorns.[12]

McCoy, as well as a great many other stock buyers and sellers, could easily distinguish interbred Texas cattle raised in the northern portion of the state from longhorns from the southern reaches. A mere year after opening his Great Western Stock Yards, McCoy made it clear that "cattle coming from the north or northwestern portion of [Texas] are as radically different in appearance from those of the lower counties." Longhorns from the southern portion of the state, south of San Antonio, always seemed to weigh less than the interbred cattle that had grazed on north Texas ranges.[13]

McCoy understood that efforts to interbreed shorthorns with longhorns in southern Texas often failed given how often Durhams and other imported shorthorn breeds succumbed to Texas fever. In northern Texas, Durhams seemed to thrive better. By 1868, McCoy had concluded that in the "northern portion of Texas the importation of Durham stock has been so successful as to radically change the cattle of the section of the country." While northern Texas ranchers sought interbreeding to improve their stock, those living to the south, given the Durham death rate there, often found, as McCoy succinctly put it, "that it would not pay for [stockmen] to take that trouble."[14]

By practicing interbreeding or not, cattlemen such as William J. Bennett, as well as Colonel Fant, managed to create extensive cattle herds under the environmental conditions prevailing in the southern half of Texas. As a young boy, Bennett had arrived in Texas with his parents in 1848. In ten years his family had established their stock operations just south of San Antonio on the Leona River. With over four hundred head of cattle, the Bennetts allowed their beeves to range far and wide over a broad expanse of grazing land. Soon other stockmen arrived in the vicinity, and cattle from various herds began mixing and dispersing as far south as the Rio Grande.

By April, the Bennetts would begin their "cow hunts" to round up their cattle for marketing. Despite the intermingling of all the herds, the Bennetts could cull their own given the brands on the animals' hides. Once William had gathered a saleable herd, he would drive it to San Antonio, where he found himself at the mercy of the Allen Company.

Sam Allen, who lived in Powder Horn, a small community near San Antonio, had cornered the shipping of cattle from there to New Orleans. Trouble quickly emerged with this system because more cattle existed than Allen could ship to port. Soon San Antonio cattlemen, such as young William Bennett, eschewed Gulf ports for the more lucrative market outlets opening up in Kansas. By 1872, William, now living in Uvalde in the broad rangeland between San Antonio and Del Rio, Texas, began driving his herds north to Wichita, Kansas.[15]

Besides the herds of cattle that freely roamed south of San Antonio, other stockmen allowed their herds to graze pastures well into northern Mexico. Much of this related to the horse trade and herding. For over two hundred years, portions of the northern grasslands in Mexico had served as a rich ground for tending hundreds of thousands of horses. These same herds provided a large portion of the animals ridden by cowboys on their way north to Abilene and other rail depots. In 1875, S. A. Hickok, who had left Ohio for the promise of riches in the Texas livestock trade, began herding sheep around San Antonio. He had "acquired" his stock from across the border and continued along these lines of ranching until switching to cattle and horses. The horses that he had purchased across the border he drove to Kansas, where they were shipped to more lucrative markets in Ohio, New York, and the south.[16]

The two regions of the state bore one trait in common. At first, cattle grazing operations depended primarily upon open rangeland. As Joseph Nimmo, the chief of the US Bureau of Statistics, phrased it, after the end of the Civil War, "almost all the cattle of [Texas] were, according to the popular phrase, 'on the range'; *i.e.*, grazed upon the public lands." But over the next twenty years, rangeland operations gradually shifted to the far western and northern portions of the state as farming took on greater extents of acreage in the eastern and central portions. As Nimmo made clear, the greater portion of cattle raising in Texas shifted to "ranch" operations, with herds "confined to the lands of the different owners or associated owners."[17]

This trend toward pasture and enclosed ranges had become evident by 1876. A report in the *New York Times* illustrated it by describing some of the largest operations clustered between Austin to the north and Corpus Christi to the south. Of the ten firms covered, three still pursued open-range grazing practices, and the others had ranches, that is, confined grazing ranges, a few of which contained around 200,000 acres. To the west of the Nueces River, M. Kennedy owned 190,000 acres in pasture upon which he grazed 8,000 horses and 130,000 head of cattle. His neighbor "Mr. King" controlled 200,000 acres of pasture that supported 160,000 cattle and 10,000 horses and mules.[18] Such smaller, yet significant operations as Allen and Son and Foster Dyer, two ranches in the Brazos River Valley, had fenced in 40,000 and 12,000 acres of pasture that supported 50,000 and 40,000 head of cattle, respectively.[19]

## *The Middle Realm*

In 1880, on his first cattle drive to Dodge City, Luther Lawhon, like many Texas cowboys of his times, called Indian Territory uncivilized, wild. Once he reached Kansas, he reentered 'God's Land.' In short, people like Lawhon regarded the resources of a "wild" country as not *owned* by anyone. Consequently, so the reasoning went, Texas cattlemen, and a great many Americans, had a right to use resources free for the taking. However, Indians considered the land theirs by right of treaty with the United States. The wild game was theirs to hunt, and the land itself was theirs to use in whatever manner they chose, whether for grazing horses or raising crops. In fact, the "civilized nations" that occupied the eastern half possessed their own cattle herds and were reluctant to share their rangelands with any drover crossing them with a herd of longhorns. The federal government, despite having carved up the area into reservations, considered the entire territory as government land and subject to federal control. Texans considered the territory to be owned by the government and open for public use. Water and grass were abundant, and cattle drovers and their outfits considered those resources free for the taking, making the realm no man's land.[20]

By the time a drover had crossed the Red River with his herd, he was often in close proximity to many other herds being driven up the Chisholm Trail. In 1868, when Jack Bailey drove his herd north, he often took note of how close the various herds were to each other. Such observation was important because preceding herds might have already eaten bare a good campground. It was also important to keep herds separated in order to keep good track of one's own cattle and horses, which at any time could be scattered miles apart while on the trail.[21]

All hell could break loose among the cowboys when herds became entangled. In 1872, Ben Drake, a seventeen-year-old cowboy, was on his second cattle drive. It had been a hard one because the cattle had had to swim swollen rivers throughout Indian Territory. Near present-day Oklahoma City, the cattle in Drake's herd stampeded into another herd grazing nearby, and the two crews had a difficult time separating them. As tempers rose, a fight broke out in the other outfit, and nine herders in that same outfit killed each other in the melee.[22]

At times cattle driving could be boring. F. M. Polk noted, "cattle driving is just about the easiest job I know of" so long as the cattle moved along calmly. There was little for a cowboy to do other than to ride his horse at a slow pace when the going was smooth. But the day to day work of herding seldom produced easy riding. W. W. Capt remembered that, after crossing the Red River, "stampedes, sleepless nights, gyp water and poor chuck, constituted our bill of fare." At the end of the day, Capt watched as cowboys often took out their frustrations on the cook, who had tucked away a Colt .45 that he often employed as a "liver regulator."[23]

While on the Chisholm Trail in 1872, F. M. Polk had the chore of riding ahead of the herd to scout for Indians and also to locate bison herds. If not careful, a drover might find his cattle headed right into a migrating herd of bison, and once intermingled, the herds became exceedingly difficult to separate. At those times, trail driving became exciting and dangerous, even deadly, for men, horses, cattle and bison.[24]

To enliven the mundane stretches, cowboys would often leave the herd to pursue wildlife. As an old man, Polk reminisced about how antelope and prairie dogs lined the entire reach of the Chisholm Trail in Indian Territory in 1881. As he put it, "We found great sport killing them." Moreover, his crew had greater "sport roping buffalo and elk," which appeared in herds of hundreds that stretched across the open grasslands. Capt similarly enjoyed the "great sport" of a bison chase.[25]

In some spots, millions of cattle and horse hooves had beaten the trail as bare and hard as a modern concrete highway. To graze cattle meant leading herds well away from routes that had become barren. To either side of the main route, prairies, once luxuriant with nutritious little bluestem, the mainstay fuel for cattle and horses, quickly became sparse pastures of buffalo grass. Buffalo grass holds up better under the heavy trampling of hooves than does little bluestem, and although buffalo grass and little bluestem possess roughly equal nutritional values, the former never produces in the quantity of the latter.[26] Quantity of forage, and access to it, was always an overriding consideration for drovers when hundreds of thousands of animals relied on the same sources.

Surveying the Chisholm Trail in the summer of 1880, Joseph McCoy commented in his diary on its broad extent. He noted how drovers in Indian Territory, while awaiting orders from their Texas bosses, routed herds far away from the trails to secure good grass and water. The valleys and flats near the main line of the trail showed the effects of overgrazing, which forced drovers to take their herds to the uplands in search of "sagegrass," or little bluestem.[27] On these uplands, the cattlemen ran the risk of poor water supplies, but they lacked alternatives. There was simply not enough grass and water to supply all the herds moving through the same vicinity at the same time.

Securing regular water sources always proved the key to a successful drive. Whenever possible, drovers avoided going more than a day without watering their stock. In Indian Territory, cowboys experienced a wide-open grassland with trees seldom in sight. When trees did come into view, cowboys knew, as W. F. Cude learned to recognize while on his first trail drive in 1868, that they were nearing a creek or river, a place where they could water their herds.[28]

In any portion of the grasslands, the watercourses could dry up during some summer seasons, and surface flow would disappear. Trail driving under such conditions always proved difficult, as it did for G. W. Mills in 1880. The herd he trailed had been well watered while crossing the Washita River. Everyone anticipated watering the herd again at the South Canadian River crossing, but once there, Mills found nothing but a sandy bottom where water had once coursed. With no recourse, Mills and his cowboys drove the herd for another thirty-five miles to Wolf Creek. The cattle suffered from thirst and during the night "'lowed' piteously" in agony.

Next day Mills and his compatriots had little ability to control the herd as it neared the flowing Wolf Creek. The parched animals broke and ran headlong toward the river, straight through a nearby Indian encampment. Those rushing, panting cattle knocked down lodges and scattered the Indian horse herd in every direction. As Mills recalled the event, under no control of the herders, "cattle and men all went off in the river together."[29]

During a typical driving season, a drover pushing a herd through this middle portion of the Chisholm Trail usually encountered pleasant spring weather. During the early driving season of April through May, herds seldom endured an average monthly temperature below 42 degrees or a high above 75 degrees. If a drover ran his herd through during the summer months, he could anticipate average monthly temperatures between 75 degrees and the low 90s for his cattle.[30]

As August was always the hottest month of the year on this part of the trail, drovers tried to have their herds well north and already grazing on Kansas rangelands by then. August was also the second-lowest month of rainfall during the growing season of April through September, which often meant worsening grazing conditions when the mixed-grass prairies that had been grazed by preceding herds neared the end of their growth and production. In other words, a pasture that was grazed off at that time of year usually would not recover until the following spring.

## *The Northern Realm*

As drovers crossed the state line into Kansas, they trailed their herds through a grassland system similar to the one they had left in Indian Territory. Texas drovers, once safely within the vicinity of Abilene or, for that matter, any shipping point in Kansas, regularly sought out ungrazed grassland pasture for their cattle. The drover might be lucky and locate a grazing ground only a few miles away from Abilene, but if arriving late in the season, he might find himself tending his herds more than fifty miles away from any shipping point. Regardless of where a drover might land his herd, he had one goal in mind: rest and fatten his stock as much as possible before weighing them on the scales at McCoy's Great Western Stock Yards. Each pound gained was more money in the drover's pocket, and he had a lot to gain by this practice so long as the grass was free for the taking and the weather remained mild.

Joseph McCoy and other buyers seldom purchased any cattle arriving near Abilene in May or June. McCoy would ride out and regularly inspect incoming herds, but his experience led him to claim that those cattle were "not fat enough to market." If these cattle were not to be grazed on Kansas rangelands, pasture men from Illinois and Indiana would buy up these underweight cattle and ship them to their midwestern pastures, where they would be fattened and placed into eastern markets the following spring or summer. McCoy rhetorically asked if this was a money-making proposition and answered, "I say that it [is], and largely, too."[31]

For those who kept their herds in Kansas, the central grassland ecosystem normally provided all the resources and conditions necessary for putting pounds on a newly arrived herd from Texas. The mixed-grass prairies that surrounded Abilene and extended westward for more than one hundred miles were a rich feeding ground for hungry longhorns. The open short-grass prairies of the High Plains, cloaked by nutritious buffalo grass, ranged from west of Hays to the foot of the Rocky Mountains in Colorado. Pound for pound of any grass growing in the grasslands of North America, buffalo grass proved to be the best source of stored solar energy for powering the vast herds of cattle arriving from Texas. The only drawback to grazing cattle on the short-grass prairies was that a herd required a greater range of grazing land than in the taller, mixed-grass prairies that dominated central Kansas.

During the growing season, the climate of central and western Kansas was much milder than that of Texas. Add to this the fact that the growing-season months of April, May, June, July, August, and September were ideally suited for producing a rich abundance of wild grasses that could sustain the hundreds of thousands of cattle awaiting shipment. Drovers who placed their herds on the open rangeland of Kansas during these months seldom, if ever, worried about finding enough pasturage to keep their cattle alive.

The weather reports recorded at two army posts, Fort Riley and Fort Hays, nicely highlight the climatic conditions between 1867 and 1885 that nourished the rich grasslands where cattlemen would graze their herds. Joseph McCoy built his Great Western Stock Yards about 30 miles due west of Fort Riley and about 110 miles east of Fort Hays. The rangeland between Abilene and Fort Hays encompassed the grazing grounds most frequently occupied by Texas drovers, and it was during the growing season, April through September, that Texas drovers most wanted to have their herds on the grasslands of Kansas.[32]

At Fort Riley, June and July stood out as the months with the highest rainfall averages. April had the lowest average, gradually increasing by July and tailing off in August and September. In comparison, the records at Fort Richardson, the northernmost post in Texas, show that May, rather than July, was the month with the greatest average rainfall. The May median monthly rainfall in northern Texas was 3.28 inches, and at Fort Riley it was 4.04 inches. In July at Fort Riley, the month with the highest rainfall, the median for the years 1867 to 1885 was 4.91 inches of rainfall. In short, the growing season in Kansas reached its peak about the same time that the bulk of Texas cattle herds arrived on the scene.

The records at Fort Hays reveal trends similar to those logged at Fort Riley. Surgeons at both posts recorded the most rainfall in July. The mean at Fort Hays was lower than that at Fort Riley, 3.41 as opposed to 4.91 inches, but the monthly trends were the same. Post surgeon records showed April with the least amount of rainfall, followed by increasing amounts recorded in May and June, peaking in July, and then tailing off in August and September.

Monthly temperatures followed similar tendencies. July was always the hottest month, with little variation in the median temperatures at either post, and April was always the coolest month during the growing season. The median at both posts varied by only a couple of degrees, 54.05 at Fort Riley, and 52.20 at Fort Hays. These Kansas median temperatures were always considerably lower than those at Fort Richardson, Texas (67.02 degrees), and, to the south, Fort Duncan (72.71 degrees).

The biggest difference in rangeland climates in Texas and Kansas occurred in the winter months. At Fort Hays, median temperatures in December and January, the two coldest months of the year, were 28.35 and 29.7 degrees, respectively. At Fort Riley, the medians for December and January were 27.2 and 24.25 degrees, respectively. In comparison, the medians at Fort Richardson and Fort Duncan were nearly 25 degrees warmer on average.

Herd owners quickly found this difference in winter temperatures between the northern and southern ranges attractive for overwintering in Kansas. Stockmen realized that cattle overwintered on Kansas rangelands seldom, if ever, spread Texas fever to any herds in the following spring or summer. Such stock was safe to intermingle with any native shorthorn breeds. With good management practices Texas cattle could be sustained on prairie grasses during the winter, and with the advent of spring, overwintered herds could take advantage of the return of fresh green prairie grasses. Fully fattened on the richest, most nutritional growth of little bluestem and buffalo grass, such cattle were ready for market in early spring long before any herds driven out of Texas arrived on the scene.

Open ranges sustained herds until the cattle were loaded onto the transportation systems leading to eastern markets. The way in which drovers used the broad prairie flats near the Great Bend of the Arkansas River to graze their herds before taking them to Wichita, Kansas, illustrates the point. In 1874, drovers wintered more than forty thousand cattle between Great Bend and Wichita in anticipation of spring markets.[33]

In a similar manner, the wide Smoky Hill River Valley provided water and grass for herds loading onto shipping points at Abilene, Hays, and Ellsworth, Kansas. This is why the Kansas Pacific Railway Company published Oakes's pamphlet devoted to extolling the grass conditions in the valley. The company spent considerable money distributing the publication among Texas drovers.[34]

When the Atchison, Topeka, and Santa Fe Railroad Company (AT&SF) began surveying its route across Kansas, people living in central Kansas took a keen interest in where the company intended to build. The route had particular consequences for the Texas cattle trade at Ellsworth. A writer from the city took comfort in how the AT&SF had mapped a line starting at Hutchinson, Kansas, that led to Fort Zarah on the tip of the Great Bend. The writer feared that the company would construct a road farther to the south, which would have bypassed rich grazing grounds in the Great Bend area.[35]

Under the pseudonym "Occasional," this writer from Ellsworth recounted how Arthur Larkin had purchased three hundred head of Texas cattle in fall 1869. Larkin overwintered the herd in the vicinity of Fort Zarah, and in the spring he had his herd driven to the Smoky Hill River Valley to await shipment. "Occasional" regaled his readers with accounts of feasting on the delicious "savory roasts and steaks" taken from a choice few of those well-fed beeves. In all, the writer championed the rich possibilities of wintertime open-range grazing around the Great Bend area and the bountiful finishing springtime grazing grounds of the Smoky Hill River Valley—along with rail connections to the Kansas Pacific. ("Occasional" did not mention the potential of the AT&SF line). Operating open-range grazing in this manner required tens of thousands of acres of unfenced grasslands, which were in abundance when "Occasional" extolled the region.[36]

## *The Urban Realm*

The vast grasslands of North America made it possible to herd cattle to Abilene with little to no regard for the cost of fueling the enterprise. Free access to the stored solar energy in the grass made it economically cost efficient to drive cattle to the Great Western Stock Yards. Simply getting a herd of cattle to Abilene, however, did not make anyone money. Joseph McCoy and his brothers realized that it was the urban demand for beef that made opening a cattle outlet in Abilene sensible, and potentially profitable, in the first place. It was the value of beeves in urban markets that promised an economic return that Texas ranchers, drovers, cowboys, and the McCoy brothers all relied upon.

After the Civil War, McCoy and like-minded cattle brokers stood to make immense profits in buying Texas cattle valued at no more than three to six dollars a head and selling them in the higher-priced northern urban markets. If during the Civil War, brokers could return a profit on Illinois cattle sold into eastern markets for ten cents per pound gross, then buying longhorns for six-tenths of one cent per pound gross could return a fortune for the person capable of facilitating the transaction.

The urban markets the McCoy brothers intended to tap were like nothing humans had ever experienced before. Something entirely new in the global economy was taking place. Changing urban demographics across the planet had a direct influence on the development of American agriculture and ranching. Before 1880, a mere 2.5 percent of the world's population lived in cities, but by 1900, over 10 percent did, and more than two-thirds of these urban dwellers lived in Europe and the United States. New York City, for example, was only one of ten cities in the United States that had a population of more than twenty thousand in 1830. Soon thereafter, the urban population of the United States doubled every decade through 1860. As this trend continued, more than fifty cities, led by New York City, had populations over 100,000 in 1860. Industrialization explains the large growth of urban areas, and by 1900, for the first time ever, the urban-industrial economy outpaced the agricultural economy.[37]

Simply comparing the populations of two American cities to that of the entire state of Kansas illustrates the magnetic power of those metropolitan markets to shape the national livestock trade. At the outbreak of the Civil War, the entire population of Kansas topped 107,000 people, whereas over 109,000 residents lived in Chicago, and 805,000 in New York City. By 1870, about 364,000 people were living in Kansas, 299,000 in Chicago, and about 1,000,000 in New York City. The demand for beef in New York City alone was easily three times greater than it was for the entire state of Kansas.

The McCoys studied the vast urban-market demands for beef in the United States carefully. In 1865, over 270,000 beeves were required to supply New Yorkers with their beefsteaks. Recall that Illinoisan ranchers and cattle buyers such as the McCoys provided the greater percentage of beeves found in the butcher shops of Lower Manhattan. After the Civil War, Illinoisan cattlemen bought and fattened cattle, a large percentage of which originated in Texas, on rich prairie grass and corn harvests before shipping the animals to New York City. In one week in September 1866, 45 percent of the beeves entering the Allerton Stockyards arrived from Illinois, and of that percentage only a small portion had been born and raised in Illinois.

During the same week, fewer than a thousand head of cattle arrived directly from Texas. Sellers simply received far less for Texas stock transported directly to East Coast markets. The cattle suffered terribly in transit, lost weight, and were typically the last purchased by the city's butchers. These low-quality steers fed the city's poor.

In 1870, over 356,000 beeves were needed to quell the growing appetite for beef in New York City. Again, Illinois stockmen supplied the majority of the cattle. In an effort to cut costs in a highly competitive market, many non-Illinoisan brokers who bought herds at Abilene and other outlets tried to place their cattle directly into the city markets without engaging Illinoisan middlemen. Indicative of this trend, in July 1870, Texas cattle accounted for the second-largest number of stock headed into the city.

Despite the rising number of longhorns arriving directly at New York, the cattle buyers at the yards still considered them the least acceptable of all breeds. As a reporter for the *New York Tribune* wrote, "It will be noticed that Texas stands second in the order of supply, thus giving us too many of that *undesirable* stock" (emphasis added).[38] Nonetheless, even the grade of beef produced by these scrawny longhorns found a ready market. Located at the foot of Catharine Street stood a market of the same name. The city's poor, who scrimped and saved all week long, would rush to the market stalls on Saturday and buy the less expensive cuts of meat and lower-quality vegetables and fruits for their once-a-week "feast." Disparaging remarks directed toward cuts of Texas beef were not uncommon, such as this one from William Rideing of *Scribner's Monthly*: "Texas beef is usually disliked, and had been classed among the poorest meats." But the lower-priced cuts of meat nearly always found willing buyers among the urban poor and working classes.[39]

As the urban population soared (the top ten cities growing by nearly a million people between 1860 and 1870), consumer demand for beef continued to grow. Among the middle and upper classes, a taste developed for exceptional tender cuts of beef served up in some of the fanciest restaurants in the United States. Chef Charles Ranhofer's recipe for his "Delmonico Sirloin Steak of Twenty Ounces,

Plain" is a good indicator of how the rich ate beef in New York City. He called for a cut of sirloin two inches thick "flattened" to an inch and a half. Then he prepared it by salting both sides, and basting the entire steak with oil or melted butter. Once seasoned, he then broiled it on a "moderate fire" for fourteen minutes to produce a rare serving. The steak was accompanied by a "little clear gravy or maître d'hotel butter." Altogether, Ranhofer had more than 160 different ways of preparing beef.[40]

A standard dinner at Delmonico's was nothing short of an elaborate affair, a leisurely repast, lasting at least a couple of hours. A typical dinner would have ten courses, the fourth course called the *relevés*, French for "removes." This was simply another way of referring to a joint of beef. More often than not, Ranhofer's menus showed a beef tenderloin for the *relevés*. This head chef regarded the cold months of November, December, January, and February the best time of year to purchase his beef. While he considered beef "in season" year round, Ranhofer probably had fewer problems purchasing unspoiled sides of beef in colder months. Whether one dined at Delmonico's or fought for a low-grade cut of beef at Catharine Market, the demand for all grades of beef was rising in the large cities of the United States.[41]

Urban demands for beef determined where cattle were driven and how they were transported, and wherever they went they also became a part, however transitory or permanent, of the ecosystems they entered. Some of these systems were far-flung in comparison with those normally associated with the drives up the Chisholm Trail. W. E. Cureton and his two brothers, for example, formed a drive that took over eleven thousand head of cattle on a two-year journey across the Southwest, past the southern rim of the Grand Canyon and over the Sierra Nevada Mountains to a wintering ground on the rich grasslands near San Bernardino, California.

In the spring of 1871, Cureton's herders drove the cattle to Owens Valley where the stock was fattened before being sold to the firm of Miller and Lux, who then shipped the cattle to their slaughterhouse and distribution networks in the rapidly growing city of San Francisco. The Curetons, who had purchased their Texas longhorns for ten dollars a head, grossed thirty dollars a head from Miller and Lux. The lure of the San Francisco market, just as surely as that of the Chicago and New York markets, shaped where cattle went and how those herds would reshape ecosystems across vast stretches of North America.[42]

Henry King, managing editor of the *Kansas State Record* (Topeka), gushed about the prospects of Kansas grasslands supplying "Eastern *and* European markets" (emphasis added) in a news item from Ellsworth, Kansas, in October 1869. King clearly understood how the Texas cattle trade had reordered the former Indian-managed landscape that had been based upon a horse-borne, bison-hunting culture and its attendant fur-trade economy. "With pure water from our numerous springs and brooks," King wrote, "this country seems to have been designed, first for the hunting ground, as it has been of the Indian, and then as the great pasturage of [cattle]." This transformation of economics and ecology, he predicted, would supply these burgeoning urban markets at *"lower prices"* (emphasis added) than cattle production done anywhere else in North America.[43]

Besides meeting the urban demands of the United States, cattle buyers eagerly sought to fill an international urban demand arising in Europe and elsewhere. Soon after the Civil War ended, buyers in Chicago and St. Louis and ranchers in Texas eagerly anticipated the rapid growth of European markets. One city in particular captured their imaginations. By 1860, London, England, with a population of nearly 3.2 million living within its immediate confines, had become the most populated city on the face of the planet. Any disruptions in supplying London and the industrial cities of Great Britain could provoke serious social unrest reminiscent of the anti-corn-law movement of the 1840s. London's growth between 1850 and 1900 outpaced the ability of English food production to meet human demands for food. This trend by itself was enough of an inducement for American exporters to keep shipping grains and meat to England, but factors other than population growth also spurred increased demand for American food products.[44]

First, summers of unusually hot weather and low rainfall, such as those of 1868 and 1870, destroyed crop production across England. Between 1868 and 1870, precipitation fell 10 to 20 percent below a long-term average for the country. Precipitation records from the Met Office of the United Kingdom show that between 1868 and 1870, the monthly rainfall averages in June and July for England and Wales were 1.06 and 1.07 inches, respectively.[45] The result: harvest failures. The lack of locally grown food reaching urban markets increased demands for imported foodstuffs, and Americans were all too ready to fill the need.

By October 1868, opportunities had clearly opened for placing American cattle into English markets. Despite the rapid and simultaneous population growth of Chicago and New York City, the operations of the Kansas Pacific and Union Pacific Railroads had delivered enough cattle into American urban markets that, as noted in *Harper's Weekly*, a surplus of animals had "left a large margin for exportation to Europe." The writer of the article had followed the effects of weather conditions in England and highlighted the importance of exporting live cattle to London. All of this influx of beef cattle was made possible by the vast improvements in railroad transportation links across the North American continent and improved ship technology that resulted in faster voyages across the Atlantic Ocean.[46]

Sometimes too much rainfall proved as troubling for English food production as did dry summers. Between 1873 and 1879, exceptionally rainy summers damaged grain crops, and English stockmen reeled from the rise of foot-and-mouth disease in their cattle herds. Records kept by the Met Office show summers considerably wetter than those between 1868 and 1870. During the decade of the 1870s, June and July monthly averages were 2.9 and 3.31 inches, much higher than the monthly averages of 1.07 and 1.06 inches recorded in June and July for 1868, 1869, and 1870.[47] American exporters, as well as those from Argentina, New Zealand, and Australia, took advantage of the situation and loaded ships bound for England with live cattle and hard grains.

By the mid-1870s, ocean freighters hauled refrigerated beef carcasses rather than transporting live cattle. The Glasgow-based Anchor Line steamship company developed efficient refrigeration technology and placed it in six of its ships. Each of the ships could handle 360 to 450 carcasses, and one of the ships arrived at the port of Glasgow every Wednesday. The steam-engine-powered fans on the ships circulated ice-chilled air that kept the meat bays at a constant 37 degrees Fahrenheit. Even in the warm summer of 1876, the Anchor Line ships did not lose a single side of beef. By 1875, the "fresh-meat" trade had transformed the operations of the butcher shops of old England. Beginning in 1875, the owners of the Anchor Line dominated the transatlantic business of shipping fresh meat.[48] Other shipping companies followed suit, and by 1900, meat imports into England accounted for half of the beef consumed in the nation.[49]

## *Sunny Prospects*

The powerful economic magnet of urban markets—in both the United States and overseas—drew Texas cattlemen north to Abilene or other Kansas towns. Profits seemed possible to anyone contemplating the trade. In 1868, Joseph McCoy explained the economic incentive to a convention of stockmen who had gathered to stop the spread of Texas fever. McCoy told the assembly that he wished he could take a herd of three hundred cattle that he had bought on average for $4.50 a head and "transport [them] through the air, and set them down in the Chicago market," where they would have fetched $75 a head.⁵⁰

Joseph McCoy knew cattle in Texas commanded no more than $6 per head in 1866. In the same year, his brother William unloaded Illinois cattle in New York City at returns ranging from $105 to $120 per head. Even the lowest-quality steers fetched fourteen cents per pound dressed; for a longhorn that might weigh nine hundred pounds, that meant about $75 per head. Under the right conditions, a savvy middleman could make considerable money in trading Texas longhorns despite losses in transit and shipping costs, and the McCoys understood this perfectly.

C. W. Ackermann's father did not have to think long and hard about driving a herd north when the local markets in San Antonio paid $8 per head weighing over one thousand pounds while, at the same time, in Wichita, Kansas, brokers were paying $23.80 per head. Soon Ackermann, only eighteen at the time, and a crew of other young men all younger than twenty-two, found themselves rounding up a herd in Bexar County in February 1873. They had it ready to head north by the middle of March.⁵¹

The contractual arrangements for putting a herd together were often loose. Sol West, one of the more famous and successful cattlemen of Jackson County, Texas, recounted how buyers in southwest Texas bought herds "on time." A buyer, simply on his word of a future payment, West explained, could purchase maybe eight thousand to ten thousand beeves. The buyer would make a count of the beeves from individual sellers, make note of the number for each seller, put the herd together, hire cowboys to manage the herd, and then see it driven to northern rail stops. It might take as long as one to three years before the buyer returned to his Texas haunts and actually paid off all the sellers—if he had the cash to do so.⁵²

Colonel J. F. Ellison followed the same method of putting together a herd that Sol West had. A bankrupt former Confederate officer, he longed to place his family on a firm financial footing. He had heard about the rich returns of the first cattle drives in 1867 and believed he could do just as well. In early 1869, he rode around the San Marcos River Valley, working to put together a herd to drive north to Abilene. By the time he had an outfit ready to go, he had assembled a herd of 750 beeves, or, as his son J. F. Jr. recalled, a collection of "mixed cattle, all kinds, from calves to grown cows." The colonel and his hands arrived in Abilene after a rather uneventful drive north. He filled his pockets with the returns of the sale and headed back to Texas via the Mississippi River, where he visited his childhood haunts. In New Orleans, Ellison boarded another boat bound to Galveston. After settling his credit accounts, he pocketed $9,000—about eighteen times the average annual income of an American worker at the time.[53]

An article in the *Kansas State Record* (Topeka), gave a much more detailed accounting of the trade for the 1869 season. In general, sellers and brokers could expect about a 30 percent return on their investments—an excellent return that spoke to growing interests in the cattle trade. The breakdown of the trade looked like this: In 1869, in a short three months, brokers shipped around 50,000 beeves out of Abilene into eastern urban markets while nearly another 19,000 were shipped from other Kansas stockyards. In June 1870 alone, 37,000 head were loaded into stock cars headed east. A market flourished to the west, too, as another 15,000 were shipped to Salt Lake City. Tens of thousands of cattle were already in stockyards near packing plants at Leavenworth, Kansas City, and Chicago. Besides these animals, mixed herds of stock cattle, cows, calves, and yearlings numbering more than 35,000 grazed the grasslands surrounding Abilene. In total, the Abilene market accounted for more than 150,000 beeves that year.[54]

How was money made from the sale of these animals? An average herd from northern Texas was called a "mixed drove" because it contained beef cattle, milk cows, and animals under three years old. The breakdowns for a hypothetical mixed drove of one thousand cattle eventually sold in Chicago would have resembled the transactions shown in the table.

Profit margins, as this table depicts, were superb. Anticipation of a 25-plus percent profit margin was enough to encourage any number of investors, knowledgeable or not, to get involved. Margins did drop some by the time beeves or packaged meats reached eastern seaboard cities. On average, the returns in New York City or Boston ranged between 20 and 30 percent. And from these port cities, Texas meats were packed and stored in ships bound for the transatlantic trade. From Waco, Texas, to Paris, France, the buying, selling, and eating of beef promised substantial returns for the big cattlemen who controlled herds ranging in size from one thousand to five thousand animals. For all others, it was more of a trickle-down gain, with the emphasis on "trickle."[55]

Although profits and riches might accrue to the herd owners, or the trail bosses, the same could never be said for the cowboys who headed the herds north. G. O. Burrows, a common cowhand who had worked herds for nearly two

**TABLE 1**

## ESTIMATED PROFITS IN THE TEXAS CATTLE TRADE, 1870

*(Assumes Texas rancher sells own herd of 1,000 animals)*

|  | Beef cattle | Milk cows | Three-year-olds | Two-year-olds | One-year-olds | Total |
|---|---|---|---|---|---|---|
| Number of Cattle | 600 | 200 | 100 | 50 | 50 | 1,000 |
| Value per Head in Texas ($) | 11.00 | 6.00 | 7.00 | 4.00 | 2.50 | |
| Market Value of Herd in Texas ($) | 6,600.00 | 1,200.00 | 700.00 | 200.00 | 125.00 | 8,825.00 |
| Total Number Reaching Abilene (assuming 20% loss during drive) | 480 | 160 | 80 | 40 | 40 | |
| Cost to Drive Herd to Great Western Stock Yards @ $2 per head | 960.00 | 320.00 | 160.00 | 80.00 | 80.00 | 1,600.00 |
| Typical Price Paid per Head at Abilene ($) | 20 | 12 | 10 | 8 | 5 | |
| Abilene Market Value of Herd ($) | 9,600.00 | 1,920.00 | 800.00 | 320.00 | 200.00 | 12,840.00 |
| Return (market value [$] minus cost of drive to Abilene) | 8,640.00 | 1,600.00 | 640.00 | 240.00 | 120 | 11,240.00 |
| Rancher's Return ($) for Selling Herd in Abilene over the Value of the Herd in Texas | 2,040.00 | 400.00 | (60.00) | 40.00 | (5.00) | 2,415.00 |
| Rancher's % Gain by Selling Herd in Abilene Rather Than in Texas | | | | | | 27.37% |

*Note:* Many variables could, at any time, affect returns for cattle buyers and sellers. The potential returns, as depicted in this table, illustrate why so many were willing to invest in cattle driving and trading.

*Source:* Estimated costs as reported in "The Texas Cattle Trade," *Kansas State Record* (Topeka), September 14, 1870.

decades, had little more to show for his work than a pair of "high-heeled boots . . . striped pants and about $4.80 worth of other clothes."[56] Though a herder might expect thirty dollars a month in pay, some riding the trail considered even fifty cents a day good wages.

Returns from the cattle trade flowed well beyond the drovers and herd owners. McCoy once recalled Abilene as he had first found it: "an obscure dingy place . . . boasting one little 'whiskey battery.'" Would-be merchants had little to brag about based on an annual sale of $500 worth of goods and services. By 1871, after three years of operating his stockyards in Abilene, McCoy had tallied over $5 million in "direct cattle trade," sales of over $1 million of "outfitting goods," a freighting business of over $200,000, and "banking business" of over $100,000 per week. All the herders, drivers, and dock loaders commanded combined incomes totaling more than $50,000 per month. Local farm families benefited from brisk sales of eggs, chickens, butter, cured meats, hay, corn, oats, potatoes, and vegetables. McCoy's testament for the economic benefits of the cattle trade was to make any opposition to it look silly and shortsighted.[57]

## Perils and Pitfalls in the Round

Joseph McCoy would have been one of the first to tell anyone inquiring about the nature of the cattle trade that besides the potential of great gains, it also carried considerable risk. Like card gamblers, stockmen were not always honorable. In fact, many were scoundrels and cheats. McCoy knew that cattle "shippers" were gamblers by nature. The "Illinoisan," as McCoy liked to call himself, succinctly referred to the trade as the "great faro game." As in any game of chance, there were always winners and losers, and also those who worked to fix the odds in their favor.

C. S. Brodbent, a Kansan who engaged in cattle selling and buying, readily told anyone who would listen that there "was some dishonesty in this trail driving." Herd owners expected drovers to arrive at a selling point with as many if not more head of cattle than when the drive started. Cattle often strayed from one herd to another, and by custom, supposedly outfits were to take the strays and reunite them with their proper owner. Sometimes protocol was not observed. And sometimes, cattle from one herd might be found "accidentally" in another herd. Brodbent learned how this worked when, on one occasion, he was informed about the sale of his "branded cattle" except that neither he nor his own agent had been the seller of the cattle. He never saw the money of that sale. Such swindles as cleaned out Brodbent were all too common.[58]

Not only would cattle drovers game each other if given the opportunity, cattle dealers and railroad magnates took the same opportunity when it presented itself. One of the more notorious stings occurred when the dust had hardly settled over the great "Erie Railroad War." In short, by 1868, Cornelius Vanderbilt had lost control of the Erie Railroad as a result of stock manipulation orchestrated by James Fisk, Daniel Drew, and Jay Gould. Two years later, Gould and Fisk had maneuvered Drew out of the Erie company and plotted to pour salt into Vanderbilt's still open economic wounds from his loss of control over the Erie line. Manipulating cattle shipping rates proved to be a good salt shaker.[59]

In 1870, Vanderbilt controlled the New York Central (NYC) and Hudson River Railroad (HRR), a line that led directly into the city along the west side of Manhattan Island. Fisk and Gould's Erie Railroad (Erie) terminated at the docks along the east bank of Jersey City. From these docks, a ferry transported cargo, livestock, and passengers to the west bank of Manhattan Island near the immense Washington Market.

In an effort to corner the flow of cattle into the city, Vanderbilt had reduced his freight charges from $120 to $40 per cattle car. He anticipated that Fisk and Gould couldn't undercut his rate without losing money. The cagey Fisk and Gould "astonished" Vanderbilt by promising to transport cattle from the suspension bridge over Niagara Falls to the city for a rate of one cent per head. Not to be outdone, Vanderbilt countered by lowering his freight rate to a mere $1 per car along the entire Erie line. At this point, Vanderbilt surely thought he had bested Fisk and Gould.

Fisk and Gould, however, had no intention of loading cattle on their own line, the Erie. They had another end in mind. They counted on Vanderbilt reacting hastily, which he did, and when they heard about his lowered rates, the two schemers ordered their agents to purchase as many head of cattle as they could and then ship them via the NYC railroad to the National Stockyard at Weehawken, New Jersey, which Fisk and Gould controlled. The Erie agents immediately went to work and soon had eight thousand head of cattle transported in Vanderbilt's stock cars from Buffalo to the Weehawken yards "on terms which would not pay for the grease on the car wheels of the stock trains." Fisk and Gould had taken Vanderbilt to the proverbial cleaners again.[60]

Like Vanderbilt, Joseph, James, and William McCoy encountered a severe economic setback when they gambled on the honorable nature of the officers of the KP. In April 1869, Joseph and James thought they had sealed a deal with John D. Perry, president of the KP, that guaranteed $2.50 for each loaded stock car of cattle at the Great Western Stock Yards in Abilene. Unfortunately for the two brothers, they had set terms with a handshake rather than with a written contract. By the end of December 1869, the McCoys had loaded 2,051 Kansas Pacific stock cars, thinking they had earned $5,127.50, payable by the Kansas Pacific.

In spring 1870, Joseph and James went to the Kansas Pacific offices in St. Louis to collect what they thought was owed to them. They entered the building, went straight to President Perry's office, and asked for their money. Perry replied that he knew nothing about a contract for loading stock cars on his line, but if he "could find any indication" of any such arrangement, he would write McCoy and let him know. As McCoy later testified in court, "I came home, got no money." But the McCoy brothers did have a lawyer, and to court they went to win a judgment against the Kansas Pacific company. The case reached the Kansas Supreme Court, and in its decision in April 1871, the court awarded the McCoys damages of $5,042.50.[61]

In the meantime, enough time had passed and enough money had been lost that the McCoy brothers had dissolved their company. By 1872, they had liquidated their holdings in their Great Western Stock Yards, and Abilene no longer served as the great Texas cattle outlet. It was not only shady behavior on the part of the railroad company that had cost the McCoys dearly. Other factors, largely beyond their control, led to their financial woe. When C. S. Brodbent averred that "the prevalent idea that the trail days were halcyon days of easy money making is erroneous," he may well have had Joseph McCoy in mind. Brodbent summed up the trade this way: "It is perhaps a surprising feature of the cattle drive that the owners of many herds that illegitimately increased the most on what they made a piratical journey north, went broke, and some of the most noted 'cattle kings' became herdsmen or dropped into oblivion."[62] McCoy never dropped into oblivion, but after 1872, he never regained the riches he had started out with in 1867.

McCoy probably had feelings that were expressed in verse by a cattleman from Cottonwood Falls, Kansas, in 1872.

> If a drove I should spy
> Either hungry or well fed
> I think I'll let them pass rite by
> I'll think of the time when I was bled
> One Consolation comes with the grief
> It does me good to tell
> I don't go heavy on the beef
> But I have hides a plenty to sell
> It gives my stricken soul relief
> That every one should know
> What I think of buying beef
> That down in Texas gro.[63]

In any faro game, even when a player thinks he or she has counted the cards well and knows the odds of winning, a loser card can appear out of the blue. While McCoy counted well enough to know when unscrupulous railroad officers were showing cards from a stacked deck, even under the best conditions, faro was still a gamble. McCoy thought he could outwit the dealer, but the dealer had other cards up his sleeve that McCoy had little, if any, ability to anticipate. When those cards—Texas fever and blizzards—appeared in combination on the faro board, McCoy, and many other cattle gamblers who had bet against these from ever showing up, lost everything.

CHAPTER 6

# Tick, Tick, Tick

TEXAS FEVER — THE 1868 EPIDEMIC — GOVERNMENTAL RESPONSES — THE MCCOY BISON SHOW — AN ABUNDANCE OF THEORIES — THE 1868 SPRINGFIELD, ILLINOIS, CONVENTION OF CATTLE COMMISSIONERS — A LINGERING PROBLEM — THEOBALD SMITH FINDS THE CAUSE

When he looked up into the nighttime heavens in the spring of 1868, Joseph McCoy surely believed that all the stars had aligned for a great start to the cattle shipping season. The weather had cooperated to produce rich grazing grounds surrounding the Great Western Stock Yards. Moderate rainfall during the spring had eliminated any concerns over "washy" grass conditions like those that had plagued the grass ranges in 1867. By June, drovers had already placed several herds on the open rangeland, fattening their cattle on the rich bluestem prairies in anticipation of strong eastern markets.

On June 10, 1868, one of those pleasant days in Kansas when late spring temperatures hover in the 70s and soft winds set clouds sailing eastward, Joseph watched as a locomotive pulled 28 stock cars loaded with cattle away from his Great Western Stock Yards. These 560 cattle, the first shipment of 1868, were all bound for eastern markets. The following day, another locomotive hauled away another 34 stock cars loaded with cattle, all destined for a connection to the Missouri Pacific line leading to St. Louis, there to be reloaded into eastbound trains. On the same day, a Texas drover moved a herd of 5,000 almost to the outskirts of Abilene, and McCoy received reports indicating that a "number of other droves of from four to six thousand head each" had already crossed into Kansas and were bound for his stockyards.[1]

Joseph McCoy had invested in buying his own herd of carefully selected beeves, and unlike the market conditions in 1867, the prospects for great returns on buying and selling cattle had never looked better. McCoy foresaw the same market conditions as those reported in the *Daily Kansas Tribune*: the "cattle trade will be very heavy this summer, as cattle are abundant and cheap in Texas, and traders can make large profits."[2] In early January 1868, the *New York Times* reprinted a piece from the *Lawrence* (Kansas) *Journal* that confidently predicted that as many as 550,000 cattle would be driven north in the spring. Moreover, the writer of the *Journal* piece expressed "grave doubts" about the existence of "so-called 'Texas cattle fever.'"[3] Based on cheery forecasts like these, McCoy calculated healthy returns on his cattle buy. He added the anticipated returns of loading cattle at his Great Western Stock Yards and an additional three dollars per stock car loaded with cattle that the Kansas Pacific company had contracted to pay him and his brothers.[4]

Everything seemed in place to reverse the losses McCoy had endured the year before. Prominent folks in Abilene had gathered to announce their support of Texas cattle. T. F. Hersey, T. C. Henry, and the mayor of "prairie dog town," the genial Josiah Jones, all good friends of McCoy at the time, resolved as "the citizens of Dickinson county" to "invite and encourage" the Texas cattle trade as "beneficial to every permanent interest of our people."[5] With this backing, McCoy confidently counted all the cards laid down on the great cattle faro table, confident he thought he knew what remained in the banker's deck.

Like McCoy, stockmen across the nation anticipated better returns in 1868. Many of the drovers were keeping their cattle on the rich prairie grasses where they were gaining weight and fat with each bite of little bluestem. Each pound was money gained for the drover readying the herd for shipment to the cornfields of Illinois, where cattlemen such as John T. Alexander, "the largest cattle shipper in the world," would further fatten beeves for eastern markets.[6] As a writer for the *Kansas State Record* (Topeka) put it, "These cattle are the machinery by which the corn should be manufactured into stall-fed beef."[7] At the same time, Texas drovers also had herds bound for New Orleans and the docks at the mouth of the Red River, where they were to be loaded onto Mississippi River steamboats bound for Cairo, Illinois.

Fast-forward to December 1868, when Joseph McCoy faced financial ruin. Convening on December 1 in Springfield, Illinois, in the statehouse Representative Hall, where President Lincoln's body had lain in state two and half years before, twenty-nine commissioners representing nine states and the Canadian province of Ontario met "to consider the history, nature and character of the disease among cattle known as Texas fever." The commissioners also sought to craft a uniform law regulating the Texas cattle trade in an effort to "secure the most perfect protection to all parties." Besides the designated commissioners, six honorary members held official seats during the convention. Joseph G. McCoy was one of them.[8]

The outbreak and spread of Texas fever throughout the Midwest and eastern stockyards in the summer and fall had incited panic throughout the entire Texas cattle market. McCoy's deep investment in the trade stood ready to collapse with the prospect of a heavy-handed nationwide inspection system to regulate the importation of Texas cattle into eastern markets. In the Illinois statehouse, McCoy found himself defending the very life of his Abilene enterprise.

From June to December, how quickly the cards on the cattle faro table had turned against McCoy. One of the banker's cards was marked by a five-micron-large protozoan. When the banker played it, McCoy and his brothers lost big time because they had wagered that it would turn up on the *loser* side, instead, it turned up on the *winner* side. It is hard to win the cattle faro game when the winner card is a disease that takes away all that you have. At the conclusion of this 1868 round of the cattle faro game, McCoy would look back upon what then seemed the winning times in 1867.

## *Texas Fever*

Texas fever progressed in the following manner: picture an adult male tick that had just finished feeding on a Texas longhorn. Humans would later give the tick the imposing name *Rhipicephalus annulatus*, two fancy words derived from the Greek *rhipis*, meaning "fan," plus *kephale*, meaning "head," and from the Latin word *annulatus*, meaning "ringed." Extensions on both sides of the tick's head give it a fan-like appearance, a characteristic defining this insect. So "Fan" the tick, who had been nourishing himself for several days, now fully satiated with its host's blood, prepared for his next adventure.

Finished eating his last meal as an adult, Fan had just enough energy and time to consummate a genetically programmed imperative: find a feeding female tick and mate with her. Let's call the female he finds "Fanny." As Fan negotiated a route along the flank of his longhorn host, fortune smiled on him when he found Fanny and began to mate with her. When Fan had finished copulating with Fanny, he unceremoniously leaves her to scour the flank of the bovine for another potential partner. Fanny, in the meantime, now done with both eating and Fan, drops from the host to the ground. Landing in the rugged Texas Hill Country, Fanny burrowed under some loose limestone and laid a batch of now fertilized eggs. Now her work finished, Fanny dies. Her forsaken, famished brood leaps, literally, at the first opportunity to latch onto any cattle passing by. Once firmly attached to cow, they begin the work of reproducing the Fan Heads.

Fanny's offspring, and all those of her species, would eventually be held culpable for spreading Texas fever, but they also had assistance for the diffusion of Texas fever. A microscopic protozoan (*Babesia bigemina*) inhabited the bodies of the Fan Head family. When the ticks starting feeding off their hosts, they injected their one-celled freeloaders into the bloodstream of their hosts. Once inside the bovine's bloodstream, the seeds of this protozoan invaded red blood cells, where they multiplied to the point of rupturing the cell membrane, releasing numerous "daughter" parasites. Newly freed, they went on a search for other red blood cells to attack, where again their spores would start multiplying. As this feeding frenzy continued, it resulted in the internal bleeding symptoms commonly associated with Texas fever.[9]

Fan Heads, and their tiny internal passengers, possessed incredible power to disrupt and wreck the cattle trade. However, Fan Heads also had one weakness—a weakness that perplexed all who entered the wreckage left behind wherever they visited. The Fan Heads could not tolerate, or even endure, cold weather. Unlike their host cattle, Fan Heads readily succumbed to freezing temperatures. Consequently, they never established a permanent home in the northern climes of the North American continent.

For decades, Fan Heads' inability to flourish in the northern reaches of the United States led observers and medical researchers to an incorrect conclusion about their responsibility for the outbreak and spread of Texas fever. When cattlemen overwintered Texas cattle in Kansas, Indiana, Illinois, or Iowa, they observed that those longhorns could always be grazed with native cattle and that no outbreak of Texas fever ever resulted from the mix. So, the logic ran, how could Texas cattle be the cause of an outbreak of the disease?

One other biological factor complicated efforts to understand how the disease spread. When a longhorn cow bore a calf, the newborn more often than not encountered an attack of Fan Heads feasting on its blood. Its mother's milk, however, provided strong nutrition and antibodies that gave the calf a lifelong immunity to the protozoan's assault on its red blood cells. The calf would bear internal signs of the disease for the rest of its life, but it would not die as a result of the Fan Heads having once latched onto its hide. Consequently, for many human observers at the time, it made little sense that longhorns were the ones transmitting the disease. Moreover, how could the Fan Heads be the ones to transmit Texas fever if longhorns never seemed to die even when completely covered by their immediate kin?

## *The 1868 Epidemic*

As if Joseph McCoy hadn't had a rough enough time starting up his cattle business in 1867, the Fan Heads' work throughout the Midwest and along the East Coast in 1868 threatened the complete destruction of his fledgling operation. As early as May, a warning of impending disaster came from D. C. Emerson of Vandalia, Illinois. He wrote a letter, which the *Chicago Tribune* published on May 26, saying in part that while at Centralia, Illinois, "I saw a very long train of stock cars filled with Texan and with Indiana oxen on their way to Iroquois County, there to be fattened on the rich prairies; and I learned that there were in the lot fourteen hundred head of old, worn-out oxen, bringing the Texas fever with them. A writer in the *Missouri Democrat* has described this disease as contagious, and says that it causes the destruction of our home cattle, wherever these Texas cattle are taken."[10] Emerson's obvious message: stockmen, beware buying Texas cattle and placing them with your native herds.

Emerson's fears were well founded, as exemplified in the "Report of the New York State Cattle Commissioners for the Year 1868."[11] A subsection of the report, titled "The Arrival of an Infected Herd from Indiana," followed the path of the disease from Texas to New Jersey.[12] On April 27, 1868, a cattle buyer purchased 930 head of longhorns in Colorado County, Texas. The cattle ranged from four to six years in age and, aside from being covered with ticks, appeared to be in good health. A drover and herders then trailed the cattle six hundred miles to the mouth of the Red River. Upon reaching the loading docks on May 31, the cattle were loaded onto steamboats and shipped up the Mississippi River to Cairo, Illinois, where the boats arrived on June 4. Within the next couple of days, the cattle were loaded into the stock cars of the Illinois Central Railroad (IC) and transported to Tolono, Illinois, where they were unloaded on June 7.

J. M. Thomas of Warren County, Indiana, had bought the herd with the intention of fattening the cattle on his prairie-grass pastures and corn harvest. By the time he drove the herd to his farm on June 12, forty-four of the animals had perished due to the rough treatment they had received while in transit. Once the herd arrived on Thomas's farm, not one more would die in the months to come. Over the same period, however, more than five hundred native cattle that had come into close proximity with Thomas's Texas cattle had died.[13]

On June 19, Thomas placed ninety-five mature native beeves, averaging 1,300 pounds each, on the same pasture where his longhorn herd had grazed. By the beginning of August, he discovered that three of his native stock had died, and eleven others showed disturbing signs of being seriously ill. Apparently, this outbreak motivated Thomas to place the rest of this native herd in the New York City markets. On August 4, he loaded the remaining eighty-four apparently healthy native cattle onto the Toledo, Wabash, and Western Railway Company (TW&W) after driving them to the station at West Lebanon. The herd reached Buffalo, New York, and was reloaded onto the Erie line headed for Campville, where the cattle were to be unloaded and given water and feed. When the cattle reached Campville, seven had died en route, and eleven others showed signs of being ill and were detained and quarantined. Within three days, all eleven had died.[14]

On August 10, the superintendent of the Bergen cattle yards in Hudson City, New Jersey, received word that five carloads of mostly diseased cattle from Campville were on their way to his facility. Dr. Moreau Morris, the sanitary inspector of the New York City Metropolitan Board of Health, was called to examine the herd before allowing it to disembark. The next day, Dr. Morris, along with two other inspectors, Dr. Stephen Smith, a professor of anatomy, and Dr. Elisha Harris, the registrar of the Metropolitan Board of Health, had the infected herd unloaded into holding pens near the Hackensack River to keep it away from the Erie Railroad endpoint in Hudson City. Morris reported observing "several fat bullocks in a dying condition," fifteen of which were in a "hopelessly diseased state." Before they could be stopped, speculators stepped in, bought fifty of the herd, and had them shipped to "parts unknown." However, Morris retained five of the cattle for careful postmortem analysis.[15]

The incident with Thomas's cattle herd illustrates a much larger story of the outbreak of Texas fever in 1868. During the spring, Texans drove cattle, originating largely from Gulf Coast counties, to Galveston, where the longhorns were loaded onto coastal boats bound for New Orleans. Other herds were driven to the shipping docks located at the mouth of the Red River. From either of these two locales, Mississippi River steamboats transported thousands of live cattle to Cairo, Illinois. Soon reports circulated in and around Cairo about the outbreak of Texas fever, but it remained largely a matter of local concern until the end of July.

Another serious outbreak of Texas fever occurred with the arrival of Texas cattle on the grazing grounds of central Illinois. In Champaign County, Illinois, perhaps as many as fifteen thousand longhorns had been placed on various pastures to fatten up before being shipped to the Chicago yards or eastern urban markets. By the end of July, newspaper reports detailed the losses suffered by local farmers with large herds of native cattle. The disease seemed to strike dairy cows the hardest, with more than one hundred already having succumbed and the spread of the disease showing no abatement. By the end of August, one estimate pegged cattle deaths in Champaign County at five thousand head of native cattle. Not long afterward, local farmers met in Tolono and demanded strict enforcement of the state quarantine law as it applied to regulating the importation of longhorns.[16]

Cattle deaths began appearing in shipments from Chicago to Pittsburgh. On July 31, a lot of two hundred cattle arrived in the East Liberty stockyards with thirty-nine having died en route. Another sixty-seven later perished in the yards. When John Alexander arrived in Pittsburgh to inspect his Illinois shipment, only three beeves in one stock car had survived the trip. Given the rapid spread of the disease, officers of the Pennsylvania Railroad (PRR) ordered a halt to any shipments of cattle that exhibited even the mere appearance of illness. Fear spread among butchers that any cattle dying from this outbreak were unfit for human consumption, and they refused to buy them.[17]

Everyone involved in the trade rightfully feared that this outbreak could wreak havoc on cattle markets across the country. At first, a few dealers believed the reports little more than an attempt to manipulate cattle prices. As reported in the *New York Tribune*, "It is believed by many that the reports [of Texas fever] are exaggerated, and that they are circulated by [Midwest] stock growers, in order to discourage the new competition [from Texas cattle] in their business."[18] It soon became distressingly clear, however, that the outbreak bore no relationship to a seller's scheme.

At the same time, farmers across Kansas resolved to keep pestilent Texas cattle far, far away from their own native herds. For some, such as Elisha Edwards and Nimrod Ridley of Lyon County, the failure of their corn crops meant a greater economic reliance on their cattle herds, especially their milk cows. Edwards and Ridley organized a meeting of fifty county farmers, and together they united to use all "lawful means" to keep Texas cattle clear of Lyon Creek Valley.[19]

Farmers in Missouri also took alarm at the appearance of Texas cattle in their neighborhoods. Joseph McCoy often described Missourians who resisted the introduction of Texas cattle as little more than bands of border ruffians who simply plundered Texas herds. S. Morgan Welch, who lived in Waverly, a small Missouri River town halfway between Kansas City and Columbia, had a different take on the situation. In a letter published in the *Prairie Farmer* in September 1868, he wrote:

> Talk to a Missourian about moderation, when a drove of Texas cattle is coming, and he will call you a fool, while he coolly loads his gun, and joins his neighbors; and they not scared, either. They mean to kill, and will and do kill, and keep killing until the drover takes the back track; and the drovers must be careful not to get between their cattle and the citizens, either, unless they are bullet-proof. No doubt this looks a good deal like border-ruffianism to you, but it is the way we keep clear of the Texas fever; and, my word for it, Illinois will have to do the same thing yet . . . Texas stock should not be allowed to cross the 35th parallel of north latitude alive.[20]

There was little hyperbole, if any, in Welch's letter. Kansas and Missouri farmers were serious about keeping Texas cattle away from their native herds and readily took matters into their own hands when the need arose.

Accordingly, when some Texas drovers attempted to drive herds along the eastern border of Kansas in an attempt to avoid quarantine enforcement, they did so at their own peril. In October, Jack Bailey, a Texan who had driven a herd into Kansas and sold it, was making his way home on the roads along the eastern border of the state. After passing by Fort Scott, Kansas, Bailey observed a "parcel of men" killing a small herd of Texas cattle. They informed him that they had destroyed "a pen full" of Texas cattle at Mound City just a few days before. They made it clear to Bailey that Texans had better not attempt to drive cattle through their part of the state.[21]

By August 5, a general panic had spread as more and more native Illinois cattle died from this "mysterious disease." As described in the *New York Tribune*, "considerable excitement" prevailed among buyers and sellers at the Chicago Union Stockyards. An IC railroad stock train loaded with Texas cattle had arrived at the yards and been unloaded. These beeves, mixed with some native ones, had been bought and loaded into stock cars bound for Pittsburgh. Before the shipment had arrived, seven head had died en route. The Pittsburgh buyers quickly telegraphed orders back to their Chicago agents to halt any further purchase of cattle.[22]

Soon dread spread among cattle dealers as the disease seemed to be inflicting death among herds arriving in eastern cities. A reporter from the *New York Tribune* referred to it as a "death-dealing malady prevailing among the cattle in Illinois and Indiana . . . more serious and alarming than at first supposed." Making matters worse, "the stock-dealers and drovers of Chicago and other Western cities are alarmed by this new and terrible visitant, whose cause they cannot explain, and against whose ravages no remedy thus far tried appear to be of any avail."[23]

The dreaded news appeared in the *New York Tribune* that diseased cattle had reached the New Jersey stockyards and the markets of the city on Saturday, August 8. George B. Lincoln, the president of the Metropolitan Board of Health, set his staff into immediate action upon hearing the news. In the afternoon, in a drenching downpour, Dr. Elisha Harris, the medical officer of the board, headed directly to the Communipaw yards in New Jersey. There he found William Fitch, the selling agent for J. T. Alexander. Fitch had separated 150 beeves shipped from Illinois. These were all that remained from an initial lot of 320. Even among those animals, several appeared to be afflicted with the disease. Harris instructed the workmen to immediately treat the ground on which the cattle stood with carbolic acid, a treatment that had worked to dissipate the spread of rinderpest, a deadly viral livestock disease, in England.[24]

When Harris returned to his office, he instructed city meat inspectors to be doubly vigilant in their efforts in detecting diseased animals. He also approved hiring of additional inspectors. Furthermore, Harris used his authority to station guards "at all railroad lines to prevent the shipment of diseased cattle" into the city markets. He then sent telegrams to New York governor Reuben Fenton, New Jersey governor Marcus Lawrence Ward, and Pennsylvania governor John W. Geary, informing each about the outbreak. The governors responded quickly, indicating their complete cooperation with the board of health. Lastly, Harris had a "competent medical" officer placed on every cattle train headed toward the city. Harris gave the officers the authority to stop any train carrying diseased cattle; he instructed that such cattle should be offloaded and "if necessary, shot, to stop the spread of the disease."[25]

In the meantime, back at the Communipaw yards, Fitch contemplated how to deal with Alexander's cattle shipment. He already knew that Henry Payson, the president of the slaughterhouse at the yards, wanted nothing to do with diseased animals. Fitch concluded that the only sensible thing to do was to have the entire shipment killed and to "throw their carcasses into the rendering kettles." This slaughter represented a more than $8,000 loss for Alexander. By Monday morning, inspectors were on guard at the stockyards at Salamanca, Buffalo, and Albany.[26]

The steps taken by Governor Fenton and the health board were not in time to prevent diseased cattle from dying in the Albany stockyards. There, cattle shipped from Chicago were usually taken out of the stock cars, driven into the yards, and provided with hay and water. On Monday, a train from Chicago loaded with cattle stopped at the Albany yards, where by common practice the animals were driven into the yards, fed, and watered. Soon, nearly thirty cattle had died, which resulted in panicked dispatches appearing in the larger city newspapers to the east.[27]

On Thursday, August 13, the Metropolitan Board of Health released a dispatch that the local papers printed in their Friday editions. It stated clearly that any attempt by stockmen to import diseased cattle into the New York market would be considered "as a gross offence against the lives of our fellow-beings." Moreover, the investigations by board personnel "confirmed the opinion that the flesh of these diseased animals cannot be safely used for food." The dispatch warned in unmistakable language that "the offering of any such diseased animals, or any portion of their flesh, for sale for food, within the Metropolitan District of New York, will be regarded as a culpable offence against the sanitary ordinance relating to markets and food articles and will be punished with the heaviest penalties the laws provide." To underscore the point, the directive stated, "No relaxation of this order of the Board can be allowed."[28]

As New York authorities worked feverishly to stop the spread of Texas fever into the state, by the middle of August, reports also flowed out from Chicago indicating that the situation might have worsened elsewhere. The inspector at the

Union Stockyards had a Texas herd of four hundred beeves killed. Some in the lot showed symptoms of the disease, and the inspector took no chances on this herd spreading Texas fever.[29]

From several cities in the Midwest and East Coast came numerous other reports of cattle deaths associated with Texas fever. Dairy cows in Cincinnati, Ohio, died from the disease. When the ailment showed up in Rhode Island, it led Governor Ambrose Burnside to appoint a five-member commission to investigate its spread.[30] On August 25, Governor (and future US president) Rutherford B. Hayes of Ohio appointed his own special commission to "prosecute all persons" who were in violation of the state law prohibiting the "introduction of Texas, and other cattle infected with disease." The commissioners were also given the authority to adopt measures to "prevent the introduction of transportation of Texas cattle through the state." With the disease continuing to spread in Cincinnati, beef and dairy consumption declined markedly.[31] The *Cincinnati Gazette* declared that there could be no doubt that Texas and Cherokee cattle, "which is a mixed breed," were "entirely unfit for human food, and should at all times be forbidden."[32]

The overall news could not have been worse for Joseph McCoy and his brothers when the *New York Tribune* (among other newspapers) reported that "the plague had materially decreased the receipts of cattle at the various yards" in and near the city.[33] Added to this report was the distressing news from the Ontario Board of Agriculture that steps were being taken to prevent any further importation of Texas cattle anywhere into Canada.[34]

The enthusiastic support at the beginning of the year for the arrival of Texas cattle in Abilene, Kansas, had turned to outright opposition by the end of August. From Junction City to Salina, cattle herds were becoming ill. Farmers around Abilene were losing a "great many native cattle." Not surprisingly, the feeling grew "very strong among the farmers against the Texas cattle business." Importation into Illinois had become nearly impossible and resulted in more than twenty thousand Texas cattle languishing between Abilene and Salina. Joseph helplessly watched as trade at his Great Western Stock Yards came to a standstill.[35]

By the end of August, Moreau Morris, the sanitary inspector for the Metropolitan Health Board, had taken several steps to ensure the safety of meat entering the city markets. Inspectors had been stationed at several entry yards into the state, and this action had largely reduced the number of diseased cattle found in the New York and New Jersey yards. Moreover, Morris noted with approval that New Jersey had hired a "competent and careful inspector" whose duty it was to carefully examine the internal organs of the slaughter steers being processed at the Communipaw Abattoirs. Not only was it important to stop diseased cattle from entering city markets, but it was equally important to discover the source of the disease.[36]

## Governmental Responses

By September, with so many governors, state commissions, cattlemen, farmers, and consumers trying to sort out how best to deal with the "plague," a wide range of observers suggested that the time had come for a more coordinated and agreed-upon approach for confronting the epidemic. Stockmen around Champaign, Illinois, reeling from deaths in their herds and crushing financial losses coupled with a bewildering array of restrictions and inspections placed on the importation of cattle into other states, gathered in an effort to create order out of the chaos engulfing them.

On Monday, August 31, several men "interested in cattle and the cattle trade" met in the Springfield office of John Williams to "devise some means for the protection of the shippers of stock to Buffalo, New York and other points." This impromptu committee crafted a letter to Governor Richard J. Oglesby asking him to give Harvey Edwards of Sangamon County and Edward Piper of Macon County the authority to proceed to Albany, New York, in an effort to "take into consideration, among the conflicting and clashing interests of the harsh speculators, the best cattle interest of the State of Illinois." The meeting attendees feared that the "interest of Illinois will be sacrificed unless this matter is promptly attended to." Time, they understood, was of the essence if they wanted to avert economic calamity.[37]

Following the Springfield commissioners' lead, Governor Oglesby wrote to Governor Fenton of New York on September 1 to inform him of his official appointment of Edwards and Piper as commissioners representing the interests of Illinois. The commissioners, the governor wrote, were authorized to inquire "into the restrictions your authorities have . . . imposed upon the trade in and shipment of cattle from [Illinois] to the eastern markets, in consequence of an apprehended epidemic among cattle, commonly known as the Spanish or Texas fever." Oglesby hoped that goodwill would prevail and that means could be found whereby the restrictions could be removed so that "both consumer and shipper may enjoy the full benefit of as free trade as is possible under the circumstances." Oglesby comprehended a couple of important components in the future well-being of the trade. First, urban consumers' demands for wholesome meat needed to be met, and second, some restrictions or regulation of the trade would be necessary for its future prosperity.[38]

In October, after the Illinois commissioners finished their work in Buffalo and Albany, New York, they made an official request to Governor Fenton. Highlighting the problems that had led them to make the request, they acknowledged the devastating prevalence of Texas fever but also lamented the "inadequacy" and "conflicting provisions" of the laws enacted by several states to counteract the spread of the disease. The commissioners hoped to create "harmonious" laws and actions that would promote the "mutual protection" of the interests of meat consumers, stockmen, and farmers alike by collectively working to find a means for curing Texas fever. In the interest of achieving these ends, they requested that the cattle commissioners of New York call for a convention of cattle commissioners from all the states and the Dominion of Canada that had an interest in the cattle trade.

The New York cattle commissioners took up the charge and recommended that a convention be assembled in Springfield, Illinois, beginning on December 1, 1868. Their stated goals were to find the cause of Texas fever, trace the history of the disease, and prepare a draft law for the consideration of the state legislatures and the Dominion of Canada represented at the convention. The governor of each invited state and the prime minister of the province of Ontario could select three commissioners to represent their respective states or province.

## *The McCoy Bison Show*

As responses and reactions to the spread of Texas fever rippled through the entire reach of the cattle trade, Joseph McCoy's initial glowing prospects for the 1868 cattle season evaporated. Not only did the emergence of Texas fever jeopardize Joseph and his brothers' investments in Abilene, they also faced growing competition from other outlets along the Union Pacific Railway Company, Eastern Division (UPED) line. Given the immense numbers of cattle headed north, cattle dealers at Junction City, Salina, and Ellsworth hoped to take a slice of the trade.[39]

The officers of the Central Branch Union Pacific Railroad (CBUP) also wanted in on the cattle action. They managed a one-hundred-mile line directly connecting Atchison, Kansas, west to Waterville, located about sixty miles slightly northeast of Abilene. At the western terminus they built a sizable stockyard, intending to intercept Texas herds bound for Abilene. Despite an additional sixty-mile cattle drive beyond Abilene, the officers promised to ship each stock car for twenty dollars less than the UPED could out of Abilene. Working for Waterville interests, and his own, A. J. Bell went to Salina and Abilene, and contracted terms that would deliver fifty thousand head of cattle to Waterville, where the CBUP would haul them to Atchison, where they would be transferred across the Missouri River to the stock cars of the H&StJ bound for Chicago.[40] All of this mounting competition for the cattle trade led McCoy to consider freighting cattle for free at his Abilene operation.[41]

Joseph and James McCoy had heavily advertised the convenience of shipping cattle from Abilene. Their deep investments in their stockyards led them to believe that they had secured good arrangements with the management of the UPED on their cut for each head boarded on UPED stock cars.[42] On June 10, the brothers loaded longhorns into 28 stock cars, the first of the season. The next day they loaded another 34 cars. On a daily average, they took receipts for over 1,000 head of cattle. Herds of 4,000 to 6,000 head of cattle were within a few days of arriving at their facility.[43] By the middle of the month, UPED locomotives were hauling trains of 35–40 stock cars loaded with cattle daily. All this stock was initially bound for St. Louis and then to markets beyond. Certainly, stock brokers in Chicago were also "striking [their] roots deeply into this soil" of the Kansas River Valley. By the end of the month, some reported at least 60,000 longhorns headed north of the Red River, with more than double that number expected for the season.[44] During the last two weeks of June, more than 270 stock cars loaded with cattle were on their way to grazing pastures in Illinois. Buyers anticipated that by the fall, these beeves would be fat enough for the slaughterhouses in St. Louis, Chicago, and New York. Everything seemed to be in place for a profitable year.

By the end of August, Joseph watched as the Texas cattle trade started to unravel. The collapse of the New York cattle market propelled by the deadly outbreak of Texas fever threatened the loss of every dollar that the McCoys had invested in their Abilene operation. Joseph saw his prospects vanish as panic arose in city after city over the purchase of diseased beef. Nearly all the beef sold in New

York City came from Illinois, Indiana, Missouri, and Texas. Moreover, much of the stock from the midwestern states had originated in Texas.

Joseph McCoy received the reports and read the articles about diseased cattle appearing in the New York stockyards and how the employees of the Metropolitan Board of Health had immediately placed all animals in quarantine, required drovers to repurchase sides of beef from butchers, and sent the cattle to the "soap-fat man," where the carcasses were boiled in steaming vats to render the fats for soap production. McCoy took alarm at the actions of Governor Reuben Fenton, who had ordered that any animal showing any signs of diseased be offloaded at all "principal railroad cities" on the western border of the state. McCoy helplessly watched as authorities in New Jersey followed suit, prohibiting the importation of Texas cattle, and then as Pittsburgh did likewise.[45]

With remarkable understatement, Joseph McCoy later recalled how competition with other railroads and Texas fever had produced a great "uneasiness" among stock buyers and Texas cattlemen at Abilene. For McCoy, the outbreak portended complete economic ruin. He knew he had to confront, as quickly as possible, the "dullness" of the Abilene market. He first advertised a semimonthly public auction of mixed herds, which produced some cattle sales. This worked well in selling cattle to stockmen who anticipated holding on to their herds in Missouri, Nebraska, Iowa, and Kansas until the market rebounded or who, hoping for better prospects in the spring, were willing to overwinter the livestock. Still, McCoy had to find a way to sell over twenty-five thousand beeves still grazing to the west in the Smoky Hill River Valley.[46]

McCoy came up with a unique, if not unusual, way to protect his cattle business from impending ruin. With a flair for P. T. Barnum–like self-promotion, he intended to round up some bison, place them in a reinforced stock car covered with large panels advertising his Abilene stockyard, and have the car hauled to cities such as St. Louis, Chicago, and New York. At each stop, he would parade the bison through the city and promote a bison hunt meant to attract well-heeled city dwellers and newspaper reporters. McCoy's ultimate goal was to have these lavishly outfitted hunting excursions stop at his outlet in Abilene, where the travelers would observe firsthand the bounty and health of Texas cattle. McCoy hoped that the resulting reports flowing back to the large cities would assuage fears of importing Texas cattle and would lead to a resumption of the trade from Abilene.[47]

On July 1, 1868, Mark A. Withers of Lockhart, Texas, had just arrived in Abilene with a herd of six hundred "big wild steers." He found a good grazing ground on Chapman Creek, some twelve miles north of Abilene, where he would keep the herd until selling it in the fall. He sent four "hands" back to Texas and kept four, along with a cook, to tend the herd. Once they were "rolling fat," Withers sold the herd to William McCoy for $28 per head, $1,000 in cash and the rest in drafts on Donald Lawson and Company of New York City, signed by William McCoy. Assuming that all the drafts would be honored—an iffy assumption given the spreading fear related to Texas fever—Withers made a nice return on cattle that had cost him $8 to $10 a head in Texas, with an added cost of $4 per head to drive them to Abilene.

While Withers camped near Abilene, he, like everyone else involved in the trade, followed what was happening with the spread of Texas fever. With an understandable interest in the future of New York cattle markets, Withers decided to join McCoy's bison publicity gambit designed to quell the panic and reopen eastern cattle markets.[48] Besides Withers, McCoy hired three other Texans, Jake Carroll, Tom Johnson, and Bill Campbell, and two unnamed "California Spaniards." First, this crew set to work reinforcing a stock car, stocking supplies, and selecting six horses "well trained to the lasso." They were later joined by six other men whom McCoy assigned to tend the supplies.[49]

Once outfitted, a UPED locomotive took McCoy and his bison-hunting outfit to the Fossil Creek station, where they disembarked. The excited Texans and Hispanics took off almost immediately on a search for bison to lasso. In the distance, they thought they saw an Indian chasing a bison. The supposed bison hunter took off at a dead run when he saw McCoy's outfit headed pell-mell straight for him. When Withers and the others caught up with him, they found him and four others barricaded in a dugout, awaiting their own attack by "Indians." Withers and the others had mistaken the man, who was trailing a regular milk cow, for an Indian chasing a bison. They all had a good laugh about it once everyone had gotten over their scare about "the savages."[50]

The following day, their hunt began to show results as they found their first bison bulls grazing near the Saline River. Two of the "Spaniards" roped one, and Withers and Campbell roped a second. Withers's horses headed his bull toward the train, and once there, the crew tied down the bull, removed the lariats, and by means of block and tackle dragged the bull into the stock car.[51] This might have been the bison bull weighing over 1,800 pounds that Joseph and James had hauled back to Abilene in the third week of August. As reported in the *Daily Kansas Tribune*, the McCoys' "party of Mexicans and Texans" was out on the plains, "lassoing and bringing alive all the buffalo" they could capture.[52] Withers would later recall that the hunting outfit captured twenty-four bulls in a week and successfully loaded twelve into UPED stock cars.[53]

On Tuesday, August 25, McCoy's stock car, filled with three bison bulls and two pronghorn deer, passed through Lawrence, Kansas, ultimately bound for New York City. Once there, McCoy intended to have the animals unloaded and then taken to the zoo in Central Park.[54] By the first week of September, McCoy had the bulls on display in St. Louis; his next stop was Chicago.[55] According to Withers and McCoy, the bison were displayed at the Chicago Fairgrounds, where Withers, Campbell, and the two "Spaniards" publicly performed lassoing the bison.[56] According to McCoy, his bison show elicited "a great amount of attention and newspaper comment," and indeed it did.[57]

But McCoy never described exactly what kind of "attention" reporters gave to his bison show. When he arrived in Chicago, the *Tribune* informed its readership about McCoy's grand bison hunt meant for "live stock men" and their spouses. As portrayed to the newspaper's readership, McCoy promised excellent quarters with "every arrangement" made for the comfort of those traveling west. The excursionists departed aboard the Chicago, Burlington, and Quincy Railroad on September 11, 1868, bound for the bison hunting grounds of the Smoky Hill River Valley in Kansas.[58]

Next McCoy made arrangements for a bison exhibition to be performed in the Equestrian Academy's rink located on Wabash Avenue. On Thursday evening, September 17, 1868, McCoy and his cowboys staged a mock "buffalo hunt." The reporter for the *Chicago Tribune*, to be sure, witnessed an amazing spectacle, one that he hoped "will not occur in this city for many years to come." He described the event as an "exhibition of brutality, such as in New York city would incur the righteous indignation of President Bergh, and which, almost, if not quite, calls for the organization in Chicago of a society for the prevention of cruelty to animals." Apparently, only one of McCoy's bison bulls remained fit, if barely so, for the show. The writer blasted McCoy and his outfit for tormenting the bull "beyond measure by a long journey on the cars and frequent transshipment under the *tender supervision* of Californian Spaniards" (emphasis added). It lay nearly motionless in the corner of the arena, and when it attempted to stand, it was "easily discovered that the unfortunate animal had lost the use of his fore legs." The "Spaniards" (or as the journalist, showing his ethnic prejudice, also called them, "half breeds") rode two "dilapidated looking horses," and attempted to stir the bull into action so that they could demonstrate their roping skills. Finally, they had provoked the animal into a state of "unforgivable fury," whereupon the bull made a "few feeble efforts to avenge himself." What followed thoroughly sickened nearly everyone in attendance. Once the bull had staggered to its feet, the cowboys "immediately lassoed and brought to the [bull] to the ground, where he was pinioned and bound and kicked, and cuffed, much, seemingly, to the delight of a few roughs from Wells street and the harrowing of the feelings of all decent people who witnessed it." Very few of the initial crowd of forty people remained to the end when afterward the bull was "hauled to a corner," as the band played "an enlivening air."[59]

McCoy's first night of entertainment, one advertised as an exhibit of wild buffalos, elks, horses, and as one "to represent the throwing of the lasso by skillful Mexicans," had failed to live up to his advance billing presented to the representatives of the Chicago Equestrian Academy. After the first night's debacle, the academy made it public in the *Tribune* that it "had nothing to do with" the McCoy's "entertainment." And to make its disgust with McCoy explicit, the academy canceled the remaining two scheduled nights.[60] Six years later, when McCoy wrote about the event, he simply said that the bison were unloaded into the "commons of the stock yards" in Chicago, and later presented to Dr. John Gamgee, who had them killed, stuffed by a taxidermist, and shipped to London.[61] The bison never reached Central Park.[62]

McCoy's flare for showmanship and publicity, however, purportedly achieved the desired result. McCoy boasted that the bison extravaganza had worked its magic in stimulating business at his Abilene yards. He claimed that he had enticed several "Illinois cattle men" to tour the plains of Kansas aboard UPED coach cars. While the Illinoisans were aboard the train, or later when they toured the vast grazing grounds surrounding Abilene by horse, McCoy showed them "many fine herds of cattle" ready for market. Still, as McCoy realized, regardless of this "brief" opening in the market, he and his brothers "were able to cover [only] a small portion" of their mounting losses.

McCoy's hope for the return of a robust eastern market was soon dealt a harsh blow by the cattle commissioners' convention scheduled to begin on December 1. His business at Abilene would be dealt a sure death blow if the commissioners crafted model legislation that further restricted or eliminated the flow of Texas cattle to the east. Given the seriousness of the situation, McCoy, along with Sarah, then pregnant with their second child, and Mary, their two-year-old daughter, took up temporary residence in Springfield, Illinois. There he began planning how best to persuade the attending commissioners that Texas cattle were safe. Most importantly, he knew that he had to demonstrate that pinning any theory of the "cattle plague" on Texas beeves was folly.

## An Abundance of Theories

In retrospect, it is easy to see how people at the time had all sorts of mistaken ideas about this plague. The editor of the *Kansas State Record* believed that the transference of the disease from Texas longhorns to domestic herds occurred only when the Texas animals were "overheated, and chased, and run, as when they are stampeded." The fix, then, was simply to adopt regulations to prevent this from happening "for the sake of those who have the feed for them, and those who expect to feed upon them."[63]

In August, when the spread of the disease had become apparent from Illinois to New York, a reporter for the *Tribune* described the symptoms and probable cause of the malady: "The animal at first becomes drowsy or stupid, which is followed by constipation of the alimentary or urinary canals. By straining and over-exertion, they seem to rupture themselves internally, and blood is discharged. The animal subsequently swells up and dies." While this reporter only partially understood the symptoms, he made a prescient observation. He noted that ticks, "resembling the wood-tick, but much larger," often covered sickened cattle. He heard from drovers that cattle shipped by rail from Chicago to New York were deprived of water for forty-eight hours and that they were subjected to overcrowded conditions in the stock cars, which, combined with "the pain suffered from the attacks of the ticks," caused the disease.[64]

J. R. Dodge, a statistician who worked for the US Department of Agriculture, had made an "extended investigation" of the disease and had come to the following conclusions. First, cattle from the southernmost regions of the Gulf states communicated the disease, but these same cattle seldom, if ever, showed symptoms of the disease. He further noted that infected native shorthorn cattle almost always died as a result of contracting the disease. Worse, Dodge pointed out, no effective medical treatments worked to cure or mitigate the disease. His recommendation—that "the movement of Texas cattle should be regulated or suppressed"—must have been distressing to Texas drovers and Joseph McCoy.[65]

Professor John Gamgee, the president of the Albert Veterinary College of London, who had gained considerable international fame for treating the "cattle plague" outbreak of rinderpest in England, quickly found himself in the middle of the cattle plague debate. When he arrived in New York City in March, Gamgee only sought to advertise his method for preserving meat over a period of months thereby making it safe for transatlantic shipments and human consumption. He made it quite clear during his public addresses that English cattlemen could no longer supply enough meat to feed such burgeoning cities such as London. He intended to persuade Americans of the virtue of using his techniques to preserve beef cut from Texas cattle, thereby furnishing meat to New Yorkers for as little as four cents per pound and creating a viable English market for American beef.[66]

Given his fame for treating European cattle diseases, he soon became embroiled in providing a "scientific" explanation for the causation of Texas fever. The Chicago stockmen understood clearly how devastating the spread of Texas fever was to their bottom line; they were just as eager as the New York authorities to find a means of preventing the disease. On Tuesday, July 12, 1868, John L. Hancock of Messrs. Cragin and Company, a Chicago livestock firm, summoned the members of the Pork Packers' Association to meet at the Tremont House in Chicago, the most elegant hotel in the city. There they hired M. E. Richardson, an editor of the *Prairie Farmer*; Dr. James V. Z. Blaney, president of Rush Medical College; and Professor Gamgee to investigate the spread of the disease in Indiana, which had no restrictions on the importation of Texas cattle. On July 29, the investigators set out to examine the central grazing prairies of Illinois, followed by an inspection of the unloading docks at Cairo. They returned to Chicago on August 5 with report in hand.

Their report indicated that the source of the problem lay with the cattle shipped up the Mississippi River to Cairo, Illinois, where the herds were transferred to the stock cars of the CI railroad. The cattle were offloaded at Tolono, a small railroad town south of Champaign-Urbana, and then driven to pastures in Indiana or to grazing grounds in Illinois where "there was the least chance of molestation from the inhabitants."[67]

The report made one acute observation and a bad conclusion based upon its findings. The investigators' experience, like that of many other careful observers of the trade, indicated correctly that Texas cattle *wintered* with native herds did not spread the disease. But the report elaborated further on this insight by erroneously concluding that the tick was harmless. Cattlemen, the report said, "now see the difference between the Summer and Winter trade, and there is not a single man, well informed on this subject, who does not recognize that, whatever other conclusions may be arrived at, it is certain that we can avail ourselves of this same trade in Texas cattle after the first frosts have withered the wild grasses of the Prairies." Authors of the report found themselves "more amused than instructed by the many popular theories as to the origin of the disease, and in some districts no amount of convincing proof suffers to divert the current of popular opinion in regard to the comparatively harmless tick."[68] Even though Texas cattle might be completely covered by ticks, most cattlemen considered the pest no more than a nuisance to cattle.

After some study, Gamgee arrived at a theory that went somewhat like this: in the spring and early summer, Texas cattle fed on certain tree shoots supposedly charged with "astringent principles." He particularly pointed toward the live oak as the culprit. He thought that cattle ate the "succulent shoots" of these trees and, given the animals' adaptation to the warmer climes of the southern states such as Texas and Florida, were unaffected. As a result, he believed, these animals carried a "peculiar form of 'enzootic haematuria'"[69] in their urine and feces that killed any domestic cattle that came into contact with it during the warm months. Gamgee noted that in the northern climes of North America, where live oaks failed to thrive, Texas fever was also absent. He was correct in noting that live oaks, the fever, and cattle had some "correlation," but he misunderstood it as "causation."

Not surprisingly, stockmen took away two main points from Professor Gamgee's conclusions. The first was that native stock in the northern states did not transmit the fever to other native stock. Only cattle from Texas seemed to transmit the disease. Second, the disease did not appear to be borne by any "animal poison" that could affect the quality of the meat of a diseased animal. Consequently, the meat from an animal stricken with the fever was still safe for human consumption. On the whole, Gamgee's report gave stockmen some reassurances that Texas cattle could be marketed without harm to consumers.[70]

Still, cattle markets along the East Coast urban corridor remained depressed.

For McCoy, even with a slight resumption of buying and selling at Abilene, the cattle seldom found markets beyond the packinghouses in Leavenworth and Kansas City, Kansas; the market in St. Louis; Indian reservations; or the stockmen who intended to overwinter the cattle with the goal of selling them in the spring. McCoy understood that these markets were not enough to carry the full potential of the Texas cattle trade or to protect his Abilene enterprise from further disruption. He realized then, more than ever, the importance of convincing the cattle commissioners attending the Springfield convention that Texas cattle should continue to be imported into large urban markets.

### *The 1868 Springfield, Illinois, Convention of Cattle Commissioners*

Writing in 1874, five years after the conclusion of the convention, McCoy called the attending commissioners little more than a collection of "quondam quacks, and impractical theorists, and imbecile ignoramuses . . . without an equal." McCoy's Abilene adventure had come to ruin little more than two years after the convention had concluded its work. Not one to forget a slight, McCoy held the work of the convention, along with the UPED's nonpayment for loading cattle in 1869, responsible for his economic failure. In his acclaimed *Historic Sketches of the Cattle Trade of the West and Southwest* (1874), he would make sure posterity understood just who the rogues were who had unjustly triggered his economic ruin.[71]

McCoy further described the commissioners as "esculapians of the most deadly type," "political bummers," and a "pestilential crew" who were "utterly unfit to deliberate on, or investigate anything." McCoy patted himself on the back as the only one attending the convention who had dared to "raise his voice in behalf of Texan cattle." Doing so, he recalled, "brought forth a storm of indignation" from the commissioners. As might be expected, McCoy overstated his own importance, but only to a degree.[72]

At the time of the convention, a report from the *Chicago Tribune* gave a more impartial portrayal of the commissioners than McCoy would in 1874. The commissioners, the reporter wrote, were "very able men, many of them having national reputation."[73] A great many were medical doctors, a few were professors specializing in the veterinary sciences, and a few were cattlemen themselves. Altogether, thirty-six commissioners attended the convention, representing twelve states and the Canadian province of Ontario. The commissioners also appointed six honorary commissioners: three representing the St. Louis Agricultural and Mechanical Association, Dr. Morris from the Metropolitan Board of Health, Dr. John Rauch from Chicago, and Joseph McCoy.[74]

Representation from one state was conspicuously absent: no official commissioner arrived from Texas. McCoy had an explanation for this nonattendance. When word of the proposed convention reached McCoy's Drovers Cottage in Abilene, the Texas cattlemen residing there met and among themselves appointed an "ex-governor" of Texas to represent their state in Illinois. However, McCoy claimed, given the "lack of public spirit and public enterprise" of Texans, the state failed to provide any funding for sending a delegate to attend the convention, which resulted in Texas being completely unrepresented.[75]

Unlike McCoy's memory, the *Chicago Tribune* reporter had a better feel at the time for the nature of the convention. He anticipated that the commissioners would probably come to terms on some means "to prevent future introduction of the disease, and yet allow the Texan cattle to be introduced under restrictions." The reporter doubted whether the commissioners would find a cause of the disease, however, given the "great many theories, and conflicting facts or facts that seem to conflict."[76]

On the first day, the convention attendees gathered in the Representative Hall of the Illinois capitol. After finding the credentials of the commissioners to be in order, the body elected Lewis Allen from Buffalo, New York, as presiding president. The commissioners also accorded Governor Oglesby of Illinois the privilege of sitting next to President Allen. A subcommittee was appointed to draft model recommendations for regulating the cattle trade, and while it went to work, the commissioners began giving testimony. Because New York was so important to North American cattle markets, John Gould, one of the commissioners from New York, gave the first report to the assembly.

Gould began by pointing out that Texas fever posed a distinct threat to the cattle and consumer interests of his state. He underscored the importance of the dairy industry while recognizing that New York cattlemen could not supply the demand of the state, much less New York City, for beef. The 1.25 million dairy cows in the state of New York, he held, were highly susceptible to Texas fever, which threatened the $25 million annual returns of the trade.[77]

When Gould came to how the disease was transmitted, he blamed the importation of Texas cattle, which, as far as he was concerned, also suffered from the disease. Furthermore, he assumed that native cattle could transmit the disease. Cause of the disease, he said, was the transmittal of "mycelia," the spores of which attacked the red blood cells of Texas cattle. Gould cited a study of the diseased cattle by Dr. Henry Reed Stiles, whose microscopic observations revealed that the diseased cattle's red blood cells appeared to be "perforated with minute holes . . . as though they had been worm-eaten." Gould concluded from this study that the "growth of these plants is at the expense of the blood discs themselves." And where did these mycelia come from? These minute plants colonized the sheaths of Texas grasses. As Texas cattle grazed, they ingested the mycelia, then deposited them through their urine and dung wherever they went. When native cattle grazed where Texas cattle had grazed, they also ingested the mycelia, which induced Texas fever.[78]

Gould's conclusion raised apprehension and dread, if not outright disagreement, among those interested in maintaining the flow of Texas cattle to eastern markets. Gould warned those cattlemen that should the causation of the disease be proved to follow the path he had outlined, then they must "give up cattle altogether; . . . you cannot raise [Texas cattle] at all." He elaborated his point:

> If there is no time when Texas cattle can safely come in, then they must be excluded, painful as it is for me to say so, for cheap meat is what we want in New York, and, from what I hear, our only hope of obtaining it is by importation of Texas cattle. But if their introduction is going to kill off all [the native cattle in the Midwest] so that you cannot supply us with any meat at all because of your prairies being so thoroughly poisoned, then it is for our interest to exclude [Texas cattle] altogether.[79]

At this point, McCoy's blood pressure and that of like-minded attendees' must have attained dangerously high levels as they contemplated the ramifications of eliminating the Texas cattle trade.

M. Eaton, the superintendent of John T. Alexander's massive Illinois cattle operation, followed Gould. Eaton said that his experience led him to believe that ticks "might have some agency in causing" Texas fever. Alexander had acquired hundreds of Texas cattle from the counties along the lower Brazos River, loaded onto Mississippi steamboats at the Red River docks. The ships unloaded the herds at Cairo, and then the animals were loaded into IC railroad stock cars and unloaded again at Tolono, Illinois. From there, the herds were driven to an Alexander operation called the Broad Lands. When Eaton saw the Texas longhorns, he noticed that they were completely covered with ticks to the point that their skin appeared grayish in color. Eaton believed that as many as ten thousand ticks might cover just one longhorn at any given time. Once the ticks were engorged, Eaton observed, they fell off the cattle and began colonizing the pastures. When a new herd was placed on pastures where Texas cattle had been, the ticks inhabiting the grass quickly attached themselves to those bovines. When that happened, native herds on those pastures began succumbing to Texas fever.

In his description of the outbreak of Texas fever around Tolono and at the Broad Lands, Eaton absolved the shipments arriving from Abilene, Kansas. These cattle seemed to be fairly free of ticks. He supposed that the ticks might have fallen off prior to arriving in Illinois and had had no chance to reattach themselves to a herd on the move. Eaton also said he was at a loss to explain why calves never seemed to acquire the disease, even though he knew that to be so.

Commissioner David Christie, a senator from Ontario, took exception to the remark that Abilene cattle were free of Texas fever. Not only a politician of some note, Christie was also well regarded as one of Canada's premier stock breeders; his farm "the Estates" in Brantford Township, Ontario, was a showplace of the latest in agricultural production.[80] He had visited McCoy's operation in Abilene and found diseased cattle on McCoy's own farm.

McCoy was not going to let this assertion stand.[81] He explained in great detail his labors in opening the Texas cattle outlet in Abilene, and laid the blame for Texas fever on the brutal methods employed for shipping cattle on Mississippi steamboats. The motive of steamboat captains, McCoy claimed, was "the more cattle the more dollars." This led to cattle being packed so tightly onto the boats that the animals had to stand for six to eight days while en route. The boat crews, according to McCoy, fed the cattle by tossing hay onto their backs, and the beeves ate "from the back of another." The crews provided the standing animals with water by spraying them through hoses. Was it any wonder, McCoy asked, that cattle transported under these conditions should be diseased upon being unloaded at Cairo or anywhere else along the Mississippi River?[82]

On the other hand, McCoy claimed, the cattle driven to his stockyards in Abilene "invariably arrived in good condition, healthy, sleek, and as a rule" without signs of disease. McCoy acknowledged that upon arrival at Abilene, these animals were seldom fit for shipping to eastern markets, but with adequate time grazing on the open rangeland surrounding his operation, the cattle gained enough weight and fat to make for good meat. As to the causes of Texas fever, McCoy made it clear to the assembly that the disease could be "traced largely to the barbarous manner in which these Texas cattle have been handled." In Texas, these longhorns, according to McCoy, were as healthy as cattle found anywhere among native herds.[83]

Following McCoy's ringing defense of his operation, Christie responded that he was not making any direct accusation against McCoy or his Abilene operation. He wanted only to "counteract the impression of some, at least, to-wit: that cattle coming from the south alone, were those which contaminated others." So ended the first day of the convention.[84]

The second day began where the first had left off. Further debates occurred among the commissioners over the nature of the disease and the history of its spread. Particular attention was given to the reports and testimonies from the Missouri commissioners, who detailed the unfolding of the disease in their state as early as 1853. In the afternoon, testimony centered on the outbreak of the disease in the Chicago Union Stockyards, whether Texas cattle were a source of wholesome beef, and how to understand what caused the red blood cells of diseased cattle to deteriorate.[85]

The heart of the second day came that evening, however, when the subcommittee appointed to make general propositions for the "legal enactments" the commissioners would ask the states to carry into law made its recommendations. The committee divided its recommendations into three sections. The first, further divided into six subsections, detailed ideas for forming commissions that would be empowered to monitor and regulate the cattle of their respective states. The second section contained eight subsections that dealt with how commissioners should be empowered to inspect and control all railroad shipments of cattle. The commissioners generally agreed with the wording of these two sections.[86]

The third section, however, raised the greatest concern and provoked the most dispute. The committee recommended the "enactment of stringent laws to prevent the transit through these states of Texan or Cherokee cattle, from the first day of April to the last day of October, inclusive." McCoy took great exception to this provision, as it made no distinction between cattle that had been overwintered and those that had not. The issue of this last section lay unresolved until the beginning of the convention's third day. Commissioner Joseph Poole from Indiana agreed with McCoy that this particular resolution worked against transporting overwintered cattle except in December, January, and February. Commissioner A. Earle of Indiana finally came up with an agreeable solution. Any Texas or Cherokee cattle that had been overwintered should be classified as native and given certification to that effect. After certification, these cattle could be shipped any time of year.[87]

The commissioners also urged that the federal government be asked formally to investigate the causation of the disease. Was the disease caused by spores, ticks, or brutal treatment of cattle while in transit? The commissioners, as anticipated, could not reach an agreement, so they shifted the responsibility for finding the cause to the federal government. At first, their recommendation was to ask Congress for an appropriation for the study, but some were concerned that congressional response to such a request would be inadequate. Some suggested the War Department carry out the study, but other commissioners thought the work should be done by the Department of Agriculture. The commissioners finally reached a consensus that it should be the War Department.[88]

Now, with the commissioners' work concluded, McCoy faced his next challenge in ensuring that the Illinois legislature did not enact laws overly restricting the importation of Texas cattle. The state senator who represented Tolono wanted to halt Texas cattle imports entirely. The Tolono area had suffered immensely, with nearly the entire number of cattle there at the beginning of 1868 dead by the end of the year. McCoy understood that passage of this bill would mean the complete ruin for his business. As he remembered, "to defeat the measure, or at least modify it" absorbed his undivided attention for the seventy-two days of that session. The Illinois legislature eventually followed the recommendation of the cattle convention and allowed the importation of Texas cattle that, upon certification, had been overwintered. The result, as McCoy drily noted, was that the following summer, "it was astonishing . . . how many 'wintered cattle' arrived in Abilene." As for the notarized certifications, a notary at Abilene, according to McCoy, had no trouble in manufacturing "certificates by the dozen, or the cart load, for a small consideration." All this assured that outbreaks of Texas fever would continue.[89]

## A Lingering Problem

At the beginning of 1868, John T. Alexander ran the largest cattle operation in Illinois and numbered among the richest cattlemen in all of North America. The outbreak of Texas fever in the summer, however, had left him nearly destitute by the end of the year. His losses for the year mounted to over $75,000 as the plummeting prices of beeves shipped into eastern markets mounted with each cattle death attributed to Texas fever. In an effort to avert complete economic collapse, he contracted with a Canadian company to sell his 26,000-acre farm, the Broad Lands. The company, however, failed to honor the contract, which left Alexander's assets highly exposed. Through the aid of some friendly bankers, Alexander eventually managed to redeem his debts, and by 1870 he had regained some of the ground lost two years before. By 1873, he had fully recovered.[90]

Although wealthy cattleman like Alexander might be able to weather the storm, families with fewer assets failed by the score. For example, many farm families in Tolono were foreign immigrants who had taken up dairying. By the end of the 1868 plague, reportedly only two dairy cows remained out of 450 numbered in the spring. During summer and fall, nearly one thousand cattle had perished, leaving families destitute. Mr. Hill, a resident of Tolono Township, warned that it might be "impossible to any longer restrain mob law" as residents gathered to prevent any passage, much less importation, of Texas cattle through or into Tolono Township. Many of the families had lost everything, including their homes and farms, and abandoned the township.[91]

The spread of Texas fever throughout the international transportation system raised fears even in England, where British authorities widely accepted the spore theory for the transmission of the disease. Despite the harsh effects of drought, crop failures, fear of food shortages, and a dangerous scarcity of forage, the English government stopped all importation of hay from the United States. The seriousness of this move is akin to the United States today cutting off oil imports. American hay supplied fuel for draft animals, especially for those in the large cities. The British justified this action by "the apprehension that the cattle disease might, by means of hay imported from the [United States], be reintroduced into England." Not until these reservations subsided did England remove the ban in February 1869.[92]

Despite the enduring prevalence of Texas fever, some people simply ignored its existence as they sought riches in the cattle trade. Baxter Springs, Kansas, could hardly have been called a town prior to 1867. A couple of cabins along one of the most beautiful, clear-flowing rivers in the state barely foretold its future. Located just a couple of miles north of Indian Territory and a few miles west of the Missouri-Kansas state line, the site was a potential stopping point for Texas cattle drovers. In 1866, anticipating the benefits of a Texas cattle trade, Captain M. Mann and J. J. Barnes surveyed the town site and made a claim to it. Herds were soon driven to the town, and in a mere five years, it had a population of more than four thousand souls.

Money flowed into Baxter Springs, and the good townsfolk indiscriminately voted a succession of large bond issues to finance the Missouri River, Fort Scott, and Gulf Railroad, a school building, a county courthouse, and city improvements. Every amusement a Texas cowboy might want could be found in the city. As one historian put it, "Saloons and bawdy and dance houses of the most virulent character were numerous, and the town, especially during the season when the cattle were being driven in, was in one continuous state of uproar, night and day."[93] Consequently, the stockmen of Baxter Springs took every opportunity to support the Texas cattle trade even to the point of questioning the existence of Texas fever.

The stockmen of Baxter Springs desired a more flourishing Texas cattle trade. To facilitate it, they petitioned the state legislatures of both Kansas and Missouri in December 1871 to revise the laws setting the dates that Texas cattle herds were allowed into the state. Prior to this, legislation reflecting the belief that cold weather prevented the spread of Texas fever, forbade Texas cattle to cross the state line prior to December 1. This viewpoint was justified, given the nature of the Fan Heads, but the town boosters remained clueless about how the disease was diffused. In fact, in their petition to the state legislatures, they held to the view that the "testimony of the best acquainted on the subject all tend to establish that the disease, *if it does exist* [italics added], does not show itself or result in contagion or death after the 15th day of October." In short, the pursuit of cattle-borne profits outweighed concern over the spread of the disease.[94]

A year later, as Wichita, Kansas, became the site of the main cattle yard in the state, similar views about Texas fever prevailed there. Some, like one writer who published a letter in the *Wichita Eagle*, took a nonchalant attitude toward Texas fever. This writer considered that the immense cattle trade and its proceeds far outweighed the prospects of an epidemic. Besides, he claimed, with proper care in driving the herds, the disease could be eliminated. Over 125,000 head of cattle, he noted, had been shipped out of Wichita by the middle of November 1872 without one instance of "Spanish fever." Hard driving practices, he theorized, produced footsore and feverish cattle. Just give the animals a little time to recover and fatten, and all traces of the disease would disappear. Texas cattlemen had convinced him that this practice would result in the ability to graze and ship cattle "with impunity anywhere." Both the writer and Texas cattlemen were in complete error, however.[95]

In the years to come, Texas fever, as the cattle commissioners formally dubbed it, would continue to hang over the entire trade like a deadly pall, although some factors eased, but by no means eliminated, its deleterious effects on the trade. By the early 1870s, for example, many large packinghouses had been built nearer the great western cattle ranges, and by the middle of the 1870s, Philip Armour and Gustavus Swift would create meat-packing empires in Milwaukee, Chicago, and Kansas City that would dominate the trade. In addition, smaller yet substantial plants were built at the ends of or on rail lines in Omaha, Nebraska; Lamar, Colorado; and Denton, Texas.

Making all the hegemony in the meat-packing business possible were refinements in refrigeration technology. Beef quarters could be transported in refrigerated freight cars and then aboard transatlantic ships equipped with refrigerated holds, bound for the immense English markets. With this development, midwestern stockmen had less to fear about live Texas cattle spreading disease.

Still, the disease posed a serious threat to the entire beef and dairy economy of the United States. The prospect of Texas fever still resulted in farmers resisting, by various means, the importation of Texas cattle anywhere near their native herds. Given the national ramifications of the continued existence of Texas fever, researchers in the Bureau of Animal Industry housed in the Department of Agriculture busily undertook the study of the disease and searched for a cure.

## *Theobald Smith Finds the Cause*

In 1868, nine-year-old Theobald Jakob Schmitt, the son of German immigrants, was attending grammar school in Albany, New York. His parents, Philipp and Theresia, carefully saved money to place Theobald in "Professor Singer's Academy," a strictly administered private school conducted solely in German. At this time, Theobald, then known as Theobald Smith, apparently paid little, if any, attention to the Texas cattle unloaded at the city stockyards and the heated concerns about the escalation of Texas fever. Rather, he applied himself to its study, and later, during his high school years, he exhibited a talent for mathematics, chemistry, and botany. He was valedictorian of his graduating class.

In 1877, Theobald, with a hefty scholarship in hand, matriculated at Cornell University in Ithaca, New York. His studies centered on preparatory work for entering Albany Medical College. Once in medical school, he found dissecting human corpses disturbing but laboratory work far more satisfying. When he graduated in 1883, the title of his final essay, "Relations between Cell-Activity in Health and in Disease," indicated where his real passion lay. With the help of a friend, he acquired an assistantship in the Bureau of Animal Industry in the Department of Agriculture, where he took an immense interest in infectious diseases among animals. German researchers such as Robert Koch and Paul Ehrlich were leading lights in microbiology, and Smith, fluent in German, was able to follow their findings and publications. Now, fifteen years after McCoy had made his grand bison tour in an effort to open eastern markets by downplaying the effects of Texas fever, Theobald Smith stood poised to find the cause of this devastating malady.[96]

In 1888, Smith isolated the cause of the disease to the protozoan *Babesia bigemina* as the transmitter. Further research showed that the protozoan lived in the tick at the time named *Boophilus annulatus*, later reclassified as *Rhipicephalus annulatus*. In a few years, the department scientists created effective means for ridding cattle of the ticks, the primary method being to dip tick-covered cattle in tanks filled with arsenic, soda, and pine tar. By 1954, the Department of Agriculture considered fifteen states to be tick-free as a result of dipping cattle on a schedule of fourteen-day intervals.

At the end of 1868 and the beginning of 1869, however, the cure for Texas fever lay in the unknowable future for stockmen like Joseph McCoy. The 1868 outbreak had seriously crippled his ability to finance his Abilene operation. By 1869, farmers around Abilene no longer had any interest in seeing either Texas cattle or Texans near their town or farms. This compounded McCoy's woes as he reeled from his protracted litigation with the KP company. And, as if these factors were not enough, prairie fires and blizzards added to his difficulties. For Joseph and his brothers, profiting from the Texas cattle trade would prove elusive at best.

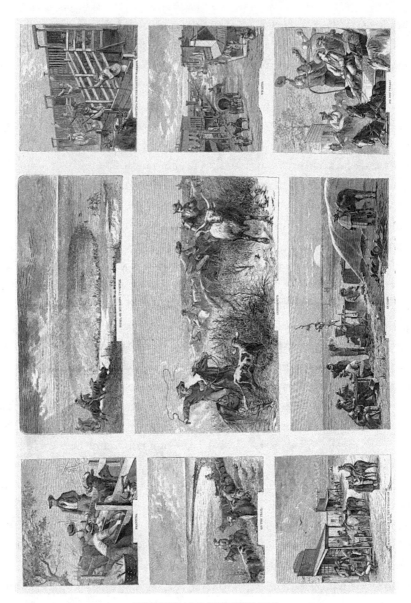

### THE TEXAS CATTLE TRADE

This is a really nice montage of nine scenes depicting a cattle drive from beginning to end. Beginning at the upper left, first caption reads "Branding," next below it, "On the Trail," and lower left, "Halting Place on the Ninnescah River." The caption to the top middle illustration reads, "Rodeo, or Rounding Up Cattle," next below it, "Cutting Out," and lower middle, "In Camp." The caption to the upper right illustration reads, "Shipping for Eastern Markets," next below it, "Wichita," and lower left, "Ho for Texas." From "The Texas Cattle Trade," *Harper's Weekly*, May 2, 1874, p. 386.

FORT HAYS, KANSAS, 1873

This lonely outpost on the short-grass prairies of Kansas is where the weather records were made of the deadly blizzard during the winter of 1871–72. Severe injuries or loss of life occurred to any person or animal caught unprotected in its deadly grip. Courtesy of the Kansas Historical Society, Topeka.

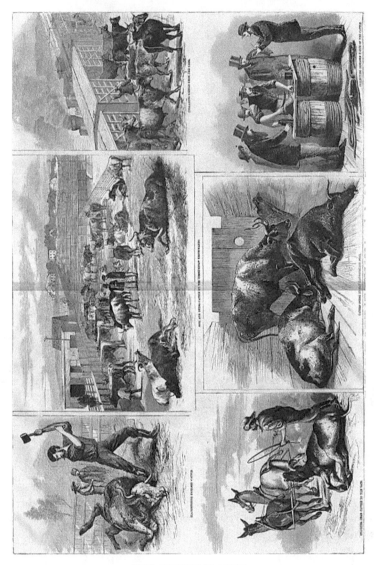

## THE CATTLE PLAGUE

The outbreak of Texas fever throughout the entire extent of the cattle trade in the summer of 1868 created panic among ranchers, farmers, cattle buyers and sellers, cattle markets, and consumers. This montage highlights how the devastation of the disease played itself out in the Communipaw facility in Jersey City. The upper frame is captioned "Slaughtering Diseased Cattle," the top center one titled "Sick and Dying Cattle at the Communipaw Drove-Yards," and the upper right hand illustration is captioned "Unloading Cattle from the Cars." The bottom illustrations, left to right, are captioned "Dragging Dead Cattle to the Vats," "Cattle Dying in the Slaughtering Pens," and "Collecting Diseased Parts of the Cattle." From "The Cattle Plague—Scenes and Incidents at the Communipaw Abattoir," *Harper's Weekly*, August 29, 1868, pp. 552–53.

### LOADING BISON

This Worrall engraving shows McCoy's crew capturing and loading bison for his dubious traveling show that ended in disaster in Chicago in 1868. In the background cowboys are lassoing bison, and in the foreground cowboys are using block and tackle to drag a bison bull into the reinforced stock car that would transport the animals for shows in Kansas City, St. Louis, and then Chicago. The obvious rough treatment of these bison resulted in horrible injuries and lameness by the time they arrived in Chicago. McCoy's glowing account of his exhibition in *Historic Sketches of the Cattle Trade* fell far short of its reality. From Joseph G. McCoy, *Historic Sketches of the Cattle Trade of the West and Southwest* (Kansas City, Mo.: Ramsey, Millett & Hudson, 1874), 183.

**LOADING CATTLE ONTO A MISSISSIPPI RIVERBOAT**

When the cattle plague of 1868 broke out, many cattlemen tried to blame it on the brutal transport of cattle on Mississippi steamboats. McCoy said the motto of ship owners was "the more cattle, the more dollars." He further elaborated by noting that cattle were so densely packed that they had "to stand for from six to eight long days—the only way in which food could be given them being, to throw it over them and let one eat from the back of another— the only water that they got being such as could be thrown over them by the hose." McCoy and others argued that cattle shipped under these conditions were the source of the plague. From *Harper's Weekly*, March 10, 1883, p. 156.

**THEOBALD SMITH**

In 1888, Theobald Smith started researching the cause of Texas fever. A pathologist, he had graduated with a medical degree from the Albany Medical College. He was working in the newly formed Bureau of Animal Industry in the Department of Agriculture, when in 1890 he identified the protozoan (*Babesia bigemina*) that caused Texas fever. This photograph was taken around the time of his discovery. Theobald Smith Photograph (n.d.), courtesy of Library of Congress, Washington, D.C.

### COWBOYS FIGHT A PRAIRIE FIRE

One of the most dreaded phenomena faced by cowboys herding cattle was the onset of a prairie fire. Whether cattle stampeded to escape the flames, or froze in their tracks and were horribly burned, the results were the same: stock losses. This Frederic Remington illustration shows cowboys frantically attempting to quash the early start of a prairie fire. "Dragging a Bull's Hide over a Prairie Fire in Northern Texas," *Harper's Weekly*, October 27, 1888, p. 815.

### WINTERING ON HAY IN CENTRAL KANSAS

Henry Worrall illustrates the rather unglamorous work of preparing a herd for overwintering on the open public range in Kansas. This engraving depicts smoke rising from the dugout in the side of the stream bank where the cowboys lived. Any herd had to be kept near a living water course, and cowboys were responsible for putting up prairie hay for both the cattle and their mounts when the weather precluded open-range grazing. Sometimes these preparations were not enough to prevent losses from severe weather, as the blizzards of 1871–72 proved. "Maj. J. S. Smiths' Herd—Wintering on Hay in Central Kansas," in Joseph G. McCoy, *Historic Sketches of the Cattle Trade of the West and Southwest* (Kansas City, Mo.: Ramsey, Millett & Hudson, 1874), 216.

### STAMPEDE OF A HERD OF CATTLE

Maintaining herd control of gasping cattle became an impossible task whenever the animals sensed a nearby water source. They would break into a stampede and rush headlong toward the water. Sometimes the herd found itself racing unaware toward dangerous steep stream banks. Those in front, unable to stop, pushed ahead by the momentum of the cattle behind them, would plunge over the side, straight down into the stream. Some lucky ones would manage to swim to the shore while many others would be crushed to death, gouged by horns, or would suffer broken bones. This engraving, while not depicting water-crazed cattle, still graphically shows what happened whenever cattle stampeded over the side of a steep river or stream bank. "New Mexico—Stampede of a Herd of Cattle," from *Frank Leslie's Weekly Illustrated*, May 12, 1877, p. 128.

CATTLE FORDING THE ARKANSAS RIVER, 1869

Cowboys knew that swimming a herd of cattle across a river was always dangerous. The Chisholm Trail was well known for its relatively safe stream crossings. This photograph taken in 1869 is of a Texas herd being led across the Arkansas River where eventually the city of Wichita would be built. Apparently, this herd was crossed during ideal river conditions as none of the cattle appear to be more than waist-deep in water. "Texas Cattle Fording Arkansas River at Wichita, Kansas, July 1869," courtesy Ignace Mead Jones Collection of James R. Mead Papers, Department of Special Collections, Wichita State University Library, Wichita, Kansas.

**AMANDA BURKS**
One of the few women to ride along on, and leave an account of, a cattle drive along the Chisholm Trail. Known as the "Queen of the Old Trail Drivers," Burks was inducted into the Texas Trail of Fame in 2000. From J. Marvin Hunter, ed., *The Trail Drivers of Texas* (1924; reprinted, Austin: University of Texas Press, 2006), 297.

**DENNIS BUSHYHEAD**

Bushyhead was the principal chief of the Cherokees from 1879 to 1887. During those years he oversaw many of the arrangements made for leasing the Cherokee Outlet to cattlemen. For a short time, he contracted Joseph McCoy, who was obligated to collect grazing fees from the cattlemen holding their herds on the land. "Portrait Photograph of Cherokee Chief Dennis W. Bushyhead," courtesy of Oklahoma Historical Society Photography Collection, Oklahoma City.

### DAVID PAYNE

David Payne led the "boomers" in an effort to remove Indian title to their lands held in Indian Territory. He organized expeditions along the southern border of Kansas, and led his followers into Indian Territory where they set up "town sites" and made claims to the land. For his efforts, the army captured him numerous times, and Payne ended up in front of federal judges, who routinely convicted on a variety of charges. Even after being jailed, Payne remained undeterred in his efforts to colonize Indian Territory although he never lived to see Oklahoma statehood. He had one outspoken proponent: Joseph G. McCoy. "Portrait Photograph of David L. Payne," courtesy of Oklahoma Historical Society Photography Collection, Oklahoma City.

SURVEYING SEDGWICK COUNTY, KANSAS, 1867

There are few photographs of federal surveys laying out the grid. This 1867 photograph is of federal territorial surveyors mapping the area that would become Sedgwick County, Kansas. Here the open mixed-grass prairies are being prepared as commodity and transferable property where Wichita would be built. This transformation of mixed-grass prairies to grid-defined land would eventually make open-range grazing impossible to do. "U.S. Surveyors Surveying Sedgwick County, Kansas, 1867," courtesy of Ignace Mead Jones Collection of James R. Mead Papers, Department of Special Collections, Wichita State University Library, Wichita, Kansas.

FIRST SANTA FE DEPOT, WICHITA, KANSAS, 1877
The grain elevators beside the tracks suggests the prevalence of the farming, rather than cattle, economy. While two stock cars appear in this view, the rest of the operation is set up to accommodate the transportation of crop production. Courtesy of Wichita Public Library Photograph Collection, Wichita, Kansas.

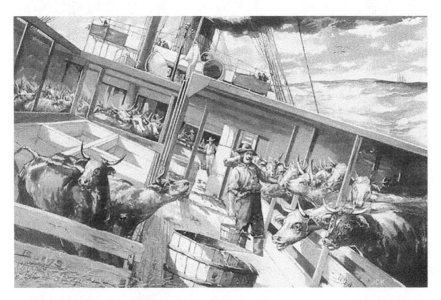

CATTLE ON A BOAT

This illustration from *Scribner's Magazine* shows live cattle on a transatlantic voyage to England. It highlights why cattle often arrived at English ports in rather rough shape. By 1890, newly designed freighters had replaced the first steamboats that had transported live cattle across the Atlantic. At the time, the National ship line's freighter, the *England*, held the record for the most live cattle shipped across the Atlantic. On September 8, 1889, it departed New York City transporting 1,022 head to England. From John H. Gould, "The Ocean Steamship as Freight Carrier," *Scribner's Magazine*, November 5, 1891, pp. 604–5.

### AMERICAN BEEF FOR OLD ENGLAND

The six scenes in this beautiful montage depict the early transporting of refrigerated sides of beef to England. The Anchor Line's steamboat the *Victoria* had been retrofitted for refrigerating beef quarters. The upper left illustration shows the blower system that chilled the room where the quarters are shown hanging. Men loading the ice room are depicted in the upper right illustration. Men are shown removing the quarters and hosting them to the deck for off-loading at the English harbor in the middle two illustrations. In the lower left a "steam lighter" receives the quarters and will transport them to where the meat will be sold in Market Hall, Cold Storage Wharf, Upper Thames Street, shown in the lower right. "American Beef for Old England," in *Harper's Weekly*, April 7, 1877, p. 277.

## FIRST NATIONAL CONVENTION OF CATTLEMEN AT ST. LOUIS, 1884

The article in *Harper's Weekly* reporting on the convention stated it was formed "as the time had come for a close and efficient organization of all the separate associations into a great deliberative body, whose delegates should meet at least once yearly for transaction of business." The main business was supporting a national cattle trail and the leasing of grasslands on the public domain. The illustrations show the convention in session, a parade of the "Mackerel" guards, and school children presenting a drum to the "Cow-boy Band (amateur)." Pictured also is the medal that the citizens of St. Louis gave to each delegate. It was this medal that McCoy proudly displayed to the editor of the *Wichita Eagle*. "First National Convention of Cattle-Men at St. Louis," from *Harper's Weekly*, December 6, 1884, p. 798.

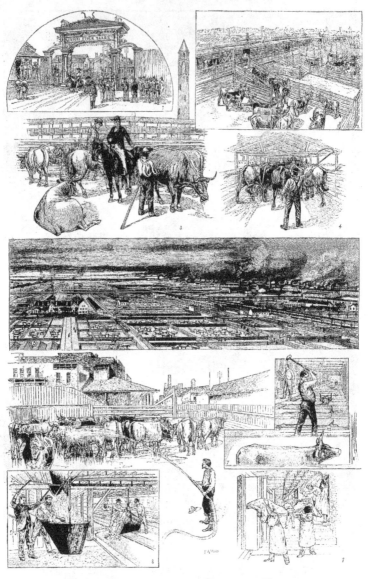

### CATTLE INDUSTRY OF CHICAGO, 1889

Refining many of the cattle marketing advances pioneered by Joseph McCoy, Chicago-based stockmen and slaughterhouse magnates such as Gustavus Swift and Philip Armour had come to dominate the cattle trade in the United States. As this illustration highlights, the Union Stockyards had become the largest in the world. Scenes are of (1) the entrance, (2) receiving cattle at the yards, (3) inspectors removing sick cattle, (4) the elevated roadways, (5) the yards and packing town from the water tower, (6) washing cattle for killing, (7) killing cattle, (8) packing refrigerated freight cars with ice, and (9) loading sides of beef into the freight cars. From *Frank Leslie's Illustrated Newspaper*, February 23, 1889, p. 33.

CHAPTER 7

# Confronting Fire and Ice

THE GREAT PRAIRIE FIRE DEBATE — INDIAN PEOPLES AND FIRE — FARMERS' FIRE STRATEGY — DROVERS AND PRAIRIE FIRES — OVERWINTERING PUT TO THE TEST: THE STORM OF 1871–1872 — THUNDER, LIGHTNING, AND HAIL

Experience taught Joseph McCoy that making money in the cattle business depended, in large part, on successfully contending with the vagaries of the natural forces that shaped the grasslands. McCoy regarded in particular prairie fires, one of the primal forces that sustained the grassland biome, as destructive to the trade. He saw no benefit derived from the flames that, prior to the arrival of American ranchers or farmers, had regularly swept the grasslands of North America. He numbered among many other ranchers and stockmen arriving on the grasslands who simply had no understanding of how grass fires preserved the treeless realm that sustained their trade in the first place. McCoy understood prairie fires only to be a "common" feature of the grasslands—in his mind, a force that ravaged the countryside.[1]

McCoy was most concerned for how prairie fires could affect the overwintering of cattle. Legislation in states such as Kansas, Missouri, and Illinois that were enacted as a result of the 1868 cattle plague had made overwintering a somewhat attractive, if not imperative stage, in the process of placing Texas cattle into eastern markets. But there had to be ample forage on the open range if cattle were to be kept on it over the winter. McCoy realized that an uncontrolled autumn prairie fire could, and at times did, destroy the prairie grass that fueled cattle on an open-range grazing ground through a winter. With effective fire guards in place, however, McCoy believed that "so long as there is no snow and the weather is fine, the cattle will get ample food on the range." When the weather turned snowy and freezing, herders needed to be sure that they had put up enough prairie hay to sustain their herds through the storm. During overwintering, if done well, a Texas bovine could gain weight and fat, and command a high selling price come the spring.²

McCoy also knew that overwintering could turn disastrous. A blizzard or freezing rain could force cattle to "fast longer than is profitable to the owner or consistent with the laws of life." More likely than not, McCoy had the winter of 1871–72 in mind when reflecting on how catastrophic overwintering could be for cattle, horses, herders, and stock traders. In November 1871, temperatures dipped below freezing, seldom rising above until February 1872. Ice and snow blanketed the plains, and cattle died by the thousands.

Not only could severe winter weather make a mess of herding cattle, thunderstorms could turn a rather uneventful trail drive into a nightmare. During such events, animals spooked and fled pell-mell in every direction. Sopping wet, hail-pounded cowboys had to round up animals no matter the location or the time of day or night.

If ever there were a drover who understood the combined perils of prairie fires, thunderstorms, and blizzards, it was Sol West. Eventually, West would become one of the wealthiest cattlemen in all of Texas. In his later years, he operated a thirty-thousand-acre spread in Jackson County, Texas. But his experience as the "youngest man who ever 'bossed' a herd up the trail" was anything but profitable. He had contracted with McCutcheon and West, a cattle company operating in Lavaca County, Texas, to drive a herd the company had assembled to Ellsworth. For his efforts, the firm offered Sol half the net profits. The first part of his drive north went without a hitch. He and his crew of cowboys, all under the age of twenty, started out in February 1874. Without any notable incidents, they crossed the Red River on March 1. Afterward, the drive through Indian Territory did not go so well.³

In the first week of April, Sol had led his cattle to Rush Creek, a small tributary to the Washita River. For some reason, he had taken a route several miles to the east of the main trail. Now, not more than one-third of the distance through Indian Territory, he encountered his first travail. As Sol recounted it, the Indians had burned off the range. For as far as he could see, the grasslands presented a forlorn black countenance. Fortunately for Sol, he had come upon a fork of the creek where the two streams had created a fire barrier. He kept his herd on this island of grass for a couple of days while he scouted ahead, looking for green pastures and water. He located a suitable site fifteen miles to the north on Hell

Roaring Creek (today known simply as Roaring Creek), and on April 8, he and his crew headed the herd hard toward greener pastures.

Before he reached his destination, however, Sol's situation turned from bad to worse. A cold front approached from the north, producing a misty rain that soon mixed with snow. Just as he reached the camp, which the cook had prepared in advance of the herd, a blizzard came on with increasing fury. At Fort Sill, south of where Sol was located, northerly winds had been increasing in velocity all throughout the day, and during the afternoon as a cold front swept across the land, the temperature dropped from 47 degrees to 39. By nightfall on April 8, Sol and his young men found themselves on a boundless grassland, completely exposed to a bone-chilling, hypothermia-inducing rain. Throughout the night, without recourse to any shelter, the outfit endured sustained rain now turned to sleet, and snows carried in winds between thirty and forty miles per hour that did not let up until after midnight. On April 9, the Fort Sill post surgeon recorded 33 degrees Fahrenheit as the low temperature for the day. Sol's outfit, even without the benefit of a thermometer, understood the cold put their herd and themselves in a precarious situation.

As soon as the northern gales hit them in the face, Sol's cattle turned in their tracks and headed south. Sol and his young crew had no option other than to stay mounted on their fatigued horses and try as best they could to keep the herd intact. Through that bitterly cold night, they lost many of their horses, and most of the cowboys found themselves drenched and afoot. By morning they had the herd "in check," but they were desperate for horses, as their remaining steeds had dropped due to fatigue and exposure. Sol hoped the "remuda" of sixty-five horses in the rear would reach them soon. These mounts were used every other day for herding so that, by alternating, the strength of the horses could be maintained through the duration of the drive. Two cowboys tended this herd. When Sol reached the hands, to his utter dismay he found them on foot. The entire horse herd had perished in the storm.

A day later, by trading with Jim Taylor, a local rancher, and with some local Indians, Sol managed to swap some steers for six horses and an ox. With this impoverished horse herd, he managed to get his cattle to Ellsworth on May 20. After selling the herd, he had to pay his cowboys and account for the loss of seventy-eight horses. Returning to Lavaca County, he provided all his receipts and expenditures to the accountant for McCutcheon and West, who happened to be his brother George. After George had paid the ranchers who had contributed cattle to the herd, and after all the expenses of the drive had been deducted from the profits of selling the herd in Ellsworth, George informed Sol that the firm had netted $1.50. Upon handing Sol his seventy-five cent share, George asked if he were going to buy his own herd or a bank. Sol probably found little humor in his brother's jest.[4]

## The Great Prairie Fire Debate

Like many cattlemen at the time, Sol West had little use for prairie fires. Still, so long as prairie grasses remained, prairie fires could and would flare up. During the years of the great Texas cattle drives, prairies fires raged as a great enigma for the people confronting them. Very few people had any idea of the ecological role the fires played in shaping and preserving the wild grasslands of North America. Enormous misconceptions about prairie fires existed among the people who studied and experienced them. A minority of observers correctly thought the fires, when properly used, had beneficial effects for farmers and ranchers alike. Other writers blamed Indians, farmers, careless travelers, and locomotives for setting the fires and creating the human woes that followed in their wake.

Samuel D. Houston, an avid abolitionist, who in the late 1850s helped found what would become the city of Manhattan, Kansas, believed himself on a divinely inspired mission. During "Bleeding Kansas," the violent struggle from 1856 to 1859 between proslavery and free-state forces over the fate of the state, he strove not only to eliminate the national blight of slavery but also to advance the cause of "civilization," which he defined as free men and women flourishing by transforming the grasslands into farmlands. In a letter written to the *Junction City* (Kansas) *Union* in 1869, he made it clear that prairie fires threatened all that he envisioned. As he put it, "The person who for any reason sets fire to the prairie grass, knowing it will extend itself, is an enemy of the State and a destroyer of the public good." Houston believed that prairie fires demolished the "productive value" of the land, and scarred and killed the earth's mantle that had been placed there by God for man's use.[5]

Houston blamed prairie fires on the settlers in the region. In the fall, some farmers plowed fireguards around their homes and outbuildings. Next, they set the prairie grass afire outside the rings surrounding their farmsteads to ensure that a prairie fire approaching from any other direction would leave their property unscathed. Houston had nothing but disdain for this practice and castigated any and all who used it. In an unmistakable reproof, he wrote that while one might save his own property from the flames with this practice, he would "lay in ruins the interest of others" and leave the land a blackened desert.[6]

Like many others at the time, Houston poorly understood, if not completely misunderstood, the ecological role prairie fires played in creating the grasslands. Contrary to the findings of grasslands ecologists today, he assumed that the fires laid bare the land, removing the cover that held the snow and rain, and in so doing destroyed "a considerable portion of the finest and best roots of the grass." Completely at odds with the findings of current ecological research, Houston proclaimed, "Let the fire be utterly discarded as the worst enemy of the grass land." Nonetheless, as contemporary grassland ecologists know, it is fire that maintains the grasslands.[7]

Houston's views found a ready forum in the *Junction City Union*, whose owner and editor harbored a similar opinion. On October 2, 1869, George Martin published an article portraying prairie fires as the enemy of Kansas and American progress. With a "forked tongue and bounding flame," Martin wrote, this destroyer of all that was good and wholesome would leave nature standing aghast and "in mournful strains sing the funeral requiem." Martin wanted to see anyone who set a match to the grass severely punished. Eliminate prairie fires, and "rich grass will so shade the earth from the scorching rays of the sun, that we shall have no more hot winds" and the earth would "fill with gladness, and make joyous the heart of man," he wrote. Prairie fires threatened any chance for happiness and prosperity to take root in the grasslands.[8]

On the same day that Martin published his prairie fire diatribe, Fort Riley post surgeon Major George Sternberg was carefully taking note of fires near Junction City and the post. He tracked the spread of the prairie fires a few miles to the northeast and southeast of where he stood. Sternberg had an excellent view of this unfolding conflagration during what was otherwise a pleasant autumn day, with temperatures in the upper 60s, not a cloud in sight, and a soft breeze blowing out of the southwest. By the next day the winds had shifted out of the north, and the prairie fires had assumed an ominous character. On October 4, when Sternberg made his daily meteorological observations, he remarked, "Prairie fires in every direction." On October 8, rains dampened the fires, and by midmonth, cooler weather prevailed, with Sternberg recording the first snowfall of the season on October 19. The weather moderated and warmed up considerably by the end of the month, and on October 27, with the temperature reaching into the 80s, Sternberg monitored a prairie on fire "in every direction day and night." Smoke filled the skies and persisted until strong westerly winds had cleared the haze by Halloween.[9]

Sternberg kept a daily meteorological record because the army required all post surgeons to do so. He made his first observation at 7 A.M., his second at 2 P.M. and his third at 9 P.M. Each time he noted the temperature, the direction and force of the prevailing winds, the amount of cloud cover, and precipitation in inches of rain or inches of melted snow. The last column in the monthly form left room for remarks. Sometimes post surgeons made insightful comments, and when they did, they often took note of unusual events such as the prairie fires that had enthralled Sternberg.

For his time, Sternberg was exceptionally well qualified not only for his duties as post surgeon but as a careful scientific observer of his surroundings. He had earned his medical degree in 1860 and practiced medicine in New Jersey until he joined the Union Army as an assistant surgeon in 1861. He participated in the first Battle of Bull Run, was captured, escaped, took part in the Peninsular Campaign, contracted yellow fever, recovered, and completed his wartime duties in hospitals. After the Civil War, the army assigned Sternberg to Fort Harker and later to Fort Riley, Kansas. While accompanying Major General Philip Sheridan's pacification operations across the High Plains in 1868, Sternberg took note of Indian peoples' habits and found time to excavate fossils of extinct sea creatures in the chalk beds of western Kansas. Through publications of his findings, Sternberg gained a national reputation as a first-class natural historian.

Sternberg not only observed and recorded prairie fires but also contributed erroneous commentaries on the nature of grass fires. He characterized the grasslands of central and western Kansas and eastern Colorado as "sterile." As reasons for this barren state, he listed a lack of rainfall, sparse plant coverage, few trees, and annual prairie fires. He viewed these factors as interwoven. He argued that if any one of these forces were eliminated, the hostile grassland environment would unravel and become conducive to the advance of "civilization."[10]

Sternberg singled out prairie fires. He asserted they destroyed the vegetative cover of the plains, impoverished soils, annihilated trees, and even consumed buffalo chips. He made a point of saying that when "the Indian has ceased to roam over the plains, one great cause of the prairie fires will be removed."[11] As Sternberg saw it, the ultimate blessing in ridding the plains of Indian peoples, and thereby preventing prairie fires, was the creation of a pathway for the emergence of wheat and corn production, which promised lucrative returns far greater than those from raising cattle and sheep. In short, Sternberg hoped prairie fires could be eradicated altogether.

When George Martin reported on the extent of the fire that Sternberg had noted on October 27, 1869, he wrote that it was "the most extensive ever known in this country." Martin continued, "The fire raged fifty miles up the Republican [River], and equal distance along the Smoky Hill, and south to beyond the Cottonwood." The flames consumed thousands of tons of hay and covered over one hundred square miles. Martin's reporting seemed to confirm Sternberg's worst fears.

## Indian Peoples and Fire

Amid the dominant fumbling of the likes of Martin and Sternberg, a few people were beginning to understand prairie fires in a manner that presaged the thinking of modern ecologists.[12] Illinoisan John Davis ventured to Junction City with the intention of transforming the wild grasslands through the planting of trees. By 1869 he had become enamored with the countryside and began establishing a business in Junction City. He still had a home in Decatur, Illinois, where he was well regarded as an accomplished horticulturalist, and he was acquainted with some of the leading lights of the American scientific community. His wife, Martha Ann, was the sister of John Wesley Powell, an acclaimed explorer of the American West, and one of the founders of the National Geographic Society in 1888. John and Martha, with eight children in their household, owned a prosperous farm in Decatur County valued at about $20,000 in 1870. Their operation specialized in raising and selling grapevines, evergreen trees, fruit trees, and a variety of "timber trees" appropriate for planting on the prairies. By September 1869 he had bought three-quarters of a section of land a few miles outside Junction City, where he established a nursery.[13]

Davis commanded respect in both Illinois and Kansas for his horticultural expertise. In Junction City he provided the trees for the fledgling city park. By April 1870 he had donated over 160 trees, including five species of evergreens and more than thirteen species of deciduous trees along with several types of roses and other bushes. In Illinois he had a reputation for a "rare ability to instruct others," and the state appointed him a member of the committee that reported on the progress of the Industrial University at Champaign (the future University of Illinois). After moving to Kansas in 1873, he was elected president of the Farmers' Co-operative Association.[14]

Like Sternberg, Houston, and Martin, Davis turned his attention to the nature and control of prairie fires, but he contributed very different insights than those of the other three contributors to the *Junction City Union*. True, he agreed that prairie fires could be highly destructive and a hindrance to the advance of civilization. In particular, he sought to end autumn fires, as in his view they did nothing more than leave the land bleak and naked. Moreover, as any cattleman would attest, these fires deprived free-range grazing cattle of "much valuable food, which, in protected localities, would remain green most of the winter." Worse, the fires "circumscribed, thinned, and eventually destroyed" the growth and spread of trees.[15]

Nonetheless, Davis described setting prairie fires in the fall, prior to the arrival of European Americans to create the state of Kansas, as a "heroic farming" practice of Indian peoples. He explained these practices in terms unlike those of any other writer who addressed prairie fires at the time:

> The wild game of the country is his crop. Autumnal fires were his reapers, to aid in collecting and harvesting. Much evil was done; also some good. Let us examine the matter a moment.
>
> Indian countries are *clean* countries. No muddy roads for want of men and vehicles to travel them. No underbrush or decayed logs and rubbish in their woods, for the annual fires clean up everything, leaving but the greenest trees with thick bark. . . . This style of farming is exhaustive and destructive tending to sterility where sterility is possible.
>
> Yet, though he exhausts the surface and banishes the rains, the Indian does not exhaust the soil *below* the surface, for he does not stir it. And in destroying everything and feeding nothing, he invariably delivers his country into the hands of white men, free from those noxious insects, which prey upon the grains and fruits of civilized culture.

One might think that Davis opposed setting the prairies on fire; on the contrary, he made a case for burning—just not in the fall but in the early summer.[16]

He warned that the suppression of fires with the "departure of the Indian" left an emerging timber culture and domesticated crop production susceptible to the proliferation of insects. Americans, Davis advised, must "not entirely abandon [Indians'] heroic treatment of the country." Burn the prairies in June, he recommended, as the fires are "easily managed because the green grass mingled with the dry moderates their progress." Davis promised that those who followed this practice would soon find a land covered by a "new coat of verdure." He recommended making May and June the "cleaning up time." Davis asserted that those who prepared for planting by plowing fields in the fall, and burned the grass in the spring, would find rich and abundant grass in the early summer. Trees would flourish, and crops would blossom free of insect infestation.[17]

The insights of one other man who wrote about fire caught the attention of some Kansas newspaper editors. Joaquin Miller's highly publicized exploits ranged from the notorious to the sublime. He had a reputation as a womanizer and as an advocate for the Indian peoples living in the Pacific Northwest and the Sierra Nevada Mountains. He also had a well-established standing as a poet and playwright. More germane to our story, in an 1882 issue of *The Independent* (New York City), Miller had penned a widely circulated piece on the virtues of the annual burning of forests and prairies.

As modern ecologists have recognized, Miller observed that an "annual fire is as natural and necessary, too, as is a rainfall at seedtime." He emphasized the value of annual forest fires, but he also noted the beneficial effects of annual prairie grass fires, and the role Indian peoples played in setting these fires. In Miller's words, autumn was "the time the Indian takes to clear off his fields for the grasses of the coming spring, and to purify them" for the advent of "the new grasses, flowers, roots, and ground fruits for the coming year." As Miller saw the situation, the prevalence of destructive insects lay with the "white man's . . . mismanagement of our plains and forests."[18]

Not surprisingly, the editor of the *Saline County Journal* (Salina, Kansas), took great exception to Miller's contention. Holding the same attitude about the virtues of prairie fires as did most contemporary commentators, the editor argued that setting the prairies on fire made as much sense as setting a farmer's barn on fire to rid it of rats and mice. The result of purposefully setting fires "by following the barbarous practices of the red man" would simply render the land "uninhabitable." Cattlemen lined up with the editor unequivocally. Farmers often practiced setting fires—but more for the protection of their property than for any ecological benefit.[19]

## *Farmers' Fire Strategy*

Farmers held ambivalent views about prairie fires. On the one hand, and with good reason, they feared the destructive force of a conflagration sweeping down on their homes and animals. So it was the wildfire they feared the most. On the other hand, farmers often employed controlled fires as a tool to protect their property. Sometimes these "controlled" blazes got out of hand and became wildfires. Regardless of whether the fires remained controlled or not, the ultimate goal was to promote the farming interests of the state to the exclusion of ranching, especially the open-range grazing practices employed by Texas drovers.

In early winter 1872, the Reverend Levi Sternberg, addressing the Farmers' Institute at Manhattan, Kansas, held that the farmer was the "guardian" of the nation's welfare, or, as he concluded, "the very paragon of humanity." Reverend Sternberg was no ordinary guest speaker. He was the father of Major George Sternberg, eventually the US Army's surgeon general, and a renowned paleontologist. Under the influence of George, who had served as post surgeon at both Fort Riley and Fort Hays, the reverend and his wife, Margaret, had moved from Iowa to take up farming near Ellsworth, Kansas. They both became enamored with their surroundings, and the reverend made it his passion to displace the "nomadic habits of mere herdsmen" with the cultivation of the soil.[20]

Reverend Sternberg made an impassioned plea for "mixed husbandry" on the central grasslands. He offered "hints" on how to achieve this goal, one of which was to improve soil productiveness. Before this could happen, however, prairie fires had to be eliminated. He blamed prairie fires for destroying young timber and consuming the "mulch and manure that nature" had spread over the land. "So to farm as to diminish the productiveness of the soil"—to not eradicate fire—was "a crime against humanity," he intoned, as it degraded the means of human subsistence.[21]

Reverend Sternberg could not have given a stronger defense of Jeffersonian agrarianism unless a reincarnated Thomas Jefferson had stood by him. Sternberg, and other like-minded farming proponents, believed that eliminating prairie fires would allow for the division "of the soil among a large number of proprietors, each cultivating his own land and surrounding himself with the comforts of home and elegances of life." The "boundless waste" of the grasslands could be redeemed so that civilization could thrive where once "savage beasts, and still more savage red men" had roamed. Moreover, the virtuous farmer would render the state more prosperous than if "Texas cattle covered our prairies like the locusts of Egypt."[22]

## Drovers and Prairie Fires

If Texas cattlemen did not agree with Reverend Sternberg that cattle were like locusts, they did agree with his opposition to prairie fires. They saw no value in setting the grasslands ablaze while driving cattle north or when grazing their herds in the central grasslands for any protracted length of time. Put simply, they had yet to understand the ecological benefit of fire in sustaining the wild grasslands. Rather, cattlemen understood that fires could depress cattle prices, destroy rangeland, and in extreme cases result in widespread death for their cattle, their horses, and themselves. Such experiences shaped a cattleman's abhorrence of prairie fires and left him unable to recognize any benefit that its flames might have in protecting a farmstead or sustaining the grasslands upon which the cattle depended.

Texans understood just how vulnerable cattle were to prairie fires. When cattle were caught in prairie fires that suddenly swept down on them while grazing on the grasslands of the open range, the results proved deadly. The Rees brothers experienced just how vulnerable cattle could be. In November 1867, the brothers had a herd of 250 cattle grazing on a divide between the Solomon River and Salt Creek. An autumn fire raced along this ridgeline and suddenly swept down on the unsuspecting herd. In short order, at least 150 animals perished horribly, the fire blinding them as they stood still until they died. Nearly as bad as the animal loss was the fire's destruction of hay mounds, leaving the settlers without winter feed for their stock.[23]

Even grass fires on the short-grass High Plains could prove deadly to cattle. In December 1885, reports from Mobeetie, Texas, in the east-central Panhandle, told of the loss of cattle to wildfires sweeping the region. One observer wrote about how common it was to "see cattle that have been overtaken by the fires wandering around with strips of baked flesh hanging in strips from their bodies, and their eyesight destroyed."[24] No ranchman ever wanted to see his herd suffering in that condition, and understandably he would take every precaution possible to avoid such a fate.

At the same time that Sternberg made his observations of the prairie fire of October 1869, cattle had flooded eastern markets, and at Abilene, prices had dropped sharply by the end of the month. In such situations, many Texas cattlemen responded by keeping their herds out on the open grasslands over the winter. They could, they thought sensibly, anticipate higher prices in the first months of spring, several weeks before any Texas herds could reach Abilene or any other shipping points on the Kansas Pacific or Union Pacific Railroad. This was the option that several Texas cattlemen opted for in the fall of 1869.

Several Texas cattlemen opted to overwinter in Kansas, but an abundance of prairie fires in that particularly dry fall of 1869 complicated the wisdom of their decision. The *Leavenworth Times* reported that although the Indians had formerly "kindled most of our prairie fires," now it was trains. The embers flying out of the smokestacks of locomotives set the "worst fires."[25]

Texas drovers who were tending several herds near or around the Kansas Pacific line many miles west of Abilene experienced several fires in mid-October that blazed over the lush grasslands near the rails. Still, enough grazing lands remained untouched to sustain the herds until a few days before the end of the month, when the situation worsened considerably. A "grand conflagration broke out," reported the *Junction City Union*, "which swept the prairie for twenty miles, consuming all grass for an immense distance."[26] Other reports revealed an even greater reach of the fires. In Saline County, the flames consumed grasslands along the south banks of the Saline River and Gypsum Creek. At Fort Riley, Major Sternberg observed how the fire initially swept to the north and east of the post but changed course to the south and west and came dangerously close to Junction City. From Riley County came reports of the fire advancing ten miles *against* the wind along Wildcat Creek in a twenty-four-hour period.[27] From as far west as Ellsworth came the story of that "bane of our country, the 'prairie fire,'" which was "devastating everything combustible" in its path.[28] This autumn fire of 1869 left a wide swath of blackened prairie and property reduced to ashes.

Texans immediately blamed Kansas dealers for setting the blaze. Given the destruction of the rangeland, they seemed to have few options and began unloading their herds for whatever the market might return. The editor of the *Junction City Union* questioned whether traders had intentionally started the blaze. Regardless of who had set the fire and for what reasons, the effects resulted in herds changing hands "at greatly reduced prices in consequence of the scarcity of feed occasioned by the fire." As the Texans saw it, better to sell well-fed beeves at a low price than to risk having to sell starved, gaunt animals in the spring.[29]

As the cattlemen understood all too well, prairie grass was the "free" fuel powering their herds. The profitability of the cattle trade required an abundance of this grass and access to it. Lacking either assured desiccated if not dead cattle, and great economic losses to cattlemen. An autumn prairie fire could, and often did, destroy a grazing ground in an instant and turn dollars to ashes.

One other variant in the grassland ecosystem—persistent freezing winter conditions—combined with prairie fires to cause even greater devastation to open-range cattle grazing. When asked what were the industrial pursuits on the plains in the winter of 1871–72, Reverend Sternberg had this response: "I should have replied that the chief pursuit of the people is skinning Texas cattle." He recounted how cattle had died by the hundreds, and those who had investments in those herds were ruined.[30]

## *Overwintering Put to the Test: The Storm of 1871–1872*

By late fall of 1870, stock prices were flat at Abilene, and despite the difficult weather affecting grazing on the open grasslands during the summer and fall, drovers and local farmers began considering overwintering approximately 350,000 beeves in anticipation of better prices in the spring of 1871. Previous experience indicated that such a strategy could prove profitable. In the *Abilene Chronicle*, Joseph McCoy, using the pseudonym "Ibex," encouraged farmers to buy unsold cattle in the fall and to winter the animals on prairie grasses. By early spring, Ibex predicted, farmers could double or triple their investment. Better yet, Ibex cheerily proclaimed, this strategy required "little labor and care." McCoy boasted that farmers who had pursued such a strategy the winter before had had ready cash to spend all year long as a result.[31]

A reporter for the *Kansas State Record* (Topeka) encouraged farmers to do likewise. They should "buy as many of these cattle as [they] can winter," the writer urged.[32] By the spring of 1871, the excitement caused by the cattle plague of 1868 had largely calmed, and drovers had become more accustomed to the legislation passed by several states limiting the importation of Texas cattle. Most laws allowed a Texas herd to enter a state during the winter subject to certification that it had been overwintered before entering the state. This resulted in the largest cattle drives to date, with more than 300,000 head of cattle driven north out of Texas. When cattle markets quickly became glutted, prices fell to the point that it became unprofitable to buy cattle at outlets such as Abilene. The recourse for most herd owners was to overwinter their livestock and hope for a rebound of prices in the spring. The winter of 1871–72, however, proved that Ibex's advice was a horrible investment strategy that season.

First of all, McCoy's assertions to the contrary, wintering a large cattle herd required hard work. Drovers had to pick a suitable location, one with reliable water, good grass, and protection for work hands during inclement weather. Often, drovers picked riparian ecosystems in the middle and western extents of the Solomon, Smoky, Saline, and later, Arkansas River Valleys. Cowboys carved dugouts in the sides of stream banks, where they would while away long winter nights. Those fellows also had to cut, cure, and stack riparian grasses for winter feed to supplement cattle grazing on the short buffalo grass. Typically, cowboys stacked about a ton of hay per animal. Protecting herds meant building a fireguard, a large circular area where they could drive and mill herds in case of a prairie fire. Cowhands also had to stockpile their own food and supplies and all the corn and oats necessary to keep their horses alive.[33]

Almost as if on schedule, fire made its annual appearance on the bluestem prairies that fall of 1871. As Reverend Sternberg described the situation, "The cattle range south [of the KP line] was mostly burned off, and [the cattle herds] were crowded into [Ellsworth] county in countless multitudes."[34] This forced drovers farther west onto the short-grass plains than they would have preferred. Moreover, many of these drovers, lacking contracts for their beeves, had taken the risk of grazing their animals on their own accounts. As noted in the *Abilene Chronicle*, the autumn fires in the Solomon River Valley alone had reduced the grazing potential to a mere ten thousand animals, but drovers had packed three times that many into the region.[35] In short, poor grazing conditions and weak markets left men and cattle in a precarious situation. It was a disaster in the making, and disaster arrived with vengeance.

November began with temperate weather across the central Kansas grasslands. Assistant surgeon John Janeway at Fort Hays recorded mild temperatures—highs between 42 and 74 degrees—for the first half of the month. A couple of rainstorms drenched the area, but most days were sunny. No one could have anticipated the arrival of three months of killing cold and blizzards.

On November 17, the temperature fell throughout the day from 25 degrees in the morning to 10 degrees by 9 P.M. The winds blew out of the northwest with speeds approaching sixty miles per hour. First, sleet coated the entire region,

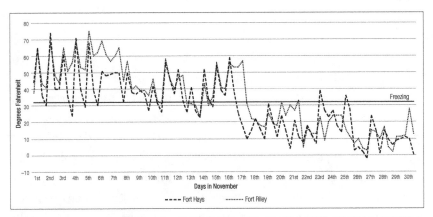

CHART 5. TEMPERATURE RANGE, FORT HAYS AND FORT RILEY, KANSAS, NOVEMBER 1871. The post surgeons' weather records taken at Forts Hays and Riley show just how brutal the blizzards of 1871–72 were.

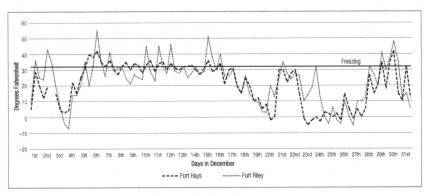

CHART 6. TEMPERATURE RANGE, FORT HAYS AND FORT RILEY, KANSAS, DECEMBER 1871.

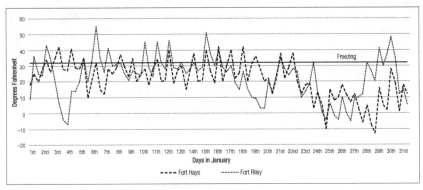

CHART 7. TEMPERATURE RANGE, FORT HAYS AND FORT RILEY, KANSAS, JANUARY 1872. Some herds on the open range had a death rate of over 90 percent during the blizzards of 1871–72. Yet it took the blizzards of 1885–86 and of 1886–87 to convince stockmen that open-range grazing over a winter was an iffy proposition at best.

followed by a snowstorm. Janeway reported at least six inches of snow at Fort Hays, with the wind whipping it into drifts two to five feet deep.[36]

From Concordia came reports of a storm that had "perhaps never been equaled in severity and suffering for years past." Bison hunters returning with their harvest of meat and hides encountered the same pounding sleet, snow, and high winds. One group sought shelter in the open as best they could, but by Saturday morning on November 18, they found themselves in a draw covered by more than four feet of snow. They joined with another small party and carved out a small dugout into which nine men crowded, trying to keep warm. During the storm, which finally abated on Sunday morning, they could hear the gunshots of others who were struggling in the freezing cold to find a place of rescue. Several buffalo hunters, who considered November the best month to hunt, paid the ultimate price with their lives.[37]

At the end of November, another severe storm pounded the region to the west of Junction City. On November 26, temperatures at Fort Hays fell to below 5 degrees, and on the morning of the 27th, when Janeway read his thermometer, the mercury indicated a bitter minus 2 degrees Fahrenheit. Soldiers left the fort in an attempt to rescue ten bison hunters, but four of the hunters died of exposure nonetheless. Stage passengers on the Smoky Hill route reported passing someone whose legs were sticking up through a snowdrift, but the stage driver did not stop to see who it was. In another instance, someone spotted a mule walking around in a circle on the open grassland; upon closer observation, it turned out that the mule was circling his owner, who lay frozen on the ground.[38]

The weather records at both Fort Riley and Fort Hays showed unremitting below-freezing conditions for the months of November and December 1871. Even though, as elsewhere, mild weather prevailed during the first half of November, with highs at posts recorded in the upper 40s, 50s, and 60s, everything changed on November 17. That day a blast of cold air greeted Janeway when he took his morning readings at Fort Hays. Just the previous day, he had enjoyed a warm, nearly 60-degree afternoon, but by the next morning, the mercury in his thermometer had plummeted to a mere 25 degrees, and it continued to fall to a frigid 17 by 2 P.M. and a downright cold 10 degrees by 9 P.M. During the rest of the month, Janeway recorded temperatures above freezing on only two days, his 2 P.M. reading on the 23rd and his 2 P.M. reading on the 25th.[39]

At Fort Riley, the cold snap began one day after its arrival at Fort Hays. On

November 19, Assistant Surgeon L. V. Loring failed to record any temperature above 19 degrees during the entire day. And for the rest of the month, he never once recorded a temperature above freezing.[40]

Conditions worsened in early December when one storm caused large herd losses in the Solomon Valley, just north of Abilene. News reached Junction City that seven hundred beeves out of a herd of nine hundred had perished. Making matters worse, sleet fell and collected as a solid sheet of ice two to three inches thick, effectively denying the cattle any fodder and water. Strong gales made it impossible for cowboys to bring their wind-driven herds to where they had hay stored and water sources freed from ice.[41]

The month of December proved equally brutal for both humans and cattle. A brief respite in the temperatures occurred during the middle of the month, but they tumbled again on December 16 and remained below freezing until the 29th. Christmas produced anything but a joyful day for soldiers at both posts, who struggled to keep warm in the lowest temperatures recorded during the entire month. The high at Fort Hays reached a bone-chilling 3 degrees, while at Fort Riley, temperatures were little better, with Loring recording 6 degrees for the high at 2 p.m.[42]

By the end of December, the losses incurred during the first stages of this freezing weather began to become apparent. From Ellsworth came reports of extreme human suffering and stock losses. One unfortunate fellow wandered for four days in a storm, and although he lived through his ordeal, he ended up losing both legs below the knees to frostbite. Only a small portion of the herds had been lost in the first wave of sleet and snow, but toward the end of the month, another onset of heavier sleet and snow covered the ground several inches deep. Cattle scattered everywhere to seek shelter, especially in ravines, and as reports filtered in to the editor at the *Ellsworth Reporter*, frozen carcasses filled those same draws. The editor predicted losses to stockmen "in the hundreds of thousands," if not a full 100 percent, should the streams and grasslands remain frozen, which they did.[43]

This blizzard lasted for a full three days and killed thousands of cattle, hundreds of horses, and several cowboys. Herd owners suffered staggering losses. McCoy estimated that more than 250,000 cattle perished. One firm working in the Republican River Valley began with more than 3,900 head; by the spring, cowboys found only 110 head of the herd remaining. Many drovers later stripped the hides from their dead cattle, and that spring they shipped more than 100,000 hides to eastern markets.[44]

In the middle of February came reports of the losses in Chapman Creek Valley, about ten miles east of Abilene. Drovers had placed three herds in the valley, and each herd had numbered about 300 animals. In one herd, 180 cattle had died; in the other two, 175 and 107 had perished respectively.[45]

Severely cold weather continued to plague drovers and their herds even into the spring. In April, a snowstorm blew through Hugo, Kansas, where the Kansas Pacific locomotives drove through cuts in the hills. Cattle swarmed into these cuts to escape the cold and blowing snow and froze to death there. Train crews had to remove scores of carcasses before they could proceed.[46]

The full effect of the winter began appearing as the severity of the storms began to subside. By early February, reports from Lawrence, Kansas, noted the "large number of hides" offered there. The hides, so the story went, had arrived from the west, where Texas cattle had "perished by hundreds and thousands." In March, a terse article in the *Leavenworth Times* described a peculiar spring harvest, a "large number of hides." The freight agent for the Kansas Pacific reported that two to four carloads of cattle hides passed the depot daily. In the Solomon Valley, where scores of herds had perished, workers dug a grave in April measuring forty feet long, eight feet deep, and eight feet wide. Into it they buried "several hundred poor Texas cattle."[47]

By any measure, cattlemen endured immense losses in cattle and capital. D. B. Long, who would later become the first Kansas fish and game commissioner, took exception to those who tried to gloss over the staggering cattle carnage. Some had claimed that a mere 1 percent of the overwintered cattle had died. Long knew better; this claim was completely unfounded, if not an outright lie. He estimated, for example, that more than half of the animals overwintered in Ellsworth County had died. And between November 1871 and May 1872, some thirteen thousand hides had been shipped east. In short, Long learned that "we must provide shelter and forage for stock if we will make stock raising pay." He calculated that at least a ton of hay and ten bushels of grain were required for each cow, steer, or bull kept over the winter in the region. He believed that stockmen must break up the prairies, sow tame grass, plant grains, and build shelters for grazing herds. Unless animals were kept this way, Long assured his readers, "we cannot raise stock with any assurances."[48]

## Thunder, Lightning, and Hail

If it were not distressing enough to be caught in the grip of a prairie fire or in the embrace of a howling blizzard, cowboys also dreaded being in the open prairies entrapped unaware in a pounding thunderstorm. Texas cowboys had their own way of describing what it was like. When lightning supercharged the atmosphere with electricity, it could, and did, produce phosphorescent glows in the grass, and even sometimes what appeared to be rolling balls of plasma coursing over the prairie. Cowboys called this phenomenon "fox fire," and during a stormy night it would often light up the tips of a cattle's horn. As electricity filled the air, and as fox fire danced between the horns of panicking cattle during a midnight "goose drownder" (a deluge) accompanied by skull-splitting hail, all made for an unforgettable if not deadly experience out on the trail.

Joseph McCoy, who described herding as a "cheerful, lively and pleasant" occupation so long as the weather remained good, empathized fully with the cowboy's plight in such circumstances. When, as McCoy said, the "night is inky dark and the lurid lightning flashes its zig-zag course athwart the heavens, and the coarse thunder jars the earth, the winds moan fresh and lively over the prairie, the electric balls dance from tip to tip of the cattle's horns," then the life of a cowboy turned anything but "romantic." Terrified herds would stampede across the prairie during the storm, and cowboys risked life and limb riding their horses hard in their efforts to pacify scattered longhorns and reestablish the herd.[49]

E. A. Robuck, known to his sidekicks as Berry, once had a herd of 2,800 beeves in the Smoky River Valley. He recollected a violent spring storm with strong winds and hail that whipped his herd into a stampeding frenzy and sent the animals off in every direction across the open grasslands. Robuck had no protection from the hail, which literally pounded his hat apart. Through the duration of the storm well into the night, he labored to round up the herd. Exacerbating his effort was fox fire. As he described the phenomenon, "The lightning played all over the horns of the cattle and the ears of my horse." By morning, he counted himself fortunate to have lost only one hundred animals to the storm.[50]

In 1891, G. W. Scott helped tend a herd gathered in the early spring and then headed to White Lake, New Mexico. The difficulties of driving this herd remained indelibly etched in his memory. The outfit started out with 2,178 two-year-old steers, and throughout southern Texas, the cattle, as well as horses and cowboys, suffered from dry conditions. In the Panhandle of Texas, when they reached Yellow Horse Draw,[51] a sudden chill followed by a pounding hailstorm resulted in severe cases of hypothermia among men and animals. Once the storm had abated, thirst, hail, and cold had killed nearly one thousand beeves out of the original herd.[52]

In 1879, G. W. Mills of Lockhart, Texas, worked a herd for M. A. Withers, one of the more successful Texas cattlemen. The herd had not been on the trail heading north for long when, on April 22, "a terrible rain" started falling at 4 P.M. and did not let up until the following morning. Mills remembered nearly "freezing to death" and seeing a number of the cattle and horses dying from exposure. It took the cowboys a few days to round up the hundreds of cattle that had drifted, following the direction of the storm.[53]

For some herders on the trail, the harsh rainstorms that pounded them on the trail simply became too much. Such was the case for J. C. Thompson. In the early spring of 1883, he rode with an outfit that rounded up a herd in the Salado River Valley in Mexico. It was a sixty-mile drive to the Rio Grande crossing near Laredo, a route largely lacking in sufficient water sources. Another forty miles to the north, a "regular blizzard," one preceded by a cold, drenching rain, came on at midnight. Typically, the cattle stampeded. Once the cowboys had quelled the excited animals, they counted more than 150 head having perished during the night. At this point, Thompson quit the outfit and, as he put it, "came back to the settlement."[54]

On August 12, 1868, while passing through the Canadian River Valley in Indian Territory, Jack Bailey recorded in his diary a terrible storm that rattled his herders, the women and children accompanying the drive, and all the cattle and horses. "Women [were] scared nearly to death," Bailey wrote, "children screaming." Dud Rogers, "the spunkiest man in the crowd when there is no danger," scampered up a tree and left the women to their fate on the ground below.[55] The next morning, Bailey, a self-confessed dull and drowsy guy, managed to keep pace with the herd before reaching the next campground a mere eight miles north of the mayhem.

Six days later, on August 18, another storm caught Bailey's outfit. Still in Indian Territory, Bailey discovered "the devil last night in shape of storm which lays over any thing of the kind I ever witnessed." His crew placed the herd in a grove of trees just as the storm broke over their heads. Bailey's tent blew down, and Annie, one of the women traveling with the outfit, cried for help to hold her tent in place. Children cried, and the women "scolded" them. The best Bailey could say for everyone was that by morning, they were "all cold wet + mad," but his herd had not scattered with the winds, as another nearby herd had done. The ground being far too wet to drive cattle, Bailey kept the camp up, dried everything out, and got ready to resume driving the following day.[56]

It was a rare drover, herder, or stock buyer or seller who did not have to contend with the vagaries of the climate. Understandably, they dreaded dealing with the aftereffects of any harsh encounter, some of which wrought economic ruin if not loss of animals and men. But there was yet another encounter that they dreaded even more than being caught without shelter in a pouring rain or having to hunker down in some dugout in a stream bank to wait out a blizzard in western Kansas. Drovers and cowboys regarded dealing with Indians as more troublesome than anything else that they endured while on the trail. Still, it was frequently the Indians in Indian Territory who suffered more.

CHAPTER 8

# Indian Cattle Travails

**CHEROKEE CATTLE — HORSE-BORNE, BISON-HUNTING CULTURE ON THE WANE — SUPPLYING GOVERNMENT CATTLE CONTRACTS — THE STRUGGLE TO CONTROL SOLAR ENERGY STORES — TOLLS, LEASES, AND LICENSES — INDIAN PASTORALISM**

Joseph McCoy was nothing if not resilient, given his many reversals of fortune. Always on the lookout for an opportunity to make a dollar, he took up a somewhat unusual occupation considering his views of Indians: the Cherokee Nation hired him to manage its cattle grazing tax. In December 1880, when the Cherokee National Legislature met, part of its agenda was to set policy for managing grazing rights on Cherokee land. Principal Chief Dennis Bushyhead instructed D. W. Lipe, the treasurer of the Cherokee Nation, to confer with Joseph McCoy "relative to Texas cattle grazing" in what was, at the time, variously called the Cherokee Outlet or the Cherokee Strip. During the session, McCoy met with a small committee appointed by Bushyhead, and the committee apparently worked out a contract that gave McCoy the authority to collect the grazing head tax levied on cattle in the Cherokee Outlet.[1]

By 1880, Indians living in present-day Oklahoma had begun making peace with the powerful cattle stockmen across their nation as well as with Texas cattle drovers and their drives through the outlet. By the end of 1880, nearly all the Five Civilized Nations had rebuilt their own cattle herds, which had been utterly destroyed during the Civil War. The Cherokee, Creek, Choctaw, Chickasaw, and Seminole Nations possessed nearly 300,000 cattle. Other tribes, such as the Osages, Kiowas, Comanches, Southern Cheyennes, and Arapahos, all labored to create cattle herds and exert control over their own grazing lands. The fledgling cattle operations of the Osages, Kiowas, and Comanches were reflected in the tiny herds each tribe controlled, respectively numbering 900, 1,089, and 500 head. Despite any advances in their livestock ventures, however small or large, cattle stealing and illegal grazing on Indian-"controlled" grasslands threatened the tribes' efforts.[2]

McCoy entered this picture when he became involved with the Cherokees' effort to rectify a bad situation. Many cattlemen routinely refused to pay any grazing fees levied by the Cherokee Nation. The fact that the federal government recognized the Cherokees' right to levy a grazing "tax" did not mean that the nation actually collected it. The situation had so worsened by the summer of 1880 that the federal government had threatened to use the army to evict any cattle owner who, without a permit, grazed his herd in the Cherokee Outlet. By December, the army had ordered Major Wordiman to patrol the Cherokee Outlet and to use "extreme measures" to remove nonpaying cattlemen who resisted expulsion. An owner could keep his herd on the land if he paid the Cherokee Nation a dollar per head, but many cattlemen apparently found that amount to be excessive.[3]

Before long the Cherokees concluded that receiving something was better than nothing. Someone like McCoy, a cattleman's cattleman, they thought, might have the standing to actually collect a grazing head tax, especially if it were reduced to forty cents per animal. McCoy, who at the time was enumerating cattle for the federal Census Bureau, took the job for a percentage of the funds he collected. What looked good on paper, however, did not work out so well in practice. By the end of July 1881, of about two hundred herds on the outlet, the owners of no more than forty had paid the Cherokee Nation. Through newspaper accounts in cities near the Cherokee Outlet, McCoy informed the loiterers to pay up or else be removed by the military if necessary.[4]

The question may be asked, why did McCoy take up this new occupation with the Cherokee Nation? After all, he seldom, if ever, had anything good to say about Indians, the several contractors who supplied the reservations, or the agents who oversaw the execution of cattle contracts. In his eyes, only Indians "excelled," his sarcastic term for "surpassed", the drunken behavior of the "half-civilized" cowboys who created mayhem in Kansas cattle towns. McCoy's descriptions of Indians mostly referred to their supposed propensity for "predatory and bloody" raids. He held in especially low esteem the Indians forced onto reservations. With their hunting cultures in shambles, they depended on receiving cattle issues, especially during the winter months. McCoy, who had probably never suffered from hunger, callously quipped that watching Indians butcher and eat beeves delivered under contract to a reservation "would perhaps go far towards dispelling that halo of sentimentality with which certain dreamy poets and maudlin writers have clothed the degraded, miserable beings." So again, why would McCoy undertake the collection of cattle taxes for the Cherokee Nation, especially given his close connections to David Payne?[5]

On the same day in July in 1881 that the *Arkansas City Weekly Traveler* printed McCoy's warning to cattlemen in the Cherokee Outlet to pay up, another article reported on "Oklahoma [David] Payne," who was in Texas to organize "another colony of dupes to again enter upon the lands in the Indian Territory"—the same land, the Cherokee Outlet, where Texas cattlemen had their herds. McCoy, a staunch Democrat like Payne, actively championed all of Payne's efforts to colonize the outlet with squatters. Over and over between 1880 and 1884, when Payne died, the army chased him and his followers out of the Cherokee Outlet, and Payne found himself in jail many times for leading filibuster operations in Indian Territory. Known as the leader of the "boomers," Payne met with constant defeats in the federal courts, especially with federal judge Isaac C. Parker, who made it clear to Payne and his minions that "no lands [in Indian Territory were] subjected to entry and settlement by citizens of the United States."[6]

Payne consistently argued that the land in Indian Territory was public domain, owned by the federal government, and hence the people, and as such was open to settlement. McCoy's support and friendship with Payne probably explains why McCoy's employment with the Cherokees lasted hardly two years. McCoy claimed that collecting the tax was in essence collecting for the federal government, an argument that would have "proved" that the outlet was indeed federally owned public domain rather than land under the sovereign control of the Cherokee Nation. McCoy's views would have certainly given the Cherokee government ample cause to fire him. By October 1882, the Cherokee Nation had replaced McCoy with George O. Saunders, a well-known Texas cattleman, and another man named Jordan (perhaps a trusted Cherokee) to collect the grazing fees levied on cattle in the Cherokee Outlet.[7]

Evidently, McCoy tried to play all sides in this contest to see who would control the land, and the stored solar energy in its grasses, in Indian Territory. On one hand, his actions seemed to undercut the rights of Texas cattlemen to contract with Indian nations for the privilege to graze their herds in the territory. Opening up the land for settlement as if it were public domain could place farming, not grazing, in the saddle. On the other hand, collecting the grazing head tax for

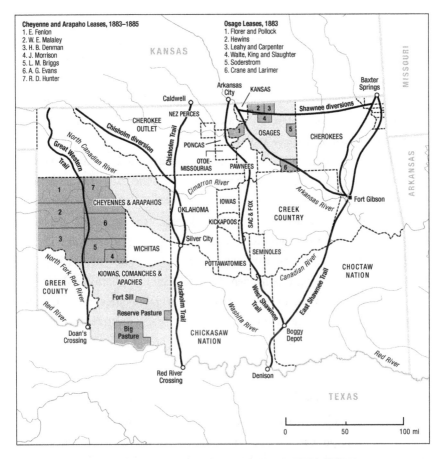

CATTLE TRADE NETWORK IN INDIAN TERRITORY

the Cherokees seemed to confirm their assertion of sovereignty over their lands, which meant that the land was not "public domain." If so, this gave the Cherokee Nation, and any other nation or tribe in the territory, the perfect legal authority to contract with cattlemen for an exclusive right to graze Indian-held land.

The key to understanding McCoy may lie in how he covered his bets on land speculation. Among many observers, it was an established fact that Payne and his like were speculators, not colonizers. McCoy may have thought that Indian Territory had room enough for both farming and ranching interests and that, if he positioned himself smartly, he could make a fortune in land speculation. McCoy seldom hesitated to place a bet on what he saw as an opportunity to make a dollar, much like the bet he placed on Abilene.

For anyone to invest in land speculation, however, the rightful occupants had to relinquish their control over their lands. Indians, whether citizens of one of the Five Nations or reservation wards, viewed things differently: the lands they occupied were theirs to govern. For a while the federal courts seemed to agree with them, and the army often enforced their rights. This was not some abstract struggle over a blot on a map; it was a campaign waged to see who would ultimately control the soil, grass, and water of the territory. By 1880, Indians had either made headway toward entering or had reentered the US cattle markets of the United States. But to fully realize the potential of the trade, they also had to control their solar and water resources. This meant their ecological relationships in the grasslands also underwent a dramatic change as they shifted from a horseborne, bison-hunting economy to a ranching and farming economy. Despite these gains, McCoy, and like-minded supporters of David Payne, the boomers, had no interest in seeing this happen. By 1900, through allotment legislation, Congress had stripped Indian control over their natural resources by dismantling their nations and reservations. For Indians, their efforts to participate in the cattle trade and large-scale ranching had come to an abrupt end.

## *Cherokee Cattle*

Joseph McCoy, like most cattlemen, employed the term "Cherokee cattle" to represent a type of bovine related to but distinct from Texas longhorns. Prior to being forced into present-day Oklahoma, Cherokees and Creeks had developed extensive cattle operations in the Blue Ridge Mountains in the Carolinas. The exact nature of the cattle that they bred and grazed using open-range herding practices is hard to trace, but certainly Iberian livestock imported by the Spanish largely dominated their herds. Incorporated into the mix were the "black cattle" that English colonists introduced into the Carolinas and that interbred with the Spanish line. In fact, "black cattle" were listed in a separate category in the Cherokee national census of 1824. In the 1840s when the Five Civilized Nations occupied present-day eastern Oklahoma, they had resumed their herding practices and any of the cattle they raised went by one classification: "Cherokee cattle."

By the 1850s, Cherokees and Creeks were well regarded for the quality of the cattle they raised. A *New York Tribune* reporter alluded to the developing market for this particular breed of cattle when, in July 1853, Ohio stockman Seymour G. Renwick shipped seventy-four Cherokee cattle into the New York markets. Not all the cattle showed a pure lineage to taurine and indicine cattle, the quintessential longhorn. The reporter noted that "these cattle are rather coarse, [and] many have the long horn peculiar to the 'Spanish Cattle'"; in essence, he observed that not all animals in the herd had "long horns," indicating that crossbreeding had occurred.[8]

Agent George Butler's annual report in 1857 highlighted the Cherokees' efforts to improve the quality of their herds by importing and crossbreeding their own cattle with "full and half-blood" stock acquired from Missourians. In the same year, the Cherokees sold thousands of cattle to the emigrants passing through their nation en route to California. It was this trade that helped to make such Cherokee men as Jesse Chisholm rich.[9] "Decidedly a stock raising country" is how agent Butler described the Cherokee Nation. In 1859, he thought that cattle raising had become the "leading occupation" among the "largest farmers." Butler reported 240,000 cattle owned by Cherokees, and it was not uncommon for "full-blooded" Cherokee women to own "most of the stock, and generally as much as their husbands."[10]

Prior to the Civil War, the Cherokees had introduced a few additional breeds into their herds. The federal government reportedly supplied cattle as part of the obligations of the removal treaties and annuity arrangements made with the Five Civilized Nations. It is not clear what breeds were introduced by those arrangements, but they were probably shorthorns. After the Civil War, the Cherokees began adding "Devon, Durham, and other improved breeds, resulting in herds of higher quality" than Texas longhorns. By 1870, a great many observers deemed Cherokee cattle to be superior to Texas longhorns. One account considered the cattle raised by the Cherokees, Creeks, Choctaws, Chickasaws, and Seminoles even "superior to the native cattle of Kansas and Missouri." Whereas a Texas rancher was lucky to receive $6 a head for longhorns driven north, a Choctaw rancher might command between $15 and $20 per head for a four-year-old steer.

Samuel Wilkison, a well-respected reporter for the *New York Tribune*, referred to the land the "Civilized Tribes" occupied as "the paradise of cattle breeders, who, with rare endowment of natural wealth, have the option any year to become cotton planters." Prior to the war, they supposedly were "so rich in herds that they did not know their wealth, and not use it. One of them was supposed to own 100,000 horned cattle and 20,000 horses and mules—but neither he nor his slaves knew exactly how many he had. Reportedly, numerous Cherokee farmers owned 10,000 head of stock."[11]

The Choctaws also occupied picturesque and productive land. As described in 1867, their realm included "beautiful table lands, heavily wooded, and oak openings, followed by prairie surface, which extends uninterruptedly south-westerly, with a gradual but continuous slope in the direction of the Texas frontier." Their antebellum farms, several of which were worked by slaves, abounded primarily in corn and cattle. One Choctaw farmer reportedly claimed that he had once sold eighteen thousand cattle for a mere one dollar per head. The great obstacle preventing Choctaws, and those in the rest of the Five Nations, from realizing the full potential returns on the cattle was difficult accessibility to midwestern or East Coast markets.[12]

Any antebellum gains in cattle raising came to an abrupt end during the Civil War, which produced nothing but suffering and destruction for the Five Nations. The plight of Jane Nave illustrates the utter ruin that befell many others living in the Five Nations. In December 1862, Daniel Ross, the nephew of John Ross, Cherokee principal chief, described to his uncle the utter ruination wrought by Stand Watie's Confederate command. "We have lost our all at home, nothing left. D. M. Gunter & Co. alone have had $100,000, merchandize, cattle, & money forcibly taken from them by [Stand] Waties men & the whites. Our houses have been pillaged & we are left destitute. . . . Mother [Elizabeth Ross] & [Eliza] Jane [Ross] have shared the same fate."[13]

In 1863, Jane Ross was well known in the Cherokee Nation, given that her father was John Ross and her stepmother Mary Stapler, the daughter of a prominent merchant family in Brandywine Springs, Delaware. Jane's second husband, Andrew Nave, had become a business partner with John Ross, and together the two men managed stores at Park Hill and Tahlequah, Cherokee Nation.

At the beginning of the war, John Ross appeared to side with the Confederacy. However, the defeat of Cherokee Confederate forces at Locust Grove in July 1862, and their desertion to the federal side, boded ill for Ross and Nave. Federal troops swooped into Park Hill, captured John Ross, and took him north. The Union troops, however, never gave Park Hill a high priority for protection and left it vulnerable to pillage, especially by the Cherokee Confederate forces led by Colonel Stand Watie, a longtime opponent of John Ross.

In October 1863, Jane still resided in Park Hill, where Andrew had abandoned attempts to maintain his mercantile business. Frequent raids in the area had endangered his life; consequently, he and his oldest son had taken refuge at Fort

Gibson. From time to time, he ran the risk of returning to Park Hill to see Jane. Andrew, as Jane described him at the time, was a "man of weakly constitution & in bad health." On October 28, 1863, Andrew was with Jane at Park Hill. The trip had worn him down, and he lay in bed feeling very ill. In the dead of night, "midnight assassins" surrounded their home, surprising Jane, Andrew, and the children. The marauders broke into the house, dragged Andrew outside, and shot him, then slashed his lifeless body with their knives. In complete distress, Jane watched as they sacked her home and robbed it of "every comfort," besides all clothing and bedding. Jane's youngest son escaped the carnage by "secreting himself in a chimney." Helpless, Jane had to endure the sight of her husband's "ghastly" mutilated body and of her house being put to the torch.[14]

The raiders did not stop with razing the Naves' home. Jane sorrowfully recalled how they burned John Ross's stately house to the ground during the same night. "Helpless women," she cried, "tender children were left that dark wintry [night], bare of clothing and houseless." As soon as she could, Jane gathered what was left of her worldly goods, her children, three of her brother's children, and her "loyal servants" (most likely house slaves), and headed north to find refuge at Fort Scott, Kansas. On the journey north, the youngest son of her brother's family fell ill and died; Jane grieved that he "now sleeps on a Kansian [sic] prairie near Ft. Scott."[15]

Jane found tragedy following her even as she sought safety near the post. Captain James Butler, the officer who had led the first raid on her home at Park Hill, found her again on a raid into Kansas. This time, his men robbed her of "*all that made life dear*," then rounded up the "servants," murdered all the men, "and carried women and children south." Again, she fled "the scene of all my woe" and made her way to Bethlehem, Pennsylvania, where her father, John Ross, lived in exile. There she stayed, tending five of her own children and the two remaining children of James, her oldest brother. Jane remained with her father until a year after the end of the Civil War, when he died on August 1, 1866.[16]

Nearly anyone living in those nations shared losses similar to Jane's. What was once a flourishing realm of livestock production devolved into a desolate landscape bereft of horses, hogs, sheep, and cattle. At the opening of the war, the leaders of the Choctaw and Chickasaw Nations had ratified agreements with the Confederacy. As a result, the "Union" faction suffered severely during the war. Article 49 of the 1866 reconciliation treaty, which the federal government compelled leaders of the Choctaw and Chickasaw Nations to sign, promised compensation to Union sympathizers who had suffered property losses during the war.[17]

Cyrus Harris, governor of the Chickasaw Nation, thought most, if not all, of the "Chickasaws, Loyal So Called have exaggerated there [sic] claims for lost property." Not surprisingly, Harris had supported the Southern cause, but in 1866, he found himself on the losing side and was now required to compensate his enemies within his own nation for their losses. Naturally, he was resentful when in July 1868, Congress appropriated $150,000 for the payment of claims made by the "loyal" Choctaws and Chickasaws.

Chickasaws such as William and Robert Patton had all their cattle and horses raided by "rebel Choctaws," in addition to seeing everything else they owned stolen. Ben Walls, among his claim of $4,763 in property losses, reported half of his small herd of twenty-five cattle stolen. Louisa Few, Willie Settle, and Celia Jacobs, each made a widow by the war, also suffered complete destruction of their homes and loss of livestock, as had Jane Nave. Among the Choctaws, Adam McCann claimed the loss of 400 head of cattle, James Elwood 25 head, John Ainsworth 30 head, Martin James 30 head, Simon Wolff 250 head, E. W. Rice 40 head, Se-no-wa 40 head, A. G. Griffith 450 head, and the brother-and-sister operation of Jane Belugshe and En-sa-te-her 220 head.[18]

Much of the loyal Choctaws' losses came in 1861. But other wholesale damages occurred in October 1864, when Confederate General Sterling Price, after his defeats at the Battles of Westport and Mine Creek, retreated south to the friendly confines of the Choctaw Nation. His "crippled and famishing army" wore out its welcome within a week as his men "collected all the corn in the nation, and either devoured or drove off its entire stock."[19]

By fall 1866, hardly any cattle remained among the Creeks, once known as the richest cattle-owning people among the Five Nations. In 1866, the Creek leadership contemplated enacting a law, "a despotic one, and prohibit, under penalty, the sale of cattle to traders" in an urgent effort to forestall widespread starvation.[20]

It would take another two decades before ranchers among the Five Nations would restore their cattle herds to their antebellum numbers. By 1875, an economic recovery was under way for the Cherokee Nation. Over 17,000 Cherokee citizens lived in the nation, and the total number of their cattle topped 103,000 head. Reportedly, all the people wore "citizens' dress" and lived in nearly 4,000 houses. The Choctaws, some 16,000 strong, managed more than 100,000 cattle.[21]

In another ten years, the citizens of the Five Nations had rebuilt their herds and homes to the pre–Civil War level. At this point, the Cherokee Nation, with a population of some 23,000 individuals, tended about 250,000 cattle in their herds, and the 18,000 Choctaws possessed 170,000 head of cattle. They appeared to have largely recovered from the devastating effects of the Civil War.[22]

## Horse-Borne, Bison-Hunting Culture on the Wane

The story of how the Plains Indians eventually took up ranching differs considerably from that of the Five Nations. For example, not long after the end of the Civil War, the Comanche and Kiowa Nations seemed to enjoy comfortable living. In the summer of 1866, they conducted successful bison hunts and stocked a good supply of meat for the winter ahead. Moreover, their take resulted in "large quantities of buffalo skins" for trade. During the winter, they remained in villages scattered along the Red River and its tributaries in a radius of about one hundred miles around the New Mexico–Texas border, and located their villages in well-wooded and well-watered river valleys. In the spring of 1866, agent Patrick Healy reported that a "luxuriant growth of grass" provided superb pasturage, and that on this range the Kiowas "raised large numbers of cattle and horses." The Kiowas and Comanches might have raised cattle to supplement their bison-meat supplies during the winter months. Interestingly, their cattle herding may also have indicated an effort on the part of a few moving away from a declining bison economy toward becoming cattle pastoralists.[23] As long as the bison herds held up, however, most Kiowas remained uninterested in cattle ranching.

One year later, the Medicine Lodge Treaty of 1867 changed all of this for the Kiowas. The treaty's terms constricted the Kiowas to a limited realm in the western portion of Indian Territory. There, along with other portions of Indian Territory set aside for the Comanches, Wichitas, Plains Apaches, Southern Cheyennes, and Arapahos, the federal government would pursue a policy of assimilation with the ultimate goal of transforming the Kiowas into Jeffersonian yeomen. This federal policy, no matter how well intended, failed to bode well for any of the nations bound by the treaty.

The halcyon days of bison hunting soon would fade away and be replaced with an effort to raise cattle. By the summer of 1874, when the Red River War broke out, James Haworth, the Kiowa agent, penned a letter to the commissioner of Indian affairs, E. P. Smith, about how easily his charges got around his prohibition against traders selling arms and ammunition to them. The traders on the reservation were livid because Haworth's restrictions put them at a disadvantage compared with traders at other agencies. Traders had acquired a mere five thousand robes from the Kiowa hunters, "while the Wichita trader got almost double that amount, the Cheyenne traders getting over thirty thousand, at least such" was Haworth's information. Although the Kiowas apparently had hunted and traded immense numbers of robes, white buffalo hunters took as many robes as they could, too. Not surprisingly, the numbers of bison plummeted quickly under this dual assault.[24]

The Kiowas adamantly opposed white bison hunters, and Haworth wrote that Kicking Bird and Big Bow of the Kiowas "had a good deal to say about white men killing their Buffalo." Perhaps Kicking Bird tried to put his concerns into words that a white man might understand, or perhaps he had already entered a full-blown market economy, one that made bison simply a natural resource subject to exploitation. Kicking Bird explained the situation this way: "Buffalo was the same to the Kiowas as the white man's money was to him. The Buffalo was their money, their only resource, with which to buy what they needed. . . . The robes they could prepare, and trade, they loved these just as the white man does his money." Kicking Bird demanded that Haworth write to the commissioner and have him put a stop to white men's robe hunting—a request that was ignored. But if the Kiowas could consider bison their money, then perhaps it would be an easy transition to get them to view cattle in the same way.[25]

By 1878, the federal government, through the agent on the Kiowa reservation, had made it a policy to put an end to bison hunting. Philemon B. Hunt, who took over as agent in February 1878, seemed dead set on enforcing the commissioner's directive. On the other hand, Lieutenant Colonel J. Davidson, the white commander of the Tenth Cavalry, in which the enlisted men, all African Americans, were called the "buffalo soldiers," made his view clear that any check on bison hunting violated the Medicine Lodge Treaty of 1867. A compromise of sorts was reached in which the Kiowas could hunt bison so long as an army escort attended the hunt to prevent trouble.[26]

By early January 1879, reports were flowing in from the hunting grounds that the Kiowa hunt had become desperate. The combined effects of white hide hunters and the Indian robe trade had already reduced the once magnificent herds to a scant remnant of their former glory. Quanah Parker and his Comanche hunters also went on this army-escorted hunt, and they decided to range far to the west of Indian Territory and yet found no bison and fell into starvation. The Kiowa expedition camped on Buck Creek, where, under horrible snowy and icy conditions, they tried to revive their horses among the riparian woodlands. Several famished hunters slaughtered some of their own horses for food.[27]

Captain Nicholas Nolan, the expedition's escort officer, assessed the dire situation. Despite the fact that the hunters often found themselves close to cattle herds and cattle ranches, federal law prohibited the army "from issuing any military supplies to Indians, and from contracting any liabilities through the purchase of cattle, even to save human life." Nolan decided to allow the hunters, under his escort, to head south deeper into the panhandle of Texas, to the Pease River Valley, where a few scattered, scanty herds of bison had been reported.[28]

With the Tenth Cavalry escort, the Kiowas crossed the Red River. While now beyond Indian Territory, eighteen Texas Rangers swooped down on White Cowbird, the brother of Chief Sun Boy, while he was alone and some distance from the camp. Rangers afforded no pity for any Indian found anywhere in Texas, and when they spied White Cowbird alone, they slaughtered him in cold blood, shooting him four times and then scalping him. They next sped toward the main camp but found themselves confronted by the African American cavalrymen escorting the hunters. The rangers decided not to confront Kiowa warriors and mounted buffalo soldiers, but resorted to heated insults before retreating to their homes without further incident. In the meantime, the army command had authorized a special agent to purchase rations for the hunters, who, empty-handed, eventually made their way back to Fort Sill.[29]

The Kiowas expected that the United States would seek justice for White Cowbird's murder. Mollified by this belief, "they molested no one" on their return to Fort Sill. As General John Pope reported, the Kiowas "did not even kill cattle from the great herds around them, though in the last stages of want and suffering." Regardless, a year before McCoy sealed arrangements with the Cherokees to collect their cattle taxes, an era of bison hunting had come to an end for the Comanches, Kiowas, and other Plains Indians.[30]

The annual report of the commissioner of Indian affairs made this clear, noting that Kiowa and Comanche revenues from bison hunting had disappeared in a short span of time. In 1876, they stood at $70,400; in 1877, they fell to $64,500; in 1878, they dropped again to $26,375; and in 1879, they plummeted to $5,068.

Realizing that bison hunting would no longer provide for them, the Kiowas and Comanches, under duress, turned their attention toward "the only other means possible of obtaining a subsistence—the cultivation of the soil and the growing of herds of cattle."[31]

As with the Kiowa experience, the collapse of bison hunting worked to propel the Osages into cattle herding farther north. For a brief time after the Civil War, the Osages enjoyed a few prosperous bison hunts. White Hair, Little Bear, Clermont, and Tall Chief, all chiefs of the Osage Nation, reported good results in bison hunting in the short-grass plains in the summer of 1867. Perhaps they enjoyed such success because of the agitated state of affairs that existed between the federal government and the Plains nations to the west, thereby opening hunting opportunities for the Osages in a region usually dominated by the Kiowas, Comanches, Southern Cheyennes, and Arapahos. Whatever the reasons, the Osage chiefs reported meeting only with "friendly" Indians while on their hunt, but on their return to their homes in southern Kansas, they received a harsh reception from white squatters and Kansas politicians such as Senator Edmund Ross, who wanted the Osages removed from the state. This state of affairs led to the drafting of a treaty with the federal government in 1868, and while its ratification languished in Congress, white squatters moved in, destroyed Osage farms and towns, and left the Osages with no recourse but to relocate to the land cut out of the Cherokee Nation that had been promised to them.

The next summer, the Osage bison hunt turned disastrous. The Plains nations had retaken control of the bison hunting grounds, causing the Osage expeditions nothing but trouble. White Hair, the principal chief, complained that his hunters "had trouble with the Plains Indians [thought to have been Arapahos] by which many of our horses and much of our property had been taken by said Indians and the profits of our hunt totally destroyed and many of our people are entirely destitute of horses, camp equipment, and provisions." In short, White Hair foretold a winter of starvation unless the federal government stepped in to relieve the Osages' situation.[32]

Isaac Gibson, the Osage agent, and several council leaders sought to keep the Osages on the reservation. They saw the rapid decline in the bison herds and hoped that those who relished the hunt would come to the same realization. The Osage leadership had picked out land from the Cherokee reserve that seemed nicely suited to cattle raising—or, for that matter, leasing to Texas or Kansas ranchers. Other areas of the reserve looked promising for farming, which a great many multiracial Osages already practiced. The Osages purchased their reserve from the Cherokees, thus gaining title in a way that would not have occurred if the land had been carved out of the public domain. But the 1874 bison hunt did not turn out as Gibson had hoped. "I have been hoping," he said, "they would get no meat, and get badly scared, which would be no inducement for others to go, but they brought in a good supply of meat, and say they were not interrupted by soldiers, or wild Indians." Nonetheless, he and other leaders among the Osages continued to encourage others to take up ranching and farming.[33]

By 1879, the Osages, much like the Plains Indians to the west, foresaw the end of bison hunting as a way of life. As a result, the fifteen bands of the nation showed considerable progress toward adapting ranching and farming. The "Half-Breed band" showed the most progress toward ranching, with a herd size of 1,430 bovines. They also had more hogs, chickens, wagons, and acres in corn and wheat than any of the other fourteen bands. Nearly all 2,400 Osages reportedly lived in peace and had "apparently given up the idea of living by the 'hunt.'" Peace would prevail as long as they had enough to eat on their own reservation and were not victimized—or did not feel victimized or abused—by non-Indian cattlemen. The key to peace, however, lay in the Indians' ability to retain possession of the solar energy stored in the grass and their access to the water sources abounding on what they believed was their sovereign domain.

## Supplying Government Cattle Contracts

At the end of the Civil War Joseph McCoy observed the rapid rise of a great "demand for cheap cattle in the Territories." McCoy boasted how this market afforded a marvelous opportunity for cattlemen to make money. He regarded the territories as a place where "any kind, sort or sized cattle could be bought and sold." The cattle market in the territories, as far as McCoy was concerned, contributed greatly to the success of his operation at Abilene. As he recalled it, driving cattle from Abilene into the "Territories became as common as driving from Texas to Abilene," or for that matter, shipping herds into eastern markets. Several Texas cattlemen, like his good friend Colonel J. J. Myers of Lockhart, Texas, made a fortune supplying the territories with cattle. There was good money to be made in supplying miners and transcontinental railroad construction crews, and in stocking the western ranges with cattle. The market in the territories also included supplying army posts and Indian reservations. One sign of the strength of this territorial market was the number of beeves required to feed reservation Indians. McCoy estimated that it required at least thirty to forty thousand beeves just to feed those living in the upper Missouri Valley.[34]

When given the opportunity, Indians, especially those residing in the Five Civilized Nations, displayed a desire and the ability to participate in the economic promise of ranching. For example, Cherokee ranchers were well aware of the opening of the territorial cattle markets immediately following the end of the Civil War. Despite the destruction and chaos that had rained down on the nation during the Civil War, a few individuals had reestablished their cattle herds. US Army posts required a regular supply of beef to keep the soldiers fed, and drovers in Kansas and the Cherokee Nation had assembled large herds of cattle to supply Fort Larned by spring 1865. In May, a small number of Kansas ranchers drove about 250 beeves through Junction City while Cherokees drove 200 beeves toward the crude town of Abilene, where these herders intended to add their stock to that of the Kansas herd.[35]

The post proposal for supplying the fort for one year beginning in August 1865 illustrates the nature of federal beef contracts and the number of cattle required to feed the soldiers stationed at Fort Larned. In June 1865, Second Lieutenant W. H. Pierce advertised for bids. He calculated that the post needed at least 30,000 pounds of edible beef of a "good and wholesome quality, in equal proportions of fore and hind quarters, necks and shanks and kidney tallow excluded." This quantity was in addition to another 200,000 pounds of steers to be delivered on the hoof as "may be required from the 1st of August, 1865, to the 31st day of October, 1865." During this time, this beef provision fed a troop strength that varied from a low of about 125 soldiers by the end of fall to a high of 475 soldiers in the summer. Of course, other forts in Kansas, Nebraska, Colorado, the Dakota Territory, and Indian Territory all required similar quantities of beef, which created a dependable cattle market for ranchers in both Kansas and Indian Territory. Several Indian stock raisers were in a position to take advantage of these fort contracts and did so when afforded the opportunity.[36]

Federal contracts for beef in the territories served another pressing need: supply Indian reservations. Indian agents purchased cattle to fill food rations for the various tribes forced onto reservations. Samuel Dunn Houston herded four thousand head of "big Texas steers" from Ogallala, Nebraska, to the Red Cloud

Agency, Dakota Territory, in 1879. Other herds were placed on the grasslands between the town of Ogallala and the reservation in anticipation of supplying reservations to the north. Not only would these herds become an important food source, they became components of a grassland ecosystem undergoing a transformation from the days when bison, rather than cattle, grazed it.[37]

McCoy also pointedly commented on how plenty of graft occurred supplying reservation contracts. In one account he detailed how a Texas drover unloaded a herd at Fort Larned for ill-gotten gain in the fall of 1867. The army had purchased the herd for supplying a reservation to the north, and supposedly the cattle weighed the equivalent of 600 pounds net. Some army contracts stipulated that the net edible meat of a steer be 50 percent of its gross weight, while other contracts called for as little as one-third of the gross to be suitable for eating. If in this case the contract called for 50 percent net, then the beeves should have weighed around 1,200 pounds. As McCoy recounted the selling of this herd, the beeves probably weighed no more than 400 pounds gross, which meant each animal provided no more than 200 pounds of edible meat. The drover had bought the cattle in this herd for $6 per head, and sold each one for $37.50 each when rightfully, at best, he should have received no more than $13.75 per head. Even $13.75 per head was an excellent return on investment.[38]

McCoy also referred to a practice called "guess off," which was when federal purchasing agents estimated the weight of cattle rather than actually putting them on scales. This was a far too common practice that put more money into a drover's pocket and less food onto an Indian's plate. In December 1867, John Q. Smith, the commissioner of Indian affairs, issued new guidelines for purchasing beeves intended for the schools on the reservations. He required that cattle be weighed "both alive, and dressed." The expectation was that the dressed meat should equal at least 50 percent of the gross weight of each of the beeves. In April 1877, William Nicholson, the superintendent of the Central Superintendency, reported the findings at the Kiowa and Comanche reservation. In the purchases made earlier in the month, in not one instance did any of the dressed meat reach 50 percent, with nearly all ranging from 40 to 45 percent of the gross weight of the beeves. The steer that weighed the heaviest came in at 770 pounds gross, a weight that would have made it nearly unmarketable in New York City. This is what McCoy meant when he said that the territories provided a market for "any kind, sort or sized cattle."[39]

## *The Struggle to Control Solar Energy Stores*

If Indians were ever to become successful ranchers and feed themselves, they had to be able to control the solar resources—the grasslands—that nourished their herds. The tribes understood themselves to be the rightful owners of their assigned realms with title to the resources therein, including timber, wildlife, water sources, horses, domestic livestock, crops, and the wild grass that blanketed the prairies and plains. Texas cattlemen, on the other hand, regarded Indian lands as federal lands and the grass free for the taking, and because of that, conflict over the control and consumption of the grass became commonplace. Despite the hard wrought gains many Indians made in cattle between 1866 and 1880, by 1890 nearly all that they had accomplished would lay in ruin.

If the 1866 cattle drive brought loss to many Texas cattlemen, it did little more for the Osages. Like other Texas cattlemen, Charles N. Baum was driving a herd through Osage lands on a route leading to Sedalia, Missouri, where the nearest railroad line leading to the great Chicago stockyards was located. For the Osages, times were tough. During the Civil War, they had formed a Kansas regiment and fought alongside other Kansas units, but after the war, in return for their loyal service to the Union, they received a tsunami of white squatters flooding their lands. The arrival of Baum's large herd only added to their distress.

Baum had his Texas cattle herd grazing near the oddly named Pumpkin Creek. During the war, cross-border raiding between Kansans and Missourians had left much of the region in ruins. Along the southern border of Kansas, the Osages had once held a sizable belt of land. An 1865 treaty had trimmed off a considerable amount of their reservation in Kansas, but they still held legal title to a strip of land thirty miles in width, even though about thirty miles had been shaved off the eastern side and another twenty off the northern side. In the southeast portion of this reservation, the Osages had one of their major villages along Pumpkin Creek near where it emptied into the Verdigris River.

Like most Texas drovers, Baum gave no thought to the destruction wrought by his cattle as they grazed freely on Osage grasslands. Given the Osages' plight in dealing with unwelcome illegal immigrants, they did not appreciate the insult added to injury caused by Texas cattle. Consequently, on September 9, 1866, several unidentified Osages simply decided to repay themselves for Baum's cattle grazing their lands by confiscating forty-five head of cattle from his herd—of course, without Baum's consent.

Like many other Texas cattlemen, Baum had business connections in Illinois. By November, he had brought his depleted herd near Danville, Illinois, and probably anticipated overwintering it there. While in the city, he visited the law and collection office of M. D. Hawes and D. D. Evans to relate his complaint to the attorneys and asked them to file a claim against the Osages with the commissioner of Indian affairs.

The partners wrote a letter to Commissioner L. V. Bogy, who had recently assumed the office, and demanded that the Osages pay $1,000 in damages. By treaty, the lawyers argued, the Osages were liable by treaty for any "depredation committed by them against . . . citizens of the United States, to an amount not exceeding thirty thousand dollars." Given their Anglicized surnames, it was often difficult to tell some Indians apart from American citizens. This treaty proviso made certain that other Indians with Scots-Irish or French surnames would not be able to seek redress for any losses incurred by Osage raids. So yes, Baum's attorneys had to aver that he was indeed a citizen of the United States.[40]

Baum knew he had been robbed, but the Osages also knew they were being robbed by Texas cattlemen such as Baum. Who was to compensate them for the destruction of their fields, their pastures, or their hunting grounds caused by hundreds if not thousands of beeves trampling across their lands? The Osages had trouble enough simply keeping squatters off their lands, much less dealing with the ecological degradation caused by herds of hungry longhorns.

The Kiowas and Comanches faced similar difficulties in protecting their grass from Texan incursions. In fact, the Kiowas and Comanches had a dim view of Texans in general even before it was compounded by the need to protect their grass from grazing longhorns. In 1868, Philip McCusker, the US translator for the Comanches, reported from their camp that they and the Kiowas generally wanted to remain friendly with all those living north of the Red River. However, he added, "this feeling of good will does not extend to the people of Texas on the contrary there is a feeling of the deadliest hatred to the people of that state."[41] In June 1870, Captain Tullius C. Tupper of the Sixth Cavalry left Fort Richardson with a command to escort herds of longhorns bound for California and outlets on the Kansas Pacific (KP) railroad. In his report, filed in August, he referred to Comanche and Kiowa raids into Texas, a "State they evidently consider *not* a portion of the United States."[42]

Given the prevailing attitude of the Kiowas and Comanches toward Texans, it seldom came as a surprise when they took retribution into their own hands, as the Kiowa warrior Satanta did during the cold winter of 1870. In the northwest corner of Indian Territory, Camp Supply, like any army post, needed a regular quantity of cattle to feed its soldiers assigned to police the territory. Texas cattlemen more often than not had the contracts to supply these outposts. Without any further need of Texan provocation, Satanta already carried a burning grudge over several miscarriages of justice. He felt that the army's recent arrest of Kicking Bird was wholly unwarranted. Moreover, the army had kept him and his band from trading for ammunition and "other supplies."[43]

Compounding these issues, Satanta had serious concerns about Texas cattle herds destroying the grass resources that his nation's domestic and wild animals depended on. The commander at Fort Sill, Brevet Major General Benjamin H. Grierson, whose sympathy for the plight of the Kiowa and Comanche Nations in Indian Territory was well known to his superiors, took note of how difficult it was for the Kiowas to travel anywhere near his post because of "the grass being all burned in this vicinity." The charred prairie offered nothing in the way of fuel sources for horse herds and made it nearly impossible for anyone to ride around near the fort without supplemental sources of fuel such as oats or corn, which the Kiowas lacked altogether. Knowing this, Grierson sent word to the Kiowa bison-hunting parties that they could remain on the plains to the west, given their struggles with hunger.[44]

On the trail leading from Fort Sill to Camp Supply, the grass range was in better shape, but the growing season was spent, and any blades grazed down would not grow back until the spring. By late January 1870, Texas cattle eating grass meant that much less available for Indian horse or bison herds through the rest of the winter. In addition, cattle, horses, and bison all needed regular recourse to water, so grazing grounds were always located near live water sources.

The route to Camp Supply led directly through the prime bison grounds where the Kiowas were hunting, and not surprisingly, Satanta adamantly objected to Texas cattle being driven to Camp Supply. In a letter to Colonel W. G. Mitchell, the acting assistant adjutant general of the army, General Grierson explained just how Satanta had made his objection known: he and his band had killed some of the cattle in the herd being driven to Camp Supply because Satanta was angry about "the cattle driven through there to eat up their grass." Satanta still had bison that he could hunt, and he did not want any Texas cattle stripping away the grass that sustained the bison herds. There was only a limited amount of stored solar fuels available in those remaining grass blades in close vicinity to water sources for grazing animals in the western portion of Indian Territory, and Satanta preferred not to share with Texas cattlemen.[45]

Indians such as Satanta seldom attacked a cattle herd simply for the fun of it. Rather, they lashed out when they had a good rationale for their actions. That did not stop people who traveled the Chisholm Trail from forming an unwarranted fear of Indians, yet most of the time, trail crews encountered little if any trouble with the occupants of Indian Territory. W. F. Burks put together a herd of one thousand cattle and began a long journey north from Banquette (now Banquete) in Nueces County, Texas. Amanda Burks accompanied her husband on the drive in 1871, and she traveled in style. Amanda rode in a buggy and was attended by Nick, a "black boy" who worked for the Burkses. Nick had the task of setting up Amanda's evening camps and cooking for her.

When about twenty miles west of the port city, Corpus Christi, Burks changed his mind and decided to turn north and head to Abilene, where he anticipated a better return from shipping by rail rather than steamboat. Nearing Austin and passing through some timber east of the Balcones Escarpment, Burks lost about thirty head of cattle in the rough and wooded terrain. Farther to the north, as the crew neared the Brazos River in Bosque County, hail pounded the herd and the heads of cowboys and their horses. Pandemonium and chaos reigned, and Amanda spent a long night in her buggy, parked somewhat safely in a grove of trees. A little farther north in this part of "civilization," Amanda encountered a lone woman drying beans on a line and pining for a return to Tennessee, but without the means to do so.

When Burks reached Fort Worth, he had to wait days on end for the Trinity River to fall before he could safely swim his herd across. In the vicinity, Amanda counted another fifteen herds and their crews waiting to cross. When the river finally fell, all the herds started north to the Red River crossing at the same time, and Amanda noted that this was where they "left all civilization behind." Now in the "savage wilderness," Amanda grieved over the disappearance of "fresh fields, green meadows, and timber lands." She boiled under a "blistering" sun and was chilled by uncomfortably cool evenings and dawns. Prairie fires threatened and terrorized both cattle and cowboys. She viewed the landscape as nothing more than a harsh, wild domain inhabited by "uncivilized," "treacherous Indians."[46]

Amanda's experiences with Indians proved largely uneventful for the most part. In fact, her benign encounters were the norm during the drive. Most of the time, she dealt with Indians who came for what she termed trade. On occasion, she thought stealthy Indians attempted to stampede the herd in the dead of night, but no one could identify who was actually inciting the ruckus. The culprits could just as easily have been Anglo or Hispanic rustlers, or wolves, for that matter. Nonetheless, the Burkses usually blamed Indians even though Burks's men did run off some non-Indian rustlers on one occasion.

The nervous, overwrought fear of Indians gave pranksters an opening to trick tenderfeet, a favorite pastime of cowboys while herding cattle on the trail. On one occasion, J. D. Jackson, who was working on a roundup in Presidio County, Texas, participated in spoofing a well-born kid from Kentucky whose family had ties to the herd's Texas owner and thought it would be a good experience for their son to work a drive. The Texas hands had little patience with the young man's airs and began to play pranks on him. They loosened his cinches so that his saddle would slide off his horse during a sudden stop. They told him that his blue shirts would become a bright target for stealthy Indians who would mistake him for a soldier.

One night, several hands disguised themselves as Indians and rode out to the horse herd some distance from camp. Around 12:30 A.M., Den Knight, the ranch manager, awakened the young man and told him to saddle up, ride out to the herd with him, and bring it closer to camp to avoid any possibility of an Indian raid. Once Den and the Kentuckian reached the herd, the other hands rushed out of their hiding spots and pretended to raid the herd. Den feigned being shot, fell off his saddle, and told the Kentuckian to save his own life and make a run for it.

The young man, needing no encouragement, made good his escape while Jackson and the hands got a good laugh from their hoax. But try as they might, they could not stop the Kentuckian as he sped out of camp on his way to sound a warning. He rode his horse hard for sixty miles, and at ten o'clock the next morning, he arrived in Marfa, Texas, exclaiming that Indians had attacked the herd and that he was the only one to have escaped alive. Soon enough, he discovered the joke was on him, and he quickly quit the drive and returned home, convinced, like the Comanches and Kiowas, that Kentucky was a more civilized place than Texas.[47]

## Tolls, Leases, and Licenses

Fording the Red River into present-day Oklahoma marked a momentous occasion as one left Texas and entered Indian Territory, the point where cowboys believed that they passed out of "civilization" and entered the "wilderness." Conversely, many who lived in the "wilderness" considered Texas and Texans to be less than "civilized." As far as they were concerned, Texas cattlemen were trespassers whose animals demolished their solar resources along a broad strip of land from the Red River to the southern Kansas border. Texas cowboys seemed never to pay for refueling charges unless hard-pressed to do so by the rightful occupants of Indian Territory. It was as if Texas cattlemen pulled into an Indian-owned gas station, topped off their tanks, and left without paying. In essence, whenever trail hands stopped a northbound herd after a day's drive, the grazing cattle were simply refueling by converting the stored solar energy in the grasses into protein and carbohydrates for their own energy needs. In doing so, these animals depleted the solar energy sources upon which other animals, such as bison, elk, deer, and antelope, as well as the Indian peoples' horses, mules, and cattle, depended. So how were cattlemen to compensate for depleting the stored solar fuels in this portion of the grasslands? Often, the simple answer was that the "civilized" ones felt no need to reimburse the "uncivilized." As far as the Texas drovers were concerned, the grass and water powering the vast herds of Texas cattle on their way to the northern markets were free for the taking. The Indian peoples, however, realized the high cost to themselves and demanded compensation.

Some cattlemen, such as J. E. Pettus of Goliad County, Texas, would often pay Indians for the right to cross their domain. As a matter of fact, Pettus viewed Indians as less troublesome to his cattle than farmers. While Indians might arrive in his camp and demand a few beeves for passage, when and if paid, they usually left contented and allowed safe passage. The "grangers," as Pettus referred to farmers, nearly always "displayed a degree of animosity toward the trail drivers that was almost unbearable." One important distinction between the two groups was that Indians and farmers employed the collected solar energy on the grasslands in different ways. It was easier for the Indian peoples to tolerate the cattlemen because they used the grasslands in a similar manner. It did neither of them any good to destroy the reproductive capacity of the wild grasses. Farmers, in contrast, sought to remove wild grasses to make way for domesticated, harvestable grasses such as wheat and corn.[48]

Several Indian leaders worked to retain good relationships with drovers. Sometimes a Texan wrote a letter of introduction for an Indian. Such letters indicated the good character of the letter holder and that if he were treated well, no trouble would come from him. Ike Pryor took herds north, and he made good connections with Indian leaders along the way. His letters read like the following:

> To the trail bosses:
>
> This man is a good Indian; I know him personally. Treat him well, give him a beef and you will have no trouble in driving through his country.
>
> (Signed) Ike T. Pryor

Bill Jackman once drove a herd that was about a week behind one being led by Pryor. Jackman's hands picked up one of Pryor's strays and added it to his herd. The custom was for the stray to be returned to its rightful owner if possible. Before Jackman reached Pryor's herd, he encountered a group of about forty Indians, and the leader had one of Pryor's letters of introduction. Jackman took the easy road and gave the leader Pryor's stray. For Jackman, Pryor's good relationships with the Indians paid off doubly.[49]

When twenty-year-old L. D. Taylor and his brothers rounded up about a thousand beeves, they embarked on an eventful drive to Abilene, Kansas. As if a bad omen for the rest of the drive, the herd stampeded through the streets of Dallas, Texas, raising havoc and causing property damage. The townspeople, of course, demanded and received payment for damages. As the herd crossed the Red River into Indian Territory, Taylor felt ill at ease, even though the first portion of Indian Territory was known to be where the friendly Indians ranged. These friendly Indians were no more disposed to accept unpaid losses for property damages than were the residents of Dallas. Unlike the folks in Dallas, however, the Indians had no enforcement powers for collecting, so they took it upon themselves to devise effective collection strategies.[50]

The first morning when Taylor woke up in "Friendly Indian Nation," which would have been the Chickasaw Nation, he realized that the herd had vanished. Taylor must have been tired because during the night, when he had been sleeping soundly, Indians had dispersed the herd by shooting arrows among the cattle. The next day, the same Indians came to Taylor and his fellow cowboys and generously—for a price—offered their services in rounding up the herd. With the paid help of the Indians, it took a couple of days to get the herd back together.[51]

Back on the trail again, Taylor and his crew joined up with a couple of other herds for additional protection in the less friendly regions of Indian Territory. After a few days of difficult crossings of swollen creeks, Taylor observed what appeared to be a line of timber on a ridge. The timber, which quickly became more than four hundred mounted Comanches, began moving down the slope, heading directly toward the herd. Before any of the Texans could give it a second thought, the Comanches had killed and begun to butcher at least twenty-five beeves. The Comanches feasted on raw meat right before the hapless Texans. Every time the cowboys attempted to start the herd, the Comanches would surround the cattle and stop it from moving. Resigned to their fate, Taylor and the others waited. The Comanches ate their fill and, once completely stuffed, finally gave the Texans permission to move on. As Taylor put it, "I felt greatly relieved, and [the Comanches] could have left us sooner without my permission."[52]

Paying tolls, whether in the form of cattle or money, is the usual explanation of what many Indian peoples wanted from Texas drovers. Bob Love's work provides a good example of toll taking. Love was an influential leader among the Choctaws and was a formal representative of the tribe in many of its deliberations with the US government. As such, he was one of the signatories for the nation's 1866 treaty with the US government, which empowered the nation to control certain aspects of trade and travel through its land. Love had a residence on Mud Creek, a stream some twenty miles north of the Red River crossing. There he stopped Texas drovers and required them to buy "passports" through the region. In 1870, while on his first cattle drive north, Pleasant Burnell Butler recalled that Love had asked ten cents per head of cattle for the right of passage and, after some negotiations, had settled for a twenty-dollar gold piece.[53]

As drovers neared the southern border of Kansas, they often encountered Osages who demanded tolls for crossing the region. The Osages had begun resettling on the land acquired from the Cherokees. The first governor of the Osage Nation, Joseph Paw-nee-no-pashe, took it upon himself to levy a tax of ten cents per head for passage through the Osage Nation. He authorized the firm of Greenway and Company to collect the tax. This firm was based several miles to the west of the Osage Nation proper, where the Chisholm Trail crossed Pond Creek. Located there was a prominent ranch and trading post known as Sewall's store where herders and Indians traded.

It did not take long for the Governor Paw-nee-no-pashe's action to attract significant opposition. James Craig, the president of the Missouri River, Fort Scott, and Gulf Railroad, made his displeasure with the tax known in a letter mailed to the US secretary of the interior. Craig wanted to know by what authority Governor Paw-nee-no-pashe could impose the tax. He warned that such a tax would allow the Osage Nation to "increase it indefinitely, and thus shut out from Market the almost inexhaustible heads of the finest Beef Cattle in the World, to the injury of the Owners of the Cattle, the Rail Road lines, and the tens of thousands of Consumers of tough, but high priced beef, in the Cities East of the Missouri River." Craig desperately wanted to reach Indian Territory before two other companies did and thereby acquire the exclusive right to build through the Cherokee Nation. His line had reached Baxter Springs, just short of the southern boundary of Kansas, and there he intended to build a slaughter facility and then pack beef quarters into refrigerated cars bound for eastern markets.[54]

Cattle coming up the Chisholm Trail would need to cross the Osage Nation to reach the railhead at Baxter Springs, and any tax levied on these herds would cut into the profit margins of the drovers. Besides, the Chickasaw Nation was already charging five cents per head for crossing its lands. The Creek Nation levied the same rate, and the Cherokee Nation imposed a tax of ten cents per head. Moreover, a Texas drover faced another charge of ten cents per head per week if he wanted to overwinter his cattle on Cherokee land. All of this, according to the superintendent of the line, would create trouble for everyone and might cause drovers to take their herds north along the Chisholm Trail toward Abilene just to avoid being taxed.[55] Of course, this is exactly why McCoy advertised the Chisholm Trail as the most cost-effective route to an outlet on a railroad line: no Indian cattle taxes, he claimed.

Craig's dreams, however, failed to materialize, as President Ulysses S. Grant awarded the right to build through Indian Territory to his competitor, the Union Pacific Railway Southern Branch (later renamed the Missouri, Kansas, and Texas Railroad, or MK&T), which terminated at Chetopa, Kansas, located about fifteen miles west of Baxter Springs and directly north of the Cherokee Nation. By terminating at Baxter Springs, Craig's engineers had inadvertently placed the line above the Quapaw Nation, through which he had no legal right to build.

Tolls could take on other forms than a head tax on transient cattle. Close to present-day Wichita, Kansas, M. A. Withers had ridden alone ahead of his main herd. At a small watering hole, he dismounted from his horse to let it drink and suddenly found himself approached rapidly by seven mounted Osages. An exceedingly nervous Withers calmed down considerably when he realized that the Osages only wanted all of his tobacco, which he gladly relinquished.

Just a few days later, Withers and his hands eagerly anticipated a feast on barbecued beef when an Indian alarm sounded in the camp. This time around thirty Osages rode down hard on the party. Indicating their peaceful intentions, the Osages dismounted and placed their rifles around a tree. Apparently, the Osages assumed that the cowboys had spent the day preparing the barbecued beef for them, and they appropriated the meat without much, if any, resistance from the Texans. The cowboys rightly figured that one grilled beef, plus one for the road, was not too much to pay the Osages for the right of passage.[56]

Regardless where Texas drovers crossed the Red River, inevitably Indians were there to collect tolls for crossing their land. In 1881, after crossing the Red River at Doan's Crossing, F. M. Polk recalled that "thousands" of Indians paid him and fellow cowboys a visit to request a steer each day. On some days, as many as 150 Indians would accompany the herders and by the end of the day request a "Wahaw," a steer, for the right of passage. Despite the Texans' obvious irritation with this routine, diplomacy reigned as the cowboys made it look as if they "were glad to give" the Indians their daily steer. Better a steer sacrificed than one of themselves.[57]

All went well for drovers and Indians alike when such tolls were paid. A foolish trail boss would refuse to pay a couple of beeves or like compensation for the right of passage. George Saunders was anything but foolish when he negotiated with several Comanches in the summer of 1884. He always offered a fair toll price, and on one notable occasion, the Comanches, in gratitude, helped Saunders swim his herd across the swollen Canadian River. Once the herd had crossed the river, Saunders paid the Comanches a horse and "some provisions."

In fact, everything was going along so smoothly, and everyone was in such a good mood, that the Comanches and cowboys in Saunders's outfit decided to engage in some fun and games. Several Comanches began riding by the cowboys and daring them to lasso them. The speeding warriors continued for some time until Saunders managed to rope one fellow and sent him flying into the air right off the back of his horse. The warrior landed hard, flat on his back, with Saunders's rope pulled tightly around his chest. At first, it appeared that the Comanche lay dead on the ground. Most of the cowboys feared the outcome of this unfortunate turn of events, and Saunders, a few hands, and the Comanches all rushed to the fallen victim. They quickly loosened the rope and prayed for the man to regain his breath. A few tense minutes passed before it became evident that the Comanche was coming around. Once he had fully regained his breathing, his fellow warriors "laughed and guffawed" over the incident. One might wonder whether the roped fellow thought it funny, but Saunders must have breathed a sigh of relief as he left his Comanche helpers and sportsmen "in fine spirits."[58]

Tolls, however, proved difficult, if not nearly impossible, for the Indians to collect on a regular basis. Despite the Osages' attempts to charge head taxes on cattle taken through or grazed on their lands, by 1883, the most that the nation had collected in a season was a mere $340. Meanwhile, Texas drovers had to confront the pervasive fear of their herds spreading Texas fever to cattle beyond the southern border of Kansas. This fear made it difficult, if not impossible, to take a herd directly into Kansas. Given that certified overwintered herds could be taken anywhere into Kansas or beyond, drovers sought to graze their cattle on Indian nation lands for at least one winter.

Rich grazing grounds abounded throughout the Indian nations. The Cherokees had little use for the six million acres in the Cherokee Outlet, and even though they wanted paying cattlemen to graze their herds there, their tax collection fell short of expectations. Reportedly, not one dollar of tax revenue reached the Cherokee treasury in 1879; in 1880, a "partial divy" was received; and in 1881, Joseph McCoy took in over $40,000, but at least $5,000 remained in arrears.[59] The Cherokee council believed there had to be a better way to derive some money from cattle grazing. They, as well as many federal officials throughout Indian Territory, hit upon the idea of "leasing" the outlet in its entirety to cattlemen.

Leasing appealed to large cattle firms that saw it as the way to control huge amounts of pasturage throughout Indian Territory. This raised a thorny issue for officials in Washington, D.C., especially those in the Bureau of Indian Affairs and the Department of the Interior: Could Indian nations legally lease or rent their reservations? In other words, did the Cherokees, Osages, Cheyennes, and Arapahos have legal title to the land, or did the federal government? The federal government's view was that whichever entity held title to the land became the sole legal agent who possessed the right to lease the land. The grass, apart from the land, was another question.

After Principal Chief Bushyhead fired McCoy as the tax collector, he and the

Cherokee legislature considered leasing the Cherokee Outlet to cattlemen as the best alternative for acquiring some return on the grass being consumed by vast herds of cattle. Cattlemen and firms were already fencing off large parts of the outlet, and the outlet had become so crowded with cattle that the herders found it nearly impossible to keep the herds separate from another. The routes of the Chisholm and Great Western Trails also created a serious problem for cattlemen in the outlet because the trails bisected the outlet, and the cattlemen feared, rightly, that longhorns driven north could spread Texas fever to their own herds if not fenced a good distance away from the trails. Moreover, small-time ranchers along the southern border of Kansas tended to allow their cattle to drift south into the outlet, especially when the county tax appraiser came around to assess their holdings. These same cattle seemed to avoid detection by hoofing it back to the sunflower state when an agent such as McCoy was in the outlet collecting the head tax for the Cherokee Nation.[60]

By the beginning of 1883, the conflicts roiling the outlet had immersed the Cherokee Nation and factions within it, the Department of the Interior, the Bureau of Indian Affairs, the Cherokee agent, and large and small stockmen. Henry Teller, the secretary of the interior, ordered H. Price, the commissioner of Indian affairs, to provide a report on the situation. Joseph McCoy caught wind of the secretary's instructions and wrote to his friend R. T. Van Horn, a congressman representing the district that included Kansas City, Missouri. McCoy thought Van Horn had enough sway to land him the job as investigator, but despite Representative Van Horn's support for McCoy, the job was given to John Tufts, the Cherokee agent.

Tufts submitted his findings to Commissioner Price on March 1, 1883. At least nineteen cattle firms had installed over 950 miles of fence. Of the 300,000 cattle grazing in the outlet, stockmen had paid head taxes on 200,000. The other 100,000 belonged to Kansans who turned "them loose on these lands" and paid no taxes. Tufts thought it wise to leave the fencing intact, since doing so would also prevent Kansans from wreaking wholesale destruction on riparian woodlands, which he believed protected the flowing water sources of the outlet. Although he had a poor ecological understanding of the effects of trees on surface water flows, he fully understood that access to living water sources determined the value of any pasture.[61]

Even before Tufts's report had reached the commissioner's office, powerful cattlemen in the outlet gathered to chart a different way of doing business with the Cherokee Nation. They formed the Cherokee Strip Live Stock Association (CSLSA), an organization with the authority and resources to lease the entire six million acres in the outlet. This would give them the power to control grazing while guaranteeing revenue to the Cherokee Nation. On March 8, 1883, after meeting for three days in Caldwell, Kansas, they approved the bylaws of the organization and elected Benjamin Miller, a stockman operating out of Kansas City, Missouri, as its president. The CSLSA, through assessments made on its membership, then offered the Cherokee Nation $100,000 a year for five years for the grazing rights to the outlet.[62]

On May 14, 1883, the Cherokee legislature passed an act authorizing the leasing of the outlet to the CSLSA, and Principal Chief Bushyhead signed it on May 19. The act provided that the treasurer of the nation would hold the proceeds until they reached $300,000 and then pay out the funds "'per capita,' under directions of the national council." In an additional act, the council voted that only those who were "Cherokee by blood" would receive per capita payments. Bushyhead vetoed the additional act, but the council overrode him. This provision excluded "adopted colored citizens, Shawnees and Delawares" based upon the reasoning that they were not of Cherokee blood.[63]

Regardless of the internal divisions within the Cherokee Nation, the ninety-eight members of the CSLSA honored their contractual obligations. Now with the authority to fence off their pastures, they also created corridors through which herds driven north along the Chisholm or Western Trails would pass. The trails, fenced on either side, ranged from one to over two miles wide and widened to around eight miles at the points where herders watered and grazed their cattle at noon and where they stopped for the night. The Osages, Comanches and Kiowas, Cheyennes, and Arapahos all used similar arrangements to govern cattle grazing on their reservations. While these arrangements did not solve all disputes—internal ones among the tribes or external ones with cattlemen lessees or with intruders—for a while, the leases provided a fairly reliable source of revenue to the tribes and slightly opened the door for their efforts to build their own cattle herds.[64]

## *Indian Pastoralism*

The federal effort to turn the Osages into a pastoral people started to show a bit of enterprise by 1877. Agent Cyrus Beede wanted to purchase twenty to twenty-five head of "half-blood Durham bulls" to begin crossbreeding with the Texas longhorn cows held on the reservation. Agent Beede had a few hundred cows and some calves on hand with the intention of stocking the reservation. Word from the Department of the Interior indicated a reluctance to purchase the Durhams because of the fear that an outbreak of Texas fever would kill the bulls in just one season. However, the department did support a stocking effort of buying twenty-five head of "native cattle" from the beef contractor. The experiment in stock raising had taken fragile root in the reservation.[65]

True, by 1880, little progress had taken place in cattle raising in the Osage Nation. More than anything, Texas fever had seriously set back the Osages' efforts to build up their stock. Slowly, however, the Osages made gains in stock raising. By 1884, they had nearly completed fencing in their own grazing lands, thereby protecting their herds from the encroachment of large Texas herds on the periphery of their own pastures or pastures that they had leased. By 1885, the Osage agent counted 9,700 head of cattle owned primarily by the mixed-blood Osages.[66]

Quite possibly, some among the Kiowa Nation had taken up cattle herding after the Civil War. Exactly when they took up this practice is an open question, and so is the extent of their herds. What is clear is that some were selling cattle in 1866. Apparently, Jesse Leavenworth, the Kiowas' agent at the time, had been questioned by D. W. Colley, the commissioner of Indian affairs, about the practice of buying Kiowa cattle. In fact, such dealings may have been spreading among many of the Indian nations in the Upper Arkansas River Valley, the portion of the valley roughly above the Great Bend of the river in Kansas. William Bent, a longtime trader with these nations, had previously reported to Colley about "parties" buying cattle from "the Indians." While Bent's account raises questions about who were the "parties" and which Indians were doing the selling, his letter clearly speaks to "Indians" possessing enough cattle to sell.[67]

Perhaps the Kiowas possessed large herds, and initially, Leavenworth believed it to be probable that they did. But the Kiowas informed Leavenworth that he was mistaken about the size of their herds, and he came to embrace that assessment. However, Elizabeth Sprague, a Kiowa captive whom Leavenworth had recovered, asked him if he had "purchased" any cattle from the Kiowas. The Kiowas had led her to believe that they possessed "quite a number" that they wanted to sell. In the end, Leavenworth held to a low estimate of the herd number because a local, unidentified trader had managed to purchase only fifty head from the Kiowas.

Regardless of the herd size and despite Colley's questions about the legality of buying cattle from Indians, the Kiowas were maintaining cattle as early as 1866.[68]

As Leavenworth took note of Kiowa cattle herds, he also started thinking about how the Kiowas might become pastoral. This idea took root among agents who followed him as well as among the Kiowas themselves. As the bison herds dwindled in size, the Kiowas saw possibilities in converting the mainstay of their economy to pastoralism. In August 1867, Leavenworth still hoped that the Kiowas could make a successful conversion to cattle raising.

Leavenworth stood as an early advocate for making this transition to pastoralism. He had serious concerns about the well-being of orphans and the elderly. These unfortunates often found themselves to be outcasts. Leavenworth wanted an agency and "home" built for them where they at least might be able to support themselves. The key to self-sufficiency, Leavenworth believed, lay in their developing a pastoral economy. As he put it, he wanted to undertake an "experiment to see if they could be made herders." He knew that the D.C. office needed to provide extraordinary funding, as a sizable purchase of cattle was needed before the enterprise could have any chance of success. In the first place, the "suffering for food" among the people was so severe that they would kill the animals immediately simply to quench their hunger. The seed had been planted regarding transitioning the Kiowas to a pastoral economy.[69]

Another prominent individual, General William Tecumseh Sherman, advocated transforming Plains Indians into pastoralists. In September 1867, as part of a peace commission designed to stop violence along the Powder River Road in Wyoming, he met with a delegation of Sioux. He put forth the following proposition: "You can own herds of cattle and horses like the Cherokees and Choctaws. You can have cornfields like the Poncas, Yanktons, and Pottawatomies . . . We want you to cultivate your land, build houses and raise cattle."[70]

By August, Leavenworth seemed to have made a little progress toward starting his experiment. He had identified the transportation fund as an appropriate source for purchasing the cattle. He still needed to find a location for an agency where the herd could be kept, but he figured that he could keep the costs reasonable by "employing the Indians to herd their own cattle." Leavenworth estimated that he required a herd of 425 beeves simply to prevent starvation among the Kiowas and Comanches. He knew that such a herd would need experienced herders who could also protect the cattle from theft. This would require employing one "head man" and three assistants for at least three months.⁷¹

Other concerns, however, interfered with implementing the herding arrangements. Leavenworth and other agents across the central grasslands were busily encouraging the various nations to convene for what would become the Medicine Lodge Treaty negotiations in October. Also, growing concerns mounted over stopping raids into Texas and protecting the first Abilene-bound herds of longhorns being driven through Indian Territory. Leavenworth nonetheless took it upon himself to see that 425 beeves were provided for feeding the Kiowas, but his move certainly failed to create any pastoralists.⁷²

Seven years later the Kiowas made little, if any, headway toward becoming pastoralists, nor had the federal government given them much encouragement or support for developing cattle ranching. In 1874, Kiowa agent J. M. Haworth pondered his charges' economic future. Many troubles plagued his agency, not the least of which was the Kiowas' unhappiness about their competition with non-Indian bison hunters. Haworth recognized that the Kiowas seemed especially good with their horse and mule herds, so why not fully encourage them to become self-sufficient as ranchers? Besides, several Kiowa chiefs had already taken the "white man's path" and willingly encouraged their kin and bands to take up farming. Their reservation contained rich grasslands suitable for sustaining large herds, and a great number of Kiowa men displayed skillful horsemanship. Theoretically they could easily adapt their bison-hunting skills to cattle herding.

In spring 1874, the grasslands around Fort Sill had responded nicely to warm weather, and lush grazing grounds abounded. While several Apache and some Comanche leaders eagerly anticipated planting corn, they also made requests for enough cattle to start their own herds. Haworth thought cattle herding a better economic alternative to bison hunting than raising corn, and he believed that the Indians would "take good care of Cattle and be greatly benefited by receiving them." The climate, he thought, was too uncertain, or rather, "the certainty of drouths makes Corn raising very doubtful." However, the environment was "very fine for grazing," and he opined that "it would be a profitable investment for this Government to give to the more reliable of the Chiefs small herds of Cattle, which can be bought with very little Capital."⁷³

Over the next two years Haworth conducted an experiment to use funds derived from selling horses taken from "hostile Indians" to fund the purchase of stock cattle in the effort to convert the Kiowas into pastoralists. In the spring of 1877, Colonel John P. Hatch, Fort Sill post commander, penned and mailed a report to Lieutenant General Sheridan. Sheridan forwarded the report to George McCrary, the secretary of war, who forwarded a copy to Zachariah Chandler, the secretary of the interior. Hatch's report acquired its significance given its subject matter: "Condition of the 'Indian Pony Fund,' and the Practical Working of the Experiment of Making the Indians at the Fort Sill Reserve a Pastoral People."[74] Hatch's report resonated through all levels of government given the expectations of seeing the Kiowas become "self-sustaining." Similar to Hatch and Chandler, many Americans accorded agriculture the hallmark of a civilized society. They believed the route toward civilization started with nomadism, which led to pastoralism, which naturally morphed into agriculture, the harbinger of civilization.

Colonel Hatch sought to show in his report how Kiowas were taking great strides toward becoming a pastoral people. As evidence, he noted how the Kiowas had taken good care of the two hundred cattle that had been bought for them in August 1876 even though a few had died during winter, and few others had been stolen. The milk cows were calving, adding to the herd. However, the native bulls purchased in Kansas had all died from Texas fever. Next time, the colonel recommended buying bulls from one of the Five Nations to the east. "A little assistance and encouragement," he recommended, "given now that we know that they are adaptable might make [the Kiowas] a pastoral people." He succinctly put the matter this way: "The ultimate advantage that [the Kiowas and Comanches] may, passing gradually through the pastoral epoch, reach that of agriculture, and possibly in the future become civilized, still possessing their distinctive features as a people." At this point, the Kiowas and Comanches could provide for their own welfare, and thereby this achievement would eliminate the need for a military peacekeeping presence.[75]

By 1885, the experiment on the Kiowa and Comanche reservation had produced mixed results. The Kiowas and Comanches owned 7,500 head of cattle, with several individual herds numbering between 20 and 200 head. But they had a difficult time protecting their herds from Texans poaching. Agent Hunt had decided that enclosing the herd in a remote area of the reserve might protect it from theft. He chose a range near the northwest corner of the Chickasaw Nation, where the grass grew abundantly, ample streams of clear water flowed, and only a couple of white settlers lived. "Boomers" overran that portion of the Chickasaw Nation in 1884 and cut the cattle fences on the Kiowa and Comanche pastures to the west. In the fall the intruders burned off the grass, making it impossible to keep the Kiowa and Comanche herd on the pasture. Their actions compelled Hunt to free-range graze the herd, which made it susceptible to raids. No wonder Hunt referred to that portion of Indian Territory as "Rustler's Bend." It is a miracle that the Kiowas and Comanches had any cattle left in their herds by 1885.[76]

Even cattle agency gave the Kiowas and Comanches fits. Cattle had their own way of doing things, and while not as capable as bison in surviving on the plains, they were smart enough to know when the grass was greener on the other side of the river. A report to the assistant adjutant general of the Department of the Missouri observed that "the Texas edge [of the Red River] is barren of grass, this side opposite in Indian Territory heavily grassed and only separated by a small stream, dry most of the summer, so cattle themselves soon make a choice." Even though this unnamed army officer had been busily "ejecting cattle men" from the reservation, he found it an impossible task, as the cattle drifted back across the river, and "their owners cannot prevent it."[77]

Like Colonel Hatch, Agent John D. Miles thought it both desirable and possible for the Cheyennes to become successful pastoralists. Despite his good intentions, in 1882 he found himself forced to take draconian measures simply to keep the Cheyennes and Arapahos from starving much less than seeing them raise stock cattle. Congress, in a budget-cutting frenzy, refused to appropriate enough money to completely fund the annual rations for Indians living on the reserve. In the effort to spread his remaining funding to the expenses of his bureau through the end of the fiscal year, the commissioner of Indian affairs, Hiram Price, directed agent Miles to reduce the beef ration to the Cheyennes and Arapahos by fully one-third. Major George M. Randall, the commanding officer at Fort Reno, saw nothing but trouble brewing as a result, and given his charge to keep the peace on the reservation, he worried about what it would take for his troops to keep starving Cheyennes and Arapahos or Kiowas and Comanches from depredating the illegal cattle herds swarming their reservation.[78]

General John Pope, who had considerable sympathy for the plight of Indians living in Indian Territory, proposed a plan to avoid trouble. He recommended conferring "with the cattlemen in Cherokee strip . . . where there are perhaps fifty thousand cattle: whether it will not be better for them to let the Indians have cattle enough to fill out their rations until appropriation is made, and take the chance of being paid hereafter by the Government? It is certainly their interest to do so as their herds will be surely raided." General Sheridan, Pope's senior officer, refused Pope's plan and callously believed that the Cheyennes and Arapahos would be unjustified in committing depredations even with their rations cut by a third. "The climate is good," Sheridan claimed, and "wild vegetables abound, and ripe at this season of the year. Many of the Arapahos and Southern Cheyennes used to have years ago fair sized cattle herds of their own." He further directed Pope to caution Major Randall "not to encourage the Indians in their demands by too much sympathy with them."[79]

Kiowa and Comanche Agent Hunt, who had to comply with the same order from Commissioner Price, took matters into his own hands. He made arrangements with Suggs and Wagoner, Texans who held their herds on the reservation under some rather questionable arrangements. He asked them to provide 150 head of cattle each to make up to the Kiowas and Comanches for the "deficiency" in rations in exchange for their allowing the Texans to remain on the reservation until at least July 1. Hunt assured them that he would do all in his power to prevent any depredations to their herds.[80]

Similar to Hunt, Agent Miles wanted to lease reservation grassland to Texas cattlemen, and use the proceeds to purchase cattle to feed the Cheyennes and Arapahos. The commissioner of Indian affairs and the secretary of the interior both rejected Miles's request even though the Cherokee Nation was leasing the outlet at the same time to several cattle companies. A letter from the headquarters of the Department of the Missouri spelled out the dire nature of the crisis confronting Miles and the Cheyennes and Arapahos. "What then are they to do? They are surrounded by herds of cattle, grazing on the Cherokee Strip, just north of them, and elsewhere in their vicinity. Are they expected to suffer the pangs of hunger in the midst of plenty without complaint? Are they to refrain from satisfying their absolute needs by levying by force, or otherwise, on the herds around them?" Commissioner Price remained unmoved. He noted that Miles's earlier effort to lease reservation grazing grounds had never returned money from the Texas ranchmen.[81]

The Cheyennes and Arapahos would be in a good position if they could have concluded an enforceable lease with the Texans. It would have provided the revenue necessary for the Indians to buy their own stock animals and would have "speedily enable[d] them to become self-self-supportive." Such a speedy solution, however, never happened.[82]

What Price, Sheridan, and the like-minded ignored was the degree to which the rations were nearly always insufficient to sustain human life. Lieutenant Colonel John Hatch, the commanding officer at Fort Sill, illustrated this fact in a letter in 1879. While diners at Delmonico's in New York City might be served a twenty-ounce steak along with a host of trimmings and side dishes, Kiowas at Fort Sill, per person, were to receive a daily average of one and a half pounds of meat (beef that pork could substitute for) and a half pound of flour with a little sugar and coffee included. Each soldier at the same post was to receive daily one and a quarter pounds of beef, two and two-thirds ounces of sugar, twenty-two ounces of bread, about four ounces of beans, and vegetables in season. The diner at Delmonico's would consume a few thousand calories, a soldier at Fort Sill would be provided daily with 3,575 calories, and a Kiowa supplied with full rations would possibly consume up to 2,140 calories. Hatch pointed out that the Kiowa ration might "prevent hunger in an indoor clerk, or a woman who did not go much in the open air, but is not enough for a child of two years of age who lives and sleeps in the fresh air of these prairies." In fact, the daily calorie content is about twice the 1,000 calories that pediatric nutritionists currently recommend for an average American two-year-old, but the rations fell woefully short of the 2,400 to 2,600 calories needed by a moderately active adult or the nearly 3,000 required by an active man.[83]

But recall, beef cattle sold to reservations seldom met contractual requirements. The cattle sold were often scrawny and lacked much in the way of meat and fat. This was especially so in the cold months when, as Joseph McCoy claimed, poor stock made up reservation deliveries more often than not. McCoy's observation was that steers often arrived reeling "as they walk with poverty and starvation."[84] Even when reservation agents tried to make sure that the beeves bought were adequate meat animals, the agents encountered powerful forces arrayed against them.

Frank Maltby found himself filling in for Agent Haworth, who took sick leave in the fall of 1876. In October, Maltby rejected 74 of the 275 beeves received at the reservation. In November he rejected 27 deficient beeves of the 195 received. However, he was ordered by the commissioner of Indian affairs to "lower his standards" and receive the steers. The controversy resulted in an inquiry, which resulted in receiving most of the rejected cattle in a November delivery. Even the cattle Maltby received were slight animals at best. The 100 steers delivered on November 9 weighed on average a mere 729 pounds, and those delivered on November 25 averaged only 789 pounds.[85]

By 1879, many of the Kiowa leaders had cattle herds of their own. The younger men, however, were largely without stock or farmsteads. Colonel Hatch strongly recommended that the Bureau of Indian Affairs purchase cows for the younger men to begin their own operations. He reminded the bureau that the federal government wanted the Kiowas to become pastoralists, and that the one hundred to two hundred calves and seven hundred cows provided to them was too little stock to get the job done. Moreover, given how often a Kiowa might find himself or herself going hungry, Hatch marveled that it was "astonishing that they have in so few instances disobeyed the order not to kill their cattle, and encourage[d] the belief that they can become pastoral people." Hatch estimated that adding one thousand animals to their existing herd would not be excessive.[86]

In July 1883, White Shield, a Southern Cheyenne chief, traveled from his village on the Washita River to Fort Supply, Indian Territory, to voice his frustration with the current state of affairs on the Cheyenne reservation. He did not go alone: Stone Calf, Little Robe, and Spotted Horse, all chiefs or prominent men among the Dog Soldier society, accompanied him. White Shield made it perfectly clear that intruding "cow boys" ruined his efforts to raise cattle. "I had 150 head of Cattle," he reported, but "I can hardly round up 50 head now." He adamantly opposed leasing or selling off any portion of the Cheyenne lands: "I don't want to trade off my land or grass." The Cheyennes living along the Washita, he emphasized, "have killed no Cattle and burned no grass." In short, White Shield explained that his village of some sixty lodges had not bothered or hindered any white man's herds, even though one near his own place had made it impossible for him to plant anything, and when he had complained to the white herder, the man had tried "to run us away."[87]

The situation that White Shield, Stone Calf, Little Robe, and Spotted Horse all endured made it impossible to protect their stock-raising efforts. By 1885, against their wishes, white stockmen were grazing over 220,000 head of cattle on the reserve.[88] Colonel J. H. Potter, the commander at Fort Supply, in an unambiguous letter to General C. C. Augur, commander of the Department of the Missouri at Fort Leavenworth, sympathized with White Shield's understanding of the situation.[89] Potter understood that White Shield and the others had never agreed to the leasing and that they never took any of the lease revenues offered to them. In 1885, this dire state of affairs led President Grover Cleveland to void all leases in the Cheyenne and Arapaho reservation and to order General Sheridan to remove "all persons, other than Indians, then on said reservation for the purpose of grazing cattle thereon."[90] Still, this would not be enough to secure Cheyenne cattle raising, as allotting the reservation under the provisions of the Dawes Act (1887) hampered all of the Indians' efforts.

From this point on, it became impossible to plug the flow of boomers into Indian Territory. The stockmen and companies would lose their leases in the Cherokee Outlet, and in the Osage, Kiowa, Comanche, Wichita, and Southern Cheyenne and Arapaho reservations. Indians would quickly, although unwillingly, find themselves relegated to 160-acre parcels that did them little good in attempts to become self-sufficient through either farming or ranching. Allotment put an end to the open-range cattle grazing and cattle driving through the new Territorial State of Oklahoma. Even though "boomer" David Payne never lived to see his followers prevail in Oklahoma, one of his main supporters did. Joseph McCoy moved there to celebrate and prosper if he could. In 1890, a Democrat like Payne, Joseph McCoy ran to represent Oklahoma in Congress. He lost.

CHAPTER 9

# The End of the Trail

THE ADVENT OF WICHITA — THE ENCROACHMENT OF FARMING: A SHIFTING CULTURAL LANDSCAPE — TECHNOLOGY AND THE OPENING OF NEW TRAILS — A CHANGING CATTLE LANDSCAPE AND THE FIRST NATIONAL CONVENTION OF CATTLEMEN, 1884 — THE END OF THE TRAIL

James Mead sold and bought cattle, just as Joseph McCoy did, but on a much smaller scale. McCoy dealt primarily with those whom he knew in Illinois, and Mead did the same in Iowa. What McCoy had done in Abilene, Mead wanted to do in Wichita. Mead knew, however, that his aspirations for Wichita had two serious shortcomings: one, Wichita lacked a railroad connection, and two, he possessed few ties to the major players in the cattle trade. He had some ideas about how to secure a railroad link, but he needed someone who could tout the virtues and advantages of Wichita to Texas cattlemen. Mead and the other Wichita promoters had one person in mind for the job: Joseph G. McCoy.

## *The Advent of Wichita*

The Wichitans had stiff competition for cornering the cattle trade. Although they had built their small assembly of buildings right on the Chisholm Trail, at best stockmen gathered there to buy and sell cattle. This location, where the Little Arkansas fed the main branch of the Arkansas River, was a major ford on the Chisholm Trail. In 1872, being a major location on the trail was the only argument that Mead could make for asserting a claim to the cattle trade. At the same time, the promoters of Ellsworth, a town well west of Abilene on the Kansas Pacific line, and notably outside the quarantine line, had made their burg a major outlet for Texas cattle.

A couple of years later, Mead's correspondence reveals the keen competition between Wichita and Ellsworth for the cattle trade. In July 1874, in a letter to Mead, E. Lucas, an Iowa cattleman, described how some of his acquaintances had paid more for 900 head of three- and four-year-old beeves than they would have if they had bought them at the Wichita stockyards. The letter underscored the fact that the news of lower prices in Wichita had arrived too late for Lucas's friends to save money. Lucas, however, now aware of more favorable pricing in Wichita, informed Mead that he was grazing 230 cattle on his bluegrass pastures and that he was contemplating buying a few more to overwinter. Lucas assured Mead that he would come to Wichita to purchase stock if he decided to overwinter any additional cattle.[1]

Town promoters in other communities also sought a cut of the Texas cattle, just like those attempting to lasso the trade in Ellsworth and Wichita. All they needed, or so they thought, was a railroad connection, ideally one south of Abilene that could grab the Texas herds first. Texas drovers did not always heed the quarantine lines drawn up by the Kansas legislature. An article that appeared in the Council Grove *Advertiser* (reprinted in the *Leavenworth Times*) noted the passing of several thousand Texas cattle through Morris County in October 1869. The county was well within the quarantine line that prohibited Texas cattle drives in the fall months. Still, the writer cheerfully predicted, "with proper precaution we might make the revenue from this source very large when the railroad is completed to this point." He did make a case for protecting farmers from the ravages of Texas fever, but he knew that if those fears could be allayed, money would flow in with the Texas cattle trade.[2]

Sam Wood, a state legislator, social reformer, and town promoter who lived in Chase County, believed Cottonwood Falls was destined for cattle greatness. By the end of 1870, he anticipated the arrival of the Atchison, Topeka, and Santa Fe Railroad. The AT&SF line led directly to Kansas City and from there connected to the great eastern beef markets. Some of the richest grazing grounds in the nation surrounded Cottonwood Falls, situated as it was in the heart of the tallgrass prairies of the Flint Hills. In a letter in the *Leavenworth Times*, Wood, confident in his prognostications, proclaimed that Cottonwood Falls would "undoubtedly be the great shipping point for cattle" in 1871. He asserted that the AT&SF would load 250,000 cattle and flood Cottonwood Falls merchants with millions of dollars. He must have sensed how far-fetched his predictions sounded, because he signed his article "Yours soberly."[3]

Whether on the sauce or not, Wood understood that the reach of railroad tracks would determine which towns in Kansas would outpace Abilene, or Ellsworth, as an outlet for Texas cattle. When Wood wrote, no railroad had reached Wichita, Kansas, yet he predicted that "the natural point for these cattle to come into our State, is Wichita or Arkansas city, and all railroads seeking this trade must point in this direction." Wood foresaw a time when the AT&SF line would reach across western Kansas and eastern Colorado, connect to Albuquerque, New Mexico, and eventually terminate in Los Angeles, California. Reasonably, Texas drovers would find outlets for their herds scattered along this line. Wood, along these lines of sober thinking, was correctly predicting the future of Texas cattle trailing.[4]

Before those people boosting Cottonwood Falls—or before anyone living in the Flint Hills who desired a cut of the Texas cattle trade—might grab it, the folks at Ellsworth, Kansas, had already captured a large portion of the trade. In their efforts to draw the cattle commerce away from Abilene, the townsfolk induced William Sigerson, a wealthy businessman from St. Louis, to build the Kansas Stock Yards. They advertised the advantages of the place as a cattle outlet over McCoy's Abilene. As a shipping point, Ellsworth did possess several advantages. For one, the city builders had located the plat just outside the quarantine line of 1867. Second, the tracks of the KP linked the commerce of the city to the eastern markets. Third, the grasslands surrounding the town were largely unsettled by farmers and as such posed no obstacle to Texas drovers wishing to graze their herds while waiting for a buyer or an opportune time to ship their herds east on their own accounts. As one writer noted, the area, "for twenty or thirty miles west, north and south of [Ellsworth], affords abundant pasturage for thousands of cattle, with living streams of water; in fact the range on the bottom and high lands is unbounded in extent."[5]

The folks in Wichita, however, saw themselves as the rightful heirs of the cattle trade. They understood the powerful lure of shipping from their locale. In the first place, the geography was good. The Chisholm Trail already crossed the Arkansas River where Mead and others were laying out the town site. The junction, famed as a trading location, was surrounded by ample water sources and grazing grounds. Moreover, like Ellsworth, it stood just barely outside the 1867 quarantine line. All that was needed to compete with Ellsworth was a rail connection and an effective marketing campaign, besides eliminating the Osage Nation's title to the land.

Even though the Osages legally owned what would become Sedgwick County, in the fall of 1868 several individuals (among them former governor Samuel

Crawford and former fur trader James Mead) met in Emporia, Kansas, and formed the Wichita Town Company. These men were premature in launching a town site, as the federal government had not yet settled the Osage land question. It would take a couple more years to iron out the question of the Osage title to land in Kansas, to gain enough population for the formation of a county, and to legally plat and start building the city of Wichita.[6]

In the fall of 1869, while Sigerson's crews were building the stockyards at Ellsworth, James R. Mead headed to Topeka to deposit the papers required for the organization of Sedgwick County. As a senator in the state house, Mead understood the formalities of creating a county and was an excellent choice to present the papers at the capitol. Even though he was still living in Towanda in Butler County, located to the east of the future Sedgwick County, Mead had an abiding interest in seeing the town of Wichita flourish. Even in its primitive state of development, cattle buyers had started meeting Texas drovers at the confluence of the Little and Big Arkansas Rivers. Mead found the trade lucrative enough that he proudly displayed his "yaller boys" (gold coins) to folks he visited on his way to Topeka.[7] By the end of 1870, 175 buildings stood in the city, populated by about 800 residents. It was then that Mead moved his family to Wichita and hitched his fortune to the fate of the town.

Some twenty miles to the north of Wichita, on July 17, 1871, the AT&SF company had extended its tracks to Newton, Kansas. This positioned Newton to intercept the Texas cattle drives before they could reach Ellsworth and created a shipping outlet lacked by Wichita. The loading yards at Newton could handle six thousand head of cattle and load six stock cars at a time.[8] The Wichita business community knew that in order to survive, it must have a rail connection to the AT&SF.

In June, Mead negotiated an agreement with Thomas Peters (the general manager of the AT&SF) and Cyrus K. Holliday (the director of the AT&SF) to connect with the Wichita and Southwestern Railway Company (W&SW). Now all that was needed was a successful bond vote to underwrite the building of the line. In August 1871, after overcoming rival town promoters in the county who also wanted the link to the AT&SF, the voters overwhelmingly approved the $200,000 Wichita-based bond issue that financed the rail line to the AT&SF. Track building followed in earnest: by the end of March 1872, the AT&SF had taken possession of the WSW company, and Peters had undertaken to build the stockyards for loading cattle into stock cars. In April, Texas drovers had several herds grazing in the Cherokee Outlet ready to sell. When May arrived, the folks in Wichita heard the shrill whistle of an AT&SF locomotive.

The next step for the town leaders of Wichita was to advertise their outlet to Texas cattlemen. They had employed runners and agents who were already scouring the Chisholm Trail for oncoming herds. The editor of the *Eagle* warned that "Newton, Abilene and the Kansas Pacific road are already making strenuous efforts" to secure the cattle trade, but Wichita had an ace up its sleeve. Joseph McCoy had arrived in town, and the Wichita promoters held him in high esteem for making Abilene "one of the best inland towns in Kansas." Now it was Wichita's turn, and the editor feared that unless the city secured the services of McCoy, "this opportunity will be flirted away." Before the end of May, the city council had hired James Bryden, "an old and experienced Texas cattle man," along with McCoy to "bring forward" the advantages of shipping cattle from Wichita.[9]

On June 8, 1872, an AT&SF locomotive pulled the first eighteen stock cars loaded with Texas cattle away from the Wichita stockyards. At about the same time, McCoy related that he had received a letter from Bryden reporting that over one hundred herds were on their way to Wichita. Mead and his cohort had transformed Wichita into the major cattle shipping point in the state.[10]

Wichitans were well positioned to take advantage of the cattle drives in 1872. By mid-July, Texas drovers had taken over 315,000 head of cattle up the Chisholm Trail. As McCoy detailed in a letter to the *Chicago Live Stock Reporter*, over 60 percent of the cattle driven north were stock cattle, and as these originated in the northern and northwestern parts of Texas, they were "comparatively short-horned, square built and well graded into the Durham and old-fashioned American cattle." These cattle, McCoy emphasized, were a fine foundation for crossing with full-blooded Durhams. Savvy Kansas farmers should buy up these cattle, breed them, overwinter them, and have on hand offspring "fit for grazing or corn feeding, and when fat, for the shambles of New York or Boston." As this drive was shaping up to be smaller than the one the year before, by fall, McCoy warned, there would be no stock cattle left to buy, so a smart investor would buy right away.[11]

Besides advising local farmers about when to buy stock cattle, McCoy wrote another letter highlighting his accomplishments boosting the Wichita cattle trade. He asserted to have "thoroughly and judiciously advertised" Wichita throughout the Northwest and West. Newspapers in cattle country had highlighted the Wichita facilities and accommodations, and "editorial notices have been accorded [to Wichita] in the livestock reports of the principal markets." More cattle had arrived in and been shipped from Wichita than from either of the two competing towns. By August, the AT&SF had hauled over 300 stock cars out of Wichita, a ratio of five to one over the competing cities. Additionally, enough cattle grazed nearby to fill another 1,200 stock cars. McCoy's letter was, in essence, a gesture to publicize the end of his contract with Wichita. He acknowledged and thanked "those who have generously contributed toward my compensation," and in closing he offered his "heartfelt wishes" for the future welfare of the city. In fact, McCoy was taken enough with Wichita that he decided to take up residence in the city.[12]

In December 1872, the AT&SF reported that up to November 21, the company had loaded and shipped 4,618 stock cars, over 3,800 of which had been loaded with about 70,000 beeves that had started out in Wichita. In total, 350,000 head of cattle grazed in the Arkansas River Valley to the west of the city, and of this number, 150,000, ranging in price from $8 to $20 a head, were bought by men from adjoining states as stock cattle "to eat up their surplus corn crops." With over $5 million changing hands in Wichita "for cattle alone," McCoy and Bryden had done their work well.[13]

Regardless of how well McCoy might perform for those engaged in the cattle business, he always seemed to be embroiled in the competition for the control and consumption of the solar energy coursing over the prairies. While his work played an important role in lessening the grip that the Indians had once held on those energy sources, he failed to forestall the advance of farms.

## The Encroachment of Farming: *A Shifting Cultural Landscape*

McCoy experienced firsthand the rising tension between those who supported the cattle trade in Abilene and those who no longer did. By 1871, the contest had boiled over into confrontation in Dickinson County. Farmers had had enough of Texas cattle trampling through their fields and spreading Texas fever to their own cattle. In May 1871, they resolved to put a stop to the trade, and they gathered in force, saddled their horses, and rode south to intercept the oncoming cattle herds. The drovers, who had no intention of turning back, engaged in some astute diplomacy. They offered the farmers $1,000 in gold and a bond of $5,000 "to make good all damages to native stock."[14]

Just days before the devastating winter of 1871–72 struck the cattle business around Abilene, a report appeared indicating that the promises of Texas cattlemen to reimburse local farmers and stockmen for their losses due to Texas fever had fallen woefully short of expectations. Texans had failed to pay up the claim fund, and those around Abilene who received payments for their losses recovered only seven cents on the dollar. This failure to fully reimburse the farmers put them in a sour mood when it came to embracing the Texas cattle trade.

While the blizzard of 1871–72 raged outside, over 140 members of the Farmers' Protective Association of Dickinson County met with the object of stopping any further importation of Texas cattle into Abilene. It must have pained McCoy to no end to think that his once good friend, T. C. Henry, then a large-scale wheat producer and leader of the association, had turned on him. In February, while cattle losses on the open range mounted from the frightful freezing weather sweeping the countryside, the association crafted a circular intended for Texas cattlemen. The members agreed to "most respectfully request all who have contemplated driving Texas Cattle to Abilene the coming season to seek some other point for shipment, as the inhabitants of Dickinson will no longer submit to the evils of the trade." In Ellsworth, Reverend L. Sternberg, along with D. B. Long, who in time became the first fish commissioner in the state, held a mass meeting of farmers opposed to the Texas cattle trade. They made it clear that "farmers and drovers of Texas cattle can not pull in the same traces." If cattlemen were to prevail, then the future of the country would fall into the hands of "a few large stock men having many poor illiterate men dependent upon them for support" and leave the land bereft of churches and schools, the marks of a truly civilized land.[15]

All of this anti–cattle trail sentiment of the farmers in both Ellis and Dickinson County spelled bad news for McCoy and eventually for the cattle transportation business of the Kansas Pacific (KP) railroad. By 1872, Joseph McCoy and his brothers had lost all connection to their venture in Abilene. It is a wonder that McCoy, reeling first from the cattle plague of 1868, then from the legal confrontation with the directors of the Kansas Pacific line, and, to add insult to injury, from the losses brought about by the blizzard of 1871–72, had any further aspirations for succeeding in the cattle business. For all practical purposes, from 1872 on, he and his brothers went their separate ways.

As was the case with Abilene, the spread of wheat farming throughout the southern counties of Kansas had further hampered trail driving up the Chisholm

Trail by the mid-1870s. Settlers had legally established Sumner County in 1871, and grain farming rapidly took hold there. By 1872, farmers had planted over 500 acres in winter wheat and harvested over 7,600 acres of their primary crop, corn. By 1874, they had planted over 3,500 acres of wheat and nearly 23,000 acres of corn.[16] In the same year, a reporter from Wellington noted that wheat farmers had harvested fields that were reportedly in "fine condition."[17] An agricultural economy had blossomed, to the distinct disadvantage of the Texas drovers who still wanted to ply the portion of the Chisholm Trail that sliced through the county.

Immediately to the north, ambitious men and women rapidly poured into Sedgwick County and competed intently with Texas cattlemen for control of the landscape. While the editor of the *Wichita Eagle* endeavored to help drovers find a better, less confrontational approach to the Arkansas River ford to reach the stockyards in the east part of town, he noted how quickly emigrants were converting open grasslands into profitable farms. J. S. McCulley, for one, had purchased 160 acres of land in the spring of 1871 and by the fall had harvested an excellent yield of sod corn grown on the same acreage. Usually farmers planted sod corn first, as the roots of the plant were good for loosening the prairie soils. The editor bragged that McCulley anticipated that after he reworked his field, the harvest the following fall would meet the costs of both land and labor. Such cost-benefit ratios for farming meant that drovers would be hard pressed to find any mixed-grass prairie grazing lands around Wichita remaining for their herds in the summer of 1873.[18]

Without a hint of the mounting conflicts arising over land use, a farmer going by the initials of J. P. H. lauded both the cattle and farming advances near Wichita in the Arkansas River Valley. In the late summer of 1872, within a circle of twenty miles around Wichita, J. P. H. counted over seventy thousand Texas cattle awaiting shipment into eastern markets. At the same time, he observed that the farmland in the valley produced abundant yields of sod corn and that farmers were racing to plant the first fields of wheat. He extolled the "luxuriant growth of grass . . . as tall as a man's head and still growing." Sunflowers lined the county roads, he boasted, like a "complete arch over the thoroughfare." All of this—people planting small grains and others grazing thousands of cattle in a mixed-grass prairie ecosystem—could not flourish together indefinitely.[19]

By the spring of 1873, rumors abounded about farmers who had banded together to oppose Texas cattle drives to Wichita. The county commissioners of Sumner and Sedgwick jointly hired a farmer, W. T. Jewett, to canvass the surrounding townships to gauge the extent of opposition to the arrival of Texas herds. Jewett went to work and issued a final report that located only one farmer who had objected to Texas cattle drives. Even this farmer, however, conceded to Jewett's request that he sign an agreement that would accept the presence of Texas herds headed to Wichita. Moreover, Jewett noted how a "great many stray dollars" could end up in the hands of those farmers trading with Texas drovers. In the end, the county commissioners were relieved to find that there existed little apparent resistance to Texas drives through the region.[20]

By the spring of 1874, the conflict between farmers and cattle had grown intense in and around Wichita. Businesspeople in Wichita anticipated a drive considerably less than the one in 1873 but still estimated an ample 250,000 beeves. However, the amount of land immediately to the west of Wichita that had been converted to corn and wheat fields stood steadfastly as an impediment to any drive of Texas longhorns through the area. This cropland covered the cattle trail leading toward the stockyards, and the town "authorities," in an effort to keep cattle from freely ranging through the streets of Wichita and to avoid "annoying" farmers to the west of town, marked out a route to a new ford across the Arkansas River, a crossing more than three miles south of the town. So that drovers would not miss the route, the townsmen marked the path leading to the ford with bright red flags emblazoned with the lone star.[21] In the end, low rainfall and plagues of Rocky Mountain locusts cut short the estimates of the cattle trade, and by year's end, only 50,253 beeves had been traded and shipped in over 2,400 cattle cars. Both farmers and stockmen were hurting.[22]

By the end of December, the members of the Ninnescah Grange, comprised of farmers living to the south of Wichita, had had enough of Texas cattle. They did not want to destroy the shipping economy of Wichita, for they recognized the importance of the stockyards and rail transport of cattle to Wichita's prosperity. Rather, they wanted the milling of the great Texas herds prior to shipment to be kept far to the west of the city. Zarah McClung, the secretary of the grange, amplified this position by illustrating the dangers that Texas longhorns posed to all domestic breeds. An exasperated McClung claimed that Texas cattle were solely responsible for over $5,000 in farmers' losses due to the deaths of their "native cattle."[23]

Agricultural improvements in the region, McClung also observed, were no less in danger from Texas cattle than were native cattle herds. Texas herds routinely trampled crops, hedges, and other farm improvements. Texas cattlemen often met the farmers' requests for compensation with "threats, violence, insult and abuse." If that were not enough, the Texans also brought with them, even if inadvertently, "an armed horde of lawless desperados" who all too often "threatened and shot down" farmers on the thresholds of their homes. McClung complained that these renegades too often escaped justice and left farmers with little recourse other than to "fight for their possessions, and to defend" themselves at their own peril. As McClung recommended, during the following session, the legislature responded by moving the quarantine line well to the west of Wichita.[24]

As agricultural production became an ever-larger share of the Wichita economy, by 1878, businesspeople hardly missed the cattle trade. Between 1875 and the end of 1877, receipts at the Atchison, Topeka, and Santa Fe yards had nearly doubled, from $230,900 to $404,360. A stockyard still operated in the city, and in 1877, the AT&SF loaded and shipped 193 stock-car loads of cattle, or 3,920 head of stock valued at $127,400. The dominance of crop farming, however, was demonstrated by the shipment out of the same facility of 859 freight car loads of wheat, or 343,600 bushels valued at $257,700.[25]

Farmsteads quickly became a more common sight in the counties to the west of Wichita and had effectively closed off open-range cattle grazing on any remaining prairie grasses in those parts. C. C. Bemis, William Bell, and W. H. VanSickle lived in Reno County and supported the farm operations there. By 1872, Reno County farmers had tilled nearly 4,500 acres, most of which were planted in corn. True, this represented only about one-half of 1 percent of the total amount of land in the county and may account for why Texas drovers thought they could drive herds indiscriminately through the county toward the grazing lands around the Great Bend of the Arkansas. But the scales had tipped in favor of agriculture. As county commissioners, Bell, VanSickle, and Bemis warned Texas cattlemen to steer clear of the county altogether. They gave notice "to all persons owning or driving Texas cattle" that "*no herds will be permitted to drive up the Arkansas river through Reno county.*" The commissioners warned drovers to avoid the settlements so they could also avoid any trouble.[26]

In 1876, Texas cattlemen still headed north, but they herded their beeves nowhere near the former cattle towns of Abilene or Wichita. They relocated their operations west to Dodge City, and the open-range grasslands near it. Along with them moved the saloons, the dance hall women, the gamblers—stockmen and card players—and lawmen like Wyatt Earp. The sedate, newly "civilized" cities of Abilene and Wichita had no need, or desire, to encourage the service businesses that addressed the demands of cowboys.

These Texans still had over 250,000 head of cattle that they intended to drive north, excluding the herds that had overwintered in Indian Territory. With the AT&SF railroad traversing the state, cattlemen had options for where to graze their herds and find outlets once they reached Kansas. Weak cattle markets, however, forced them to hold their herds in the state and to anticipate moving only about a third of the animals east while they hoped that they could sell half as "stock cattle." That still left a sizable number lingering in the state with no particular place to go. The grasslands between Dodge City and Ellis offered the most promising region to keep the herds until the market conditions improved. These open rangelands were close to outlets along the western portions of both the Kansas Pacific and the Atchison, Topeka, and Santa Fe lines. If the markets advanced, a drover could move a herd fairly quickly from there to one of the shipping yards.[27]

The counties between Ellis and Dodge City had hardly any agricultural development by 1876. A quick look at the acreage under cultivation from south to north indicates just how little farming had spread through the region. In Ellis County, less than one-half of 1 percent of the land was in crops. Trego County, just to the west of Ellis, had barely been organized. Farmers in the three counties in a tier below Ellis, Rush, Pawnee, and Edwards had planted less than 1 percent of the total combined acreage making up the counties.

This area of the High Plains grasslands, most of which still remained in the public domain, was prime grazing land, ideal for keeping Texas cattle at bay while waiting to load them into eastbound railcars. In Ford County, where the AT&SF shipping point was at Dodge City, a mere one-third of 1 percent of the land was in crops. Even this number is distorted by the farmers' experimentation with growing corn, which failed as the 1,040 acres planted in 1876 fell to 154 and then rose only to 300 in the two years that followed. The Kansas Board of Agriculture reported no old corn on hand in the county in 1878, which implies that all of it had been consumed, so the county hardly represented a flourishing commercial agricultural economy in the making.[28]

This realm of Kansas, as many understood it at the time, was good for little but cattle grazing. In 1882, a special correspondent for the *San Marcos Free Press* writing from Wichita confirmed this belief for his readers back in Texas. "The large area of land comprised in the unorganized counties of Kansas has been found after repeated trials to be only a potters' field for diversified farming, and hence all this vast country has long since been turned over to the stock raiser, and vast herds of cattle now range on the rich and extensive pasturage."[29] In this, the heart of the Great Plains blanketed by nutritious buffalo grass, the AT&SF channeled the flow of cattle out of its yards located in Dodge City. The cattle drives to Dodge City, however, would soon become a thing of the past. Changes in the technology of shipping beef and the consolidation of the packing industry would play major factors in rendering cattle driving obsolete.

## *Technology and the Opening of New Trails*

Ice could solve a lot of problems in transporting beef and appeasing cranky farmers as well as opening new trails and destinations for American roasts and steaks. Things were literally heating up in Texas during the Civil War. The war not only cut Texas cattlemen out of northern markets but also eliminated the importation of natural ice into Texas.[30] This situation led Texans to embrace artificial ice making during the war.

Ferdinand Carré had patented an ice-making machine in France in 1859. He refined the technique of heat absorption in his machine, which he displayed at the Universal London Exhibition in 1862. His machine, which could produce up to 440 pounds of ice an hour, caught the attention of visiting Texans. Confederate blockade runners delivered one of his machines to Mexico, and it was transported from there overland to San Antonio, Texas. Ice was a valuable commodity in Texas. In San Antonio, where ice was manufactured, a person could dine on beefsteak costing two cents a pound, whereas one pound of ice cost ten cents per pound.[31] By 1866, led by innovators such as Andrew Muhl, ice manufacturing in San Antonio had reached a rate of 1,200 pounds daily.[32]

Other cities suffered worse from an ice shortage than San Antonio. In Matamoros, manufactured ice of "poor quality" sold for fifty cents a pound. The Galveston firm of Allen, Poole, and Company—the same one that had a tight hold on shipping cattle to New Orleans or Havana—also largely controlled the importation of "natural ice." In the summer of 1865, residents of Galveston complained of an "ice famine" and the usurious price of ten cents per pound when

Allen and Poole could acquire it for $9.50 per ton. A writer in the *Galveston Daily News* hoped that artificial ice making might increase and that he might "yet be independent of the monopolists for our sherberts, ices and juleps."[33]

Developments in artificial ice making quickly caught the attention of many, both southerners and northerners, who wanted to see an alternative to the live shipment of cattle either by rail or by steamboat. In 1866, a writer in the *New Orleans Times-Picayune* thought that "if fast sailing vessels can be fitted up as refrigerators, and take the beef through fresh and sweet, some of the superabundance of Northern capital could find a profitable investment in the enterprise, and do a wonderful deal of good by furnishing cheap beef to the poor of the crowed cities of the North."[34] Six months later, a correspondent for the *New York Times* writing from San Antonio noted that "the late introduction of 'ice machines' will create a vast change in the supply of salt beef throughout the world." The implications, according to the writer, were immense, with Texas alone capable of supplying Europe, "and at a price far below the present market." He touted a shipment of beef, "fully equal to the best Western or Fulton Market beef," kept at an "even temperature" by ice made on board a ship that sailed from New Orleans to New York.[35]

In February 1869, Dr. H. P. Howard and General Walter A. Bennett of San Antonio, who represented several ranchers, headed north, traveling through several states on a quest "to perfect arrangements whereby the beef of Texas should find a market." Their initial idea was to construct a "packery" in Kansas City to which Texas cattle could be driven and where the animals could be slaughtered, packed, and shipped to eastern urban markets.[36] During their travels, they made their way to Philadelphia, where they met Wilson Bray, a skillful mechanic and inventor who had perfected a refrigerating technique. Bray had designed a device with two chambers, one containing salted ice and the other heavily insulated. A small steam engine blew a strong current of air across the ice mixture, and this rapidly chilled air then became the coolant that removed the heat from the insulated chamber. Bray's operation could reduce the air temperature in the insulated chamber to 30 degrees below zero Fahrenheit, which was more than enough to keep meat fresh during transit.[37]

Thoroughly impressed by Bray's demonstration, Howard and Bennett acquired a half interest in Bray's patent, gained the interest of several eastern investors, and incorporated the United States and West India Meat and Fruit

Company. With $1 million in stock, $600,000 of which was working capital, the company retrofitted the steamship *Agnes* with Bray's refrigeration machine. The forward hold of the ship could keep chilled 150 dressed beeves. The directors estimated that their company could deliver beeves into the New Orleans market for six cents per pound and into the New York market for ten cents per pound, well below the profit margin for McCoy or any cattle shipper from the Midwest.[38]

Toward the end of June 1869, the *Agnes* docked at Indianola, Texas, and was loaded with beef destined for New Orleans. This trip proved a disaster, as not enough ice was loaded into the *Agnes* to keep the meat chilled during the entire voyage. The second voyage fared better. On July 5, the *Agnes* again departed from Indianola, bound for New Orleans. On Saturday, July 9, on a cool and pleasant day by New Orleans standards, the *Agnes* docked with its cargo of Texas beef.

The *Times-Picayune* declared the beginning of "a new era." The successful delivery of the meat "has established beyond all peradventure the very important fact that beef may be brought from the prairies of Texas and laid down in the markets of the world perfectly fresh and juicy, greatly cheaper than that now offered for sale, and vastly superior in quality." Moreover, the owners of the Meat and Fruit Company anticipated a net profit of $20,000 on the delivery to New Orleans of 1,000 choice beeves, and 2,000 beeves delivered to New York could return nearly $85,000.[39] Soon the company planned to ship 200 animals a week to Mobile, Alabama, and another 300 a week to Havana. The reporter for the *Times-Picayune* gleefully noted that Bray's "apparatus is alike applicable to railroad and steamers."[40] But one aspect of Bray's technology hindered its application: it relied on the application of ice, two tons of it per day to keep one hundred hanging beeves chilled.[41] Any amount of ice less than this would result in higher temperatures than 40 degrees in the cargo holds and meat spoilage.

At the same time, another refrigeration technique was in the works. "Professor" Thaddeus S. C. Lowe had devised a cooling system employing a compressor, which eliminated the need for ice as a coolant. He used carbonic acid gas as the coolant and produced chilling temperatures that plummeted as low as 160 degrees below zero Fahrenheit. Not only did Lowe's technology dispense with the need for ice but it could manufacture ice for as little as three dollars per ton. In New York City, Lowe and investors incorporated the Lowe Refrigerated Steamship Company, and by the spring of 1869, they had fitted the steamship *William Taber* with the Lowe cooling system and the capacity to haul three hundred beeves.[42]

The ship, docked at the foot of East Nineteenth Street and readied to leave port on May 15, was to steam to the Allen, Poole, and Company's docks at Galveston and bring Texas beef back to New York City. However, the *William Taber* sprang a leak off the coast of Florida and never reached its destination.[43] Nonetheless, Lowe's technology, employing compressed gas rather than ice as the coolant, would become the future standard by which refrigeration would be accomplished by either railroad or steamboat. It would not take long for slaughterhouses and shipping companies to see the utility and economy in transporting refrigerated beef. In short order, new cattle trails appeared that sharply competed with those originated and championed by McCoy.

Joseph McCoy was an astute student of the cattle trade, and he recognized, if not experienced, firsthand how technology and ecological change could rapidly transform the nature of the cattle trade. Given his business ties to New York City, he may have been a regular reader of the *New York Tribune*, and if so, he might have read an article titled "The Cattle Trade" in June 1868. It was a short piece that in part highlighted the brisk business of the KP company in transporting cattle from Abilene, "that point on the Kansas Pacific Road most accessible from the cattle-growing region of Texas." In fact, the railroad company found its capacity so overtaxed in transporting cattle that it was "blocked up at the State line, unable to take the stock away as fast as delivered."[44]

But McCoy would also have noted something else in the piece, an insight that probably came as no surprise to him. The situation, the journalist opined, clearly pointed "to the not distant day when cattle must be slaughtered on or near the prairies that fed them, and only their meat, &c., brought to market, dropping their hides by the way at the tanneries in the great hemlock woods, and leaving their offal to fertilize the soil whence it was drawn." Others besides this New York correspondent envisioned a similar future of dressed meat shipped long distances, which was why a packing plant was built at Junction City, Kansas, and another at Leavenworth, followed by one built at Kansas City. But these companies failed as there was a reluctance on the part of consumers to purchase canned or salted beef, the mainstay of the packers' production, when and if fresh meat was available.

Consumers' preference for fresh meat over canned and salted provided, at least in theory, an economic incentive to engage in refrigerated fresh meat delivery. It took several days to transport fresh meat from the docks of Indianola, Texas, to dining tables in New Orleans. During transit, without refrigeration, fresh meat from a Texas slaughterhouse would surely spoil in the heat and humidity along the Gulf shore before ever reaching New Orleans. But refrigerated meat could be kept as fresh as the day the beef was slaughtered.

Nonetheless, one problem remained: consumers remained skeptical that refrigerated meat that had been in transit for several days was safe to eat. They needed convincing, which the United States and West India Meat and Fruit Company was happy to provide. The company's new steamship, the *Fire Fly*, could haul a much larger cargo than the *Agnes*. Once the meat arrived in New Orleans and was unloaded into the company's refrigerated warehouse, it was important to sell it before the next shipment arrived. Testimonials regarding the quality of the meat became important to the company, such as one from Colonel R. S. Morse, who owned two of the best hotels in the city, the City Hotel and the St. James Hotel, both known for fine dining. He praised the beef delivered to his City Hotel as keeping longer and better than beef slaughtered in the city and "treated in the ordinary way." He insisted that his "experiment" removed any doubt that "this beef might not keep long after being removed from the refrigerator." He claimed the meat possessed rich "juiciness and excellence of flavor."[45]

In 1872, Denison, Texas, became an incorporated town whose founders anticipated the arrival of the Missouri, Kansas, and Texas Railroad (MK&T), commonly referred to as the Katy. Like a present to the city, the first train arrived on Christmas Eve 1872. By July 1873, the town boasted four thousand residents, three newspapers, the first public school in Texas, and forty saloons. Like McCoy in Kansas, T. S. Rankin, who hailed from Emporia, Kansas, saw an opportunity to establish an outlet on the Katy line that fed into the national cattle trade. In contrast to McCoy's Abilene, Rankin added two additional components to his outlet: a slaughterhouse and refrigerated transportation of beef sides into eastern markets.

McCoy and Rankin were aware of each other before Rankin even undertook to build his enterprise. By the end of 1873, McCoy had moved to Denison, and Rankin employed him to advertise his facility to Texas cattlemen. McCoy went right to work and in February presented the Denison Board of Trade with his plans for advertising the advantages of Rankin's slaughterhouse. The board members made a few modifications to McCoy's circular and immediately ordered five hundred copies of it printed and prepared for distribution.[46]

Before McCoy saddled up to round up Texas ranchers, on November 25, 1873,

Rankin, having purchased his own herd of cattle, launched the first rail shipment of dressed beef to New York City. The Wason Car Company, located in Springfield, Massachusetts, had manufactured the refrigerated freight cars for Rankin at $1,100 apiece. The cars, approximately thirty feet in length and "sufficiently high to admit the beeves being hung up," were heavily insulated and entered through airtight doors on either side. Each car could hold the equivalent of thirty beeves closely packed together, which amounted to ten tons in hanging weight.[47]

Along the top of each car were two chambers, the upper measuring two feet deep and four feet wide and the one below about ten inches deep. The upper chamber was packed with about a ton of ice, and the lower chamber was designed to remove the water from the melting ice above. A box filled with one hundred pounds of salt was placed at one end of the upper chamber. The crew would disperse the salt "at intervals during the journey, to keep the ice in a thawing condition, without affecting the temperature to any great extent."[48]

In short, Rankin's refrigerator cars employed a Bray-like cooling technique. At the time, any compressor unit would have been much too bulky to be incorporated into a freight car. This left ice as the most efficient means to chill hanging dressed beef, but as we have seen, this method came with limitations. Even though Rankin hoped to ship year-round, he quickly found that he could reliably transport chilled beef only during the cold months of October, November, December, January, and perhaps part of February.[49]

Compounding the difficulty in maintaining enough ice to keep the cargo chilled was the time it took to transport the dressed beef from Denison to New York City. Rankin's first load took eight days. The train averaged fifteen to eighteen miles an hour, and it required passage on four railroad lines. From Denison to Hannibal, Missouri, the train traveled the Missouri, Kansas, and Texas Railroad line (MK&T); from Hannibal to Toledo, Ohio, on the Toledo, Wabash, and Western Railroad (TW&W); from Toledo to Buffalo, New York, the train skirted the northern shore of Lake Erie on the Canada Southern Railroad (CS); and finally, from Buffalo to Jersey City, it took the Erie Railroad.[50]

A cold day greeted the workers when they arrived at the Erie freight yard in Jersey City on December 6. The day turned sour when John Connors, a switchman, lost a leg at the knee joint after an engine ran over it, and Arthur Hawes, a brakeman, lost his right hand while coupling cars. Such all-too-frequent accidents left workers disabled for life, with few prospects for future employment. Worse yet, Connors and Hawes lost their limbs during one of the severest economic collapses in American history. On September 18, 1873, the banking firm of Jay Cooke and Company had closed its doors, resulting in thousands of failed businesses and sharply rising unemployment. On December 6, 1873, those who lost their jobs in Jersey City found little more relief than a restaurant opened on the same day by the YMCA that provided meals, or a quart of soup, for five cents. Rankin's beef delivery had arrived at an inauspicious time.

But not all was gloom and doom for Rankin—at least not at the start. Despite the difficulties in reaching New York City, the *New York Times* heralded the experiment as a success. Rankin's method of transporting beef eliminated the importation of live cattle, which had routinely resulted in losses caused by injured, debilitated animals arriving in overcrowded stock cars. When the ten refrigerated freight cars arrived in Jersey City on Saturday, December 6, inspectors found the quarter sections in "excellent condition." Reportedly, all the New York City buyers who saw or bought the meat pronounced the "enterprise a decided success."[51]

Other agents representing shippers who delivered live cattle into the city markets could not help but notice the effect that Rankin's experiment could have on their trade. A Mr. Thirston acted as the New York selling agent for the Atlantic and Texas Refrigerator Cattle Company, and while returns on common to prime dressed beef derived from live cattle shipments averaged between ten cents and twelve and a half cents per pound, Thirston unloaded two carloads across the river directly into Washington Market for six cents per pound. Even fair- to poor-quality *live* longhorns shipped to the Erie yard sold for ten cents per pound once dressed. No wonder the headline in the *New York Times* read "Cheaper Beef for the East." During such harsh economic conditions, this came as especially welcome news to urban consumers.[52]

Shippers of live cattle knew that Rankin's enterprise would hurt their profit margins. By the end of February, Rankin had supplied New York City with seventy-five carloads of refrigerated beef that sold to retailers for six cents to seven cents per pound, or $40 to $46 per dressed beef on average. For those dealing in the livestock trade, once a steer had been slaughtered and dressed, markets that had returned $94 to $100 per dressed beef in December 1873 had fallen to $78 to $84 for the same quality of beef by February 1874.

Once May arrived, McCoy headed out to intercept Texas drovers and encouraged them not to drive their herds north but to route them to the pastures near

Denison. Other pasture grounds abounded even if those around Denison filled up, as Rankin had made arrangements with the Chickasaw Nation to graze any Texas cattle awaiting their journey to his slaughterhouse.

Rankin's experiment stood on the brink of reordering the nature of the livestock trade across the entire continent. With its continued success, the long drive up the Chisholm Trail would no longer be necessary or profitable. Cattle outlets such as Ellsworth, Wichita, Chetopa, and Dodge City would no longer serve any purpose, even without the competition from farmers for control of the land. Moreover, refrigerated beef posed no danger of spreading Texas fever to native herds.

Rankin's success, however, rested on shipping year-round, and his company lacked the technology and capital to make that happen. As a reporter for the *New York Times* noted, "the company do not propose to work this trade during the Summer months, as the patent requires some improvements before this can be undertaken." Most likely, in warm weather the refrigerated cars could not keep the hanging beef quarters chilled during the five days it took for the meat to arrive at Washington Market after being shipped from Denison. During the downtime, Rankin still had to pay the fixed capital costs of his slaughterhouse and the refrigerated freight cars, whether in use or not.[53]

Compounding Rankin's difficulty was the panic of 1873, which dried up capital investment throughout the nation. The city government of Denison attempted to assist Rankin's company by issuing public bonds to create capital for the refrigerator company, in essence creating a private-public partnership. But this was not enough to forestall insolvency. By 1875, Rankin had lost control of the company.

Before 1878, the company had ceased operation altogether, and in October, a fire broke out in the abandoned slaughterhouse, burning it to the ground. But the Atlantic and Texas Refrigerator Cattle Company had demonstrated that with the right refrigeration technology, dressed beef, as opposed to livestock, could be efficiently and economically transported year-round into any urban market in the nation. In short, it served as the prototype for the great slaughter-shipping corporations that would later dominate the trade to come into Chicago and Kansas City.

By 1882, as an article in the *Austin Weekly Statesman* made clear, a refrigerated shipment of dressed beef from Chicago to New York sold for "two cents a pound cheaper than the New York butchers can lay it on the block." The reporter continued, "A revolution is taking place," and the question was not whether refrigerated shipments would be profitable but "Where would the cattle be slaughtered?" In this respect, the reporter highlighted the fast-expanding work of Armour and Company in Kansas City and Chicago.[54] By the mid-1880s, refrigerated shipping of dressed beef made it possible for Philip Armour and Gustavus Swift to centralize and dominate the packing and shipping of meat from Chicago and Kansas City to urban markets in the East.

The writer also pointed to the international aspects of refrigerated shipments. The Atlantic and Texas Company had demonstrated the safety of transporting refrigerated beef over great distances and time, and this fact would open the door to transatlantic beef markets. By 1882, as the *Statesman* reporter observed, "the fact that Australia and New Zealand are to-day shipping dressed meats—both beef and mutton—to England, is but a suggestion of what may be expected in America." Somehow, however, this reporter had missed the fact that for some time, American firms had already been working the transatlantic beef trade.

Nelson Morris well understood that serious food shortages in England also opened the door for American beef imports. In 1867, the wheat harvests in England and on the continent failed to meet the demand. In 1868, the harvests rebounded a bit, but as one correspondent summarized the food situation in Great Britain at the beginning of 1869, there would continue to be a "demand at better prices from this country, whatever may be the immediate effect of the firm limits which England affixes and maintains while living from hand to mouth and witnessing the certain diminution of her store of food." Morris understood this situation and saw a way to skirt around the "firm limits which England affixes."[55]

In 1868, while working out of his office in the Exchange Building at the Chicago Union Stockyards, Morris foresaw that he could make a killing on shipping Texas beef into the English markets if he could figure out a way to get a high enough volume of either dressed or live cattle there. By this time, several packing firms in the Midwest had already perfected methods of preserving beef by pickling, canning, or smoking it. However, the taste and tenderness of these cured meats compared poorly to those of a freshly slaughtered fat steer. The meat from freshly slaughtered cattle always had a greater consumer appeal than preserved meat.

Morris decided to gamble on exporting some live cattle to London and Glasgow. The risks were high, but so were the potential returns. The cattle plague had already begun depressing cattle markets across North America, leaving unsold a growing surplus of cattle that remained on prairie grazing grounds. On the English side of the equation, a drought had produced serious food shortages on the island and opened a need for imported foodstuffs.

The returns on shipping cattle to England looked promising if everything fell nicely into place. In September, for example, Morris knew he could buy "good to smooth shipping steers" for $63 to $68 per head. In London, the largest city in the world at the time, a steer of that quality could bring £14 to £18, or the equivalent of US $91 to $117. Even if Morris suffered the loss of 25 percent of his shipment of four hundred steers, the surviving three hundred beeves could have returned nearly 30 percent on Morris's initial investment in Chicago. Of course, there were the rail and transatlantic shipping charges of about $17 per head that Morris had to factor in, but still, he considered the risk acceptable.[56]

Soon English investors also saw the same potential for importing Texas cattle. The idea behind one firm, which apparently never got off the ground, was to import live steers directly from Texas to an English port. However, reporters for both the *Galveston Daily News* and the *New Orleans Picayune* found the "idea of an Englishman sitting down to a roast cut from the lean side of a Texas beef, which has suffered all the horrors of a long, rough Atlantic passage . . . decidedly amusing." They found it nearly impossible to believe that a company would attempt to transport live beef, especially when simply transporting livestock from Galveston to New Orleans resulted in losses approaching 20 percent. The two writers agreed that the key to transporting beef into England lay not in canned meat but rather in refrigerating fresh sides while in transit.[57]

The owners of some shipping lines understood the advantage of shipping dressed beef in refrigerated holds over shipping live cattle. One firm, Martin Fuller and Company of Philadelphia, transported 30 dressed beeves, 150 dressed sheep, poultry, and oysters to Liverpool in the refrigerated hold of the steamship *Illinois*. The Anchor Line, of Glasgow, Scotland, employed refrigeration technology similar to that used on the *Illinois* in its steamship the *Olympia*. The *Olympia* was outfitted with two holds capable of containing 360 to 450 dressed beeves and keeping them chilled at 37 degrees Fahrenheit. In 1876, the Anchor firm had six steamers carrying beef plying the Atlantic Ocean between New York and Glasgow, and reportedly "not a single invoice was lost" when the crews properly attended to the refrigeration units. It was also reported that "where this matter did not receive proper attention, whole shipments were lost."⁵⁸

By 1875, a few shipping firms had made enough refinements to the methods of conveying both live and dressed beef that England began to rely heavily on American exports. In 1877, the United States exported over 49 million pounds of dressed beef into Great Britain, and in 1884, the total had climbed to nearly 116 million pounds. American cattle shippers such as Morris dominated the trade with Great Britain. Although twenty countries were exporting beef to Great Britain, US exports amounted to about 90 percent of the total. By 1885, a major exporter such as Nelson Morris could count on a 1 to 5 percent loss on any shipment to Great Britain, a remarkable improvement over the 25 percent losses usually anticipated before 1875. Of course, this reduction also assured a much higher return on the initial investment, especially with the improved exchange rate of US $4.80 to £1 sterling, which favored American exporters.⁵⁹

## *A Changing Cattle Landscape and the First National Convention of Cattlemen, 1884*

As people continued to push the agricultural landscape farther westward into the grasslands, the cattle shipping points and rangeland also gravitated farther west into the short-grass High Plains. Cattlemen found promising haunts in places such as the Arkansas River Valley of southeastern Colorado and western Kansas. By 1876, cattlemen had enough experience in overwintering herds in the area that they considered it to be an excellent location for fattening and preparing their herds for the spring roundups in addition to alleviating fears that their cattle might spread Texas fever. By this time, between Dodge City, Kansas, and Fort Lyon, Colorado, over 125,000 cattle grazed the rich buffalo grass in the valley. By 1878, Dodge City had gained prominence as the largest cattle outlet in Kansas. Local businessman Robert Wright, who also served as a representative in the Kansas legislature, led the effort to secure and enhance Dodge City's cattle trade. In his political capacity, between 1880 and 1884, he successfully staved off legislation to quarantine the entire state.

In Colorado, a consolidation occurred of packinghouses tied to railroad shipping facilities. The fast-growing city of Las Animas, Colorado, located in the Arkansas River Valley, rapidly became a center of the regional cattle trade on the High Plains. The AT&SF railroad and the KP railroad met there and provided ready access to eastern markets. As a result, the modernization of the modern beef industry began to mature there. In 1876, over 40,000 dressed beef carcasses left Colorado in refrigerated freight cars bound for the eastern markets. Entrepreneurs in Las Animas led the way in this manner of shipping. Taking advantage of this transportation hub, three slaughterhouses operated in the city, employing around ninety men, and processed on average 700 to 800 animals per day. From these packinghouses, men loaded somewhere between 40 and 50 dressed carcasses into each refrigerated car. In the short span of ten years, railroad companies had doubled the number of animals per car.[60]

By 1878, another change began to set into motion a distinctive change in Texas cattle driving. No longer did Texas cattlemen intend to send their herds directly to eastern or foreign markets. Most drovers sold their herds to ranchers operating on vast grazing grounds north of Texas and throughout the High Plains. In short, Texas came to resemble the breeding grounds for cattle and the northern ranges the "maturing and fattening ground."[61]

This shift in cattle raising, however, faced a host of opponents. Boomers such as David Payne wanted the Cherokee Outlet opened for adventures in speculation, which portended eliminating the cattle firms' ability to lease grazing grounds in the outlet. The members of the Cherokee Strip Live Stock Association also had qualms about any Texas cattle being driven anywhere near their own herds in the outlet. Then there were the Comanches, Kiowas, Southern Arapahos, and Cheyennes who wanted their reserves actually *reserved* for their own stock raising and farms or leasing arrangements. In Kansas, the new arrivals who kept taking up more and more land for farms and crops resisted Texas cattle trampling their fields, and in cases where farmers and drovers came to blows, as they did in Abilene and Wichita, the Texas cattlemen always lost out. Needless to say, Texas drovers intent on reaching an outlet such as Dodge City or grazing grounds on the northern High Plains encountered mounting trail blocks from boomers, the CSLSA, the Indian nations, the federal government, and farmers.

By 1884, the changing nature of cattle dealing and the markets had become so pronounced that stock dealers and raisers across the nation knew that they needed to organize and reach a consensus on how to treat the most pressing issues confronting them. One was how to get cattle from Texas to the public-domain grazing grounds to the north. Another was the thorny question of who controlled grazing on the public domain or Indian reservations.

In January 1884, a group of some of the most influential stockmen in the country met and called for a national convention of cattlemen. Among them were such luminaries as Colonel R. D. Hunter of St. Louis; William Hughes and John Simpson of the Continental Cattle Company, with offices in both Dallas and St. Louis; C. C. Slaughter, who owned and operated a forty-thousand-acre ranch in west Texas; Alexander Swan, who with his brother formed the massive Swan Cattle Company near Chugwater, Wyoming; and Charles Goodnight, a famous cattleman in the panhandle of Texas. They declared the object of the convention to be securing "advantages and recognition which are now denied [cattlemen], but which are accorded railroad and manufacturing companies . . . simply because such interests are guarded and recognized by a national protective system, secured only by National Organizations."[62]

On November 17, 1884, over four hundred delegates representing every state, every territory, Great Britain, the Republic of Mexico, and a great many of the cattle associations organized throughout the nation descended upon St. Louis and gathered in the east nave of the Exposition Building. Among more than sixty delegates from Kansas stood Joseph G. McCoy, who now represented the Arkansas Valley Stock Breeders' Association and who also served with seventy-nine others on the committee of resolutions.

The delegates were greeted by Governor Thomas Crittenden and famous general William T. Sherman. The governor indicated that the most pressing issue, at least in his view, was the need for Congress to create a "national or an international trail or highway for cattle, of ample width, from the Red River on the south to the Red River on the north," a trail that could accommodate the drive of a million cattle annually.[63] Another major question before the delegates was the leasing of the public domain to cattlemen.

Judge J. A. Carroll of Texas offered the first motion of real business to this huge assembly when he moved to create a "National Stock Trail" that would link the "extensive breeding grounds of the South to the extensive maturing grounds of the Northwest." When a delegate from Missouri wanted to remove the motion from consideration by the committee on resolutions, McCoy leaped into action and pointed out that the committee on resolutions was well equipped to deal with the issue because on it was "a man who laid out the first trail that was ever laid from Central Kansas and made the first cattle shipping depot on the Kansas Pacific Road; the first one that was made in this United States to bring cattle from Texas; with his own money and with men in his own employ . . . a trail across from Texas over which to-day have passed more than five million head of Texas cattle." Of course, McCoy was talking about himself. Apparently, that was enough to resolve the issue, and Judge Carroll's motion was sent to the committee on resolutions with instructions to report as early as possible.[64]

While the delegates generally supported the creation of the trail, several from the state of Kansas did not—and they clearly saw why the proposal would never see the light of day. Ed Russell, a representative of the Western Kansas Cattle Growers Association, stood and recited an old saying: a "burnt child shuns the fire." Pointedly, he blamed the cattle from Texas for spreading disease among native and high-value imported stock. "We have had some experience with the cattle trail in Kansas," Russell averred, "and we are sick of it; we don't want any more of it." Not surprisingly, several Texans took issue with Russell, but the Kansan, undeterred, continued his indictment. He pointed out that southwest Kansas had filled with "improved" cattle breeds. He asked, "Because I want to grade up my stock, have I to lose it in order that you may sell your cattle?" He warned all the delegates that they could pass a resolution to create a national trail, but such a project would have to meet with congressional approval, and the Kansas congressional delegation would be there to defeat it.[65]

Russell also noted a fact that had already ended the cattle trail business in Abilene and Wichita: the landscape in southwest Kansas was undergoing a rapid ecological transformation that precluded cattle trail driving. "Thousands upon thousands of settlers have gone upon the plains of Southwest Kansas this season," he said, "one can scarcely find a section of land along the line of the present cattle trail that has no squatters upon it south of Dodge City." If they tried to establish a national trail, he warned the Texans in attendance, "in the face of thousands of settlers, is there one among you who could get your cattle through there . . . without congressional action . . . unless there is an army of bayonets to sustain that action?"[66]

Russell and like-minded delegates meant trouble for McCoy's hope for a national trail. In the end, McCoy helped to work out compromises that in effect amounted to a call for a federally funded internal improvement act: fence the trail on either side to keep the driven cattle from mixing with native herds. Leave the trail wide enough in places to graze over a million cattle a year. Narrow the trail in places to a hundred feet and build bridges over it at those locations so local herds could cross the trail without coming into contact with any herds being driven north. All these modifications to the initial resolution met with the approval of a majority of the delegates. Yet it was Russell, not McCoy, who proved to hold the winning hand.

Just two months later, in January 1885, a bill was introduced in the Kansas legislature that favored farmers and stockmen who raised domestic cattle over Texas drovers trailing longhorns into the state. Farmers had mounted enough pressure in the state house that even Wright could not forestall the passage of the quarantine act that eliminated Texas drives into the state other than in the months of December, January, and February. Soon afterward, Kansas enacted a statewide quarantine,[67] and Colorado followed suit with similar legislation. The stringent quarantine lines that all but eliminated the possibility of driving Texas cattle into either state during the spring, summer, or fall.

In March 1885, a notice in the *Dodge City Times* simply stated, "The Texas cattle quarantine law passed the legislature. No more Texas cattle to Dodge City." In October, the editor of the *Dodge City Times* compared the fate of his city to that of Wichita. He encouraged his readers not to fear: "While one source of business has fallen off another takes its place, until we have gone through from a trading buffalo point to a commercial metropolis, when cattle as well as grain shipments afford a business." Dodge City was passing through a phase, as Wichita had, starting out "uncouth" and emerging "cultured."[68]

Besides considering the value of a national cattle trail, the delegates in St. Louis addressed the issue of leasing the remaining public domain. This issue proved to be the most contentious addressed by the delegates, and again, McCoy found himself with a losing hand. The resolution called for the lands in the arid region to be leased to cattlemen for a term of years while reserving the rights of people to acquire land through the Homestead and Preemption Acts. McCoy, whose success in the cattle trade had more often than not rested upon free access to the grazing lands in the public domain, joined a small group of delegates to oppose leasing the public domain. McCoy had no truck with the view that leasing the public domain would provide better conservation of its grazing grounds and provide an economic return to the federal government.

McCoy tried to persuade the delegates that the federal government, being "representative in character," had no right to go into the landlord business of renting lands and collecting rents. He further alleged that such actions were "contrary to the genius of our institutions, and abhorrent to almost every American citizen who . . . fled from the old world . . . in order to escape hated landlordism." He also took John Wesley Powell, a famous explorer of the American West who was the director of the United States Geological Survey at the time, to task for his *Report on the Lands of the Arid Region of the United States* (1879) for its recommendation for federal leasing of the public domain. McCoy pointed out that Powell had failed on several occasions to induce any congressman to introduce a measure for leasing the public domain. In short, putting forth such a measure in Congress, according to McCoy, was nothing short of "political suicide."[69] Nonetheless, the delegates favored the resolution even though another sixty years would pass before Congress would enact the Taylor Grazing Act of 1934, which established a fee structure and regulations for grazing on the public domain.

## *The End of the Trail*

After the Kansas legislature enacted the quarantine-line law of 1885, the era of great cattle drives into the state came to an end. Dodge City, the last of the great cattle towns, no longer resembled its reckless youth as a wild and woolly playground for Texas cowboys. By 1915, the city had matured and taken on the characteristics of a sedate Victorian if provincial town. Civilization had come to the city. The days of soldiers and Indian prisoners were all but faded memories aside from those images preserved in photographs. Gone were the Long Branch Saloon, the dancing girls, and the gambling tables that had entertained Texas cowboys and taken their money.[70]

In September 1915, a large crowd gathered to celebrate the old days during the "southwestern Old Soldiers' Reunion." Tuesday was "Sunday school day," a celebration with apparent religious overtones and instruction; Wednesday was Democratic day, with speeches from Senator William H. Thompson, one of the few Democrats to have ever served the state in the Senate, and fellow Democratic congressmen Jouett Shouse and Willis L. Brown. As opposed to Republican day on Thursday, Wednesday must have been Joseph McCoy's favorite day of the celebration.

McCoy, not quite seventy-eight years old, and still an unrepentant Jeffersonian Democrat, undoubtedly enjoyed the speeches by Senator Thompson and Representatives Shouse and Brown. Also making the day more enjoyable for him was the company of his daughters, Dr. Florence McCoy, a practicing physician in Kansas City, and Mamie (Mary) McCoy, a teacher in Wichita. The mild

80-degree days that occasionally grace the High Plains in the fall probably made it easier for the daughters to care for their ailing father. For a couple of weeks, fluid had been building up in Joseph's lungs, making it harder with each passing day for him to catch his breath. Still, he reveled in the acclaim that he often received for his pioneering work in developing the cattle trade of the United States.

In October, Joseph traveled to Kansas City to be with Florence. He had come to relish his role as a cattleman's sage, a man of wisdom in all aspects of the cattle trade. He refused to heed the debilitating symptoms of his weakening lungs as he prepared for a talk slated for a gathering in Wichita, and most people who knew him were unaware of how serious his health issue had become. Over the previous month and a half, despite McCoy's self-confident outlook, his illness had gathered enough strength to overwhelm him. On October 19, 1915, in his daughter's home, McCoy took his last breath.[71]

CONCLUSION

# Shifting Trails

EMERGENCE OF THE DOMESTICATED GRASSLANDS — EXCEEDING
THRESHOLDS — HUMANS AS A KEYSTONE SPECIES — A GAMBLING MAN'S LEGACY

Upon Joseph McCoy's death, Victor Murdock, the editor and owner of the *Wichita Eagle*, published a sterling tribute to McCoy. Murdock waxed eloquent, in keeping with the lofty language expected of a proper Victorian gentleman. He described McCoy as "towering in stature," an individual "who kept the tenor of his way, gazing into the mirage of the plains with the soft and dreaming eye of a poet." McCoy had a vision, Murdock averred, of the prairie "full of glistening cities, criss-crossing it with giant highways, peopling it with teeming millions."[1]

By the 1900s, Murdock declared that McCoy's dream had largely become reality. Murdock also praised McCoy's proclivity toward perpetual human improvement. Murdock saw in McCoy a booster "quick to scent out and untiring to follow a speculation, fully possessed with an earnest desire to do something that would alike benefit humanity as well as himself—something that, when life's rugged battles were over, could be pointed to as an evidence that he had lived to some good purpose and that world, or a portion thereof, was benefited by his having lived." Murdock admired this trait in McCoy, a man who sought "always that which was to be, indifferent to that which had come to be."[2]

## *Emergence of the Domesticated Grasslands*

Almost as an aside, Murdock, in his own way, also acknowledged the ecological transformation wrought by McCoy's endeavors: "The prairies went long ago," he wrote, "but Joseph G. McCoy went on dreaming of them and of their tomorrow to the end."[3] McCoy's dreams had led to the Chisholm Trail cattle drives, and in an ecological sense, they had also formed an "ecotone," that is, a moment in time when the wild grassland, a biome once managed and shaped by Indians, gave way to a domesticated grassland, one managed and shaped by the values of an American farm culture.[4]

In the spring of 1872, Joseph McCoy began to see the advance of American "civilization" accompanying the rise of Wichita, Kansas. While riding around Sedgwick County, a parcel of Kansas rapidly undergoing a transformation from mixed-grass prairie to cattle pastures and farmland, McCoy observed "large patches of genuine Kentucky blue grass." Like the appearance of the honeybee, bluegrass always seemed to follow the arrival of Euro-American farmers and ranchers. For a great many Americans, bluegrass marked the arrival of civilization and the retreat of the wilderness.[5]

In a moment of reflection on the rapidly changing landscape of Kansas, James Mead, a Wichita acquaintance of McCoy's, pondered how human cultural values had rapidly reordered the once prevalent grassland ecosystem. In 1875, when Mead recorded his observations, he owned a splendid home in the city where, a mere five years earlier, wide-open grasslands had prevailed. Mead sorrowfully looked around the countryside and saw bleached bison bones covering the plains. This sight brought back memories of when the "monarch of the plains" had abounded in the region. But now he watched as people gathered up bison bones, a ton of which could buy nearly a ton of coal to heat their homes in the winter.[6]

Mead loved the look and feel of the Kansas grasslands as they had been prior to the advent of ranching and farming. He lamented the arrival of "white men," whom he indicted with "destroying everything, Animals, Birds, Fish, and timber." He said "in the gap between the time when they have destroyed all that Providence placed on the earth for their sustenance, and the time when they can again stock the Earth . . . they are apt to starve." Kansans, he thought, were living in that gap, a time of rapid ecological transformation during which people had "destroyed all the natural products of the Country, and have not had time to replace them with others suited to their ideas." His wording, "suited to their ideas," tacitly recognized the power of cultural values to function as an ecological force interacting with the geology, climate, and solar energy that brought about the domesticated landscape of farms and towns.[7]

Two years later, Colonel John P. Hatch, post commander at Fort Sill, noticed significant landscape changes occurring over large areas of northern Texas and present-day south-central Oklahoma. In particular, Hatch observed that cattle herding seemed to be changing the plant composition throughout an "immense tract of country" in the state of Texas. The tallgrasses (he called them "the tall 'Sedge Grass'") were rapidly being replaced by shorter grasses such as buffalo grass and Texas mesquite.[8] Under heavy grazing pressures, tallgrasses give way to the more resilient short-grasses, such as buffalo grass. Hatch had correctly attributed the displacement of the tallgrasses to cattle grazing.

Hatch also thought the expansion of the short-grass range ultimately created a pathway for Indian farming to emerge. The colonel was clear in viewing agriculture as a higher form of civilization than cattle herding; for him, this change had positive implications for the future of the Kiowa and Comanche Nations. He also noted that the short-grass range produced a small fire load, and given the low intensity of this type of "annual fire," bushes began encroaching upon the land.

In this part of his report, like so many of his contemporaries, he believed that rain followed the plow. With "bushes" making an appearance throughout the region, Hatch thought that they would contribute to soil water retention and increase the "quantity and frequency of the rain," which altogether would result in "sections of County formerly unsuited for cultivation now producing crops." Based on this observation, Hatch concluded that once the Kiowas and Comanches became pastoralists that they would be "sufficiently civilized to become thrifty farmers," and "the land will have become adapted to cultivation."

## Exceeding Thresholds

Grassland ecologists today have a better understanding of the drivers that exceed the threshold of an ecosystem to sustain itself. The drivers Hatch saw at work were the suppression of prairie fires coupled with cattle grazing. A threshold may be usefully defined as "a point at which an (ecological) system experiences a qualitative change, mostly in an abrupt and discontinuous way."[9] The transition from a wild grassland ecosystem to farmland is an example of hysteresis, or the point at which it becomes difficult, if not impossible, for the former ecosystem, the wild grassland system, to recover or be re-created because the new system possesses its own self-sustaining mechanisms.

Ecologists now recognize that wild grassland ecosystems can be replaced by an "alternative stable community," such as cedar woodlands or farms. Rangeland and soil ecologists D. D. Briske, S. D. Furlendorf, and F. E. Smeins argue that "thresholds often define management, rather than ecological threshold, because the time frame for vegetation change is based primarily on management alternatives bounded by human longevity." The rapid ecological changes to the wild grasslands did not take place because of the advance of glaciers, a lack of rainfall during the Altithermal period (9,000 to 5,000 B.P.), or the cooling effects of the "Little Ice Age" (ca. 1400 to ca. 1850). Rather, they occurred as a result of how humans decided to manage the resources in the region. What Hatch witnessed was cattle herding and the suppression of prairie fires driving the ecosystem across an ecological threshold, one that opened a pathway for farming.[10] Cattle driving and herding led to the suppression of prairie fires, thereby creating an opening for the planting of crops like corn and wheat. As in the case with Abilene, the cattle trade also provided an initial market for locally produced agricultural products, and development of small-scale cattle raising. Once this agricultural economy had taken root, it could no longer coexist with the seasonal intrusions of Texas cattle herds.

The suppression of prairie fires opened a pathway for more than farming. Invasive plants started displacing wild prairie grasses. The Indian practice of setting annual grass fires had kept brush from taking root in the plains and favored the growth of $C_4$ grasses. With the suppression of annual grass fires, brush became firmly established. Moreover, cattle grazing practices further reduced the grass-fire load, which lessened the intensity of fires that could have destroyed a brush intrusion. Current research has demonstrated that even a periodic grass fire at four-year or longer intervals will not eliminate the presence of brush. Once brush is firmly established, cedar begins to invade wild grasslands where farming is not practiced.[11]

## *Humans as a Keystone Species*

In 1877, as Colonel Hatch penned his letter to General Sherman on the "practical working of the experiment of making the Indians at the [Kiowa, Comanche, and Apache] reservation a pastoral people," he described how cattle ranching functioned as a transitional ecosystem to farming. Hatch's report took on greater importance at all levels of the federal government because it helped to fulfill the hopeful expectations of the government's social experiment. Like Hatch, Zachariah Chandler, the secretary of the interior, who also received the report, assumed that agriculture was the hallmark of a civilized society. They believed that the path toward civilization started with nomadism, which led to pastoralism, which, when given enough time and the right conditions, morphed into agriculture, the harbinger of civilization. Colonel Hatch had great hopes for "civilizing" Kiowas and Comanches by providing them with the means to become pastoral people. He succinctly put the matter this way: the Kiowas and Comanches "may, passing gradually through the pastoral epoch, reach that of agriculture, and possibly in the future become civilized, still possessing their distinctive features as a people."[12] As a contemporary ecologist would put it, the process of exceeding the threshold of grassland sustainability by replacing it with farming, "an anthropogenic activity," would be "rapid, nonlinear, and perhaps difficult to reverse." In this case, the ecological driver of cattle grazing, a human-managed force, produced the tipping point at which the wild grassland system yielded to farming, and created a domesticated grassland.

Ecologically speaking, Hatch, Mead, and McCoy recognized human beings as a "keystone species" with the potential to alter the structure of any biome, a life community, in which it lives. Robert V. O'Neill, an award-winning ecologist, made this concept explicit in an article published in *Ecology* in 2001. "*Homo sapiens*," he wrote, "is a keystone species that changes system stability by altering environmental constraints, rate processes, and biotic structures." O'Neill further argued that people change the physical and chemical conditions of how ecosystems function. In this case, cattlemen and farmers moved ecological systems, such as the wild grasslands previously managed by Indians, "outside the envelope of conditions" that had created the grasslands in the first place.[13]

The story of Joseph McCoy and the Chisholm Trail can be viewed as ecological explication. Ecologists such as O'Neill often explain that humans have created "dispersal barriers" that shape ecosystems.[14] The Chisholm Trail is a good example of this concept. The arrival of cattle in the grasslands established barriers to bison grazing on the same prairie grasses. Farmers, with their domestic herds of cattle and domesticated grasses like wheat, corn, and oats established barriers to longhorns and little bluestem.

People, O'Neill points out, also create ecological "invasion pathways" for other plants and animals to occupy in the grasslands.[15] The most historically important of these were the pathways that humans created by building railroads across the continent and piloting steam-powered freighters across the Gulf of Mexico and the Atlantic Ocean. These transportation systems opened the door for competing plants, animals, and cultural values to invade and overtake the wild prairie grasslands. Railroads and steamships also created an intricate web of connections throughout the nation and beyond, which reshaped ecosystems on a global scale. Hereford and Durham cattle from England were transported into the United States and interbred with longhorns, and these new breeds filled the grazing niche once held by bison. American cattle were shipped to English markets, thereby sustaining the powerful urban industrial centers of Great Britain.

These same invasion pathways also transported disease. The cattle plague of 1868, made possible by continental transportation systems, created a virgin soil epidemic throughout the Midwest and North. During the entire period of the great western cattle drives, 1866 to 1884, Texas fever ravaged domestic cattle herds raised anywhere outside the Deep South and Texas. Texas longhorns, with their evolved resistance, carried the ticks bearing the protozoan that struck down Durham bulls and Jersey dairy cows with indiscriminate vigor. Just as Euro-Americans had some immunity to the smallpox and measles that devastated the Indian populations in North America, northern native cattle's lack of immunity to the protozoan made their deaths inevitable.

## *A Gambling Man's Legacy*

Through the dramatic role he played in the cattle trade from the end of the Civil War to his dying day, Joseph McCoy, representing the keystone species of *Homo sapiens*, stood in the midst of the upheaval and flux that reshaped ecosystems throughout North America. Looking back, we may view McCoy, as folklorist Jim Hoy does, as one of the primary creators of "the pervasive mythology of the American West." What were the elements of this myth? According to Hoy, at the center is the image—perpetuated to this day by more than a century's worth of dime novels and western movies—of a "roving cowboy who symbolizes freedom in a classless society where a person's worth is determined by character not birth." Hoy's cowhands were "knight-errants of the prairies" who always prevailed over the forces of evil.[16]

But it is also important to realize that McCoy held a dim view of cowboys. Although he may have considered the life of a cowboy "wild and free," it was not the civilized life that he valued. The cowboy lived hard, had little taste for reading, abhorred menial labor, and would rather fight than pray—and his holy trinity consisted of tobacco, liquor, and women. "His life," McCoy wrote, "borders nearly upon that of an Indian," and McCoy had no use for Indians.

Moreover, McCoy considered Texas drovers, the ones who led and managed the great cattle drives north, hardly better than the cowboys who worked the herds. Of drovers, and Texans in general, McCoy believed that "great as the wealth of some of its citizens were ... to this day [1874] we know of no other state which has so few public-spirited citizens, so few that are willing to do an act or develop an enterprise which has for its object the benefit of the whole people."[17]

McCoy revered the ranchman and the stockman, calling them "from the beginning of history, nature's uncrowned Knights of Navarro." There was a distinct class bias in McCoy's view of the cattle world. There were the cow*boys* and the stock*men*. Stockmen owned land and cattle and amassed fortunes. Cowboys herded and worked the trails. In fact, contemporary observers and reporters often employed the term "herder" rather than "cowboy" to describe those who were employed to tend or drive cattle.

So what may be said about Joseph G. McCoy's life? He was a gambling man, willing to take risks, always looking for the next big opportunity in the field of business that he knew best: the cattle trade. His social aspirations paralleled those of his idol and Illinois neighbor, Abraham Lincoln, who sought "improvement" in the realm of human affairs. In quoting a remarkable speech of Lincoln's, historian Mark Fiege illustrates well how Lincoln defined "improvement," a human aspiration that McCoy readily embraced: "All nature is a mine, and every man, a miner. The whole earth, and all *within* it, and *round* about it, including *himself* ... are the infinitely varied 'leads' from which, man, from the first, was to dig out his destiny." McCoy saw his labor resulting in a public good, one that transcended his own gain from the trade and improved people's lives.

McCoy always considered the creation of the outlet in Abilene and the marking out of the Chisholm Trail to be his greatest accomplishment. But even the Great Western Stock Yards of Abilene failed to make him and his brothers, James and William, rich. As Joseph McCoy's opportunities in the cattle business closed in one place, he was quick to seize real or imagined openings in others. When farmers closed the door to the cattle trade in Abilene, McCoy went to Wichita, Kansas, and helped build the cattle-shipping economy there. As farmers encroached upon the Wichita cattle trade, he saw another opening in Denison, Texas. McCoy could sense how technological advances in refrigeration, freight transportation, and packinghouse systems were rapidly transforming the beef industry of the United States. These changes led Rankin and McCoy to build the prototype beef operation that characterizes the cattle and beef markets today at massive packing firms such as National Beef and Tyson in western Kansas.

McCoy's aim, however, always seemed to overshoot the horizon. He lost money in creating the Abilene outlet in large part because of a two-year legal confrontation with the management of the Kansas Pacific Railway Company. The devastation of the 1868 cattle plague and losses brought on by the blizzards of 1871–72 compounded his problems in Abilene. His stint in the Wichita cattle business was short-lived as well. His timing for becoming a stock buyer and seller in Kansas City was poor, as it coincided with the panic of 1873. The Denison, Texas, operation failed after a few years, as its capital costs outpaced its income. In the early 1880s, McCoy's work collecting grazing taxes for the Cherokee Nation also proved short-lived. His support of David Payne and the boomer movement prior to 1890, when Congress created the Territory of Oklahoma, did little to advance his speculative aspirations there. McCoy also came up short as an aspiring politician, losing his bid to win the congressional seat representing the Territory of Oklahoma in 1890. The only line of work that proved reliable and steady for McCoy was public employment. The federal Census Bureau hired him to enumerate livestock figures in 1880 and again in 1890. In 1897, the Populist governor of Kansas, John Leedy, appointed McCoy as the Kansas livestock inspector.

McCoy's family life appears to have been far more stable than his business career. In November 1911, he lost Sarah, his dear wife of fifty years. She had arrived in Wichita with Joseph in the 1870s and remained there for the rest of her life, weathering the swings from adversity to prosperity that marked her years in the city. After Sarah's death, Joseph remained in Wichita, keeping close company with his daughters but with little evident connection to his brothers, each of whom died before him.

Joseph's oldest brother, William McCoy, spent his last days in Pendleton, Oregon. He does not appear to have prospered in either cattle or real estate. He married late in life, when at age fifty, he wed thirty-seven-year-old Caroline, known in Pendleton as Carrie. They had one son, Virgil, who lived a tragic life and struggled with alcoholism. In 1910, when attempting to jump aboard a moving freight train, Virgil fell between two cars and lost both legs as a result. When William died in October 1898, Carrie had little property to support herself. In 1909, she fell and broke a hip. Her accident triggered the onset of the dementia that eventually claimed her life in March 1913. She died with virtually no property to her name.[18]

Joseph's older brother, James McCoy, fared better in life. He flourished as a cattle buyer and seller. He and his wife, Jane, lived a comfortable life in Topeka, Kansas. People in the city regarded the couple as stalwarts in the community. Late in life, James suffered a broken hip when thrown from a horse in 1881. Although he never fully recovered, he still successfully engaged in the cattle trade. He and Jane managed to build a new house in Topeka in 1882, where he lived until dying from complications from liver failure in July 1886. Jane remained in Topeka until her death in April 1911.[19]

In his later years, Joseph McCoy was a man seeking, even craving, constant affirmation and recognition as the prime innovator of the cattle trade of the United States. When he returned to Wichita after the conclusion of the St. Louis National Cattlemen's Association meeting in 1884, he made a point of visiting the office of Marshall Murdock (Victor's father) at the *Wichita Eagle*. McCoy proudly displayed the medal he had received as one of the more than four hundred delegates attending the convention, and Murdock duly noted it in the *Eagle* so that all would know of McCoy's importance.[20] It is clear that in his later years, McCoy relished his fame as an elder statesman of the cattle trade.

If McCoy and the Texas ranchers, drovers, and cowboys he promoted should be remembered for anything, it should be for how they transformed the American diet and landscape. McCoy should be remembered for creating the outlet in Abilene that led to a revolution in cattle markets, creating the ecological transition that transformed the sweeping grasslands of North America into the breadbasket of the world. In reading the reminiscences of cattlemen, it is easy to understand how they thought of themselves as the harbingers of civilization. They cleared the wilderness and paved the path for American civilization to follow. J. E. Pettus, a successful cattleman who had his operation in Goliad County, Texas, gave a direct testimonial to this effect. When his father arrived in Texas, the country, he said, was "almost a wilderness." Within a span of fifty years, the "cowman" had transformed the land into a "glorious country." The cowman "was the advance guard of the high state of civilization" that he and his neighbors now enjoyed.[21]

McCoy's adventures in the cattle trade, and the story of how that industry transformed the grasslands, both illustrate that history is ecological, and ecology is historical. In the end, McCoy finally drew the winning faro card he had always sought—the rise of a vast, consolidated, and highly profitable beef empire—but he did not live to play it.

# Appendix
*Explanation of Weather Statistics*

The data used to compile the temperature trends for the southern, middle, and northern regions of the Chisholm Trail system were taken from the online records housed by the National Oceanic and Atmospheric Administration. The specific records that I used are taken from the online data set "Forts." During the time of this study, the post surgeons were responsible for recording the daily weather. How they were instructed and trained to make their readings is nicely described in *Army Meteorological Register for Twelve Years, from 1843 to 1854, Inclusive*, prepared under direction of Brevet Brigadier General Thomas Lawson, Surgeon General, United States Army (Washington: A. O. P. Nicholson, Public Printer, 1855), and the *Annual Report of the Signal-Officer to the Secretary of War for the Year 1872* (Washington: Government Printing Office, 1873).

The adjacent figure is a copy of the form used by Captain William Forwood, the post surgeon at Fort Richardson, Texas, to record the weather conditions at the post in July 1875. The columns are, from left to right, date, thermometer, self-registering thermometer, movements of the atmosphere, amount of cloudiness, rain and melted snow, and remarks. Captain Forwood recorded his observations of the temperature in Fahrenheit, wind directions and speed, and cloudiness three times a day: 7 A.M., 2 P.M., and 9 P.M. He noted the time when rain and snow began and ended, and then provided the amount of precipitation recorded. Officers made various comments in the remarks column, sometimes noting the migration of birds, the occurrence of prairie fires, meteors, auroras, or the nature of a storm.

Each day Forwood averaged the three daily readings, and at the end of the month he averaged all the daily averages to produce a monthly average temperature

METEOROLOGICAL REGISTER, FORT RICHARDSON, TEXAS, July 1875. Courtesy National Archives and Records Administration, Washington, D.C.

for the month of July. As is also apparent, the monthly average temperature is not a reflection of the high and low temperatures that he recorded for the month. Forwood followed this procedure for noting the weather in each and every month that he was on post.

Take, for example, two days of Captain Forwood's records: July 4 and July 11, and the end of month averages (see table 2). Forwood used a modified Beaufort scale for recording wind speeds as shown in table 3. The Army Signal Corps used the scale shown in table 4 for recording cloudiness.

Table 5 shows the July monthly averages of temperature at Fort Richardson from 1868 to 1877. As evident, the post surgeon did not record anything for July in 1870 and 1871. The lack of records for those months indicates that the post surgeon was most likely in the field along with troop movements. The monthly averages for each year are used to produce the trend of temperature over the time period being studied, in this case, 1868–77.

## TABLE 2
## SAMPLE AND AVERAGES FROM METEOROLOGICAL REGISTER FORT RICHARDSON, JULY 1875

|  | Temperature | | | Daily | Winds | | | Cloudiness | | | Rain | |
| --- | --- | --- | --- | --- | --- | --- | --- | --- | --- | --- | --- | --- |
|  | 7 A.M. | 2 P.M. | 9 P.M | Mean | 7 A.M. | 2 P.M | 9 P.M | 7 A.M. | 2 P.M | 9 P.M. | Start | End |
| July 4 | 79 | 94 | 84 | 85.66 | SE3 | SE3 | E2 | 1 | 2 | 4 | | |
| July 11 | 81 | 86 | 77 | 81.33 | SW1 | W2 | W1 | 4 | 8 | 6 | 2 P.M | 2:30 P.M |
| Monthly Average | 77.84 | 93.68 | 81.64 | 84.39 | | | | 3.06 | 2.97 | 4.97 | | |
| Maximum | | 103 | | | | | | | | | | |
| Minimum | | 63 | | | | | | | | | | |

## TABLE 3
## WIND SPEED SCALE

| 0 | A calm day |
| --- | --- |
| 1 | A barely perceptible breeze |
| 2 | A gentle breeze, 5 to 10 mph |
| 3 | A moderate breeze, 10 to 15 mph |
| 4 | A brisk breeze, 15 to 20 mph |
| 5 | A strong wind, 20 to 30 mph |
| 6 | A very strong wind, 30 to 40 mph |
| 7 | A storm, 40 to 50 mph |
| 8 | A great storm, 50 to 60 mph |
| 9 | A hurricane |
| 10 | A violent hurricane |

## TABLE 4
## CLOUDINESS SCALE

| Absence of lower clouds | 1 |
| --- | --- |
| Hazy atmosphere | 2 |
| Foggy atmosphere | 3 |
| Smoky atmosphere | 4 |
| Clear sky to ¼ covered with stratus clouds | 5 |
| Sky ¼ to ½ covered with stratus clouds | 6 |
| Sky ½ to total covered with stratus clouds | 7 |
| Sky clear to ¼ covered with nimbus clouds | 8 |
| Sky ¼ to ½ covered with nimbus clouds | 9 |
| Sky ½ to total covered with nimbus clouds | 10 |

## TABLE 5
## JULY TEMPERATURES, FORT RICHARDSON, 1868–1877

| Year | Monthly Average |
| --- | --- |
| 1868 | 86 |
| 1869 | 83.02 |
| 1870 | no record |
| 1871 | no record |
| 1872 | 85.78 |
| 1873 | 83.45 |
| 1874 | 86.96 |
| 1875 | 84.39 |
| 1876 | 82.35 |
| 1877 | 82.05 |

I have used box-and-whisker statistical analysis to create the trends noted in this work, to represent the range of average temperatures for each month. A box-and-whisker plot is shown below for all the months at Fort Richardson for the years 1868–78. Take July, for example. The square box has three data points. The median for July is 83.92 degrees Fahrenheit. The median is represented by a line cutting across the box and is the point at which half of the average monthly temperatures are above 83.92 degrees, and the other half are below 83.92 degrees.

The box has two other data points, one at the top of the box, and the other at the bottom end of the box. The top end value is 85.95 degrees Fahrenheit, which means that 75 percent of the monthly July averages are less than that amount. Conversely, the bottom number of the box, 82.05 degrees Fahrenheit, means that 75 percent of the monthly July averages are greater than this temperature.

Above and below the box are horizontal lines indicating the low and high July monthly averages. Referring to table 5, the lowest monthly July average was 82.05 degrees Fahrenheit, and the highest was 86.96 degrees Fahrenheit. These horizontal lines are connected to the box with vertical lines called the "whiskers."

Each month has a similar set of numerical values. When plotted out over the year, the temperature trends for the time period under study become evident. It is possible to see which was the hottest or coldest month of the year. When the records from various posts are compared, the medians give a general indication of how much warmer or colder a particular month in one locale might be compared to the same month in another locale during the same span of years.

WEATHER STATISTICS 291

CHART 8. RANGE OF AVERAGE MONTHLY TEMPERATURES, FORT RICHARDSON, TEXAS, MARCH 1868–MAY 1878.

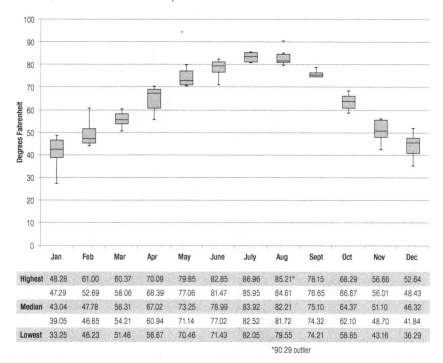

| | Jan | Feb | Mar | Apr | May | June | July | Aug | Sept | Oct | Nov | Dec |
|---|---|---|---|---|---|---|---|---|---|---|---|---|
| Highest | 48.28 | 61.00 | 60.37 | 70.09 | 79.85 | 82.85 | 86.96 | 85.21* | 78.15 | 68.29 | 56.66 | 52.64 |
| | 47.29 | 52.69 | 58.06 | 68.39 | 77.06 | 81.47 | 85.95 | 84.61 | 76.65 | 66.67 | 56.01 | 48.43 |
| Median | 43.04 | 47.78 | 56.31 | 67.02 | 73.25 | 78.99 | 83.92 | 82.21 | 75.10 | 64.37 | 51.10 | 46.32 |
| | 39.05 | 46.65 | 54.21 | 60.94 | 71.14 | 77.02 | 82.52 | 81.72 | 74.32 | 62.10 | 48.70 | 41.84 |
| Lowest | 33.25 | 46.23 | 51.46 | 56.67 | 70.46 | 71.43 | 82.05 | 79.55 | 74.21 | 58.85 | 43.16 | 36.29 |

*90.29 outlier

# Notes

**PREFACE**

1. The cowboy lingo incorporated in this paragraph comes from John J. Lomax, "Cowboy Life in West Texas," in *The Trail Drivers of Texas: Interesting Sketches of Early Cowboys and Their Experiences on the Range and on the Trail during the Days That Tried Men's Souls—True Narratives Related by Real Cowpunchers and Men Who Fathered the Cattle Industry in Texas*, comp. and ed. J. Marvin Hunter (Austin: University of Texas Press, 1924, 2006), 329–35.

2. Ibid., 331, 333. "Has taken a little more hair off the dog" means that a person has gained a little more experience in a proposition, and a "waddy" is an ordinary cowboy, in this case an ordinary scholar.

3. Ibid., 333. "Ain't got any medicine" means a person lacks information on the subject matter that he or she is discussing.

4. The phrase "as dangerous as walkin' quicksand over hell" refers to attempting something dangerous. See Ramon F. Adams, *Cowboy Lingo: A Dictionary of the Slack-Jaw Words and Whangdoodle Ways of the American West* (New York: Houghton Mifflin, 1936, 2000), 233.

5. Ibid., 231. The phrase "grabbin' the brandin' iron" refers to taking a chance.

6. Ibid., 210. The phrase is a cowboy reference to someone who has grown older and wiser in experience, and given Chuck Rankin's vast experience in editing, this phrase certainly applies.

7. Ibid., 215.

8. Lomax, "Cowboy Life in West Texas," in *Trail Drivers of Texas*, 333. The phrase refers to something said or written that raises doubt.

9. Ibid., 333. The phrase, according to Lomax, means "doing your best."

**INTRODUCTION**

1. Gary and Margaret Kraisinger, *The Shawnee-Arbuckle Trail, 1867–1870: The Predecessor of the Chisholm Trail to Abilene, Kansas* (Gary and Margaret Kraisinger, 2016); and their prior work, *The Western Cattle Trail, 1874–1897: Its Rise, Collapse, and Revival* (Newton, KS: Mennonite Press, 2014), are good introductions to the routes and names of various cattle trails that in common usage have been subsumed by one name: the Chisholm Trail.

In general, several cattle trails led through Texas, nearly all of which headed north toward the Red River, the border between Texas and present-day Oklahoma. In this work, the trail system initially leading through the central portion of present-day Oklahoma and connecting with Abilene, Kansas, will be referred to as the Chisholm Trail. The trail system crossing through the eastern portion of present-day Oklahoma will be referred to as the Shawnee Trail. The cattle trail system through the western portion of present-day Oklahoma will be referred to as the Western Cattle Trail.

2. *Proceedings of the Second Annual Convention of the National Live Stock Association, Denver, Colorado, January 24, 25, 26 and 27* (Denver: News Job Printing Company, 1899), 324.

3. Ibid., 109–10, 234.

4. "Miss M'Coy Surprised," *Wichita Daily Eagle*, May 29, 1898; "Topics of the Town," *Wichita Beacon*, August 26, 1903; "Pioneer Physician [Florence McCoy] Dies at Home," *Wichita Daily Eagle*, April 2, 1957.

5. *Proceedings of the Second Annual Convention of the National Live Stock Association*, 109–10, 153, 256–58.

6. Ibid., 110.

7. Ibid.

8. Ibid.

9. Ibid., 232.

10. Ibid., 235.

**CHAPTER 1**

1. "Death and the Tenements," *New York Tribune*, May 16, 1867.

2. The older spelling of Catharine Street and Catharine Market, found in press and maps during the heyday of the Texas cattle drives, later evolved into the modern spelling of Catherine.

3. For excellent accounting of the early formation of markets in New York City and other East Coast cities see Thomas F. De Voe, *The Market Book, Containing a Historical Account of the Public Markets in the Cities of New York, Boston, Philadelphia and Brooklyn*, 2 vols. (New York: printed for the author, 1862), and De Voe, *The Market Assistant: Containing a Brief Description of Every Article of Human Food Sold in the Public Markets of the Cities of New York, Boston, Philadelphia, and Brooklyn* (New York: Hurd and Houghton, 1867).

4. William Rideing, "How New York Is Fed," *Scribner's Monthly* 14 (October 1877): 729–30; and "The Public Health: Annual Report of the Metropolitan Board of Health," *New York Tribune*, January 3, 1867.

5. "The Relief of Broadway," *Harper's Weekly*, January 6, 1866, 3.

6. "Annual Statistics of the New York Cattle Market, 1866," *New York Tribune*, January 9, 1867.

7. See Judith Choate, *Dining at Delmonico's: The Story of America's Oldest Restaurant* (New York: Stewart, Tabori & Chang, 2008). The menu for President Andrew Johnson's banquet comes from Charles Ranhofer, *The Epicurean: A Complete Treatise of Analytical and Practical Studies on the Culinary Art* (New York: Charles Ranhofer, 1894), 1082.

8. "Bull's Head," *New York Tribune*, March 6, 1866.

9. M. R. Patrick, Lewis F. Allen, and Jonathan Stanton Gould, *Report of the New York*

*State Cattle Commissioners in Connection with the Report of the Metropolitan Board of Health, in Relation to the Texas Cattle Disease*, State of New York, no. 9, in Senate (March 12, 1869): 14.

10. "The Health of the City," *Harper's Weekly*, January 20, 1866, 35. In many ways, the creation of this board was very similar to the professional organizations often attributed to the beginnings of the "progressive movement."

11. "Health Queries," *New York Tribune*, March 10, 1866.

12. "The Board of Health and the Butchers," *New York Tribune*, March 13, 1866.

13. See Clay McShane and Joel Tarr, *The Horse in the City: Living Machines in the Nineteenth Century* (Baltimore: Johns Hopkins University Press, 2007).

14. "The Board of Health and the Butchers."

15. Rideing, "How New York Is Fed," 736.

16. "About the Butchers," *New York Times*, March 18, 1866.

17. Ibid.

18. "Enraged Bull," *New York Times*, March 14, 1866.

19. "The Metropolitan Board of Health," *New York Tribune*, March 17, 1866.

20. "Doings of the Sanitary Police," *New York Times*, March 14, 1866.

21. The following information about Samuel Allerton is taken from David S. Rotenstein, "Hudson River Cowboys: The Origins of Modern Livestock Shipping," *Hudson Valley Regional Review* 19 (March 2002): 1–15.

22. "Views of the Communipaw Abattoir," *History Sidebar* (historical blog), November 1, 2012, http://blog.historian4hire.net/2012/11/01/views-of-communipaw/.

23. "Opening of the New Abbattoirs—Great Celebration at Communipaw," *New York Times*, October 18, 1866.

24. "Statistics of the New-York Cattle Market for 1865," *New York Tribune*, January 21, 1866.

25. "Annual Statistics of the New York Cattle Market, 1866," *New York Tribune*, January 9, 1867.

26. "New York Cattle Market," *New York Tribune*, March 14, 1866.

27. "Cattle Markets," *New York Times*, January 14, 1866.

28. See ads like the following published in Kansas newspapers for their Abilene stockyard facilities: "W. K. McCoy & Bros., Live Stock Dealers, Abilene, Kansas," *Daily* (Lawrence) *Kansas Tribune*, November 12, 1867.

29. "New York Cattle Market," *New York Tribune*, June 20, 1866; and "New York Cattle Market," *New York Tribune*, September 3, 1866.

30. "Local News," *New York Times*, October 17, 1866.

31. A good biography of Bergh is Mildred Mastin Pace, *Friend of Animals: The Story of Henry Bergh* (Ashland, KY: Jesse Stuart Foundation, 1995).

32. "Cruelty to Animals," *New York Tribune*, March 31, 1866.

33. "Cruelty to Animals. How Cattle Are Transported from the West to New-York City," *New York Times*, November 13, 1866.

34. Ibid.

35. "The Wrongs of the Lower Creation," *New York Times*, November 13, 1866.

36. "The Cattle Plague," *New York Times*, January 5, 1866.

37. "The Cattle Plague," *Harper's Weekly*, February 17, 1866, 99.

38. "Metropolitan Board of Health. Adoption of the Code—the Rinderpest—Timely Precautions—No Cholera Here Yet," *New York Times*, April 11, 1866.

39. "Disease among the Cattle in Kansas," *New York Times*, August 11, 1866.

## CHAPTER 2

1. A. C. Wheeler, "On the Iron Trail," *Scribner's Monthly*, August 1876, 532.

2. William J. Bennett, "Sixty Years in Texas," in *Trail Drivers of Texas*, 123.

3. Territorial Survey Map, Township 13 South, Range 2 East, July 1857, Kansas Historical Society, Topeka.

4. A. T. Andreas, *History of the State of Kansas* (Chicago: A. T. Andreas, 1883), 684–85, 688; and Kansas State Census, 1865.

5. *Report of Lieut. Col. James H. Simpson, Corps of Engineers, U.S.A., on the Union Pacific Railroad and Branches, Central Pacific Railroad of California, Northern Pacific Railroad, Wagon Roads in the Territories of Idaho, Montana, Dakota, and Nebraska, and the Washington Aqueduct. Made to Honorable James Harlan, Secretary of the Interior, November 23, 1865* (Washington, DC: Government Printing Office, 1865), 96–111.

6. John D. Perry, President of the Union Pacific Railway Company, Eastern Division, to Honorable O. H. Browning, Secretary of the Interior, December 31, 1868, Manuscript Division, Kansas State Historical Society, Topeka.

7. Horace Traubel, *With Walt Whitman in Camden* (New York: Mitchell Kennerley, 1914), 346.

8. Anne E. Peterson, "Alexander Gardner in Review," *History of Photography* 34 (November 2010): 357–58.

9. Josephine Cobb, "Alexander Gardner," *Image* 7 (June 1958): 124–36.

10. Ibid., 124–36.

11. Joseph G. McCoy, *Historic Sketches of the Cattle Trade of the West and Southwest* (Kansas City, MO: Ramsey, Millett & Hudson, 1874; Columbus, OH: Long's College Book, 1951), 44.

12. *Daily* (Lawrence) *Kansas Tribune*, August 24, 1867.

13. Andreas, *History of the State of Kansas*, 688.

14. McCoy, *Historic Sketches of the Cattle Trade*, 120–21.

15. *Junction City* (KS) *Weekly Union*, July 17, 1869.

16. US Bureau of the Census, "Inhabitants in Grant Township, in the County of Dickinson, Kansas, Enumerated . . . on the 25th day of July, 1870," 21.

17. *The Kansas Pacific Railway Company v. Joseph G. McCoy*, transcript, Manuscript Division, Kansas State Historical Society, Topeka.

18. "Texas Cattle Trade," *Lawrence* (KS) *Daily Journal*, August 6, 1869.

19. McCoy, *Historic Sketches of the Cattle Trade*, 42.

20. *Daily* (Lawrence) *Kansas Tribune*, September 5, 1867.

21. McCoy, *Historic Sketches of the Cattle Trade*, 43.

22. Joseph G. Knapp, "A Review of Chicago Stock Yards History," *University Journal of Business* 2 (June 1924): 332.

23. Ibid., 333–35.

24. "Lyman's Ventilated Car for the Transportation of Dressed Beef," *New York Times*, June 7, 1867.

25. Ibid.
26. "Enraged Bull," *New York Times*, March 14, 1866.
27. "City Slaughter-Houses," *New York Times*, August 29, 1866.
28. "The New Harlem Abattoirs," *New York Times*, August 5, 1866.
29. William David Zimmerman, "Live Cattle Export Trade between United States and Great Britain, 1868–1885," *Agricultural History* 36 (January 1962): 46; Joseph Nimmo Jr., *Report in Regard to the Range and Ranch Cattle Business of the United States* (Washington, DC: Government Printing Office, 1885), 66–71; and "Cattle Trade for Europe," *Harper's Weekly* 23 (September 27, 1879): 774.
30. Zimmerman, "Live Cattle Export Trade," 47.
31. "American Beef for Old England," *Harper's Weekly* 21 (April 7, 1877): 277–79.
32. *Galveston Daily News*, May 17, 1866.
33. Nimmo, *Report*, 69.
34. McCoy, *Historic Sketches of the Cattle Trade*, 65–73.
35. James Sherow, "Water, Sun, and Cattle: The Chisholm Trail as an Ephemeral Ecosystem," in *Fluid Arguments: Five Centuries of Western Water Conflict*, ed. Char Miller (Tucson: University of Arizona Press, 2001), 141–55.

## CHAPTER 3

1. McCoy, *Historic Sketches of the Cattle Trade*, 52–54.
2. US Department of Commerce, National Oceanic and Atmospheric Administration, National Centers for Environmental Information, Publications, Forts, Fort Riley, 5–6, https://www.ncdc.noaa.gov/EdadsV2/library/FORTS.
3. "Spanish Fever," *Emporia* (KS) *Weekly News*, September 8, 1860.
4. "The Cattle Disease," *Emporia Weekly News*, September 1, 1860.
5. *Emporia Weekly News*, May 19, 1860.
6. *General Laws of the State of Kansas Passed at the First Session of the Legislature, Commenced at the Capital, March 26, 1816* (Lawrence: Kansas State Journal Steam Power Press Print, 1861), 280.
7. "Our Markets," *New Orleans Picayune*, June 19, 1862.
8. *New Orleans Picayune*, July 11, 1865.
9. Ibid.
10. W. D. H. Saunders, "Drove a Herd to Mississippi and Alabama," in *Trail Drivers of Texas*, 267–68.
11. E. M. Daggett, "Worked with Cattle for Over Sixty Years," in *Trail Drivers of Texas*, 532.
12. "Our Markets," *New Orleans Picayune*, June 19, 1862.
13. "Our Markets," *New Orleans Times-Picayune*, October 11, 1865; "Something New," *New Orleans Times-Picayune*, July 12, 1865.
14. *Olathe* (KS) *Mirror*, July 20, 1865.
15. "Powder Horn, TX," *Handbook of Texas Online*, accessed February 25, 2016, http://www.tshaonline.org/handbook/online/articles/hvp80.
16. Bennett, "Sixty Years in Texas," in *Trail Drivers of Texas*, 122.
17. *Howard Union* (Glasgow, MO), October 12, 1865.
18. "The Texas Cattle Trade," *Inter Ocean* (Chicago), June 17, 1873.

19. "Letter from Travis," *Galveston Daily News*, June 9, 1866; "Letter from Bell County," *Galveston Daily News*, June 28, 1866.
20. "The Texas Cattle Law," *Daily* (Lawrence) *Kansas Tribune*, January 25, 1866; "Southern Cattle," *Emporia Weekly News*, March 17, 1866.
21. "The Wyandotte *Gazette* says," *Daily Kansas Tribune*, April 29, 1866.
22. *Daily Kansas Tribune*, August 8, 1866.
23. Ibid.
24. "Southern Cattle," *Emporia Weekly News*, March 17, 1866.
25. "Texas Cattle," *Daily Kansas Tribune*, May 22, 1866.
26. "To Whom It May Concern," *Olathe* (KS) *Mirror*, May 17, 1866.
27. *Daily Kansas Tribune*, May 26, 1866.
28. *Daily Kansas Tribune*, June 27, 1866.
29. *Daily Kansas Tribune*, July 22, 1866.
30. *Junction City* (KS) *Weekly Union*, August 4, 1866.
31. McCoy, *Historic Sketches of the Cattle Trade*, 26–27.
32. Dr. J. Hargus, "Noted Quantrell Was with Herd on Trail," in *Trail Drivers of Texas*, 591–92.
33. "Texas Cattle," *Lincoln County Herald* (Troy, MO), September 21, 1866.
34. "Cattle and Railroads—An Item of Importance to St. Louis," *Daily Kansas Tribune*, September 26, 1866; and *Wyandotte* (KS) *Commercial Gazette*, November 10, 1866.
35. "Southern Cattle," *Wyandotte Commercial Gazette*, October 16, 1866.
36. McCoy, *Historic Sketches of the Cattle Trade*, 23, 37.
37. Ibid., 122–24.
38. Ibid., 73–75.
39. Samuel Wilkison, "Beef from Texas," *New York Tribune*, November 6, 1867.
40. McCoy, *Historic Sketches of the Cattle Trade*, 103.
41. See "From the Capital," *Emporia Weekly News*, February 15, 1867; "Members and Officers of the House of Representatives," in *The Annals of Kansas, New Edition, 1541–1885*, ed. D. W. Wilder (Topeka: T. Dwight Thacher, Kansas Publishing House, 1886), 450; and "An Act for the Protection of Stock from Disease," in *The Laws of the State of Kansas Passed at the Seventh Session of the Legislature Commenced at the State Capitol on January 8, 1867* (Leavenworth, KS: Bulletin Book and Job Office, 1867), 263–65.
42. McCoy, *Historic Sketches of the Cattle Trade*, 41.
43. Ibid., 44.
44. William Lamb and "Others" to Governor Samuel Crawford, September 10, 1867, Letters received, Governor Samuel Crawford, Archives, Kansas State Historical Society, Topeka.
45. William Lamb and "Others" to Governor Samuel Crawford, August 31, 1867, Letters received, Governor Samuel Crawford, Archives, Kansas State Historical Society, Topeka.
46. Newton Blair to Governor Samuel Crawford, October 7, 1867, Letters received, Governor Samuel Crawford, Archives, Kansas State Historical Society, Topeka.
47. *New York Tribune*, August 14, 1867.
48. McCoy, *Historic Sketches of the Cattle Trade*, 41–42.
49. McCoy, Joseph vs. the Kansas Pacific, J. G. McCoy Collection, Archive Division, Kansas Historical Society, Topeka, 47.
50. McCoy, *Historic Sketches of the Cattle Trade*, 212.

## CHAPTER 4

1. The biographical material on Black Beaver is taken from Carolyn Thomas Foreman, "Black Beaver," *Chronicles of Oklahoma* 24 (1946): 269–91.

2. John Rossel, "The Chisholm Trail," *Kansas Historical Quarterly* 5 (February 1936): 5–7; *Wichita Eagle*, March 1, 1890; "Beginning and End of the Old Chisholm Trail," *Kansas City Times*, December 9, 1924; and *The War of the Rebellion: A Compilation of the Official Records of the Union and Confederate Armies*, series 1, volume 1 (Washington, DC: Government Printing Office, 1880), 648–49.

3. *War of the Rebellion*, 648–49.

4. Rossel, "Chisholm Trail," 5–7; *Wichita Eagle*, March 1, 1890; "Beginning and End of the Old Chisholm Cattle Trail," *Kansas City Times*, December 9, 1924.

5. *Reports of Explorations and Surveys, to Ascertain the Most Practicable and Economical Route for a Railroad from the Mississippi River to the Pacific Ocean. Made under the Direction of the Secretary of War, in 1853–4*, vol. 3. Washington: A. O. P. Nicholson, Printer, 1856.

6. Rossel, "Chisholm Trail," 5–7; *Wichita Eagle*, March 1, 1890; and "Beginning and End of the Old Chisholm Cattle Trail," *Kansas City Times*, December 9, 1924.

7. Adams, *Cowboy Lingo*, 200–201, 216.

8. Luc Brouillet and R. David Whetstone, "Climate and Physiography of North America," in *Flora of North America*, vol. 1 (New York: Oxford University Press, 1993), http://flora.huh.harvard.edu/FNA/Volume/V01/_old/Chapter01.html.

9. Bruce P. Hayden, "Regional Climate and the Distribution of Tallgrass Prairie," in *Grassland Dynamics: Long-Term Ecological Research in Tallgrass Prairie*, ed. Alan K. Knapp, John M. Briggs, David C. Hartnett, and Scott L. Collins (New York: Oxford University Press, 1998), 19–34.

10. Jasper (Bob) Lauderdale, "Reminiscences of the Trail," in *Trail Drivers of Texas*, 409–10.

11. Richard Withers, "The Experience of an Old Trail Driver," in *Trail Drivers of Texas*, 314.

12. "Live Stock," *Galveston Daily News*, September 13, 1881.

13. Joseph G. McCoy, *Historic Sketches of the Cattle Trade*, 121; C. W. Ackermann, "Exciting Experiences on the Frontier and on the Trail," in *Trail Drivers of Texas*, 157.

14. K. A. Valentine, "Distance from Water as a Factor in Grazing Capacity of Rangeland," *Journal of Forestry* 45 (October 1947): 749.

15. Ibid., 751.

16. Gustavo Caetano-Anollés, "Grass Evolution Inferred from Chromosomal Rearrangements and Geometrical and Statistical Features in RNA Structure," *Journal of Molecular Evolution* 60 (2005): 635–52.

17. William Dayton, "The Family Tree of Gramineae," in *Grass: The Yearbook of Agriculture*, ed. Alfred Stefferud (Washington, DC: Government Printing Office, 1948), 637–39.

18. John James Ingalls, "In Praise of Bluegrass," in *Grass: The Yearbook of Agriculture*, ed. Alfred Stefferud (Washington, DC: Government Printing Office, 1948), 6–8.

19. R. E. Redman and E. G. Reekie, "Carbon Balance in Grasses," in *Grasses and Grasslands: Systematics and Ecology*, edited by James R. Estes, Ronald J. Tyrl, and Jere N. Brunken (Norman: University of Oklahoma Press, 1982), 195–231.

20. O. J. Reichman, *Konza Prairie: A Tallgrass Natural History* (Lawrence: University Press of Kansas, 1987), 76–82.

21. Mycorrhiza is pronounced mahy-kuh-rahy-zuh.

22. Interview with John Briggs, Director of Konza Biological Research Station, September 16, 2016.

23. McCoy, *Historic Sketches of the Cattle Trade*, 5–6.

24. Joseph Barrell, *The Red Hills of Kansas: Crossroads of Plant Migrations* (Rockford, IL: Natural Land Institute, 1975).

25. J. M. Hankins, "Reminiscences of Old Trail Driving," in *Trail Drivers of Texas*, 110.

26. Territorial Survey Map, Township 32 South, Range 2 West, February and March 1871, Kansas State Historical Society, Topeka.

27. B. W. Allred, "Bluestem on the Longhorn Trails," *Journal of Soil and Water Conservation* 5 (October 1950): 150–57, 198.

28. Joseph Geating McCoy, Diary, 1880–81, MS 406, entries for June 21–22, 1880, Kansas Historical Society, Topeka.

29. *Sumner County* (KS) *Press*, July 3, 1874.

30. Kevin Kelly, *What Technology Wants* (New York: Viking, 2010), 11. A good overview of theories about technology is Richard Rhodes, ed., *Visions of Technology: A Century of Vital Debate About Machines, Systems, and the Human World* (New York: Simon & Schuster, 1999). See also W. Brian Arthur, *The Nature of Technology: What It Is and How It Evolves* (New York: Free Press, 2009); and Roe Smith and Leo Marx, eds., *Does Technology Drive History? The Dilemma of Technological Determinism* (Cambridge, MA: MIT Press, 1994).

31. Charles Godfrey Leland, *The Union Pacific Railway, Eastern Division, or, Three Thousand Miles in a Railway Car* (Philadelphia: Ringwalt & Brown, 1867), 13.

32. Kate Brown, "Gridded Lives: Why Kazakhstan and Montana Are Nearly the Same Place," *American Historical Review* 106 (February 2001): 17–48.

33. Robert V. O'Neill discusses the role of human beings as keystone species in his article "Is It Time to Bury the Ecosystem Concept? (With Full Military Honors, of Course!)," *Ecology* 82 (December 2001): 3281–82. The quote defining keystone species is taken from Sergio Cristancho and Joanne Vining, "Culturally Defined Keystone Species," *Human Ecology Review* 11, no. 2 (2004): 153. The one most associated with developing this concept is Robert T. Paine. See Paine, "A Conversation on Refining the Concept of Keystone Species," *Conservation Biology* 9 (1995): 962–64.

34. O'Neill, "Is It Time to Bury the Ecosystem Concept?," 3279.

35. Kelly, *What Technology Wants*, 103.

36. Ibid., 180.

37. Josiah Copley, *Kansas and the Country Beyond on the Line of the Union Pacific Railway, Eastern Division, From the Missouri to the Pacific Ocean* (Philadelphia: J. B. Lippincott, 1867), 8.

38. Richard Yates, "Speech of Senator Yates, of Illinois," in *Senatorial Excursion Party over the Union Pacific Railway, E.D.* (St. Louis: S. Levison, 1867), 15. Italics added for emphasis.

39. Copley, *Kansas and the Country Beyond*, 8.

40. William A. Bell, *New Tracks in North America: A Journal of Travel and Adventure Whilst Engaged in the Survey for a Southern Railroad to the Pacific Ocean During 1867–8* (London: Chapman and Hall, 1870; Albuquerque: Horn and Wallace, 1965), xxv.

41. *Emporia* (KS) *Weekly News*, September 20, 1867.

42. *Junction City* (KS) *Union*, November 30, 1867.

43. McCoy, *Historic Sketches of the Cattle Trade*, 106.
44. *Junction City* (KS) *Union*, November 16, 1867; and *Emporia* (KS) *Weekly News*, December 13, 1867.
45. *Junction City* (KS) *Union*, November 2, 1867.
46. McCoy, *Historic Sketches of the Cattle Trade*, 107.
47. *Kansas State Record* (Topeka), November 20, 1867.
48. Samuel Wilkison, "Beef from Texas," *New York Tribune*, November 6, 1867.

## CHAPTER 5

1. T. F. Oakes, *Guide Map of the Great Texas Cattle Trail from the Red River Crossing to the Old Reliable Kansas Pacific Railway* (Kansas Pacific Railway, 1874).
2. C. H. Rust, "Location of the Old Chisholm Trail," in *Trail Drivers of Texas*, 38–39.
3. John P. Burkhart, "The Texas Cattle Trade," *Galveston Daily News*, December 23, 1869.
4. "Frio," *Dallas Daily Herald*, September 1, 1882.
5. See appendix for an explanation of the statistical methods used for analyzing the weather records of army posts for determining temperature trends and variations in southern, middle, and northern regions of the Chisholm Trail system.
6. United States Army, "Meteorological Register, Fort Duncan, Texas, 1873–1879"; and United States Army, "Meteorological Register, Fort Richardson, Texas, 1868–1878," www.ncdc.noaa.gov/EdadsV2/library/FORTS.
7. "Profits on Texas Cattle," *Galveston Daily News*, January 21, 1869.
8. *Proceedings and Debates of the American Convention of Cattle Commissioners, Held at Springfield, Ill., December 1st, 2nd and 3d, 1868*. Ely, Burnham, and Bartlett, Official Reporters. (Springfield: Illinois Journal Printing Office, 1869), 49–50.
9. "Cattle Items," *Atchison* (KS) *Daily Patriot*, December 31, 1870; *Junction City* (KS) *Weekly Union*, December 31, 1870; and Joseph Nimmo, *Report*, 22–23.
10. "Colonel Dillard R. Fant: Sketch of One of the Most Prominent of All Trail Drivers," in *Trail Drivers of Texas*, 517–18.
11. "Registered Members of the Texas LiveStock Association," *Austin Weekly Statesman*, February 23, 1882.
12. *Proceedings and Debates of the American Convention of Cattle Commissioners*, 50.
13. Ibid., 131.
14. Ibid., 49–50.
15. Bennett, "Sixty Years in Texas," in *Trail Drivers of Texas*, 21–22.
16. S. A. Hickok, "Mistaken for Cole Younger and Arrested," in *Trail Drivers of Texas*, 47.
17. Nimmo, *Report*, 2–5.
18. The *New York Times* reporter failed to give the first name of "Mr. King," who in all likelihood was Richard King, a leading Texas rancher and entrepreneur. Upon his death he reportedly owned more than 500,000 acres of land. See "Richard King," in *Trail Drivers of Texas*, 529–30.
19. "Cattle Kings of Texas," *New York Times*, November 12, 1876.
20. Luther A. Lawhon, "The Men Who Made the Trail," in *Trail Drivers of Texas*, 201.
21. Jack Bailey, *A Texas Cowboy's Journal: Up the Trail to Kansas in 1868*, ed. David Dary (Norman: University of Oklahoma Press, 2006), 9–10.

22. Ben Drake, "Ate Terrapin and Dog Meat, and Was Glad to Get It," in *Trail Drivers of Texas*, 626.

23. A. W. Capt, "The Early Cattle Days in Texas," in *Trail Drivers of Texas*, 365.

24. F. M. Polk, "My Experience on the Cow Trail," in *Trail Drivers of Texas*, 141.

25. Capt, "The Early Cattle Days in Texas," in *Trail Drivers of Texas*, 366.

26. Allred, "Bluestem on the Longhorn Trails," 150–57, 198.

27. Joseph Geating McCoy, Diary, 1880–81, MS 406, entries for June 21–22, 1880, Kansas Historical Society, Topeka.

28. W. F. Cude, "Trail Driving to Kansas and Elsewhere," in *Trail Drivers of Texas*, 216.

29. G. W. Mills, "Experiences 'Tenderfeet' Could Not Survive," in *Trail Drivers of Texas*, 239.

30. The weather information was compiled from United States Army, "Meteorological Register, Fort Arbuckle, Indian Territory," 1867–70; and "Meteorological Register, Fort Sill, Indian Territory," 1870–85.

31. *Proceedings and Debates of the American Convention of Cattle Commissioners*, 24.

32. The weather information was compiled from United States Army, "Meteorological Register, Fort Riley, Kansas," 1867–83; and "Meteorological Register, Fort Hays, Kansas," 1867–79.

33. *Sumner County* (KS) *Press*, July 3, 1874.

34. Kansas Pacific Railway Company, *Guide Map of the Great Texas Cattle Trail from the Red River Crossing to the Old Reliable Kansas Pacific Railway* (Kansas Pacific Railway, 1874).

35. "From the West," *Kansas State Record* (Topeka), June 22, 1870, 2.

36. Ibid.

37. Clive Ponting, *A Green History of the World: The Environment and the Collapse of Great Civilizations* (New York: St. Martin's Press, 1991), 301–9.

38. *New York Tribune*, July 12, 1870.

39. Rideing, "How New York Is Fed," 732–33.

40. Ranhofer, *Epicurean*, 487; and Paul Freedman and James Warlick, "High-End Dining in the Nineteenth-Century United States," *Gastronomica* 11 (Spring 2011): 44–52.

41. Ibid., 2, 19.

42. W. E. Cureton, "Drove a Herd over the Trail to California," in *Trail Drivers of Texas*, 51–52; and David Igler, "Miller and Lux and the Transformation of the Far West, 1850–1920," *Pacific Historical Review* 69 (May 2000): 159–92.

43. "From the West," *Kansas State Record* (Topeka), November 3, 1869.

44. Clive Emsley, Tim Hitchcock, and Robert Shoemaker, "London History: A Population History of London," Old Bailey Proceedings Online, accessed February 3, 2015, version 7.0, http://www.oldbaileyonline.org/static/Population-history-of-london.jsp.

45. These June and July averages are considerably lower than that recorded for 1860–67, and those recorded in the following decade, 1871–80. The average for June 1860–67 was 3.18 inches, for the same month, 1871–80, the average was 3.05 inches. For July 1860–67, the average was 2.83 inches, and for July 1871–80, the average rainfall for the month was 3.85 inches. All these averages are around three times the average that fell in June and July in 1868, 1869, and 1870. See Monthly England and Wales Precipitation, 1766–2014, accessed February 5, 2015, www.metoffice.gov.uk/hadobs/hadukp/data/monthly/HadEWP_monthly_qc.txt.

46. "Chicago Grain and Cattle Markets," *Harper's Weekly* 12 (October 31, 1868): 702.

47. Monthly England and Wales Precipitation.
48. "American Beef for Old England," 277–79.
49. Regarding English meat markets see *New York Times*, February 2, 1869; "Texas Beef—Its Transportation," *Galveston Daily News*, November 19, 1869; "There Is Nothing in the Pot," *Galveston Daily News*, September 12, 1872; "American Beef for Old England," 277–79; Nelson Morris, "Statement in Regard to the Early Shipments of Cattle and Dressed Beef to Europe," in Nimmo, *Report*, 198; "The Exportation of Cattle and Beef Products to Foreign Countries," in Nimmo, *Report*, 65; and Zimmerman, "Live Cattle Export Trade," 46–52.
50. *Proceedings and Debates of the American Convention of Cattle Commissioners*, 23.
51. Ackermann, "Exciting Experiences," in *Trail Drivers of Texas*, 154–55.
52. Sol West, "Courage and Hardihood on the Old Texas Cattle Trail," in *Trail Drivers of Texas*, 127–28.
53. J. F. Ellison Jr., "Sketch of Col. J. F. Ellison," in *Trail Drivers of Texas*, 476–77.
54. "The Texas Cattle Trade," *Kansas State Record* (Topeka), September 14, 1870.
55. Ibid.
56. G. O. Burrows, "High-Heeled Boots and Striped Breeches," in *Trail Drivers of Texas*, 120.
57. "The Facts and Figures about the Cattle Trade—Common-Sense View," *Abilene* (KS) *Chronicle*, February 2, 1871.
58. C. S. Brodbent, "Lost Many Thousands of Dollars," in *Trail Drivers of Texas*, 592–93.
59. For some background on Jay Gould and Cornelius Vanderbilt, see Maury Klein, *The Life and Legend of Jay Gould* (Baltimore: Johns Hopkins University Press, 1986); and Edward J. Renehan Jr., *Commodore: The Life of Cornelius Vanderbilt* (New York: Basic Books, 2009).
60. "Vanderbilt's Cattle Trade," *Belvidere* (IL) *Standard*, August 9, 1870.
61. See McCoy, Joseph vs. the Kansas Pacific, J. G. McCoy Collection, Archive Division, Kansas Historical Society, Topeka.
62. Brodbent, "Lost Many Thousands," in *Trail Drivers of Texas*, 593.
63. "The Lemontation or Confession of a Dealer in Texas Cattle," *Emporia* (KS) *Weekly News*, January 19, 1872.

## CHAPTER 6

1. "Stock Shipment," *Daily* (Lawrence) *Kansas Tribune*, June 12, 1868.
2. Ibid.
3. "The Kansas Law Prohibiting the Importation of Texas Cattle," *New York Times*, January 5, 1868.
4. McCoy, Joseph vs. the Kansas Pacific, "Petition, Joseph G. McCoy, Plaintiff," 11, Archive Division, Kansas Historical Society, Topeka.
5. *Junction City* (KS) *Weekly Union*, April 11, 1868.
6. *Junction City* (KS) *Weekly Union*, June 27, 1868.
7. "Chicago and the Extension of the Union Pacific Railway E.D.," *Kansas State Record* (Topeka), June 17, 1868.
8. *Proceedings and Debates of the American Convention of Cattle Commissioners*, 1.
9. M. Arcari, A. Baxendine, and C. E. Bennett, "Babesia, Trypanosomes & Leishmania," Diagnosing Medical Parasites through Coprological Techniques 11, copyright 2000, http://www.soton.ac.uk/~ceb/Diagnosis/Vol11.htm. See also Tamara Miner Haygood, "Cows,

Ticks, and Disease: A Medical Interpretation of the Southern Cattle Industry," *Journal of Southern History* 52 (November 1986): 551–64.

10. *Reports on the Diseases of Cattle in the United States: Made to the Commissioner of Agriculture, with Accompanying Documents* (Washington, DC: Government Printing Office, 1869), 89.

11. Patrick, Allen, and Gould, *Report of the New York State Cattle Commissioners*, 3–148.

12. Ibid., 47–49.

13. Ibid., 48.

14. Ibid., 49.

15. Ibid., 47.

16. *New York Times*, July 31, 1868; and Patrick, Allen, and Gould, *Report of the New York State Cattle Commissioners*, 4.

17. "The Cattle Plague: The Plague at the West—Diseased Meat in the New York Market," *New York Tribune*, August 8, 1868.

18. "Illinois Farmers and Texas Cattle," *New York Tribune*, August 1, 1868.

19. *Junction City* (KS) *Union*, August 1, 1868.

20. *Reports on the Diseases of Cattle in the United States*, 89.

21. Bailey, *Texas Cowboy's Journal*, 66–67. An article in the *Junction City* (KS) *Weekly Union*, October 10, 1868, reported that the "citizens" of Mound City had killed forty head of Texas cattle.

22. "The Cattle Plague in Illinois," *New York Tribune*, August 5, 1868.

23. "The Cattle Plague," *New York Tribune*, August 8, 1868.

24. "The Cattle Plague within the Metropolitan District," *New York Tribune*, August 10, 1868.

25. Ibid.

26. Ibid.

27. *New York Times*, August 12, 1868.

28. "The Cattle Plague: Report of the Health Board Sanitary Committee—Action of Govs. Fenton and Ward," *New York Times*, August 14, 1868.

29. *Junction City* (KS) *Weekly Union*, August 15, 1868.

30. "The Cattle Plague," *New York Tribune*, August 25, 1868.

31. "The Cattle Plague: The Disease Still Prevailing in Ford County, Ill.—Diseased Meat in the New York Market," *Chicago Tribune*, August 26, 1868.

32. "The Cattle Disease, Its Appearance in the Dairies in the Vicinity of Cincinnati: From the *Cincinnati Gazette*, Aug. 24," *New York Times*, August 28, 1868.

33. "The Cattle Plague," *New York Tribune*, August 27, 1868.

34. "An Opinion from Canada," *New York Tribune*, August 31, 1868.

35. *Junction City* (KS) *Weekly Union*, August 29, 1868.

36. "Report of Dr. Moreau Morris," *New York Times*, August 28, 1868.

37. The letters are reprinted in both "The Cattle Disease: Illinois Complains of the Action of the New York Authorities," *New York Times*, September 5, 1868; and Patrick, Allen, and Gould, *Report of the New York State Cattle Commissioners*, 35.

38. Patrick, Allen, and Gould, *Report of the New York State Cattle Commissioners*, 36.

39. *Junction City* (KS) *Weekly Union*, August 1, 1868, 3.

40. "An Important Enterprise: Atchison and Waterville, the Great Cattle Depots of the West," *Olathe* (KS) *Mirror*, July 2, 1868.

41. *Junction City* (KS) *Union*, April 25, 1868.

42. McCoy, Joseph vs. the Kansas Pacific, "Petition, Joseph G. McCoy, Plaintiff," 11–12, Archive Division, Kansas Historical Society, Topeka.

43. *Daily* (Lawrence) *Kansas Tribune*, June 12, 1868, 3.

44. *Daily* (Lawrence) *Kansas Tribune*, June 26, 1868, 3.

45. "The Cattle Plague," *Harper's Weekly*, August 29, 1868, 554.

46. McCoy, *Historic Sketches of the Cattle Trade*, 179–80.

47. McCoy, *Historic Sketches of the Cattle Trade*, 179–82.

48. M. A. Withers, "Killing and Capturing Buffalo in Kansas," in *Trail Drivers of Texas*, 99.

49. Ibid.

50. Ibid., 99–100.

51. Ibid., 100–101.

52. *Daily* (Lawrence) *Kansas Tribune*, August 25, 1868.

53. Withers, "Killing and Capturing Buffalo," in *Trail Drivers of Texas*, 101.

54. *Macon* (MO) *Argus*, September 9, 1868.

55. *The Sun* (New York City), September 9, 1868.

56. Withers, "Killing and Capturing Buffalo," in *Trail Drivers of Texas*, 101.

57. McCoy, *Historic Sketches of the Cattle Trade*, 182.

58. "Grand Buffalo Excursion," *Chicago Tribune*, September 11, 1868.

59. "An Inhuman Entertainment," *Chicago Tribune*, September 18, 1868.

60. "That Buffalo Hunt," *Chicago Tribune*, September 20, 1868.

61. McCoy, *Historic Sketches of the Cattle Trade*, 182.

62. A search of the *Twelfth Annual Report of the Board of Commissioners of the Central Park for the Year Ending December 31, 1868* (New York: Evening Post Steam Presses, 1869), reveals no bison donation made by McCoy.

63. "Texas Cattle," *Kansas State Record* (Topeka), October 19, 1870.

64. "The Cattle Plague," *New York Tribune*, August 8, 1868.

65. *New York Times*, August 15, 1868.

66. "The Gamgee Banquet," *New York Tribune*, March 4, 1868.

67. "Illinois," *New York Tribune*, August 21, 1868; and Richardson, W. E., "Cattle Plague: Another Report by Mr. Richardson," *Chicago Tribune*, August 18, 1868.

68. Richardson, W. E., "Cattle Plague."

69. "Enzootic" meaning animal disease, and "haematuria" meaning blood in the urine.

70. "The Cattle Disease: Prof. Gamgee's Report," *New York Times*, August 9, 1868.

71. McCoy, *Historic Sketches of the Cattle Trade*, 151.

72. Ibid., 152.

73. "Second Day's Proceeding in the Cattle Commissioners' Convention," *Chicago Daily Tribune*, December 3, 1868.

74. *Proceedings and Debates of the American Convention of Cattle Commissioners*, 2, 24–25.

75. McCoy, *Historic Sketches of the Cattle Trade*, 156–57.

76. "Second Day's Proceeding in the Cattle Commissioners' Convention," *Chicago Daily Tribune*, December 3, 1868.

77. *Proceedings and Debates of the American Convention of Cattle Commissioners*, 3.
78. Ibid., 6–10.
79. Ibid., 14.
80. J. M. S. Careless, "Christie, David," in *Dictionary of Canadian Biography*, vol. 10 (Toronto: University of Toronto Press, 1972), http://www.biographi.ca/en/bio/christie_david_10E.html.
81. *Proceedings and Debates of the American Convention of Cattle Commissioners*, 21.
82. Ibid., 23.
83. Ibid., 23–24.
84. Ibid., 24.
85. Ibid., 24–50.
86. Ibid., 50.
87. Ibid., 55–59.
88. Ibid., 60.
89. McCoy, *Historic Sketches of the Cattle Trade*, 187–88.
90. Ibid., 171–78.
91. *Proceedings and Debates of the American Convention of Cattle Commissioners*, 46–48.
92. "Hay and Food for Great Britain," *New York Times*, February 2, 1869.
93. Andreas, *History of the State of Kansas*, 1161.
94. "The Texas Cattle Law," *Kansas State Record* (Topeka), December 20, 1871, 4.
95. *Wichita Eagle*, November 14, 1872.
96. The best biography of Theobald Smith is Claude E. Doman and Richard J. Wolfe's *Suppressing the Diseases of Animals and Man: Theobald Smith, Microbiologist* (Boston: Boston Medical Library, Francis A. Countway Library of Medicine, Distributed by Harvard University Press, 2003). The first three chapters, pp. 1–58, cover Smith's early years and university training.

**CHAPTER 7**

1. McCoy, *Historic Sketches of the Cattle Trade*, 282–84.
2. Ibid.
3. West, "Courage and Hardihood," in *Trail Drivers of Texas*, 129.
4. Ibid., 128–29.
5. S. D. Houston, "Prairie Fire," *Junction City* (KS) *Union*, October 9, 1869.
6. Ibid.
7. For starters, see Scott L. Collins and Linda L. Wallace, eds., *Fire in North American Tallgrass Prairies* (Norman: University of Oklahoma Press, 1990); and Julie Courtwright, *Prairie Fire: A Great Plains History* (Lawrence: University Press of Kansas, 2011).
8. "Prairie Fires," *Junction City* (KS) *Union*, October 2, 1869.
9. Brevet Major George Sternberg, Assistant Surgeon, Meteorological Register, Fort Riley, Kansas, October 1869, National Centers for Environmental Information, National Oceanic and Atmospheric Administration, https://www.ncdc.noaa.gov/EdadsV2/.
10. George M. Sternberg, "Sterility of the Plains," *Junction City* (KS) *Weekly Union*, February 5, 1870.
11. Ibid.
12. S. D. Houston, "Prairie Fires," *Junction City* (KS) *Union*, November 6, 1869.

13. *Junction City* (KS) *Union*, September 25, 1869.
14. "From Kansas," *Decatur* (IL) *Weekly Republican*, October 2, 1873.
15. *Junction City* (KS) *Union*, February 7, 1870.
16. Ibid.
17. Ibid.
18. *Saline County Journal* (Salina, KS), February 9, 1882.
19. "Prairie Fires," *Saline County Journal* (Salina, KS), February 23, 1882.
20. Martha L. Sternberg, *George Miller Sternberg: A Biography by His Wife* (Chicago: American Medical Association, 1920), 18–20.
21. Rev. Dr. Sternberg, "Industrial Pursuits on the Plains in 1871," *Lawrence* (KS) *Daily Journal*, January 23, 1872.
22. Ibid.
23. *Saline County Journal* (Salina, KS), November 30, 1867.
24. *Dodge City Times*, December 31, 1885.
25. "Prairie Fires," *Leavenworth* (KS) *Times*, November 4, 1869.
26. *Junction City* (KS) *Union*, October 30, 1869.
27. *Kansas State Record* (Topeka), November 3, 1869.
28. "From the West," *Kansas State Record* (Topeka), November 3, 1869.
29. *Junction City* (KS) *Weekly Union*, October 30, 1869.
30. Sternberg, "Industrial Pursuits on the Plains in 1871."
31. *Abilene* (KS) *Chronicle*, February 2, 1871.
32. *Kansas State Record* (Topeka), June 14, 1871.
33. McCoy, *Historic Sketches of the Cattle Trade*, 217.
34. Sternberg, "Industrial Pursuits on the Plains in 1871."
35. *Junction City* (KS) *Union*, December 2, 1871.
36. Captain John Janeway, Assistant Surgeon, Meteorological Register, Fort Hays, Kansas, November 1871, National Centers for Environmental Information, National Oceanic and Atmospheric Administration, https://www.ncdc.noaa.gov/EdadsV2/.
37. "From Sciota," *Junction City* (KS) *Union*, December 2, 1871.
38. *Junction City* (KS) *Union*, November 25, 1871.
39. Janeway, Meteorological Register, Fort Hays, November 1871.
40. Captain L. V. Loring, Assistant Surgeon, Meteorological Register, Fort Riley, Kansas, November 1871, National Centers for Environmental Information, National Oceanic and Atmospheric Administration, https://www.ncdc.noaa.gov/EdadsV2/.
41. Ibid., 226–28.
42. Janeway, Meteorological Register, Fort Hays, December 1871; and Loring, Meteorological Register, December 1871.
43. "The Late Snow Storm," *Ellsworth* (KS) *Reporter*, December 28, 1871.
44. Ibid.
45. *Ellsworth* (KS) *Reporter*, February 17, 1871.
46. *Ellsworth* (KS) *Reporter*, April 27, 1872.
47. "The Markets for the Week," *Daily* (Lawrence) *Kansas Tribune*, February 8, 1872; "Texas Cattle," *Leavenworth* (KS) *Times*, March 21, 1872; *Junction City* (KS) *Union*, April 6, 1868.

48. D. B. L., "Loss of Stock on the Plains," *Ellsworth* (KS) *Reporter*, May 16, 1872.

49. McCoy, *Historic Sketches of the Cattle Trade*, 99–100.

50. E. A. (Berry) Robuck, "Dodging Indians Near Packsaddle Mountain," in *Trail Drivers of Texas*, 33.

51. Cowboys like Scott referred to a dry stream bed as a "draw."

52. G. W. Scott, "With Herds to Colorado and New Mexico," in *Trail Drivers of Texas*, 116–17. The date printed in the book is 1881, but it is more likely that the actual date was 1891, when Scott would have been twenty years old. The description of this event follows Scott's recollection of his first drive, which occurred in 1890.

53. Mills, "Experiences," in *Trail Drivers of Texas*, 236.

54. J. C. Thompson, "'Chawed' the Earmarks," in *Trail Drivers of Texas*, 667.

55. Bailey, *Texas Cowboy's Journal*.

56. Ibid., 26.

## CHAPTER 8

1. "Proceedings of the National Council," *Cherokee Advocate* (Tahlequah, Cherokee Nation), December 8, 1880.

2. US Department of the Interior, *Report of Commissioner of Indian Affairs* (1880), 83–93, 98, 189, 385.

3. "A Fight or a Foot-Race," *Walnut Valley Times* (El Dorado, KS), December 10, 1880.

4. *Arkansas City* (KS) *Weekly*, July 27, 1881.

5. McCoy, *Historic Sketches of the Cattle Trade* (1874), 138, 380, 67–70.

6. *Arkansas City Weekly*, July 27, 1881.

7. "Oklahoma. A Few Words About the Boomers and Their Attitude," *Wichita Eagle*, September 19, 1884.

8. "Cattle from the Cherokee and Creek Nation," *New York Tribune*, July 12, 1853.

9. US Department of the Interior, *Report of Commissioner of Indian Affairs* (1857), 499.

10. US Department of the Interior, *Report of Commissioner of Indian Affairs* (1859), 540–41; *Condition of the Indian Tribes: Report of the Joint Special Committee, Appointed under Joint Resolution of March 3, 1865* (Washington, DC: Government Printing Office, 1867), 445.

11. "Beef from Texas," *New York Tribune*, November 6, 1867.

12. "Indian Affairs: The Choctaw Tribe—Their Agricultural Pursuits and Their Civilization," *New York Times*, September 16, 1867.

13. John Ross, *The Papers of Chief John Ross*, vol. 2, ed. Gary E. Moulton (Norman: University of Oklahoma Press, 1985), 523–24.

14. Jane Nave to Oliver H. Browning, Secretary of Interior, September 21, 1866, US Department of the Interior, Bureau of Indian Affairs, Letters Received by the Office of Indian Affairs, 1824 to 1881, Cherokee Agency, 1865–66, Record Group 75, M234, roll 100.

15. Ibid.

16. Ibid.

17. "Special Files of the Office of Indian Affairs, 1807–1904," files 134–38, Office of Indian Affairs, Record Group 75, M574, roll 27; and US Department of the Interior, *Report of the Commissioner of Indian Affairs* (1868), 781.

18. "Special Files of the Office of Indian Affairs, 1807–1904," files 134–38.

19. "Indian Affairs: The Choctaw Tribe—Their Agricultural Pursuits and Their Civilization," *New York Times*, September 16, 1867.

20. US Department of the Interior, *Report of the Commissioner of Indian Affairs* (1866), 319.

21. *Report of the Secretary of the Interior*, H. Ex. Doc. 1, 44th Cong., 1st sess., 1875, 612–13, 628.

22. *Report of the Secretary of the Interior*, H. Ex. Doc. 1, Part 5, 49th Cong., 1st sess., 1885, 612–13.

23. Patrick Henry Healy to Commissioner of Indian Affairs, October 15, 1866, US Department of the Interior, Bureau of Indian Affairs, Letters Received by the Office of Indian Affairs, 1824 to 1881, Kiowa Agency, 1869–70, Record Group 75, M234, roll 375.

24. J. M. Haworth, US Indian Agent, to E. P. Smith, Commissioner of Indian Affairs, May 15, 1874, Office of Indian Affairs, Kiowa Agency, 1874, Record Group 75, M234, roll 379.

25. J. M. Haworth, US Indian Agent, to E. Hoag, Superintendent, Central Superintendency, June 6, 1874, Office of Indian Affairs, Kiowa Agency, 1874, Record Group 75, M234, roll 379.

26. Colonel J. Davidson to P. B. Hunt, May 11, 1878, Office of Indian Affairs, Kiowa Agency, 1878, Record Group 75, M234, roll 384.

27. Captain Nicholas Nolan to Post Adjutant, Fort Sill, Indian Territory, January 8, 1879, Office of Indian Affairs, Kiowa Agency, 1879, Record Group 75, M234, roll 385.

28. General John Pope, Commander, Department of the Missouri, to Colonel W. D. Whipple, Assistant Adjutant General, March 14, 1879, Office of Indian Affairs, Kiowa Agency, 1879, Record Group 75, M234, roll 385.

29. Captain John A. Wilcox to Assistant Adjutant General, Department of the Missouri, January 17, 1879, Office of Indian Affairs, Kiowa Agency, 1879, Record Group 75, M234, roll 385.

30. US Congress, House, "Kiowa, Comanche, and Wichita Agency, August 30, 1879," in *Report of the Secretary of the Interior*, November 1, 1879, H. Ex. Doc. 1, 46th Cong., 2nd sess., 1879, 171.

31. Ibid.

32. White Hair, Little Beaver, et al., June 10, 1868, US Department of the Interior, Bureau of Indian Affairs, Letters Received by the Office of Indian Affairs, 1824 to 1881, Neosho Agency, 1868–69, Record Group 75, M234, roll 535.

33. Isaac Gibson, Osage Agent to Enoch Hoag, Superintendent of Indian Affairs, October 4, 1874, Office of Indian Affairs, Neosho Agency, 1872–75, Record Group 75, M234, roll 537.

34. McCoy, *Historic Sketches of the Cattle Trade*, 73–74.

35. "Cattle," *Junction City* (KS) *Union*, May 27, 1865.

36. "Proposals for Beef," *Junction City* (KS) *Union*, June 10, 1865.

37. Samuel Dunn Houston, "A Trying Trip Alone through the Wilderness," in *Trail Drivers of Texas*, 78–79.

38. Ibid., 69.

39. William Nicholson to John Q. Smith, April 23, 1877, US Department of the Interior, Bureau of Indian Affairs, Letters Received by the Office of Indian Affairs, 1824 to 1881, Kiowa Agency, 1877, Record Group 75, M234, roll 382. For a further discussion of cattle buying for Indian reservations see Jeffrey D. Means, "'Indians Shall Do Things in Common': Oglala

Lakota Identity and Cattle-Raising on the Pine Ridge Reservation," *Montana: The Magazine of Western History* 61 (Autumn 2011): 3–21; and Catharine Franklin, "'If the Government Will Only . . . Fulfill Its Obligations': Colonel Benjamin Grierson, Rations Policy, and the Kiowa Indians, 1868–1872," *Southwestern Historical Quarterly* 118 (October 2014): 179–99.

40. Hawes and Evans to Commissioner of Indian Affairs, November 28, 1866, US Department of the Interior, Bureau of Indian Affairs, Letters Received by the Office of Indian Affairs, 1824 to 1881, Neosho Agency, 1866–67, Record Group 75, M234, roll 534.

41. Philip McCusker to Colonel J. H. Leavenworth, April 6, 1868, Office of Indian Affairs, Kiowa Agency, 1864–68, Record Group 75, M234, roll 375.

42. Captain Tullius C. Tuffer, Report, August 7, 1870, Office of Indian Affairs, Kiowa Agency, 1869–70, Record Group 75, M234, roll 376.

43. General Benjamin H. Grierson to Assistant Adjutant General, Department of the Missouri, January 28, 1870, Office of Indian Affairs, Kiowa Agency, 1870, Record Group 75, M234, roll 377.

44. Ibid.

45. Ibid.

46. Mrs. A. Burks, "A Woman Trail Driver," in *Trail Drivers of Texas*, 296–300.

47. J. D. Jackson, "A Tenderfoot From Kentucky," in *Trail Drivers of Texas*, 536–37.

48. J. E. Pettus, "Had Less Trouble with Indians than with the Grangers on the Trail," in *Trail Drivers of Texas*, 526.

49. "A True Story of Trail Days," in *Trail Drivers of Texas*, 537–38.

50. L. D. Taylor, "Some Thrilling Experiences of an Old Trailer," in *Trail Drivers of Texas*, 498–99.

51. Ibid.

52. Ibid., 501.

53. Pleasant Burnell Butler, "Sixty-Eight Years in Texas," in *Trail Drivers of Texas*, 481–82.

54. James Craig to J. D. Cox, Secretary of Interior, May 14, 1870, US Department of the Interior, Bureau of Indian Affairs, Letters Received by the Office of Indian Affairs, 1824 to 1881, Neosho Agency, 1870–71, Record Group 75, M234, roll 536.

55. B. S. Henning, Superintendent to President James Craig, May 9, 1870, Office of Indian Affairs, Neosho Agency, 1870–71, Record Group 75, M234, roll 536; T. J. Dillard, "The Texas Cattle Trade," *Daily* (Lawrence) *Kansas Tribune*, August 28, 1869; and US Congress, Senate, "Report: The Committee on Indian Affairs, to Whom Was Referred Sundry Petitions of Certain Citizens of the State of Kansas Remonstrating against the Imposition, by the Cherokee Nation, of a Tax upon Cattle Driven through Their Territory from Texas to Northern Markets," Report no. 225, 41st Cong., 2nd sess., June 22, 1870, 1–3.

56. Withers, "Killing and Capturing Buffalo," in *Trail Drivers of Texas*, 97.

57. Polk, "My Experience," in *Trail Drivers of Texas*, 143–44.

58. T. T. Hawkins, "When George Saunders Made a Bluff 'Stick,'" in *Trail Drivers of Texas*, 391–92.

59. *Daily Commonwealth* (Topeka), April 29, 1882.

60. US Congress, Senate, *Testimony Taken by the Committee on Indian Affairs of the Senate in Relation to Leases of Lands in the Indian Territory and Other Reservations*, S. Rep. 1278, 49th cong., 1st sess., 1886, 81.

61. US Congress, Senate, *Letter from the Secretary of the Interior, Transmitting, in Compliance with Senate Resolution of December 4, 1883, Copies of Documents and Correspondence Relating to Leases of Lands in the Indian Territory to Citizens of the United States for Cattle-Grazing and Other Purposes*, S. Ex. Doc. 54, 48th cong., 1st sess., 1884, 148–49.

62. US Congress, Senate, *Testimony Taken by the Committee on Indian Affairs of the Senate in Relation to Leases of Lands in the Indian Territory and other Reservations*, S. Rep. 1278, 49th cong., 1st sess., 1886, 79–82.

63. "The Indian Council," *Leavenworth (KS) Times*, May 20, 1883; and US Congress, H. Rep. 1345, *Leasing Indian Lands to Citizens of the United States, Etc.*, 48th Cong., 1st Sess., 1884.

64. US Congress, Senate, *Testimony Taken by the Committee on Indian Affairs of the Senate in Relation to Leases of Lands in the Indian Territory*, 86.

65. Carl Schurz, Secretary of the Interior to S. E. Lawrence, Commissioner of the Central Superintendency, November 14, 1877; Cyrus Beede to Ezra A. Hayt, Commissioner of Indian Affairs, October 31, 1877; and Cyrus Beede to Ezra A. Hayt, December 5, 1877, US Department of the Interior, Bureau of Indian Affairs, Letters Received by the Office of Indian Affairs, 1824 to 1881, Osage Agency, 1877, Record Group 75, M234, roll 637.

66. US Congress, House, "Osage Agency," in *Report of the Secretary of the Interior*, November 1, 1884, H. Ex. Doc. 1, 48th Cong., 2nd sess., 1884, 127; and "Osage Agency," in *Report of the Secretary of the Interior*, November 1, 1885, H. Ex. Doc. 1, 49th Cong., 1st sess., 1885, 610–11.

67. Jesse Leavenworth, Agent of the Kiowa, Comanche & Apache Indians of the Upper Arkansas to D. W. Colley, Commissioner of Indian Affairs, May 1, 1866, US Department of the Interior, Bureau of Indian Affairs, Letters Received by the Office of Indian Affairs, 1824 to 1881, Kiowa Agency, 1864–68, Record Group 75, M234, roll 375.

68. Ibid.

69. Jesse Leavenworth to N. G. Taylor, Commissioner of Indian Affairs, May 22, 1867, Office of Indian Affairs, Kiowa Agency, 1864–68, Record Group 75, M234, roll 375.

70. "Indian Peace Commission," *New York Times*, September 29, 1867, 4.

71. Jesse Leavenworth to Charles E. Mix, Acting Commissioner of Indian Affairs, August 18, 1867, US Department of the Interior, Bureau of Indian Affairs, Letters Received by the Office of Indian Affairs, 1824 to 1881, Kiowa Agency, 1864–68, Record Group 75, M234, roll 375.

72. Jesse Leavenworth to the Commissioner of Indian Affairs, September 2, 1867, and Jesse Leavenworth to N. G. Taylor, Commissioner of Indian Affairs, November 27, 1867, Office of Indian Affairs, Kiowa Agency, 1864–68, Record Group 75, M234, roll 375.

73. J. M. Haworth to E. P. Smith, Commissioner of Indian Affairs, April 8, 1874, Office of Indian Affairs, Kiowa Agency, 1874, Record Group 75, M234, roll 379.

74. Colonel John P. Hatch, "Condition of the 'Indian Pony Fund,' and the Practical Working of the Experiment of Making the Indians at the Reservation a Pastoral People," March 31, 1877, Office of Indian Affairs, Kiowa Agency, 1877, Record Group 75, M234, roll 382.

75. Ibid.

76. *Report of the Secretary of the Interior*, November 1, 1885, H. Ex. Doc. 1, 49th Cong., 1st sess., 1885, 310–11.

77. To the Assistant Adjutant General, Department of the Missouri, August 26, 1882, Letters Received by the Office of the Adjutant General, 1881–1889, M689, roll 88.

78. Major Randall, Commanding Officer, Fort Sill to General John Pope, Commander, Department of the Missouri, March 20, 1882, Letters Received by the Office of the Adjutant General, 1881–1889, M689, roll 88.

79. General John Pope, Commander, District of the Missouri to Colonel R. Williams, Assistant Adjutant General, April 2, 1882; and General P. H. Sheridan to General R. G. Drum, April 6, 1882, Letters Received by the Office of the Adjutant General, 1881–1889, M689, roll 88.

80. Agent Hunt to Colonel G. V. Henry, Commander, Fort Sill, I.T., March 20, 1882, Letters Received by the Office of the Adjutant General, 1881–1889, M689, roll 88.

81. Headquarters Department of the Missouri to Colonel R. Williams, Assistant Adjutant General, April 3, 1883, and Hiram Price, Commissioner of Indian Affairs to Henry Teller, Secretary of the Interior, August 3, 1882, Letters Received by the Office of the Adjutant General, 1881–1889, M689, roll 88.

82. Ibid.

83. Lieutenant Colonel John P. Hatch, 4th Cavalry to Assistant Adjutant General, Department of the Missouri, April 12, 1879, US Department of the Interior, Bureau of Indian Affairs, Letters Received by the Office of Indian Affairs, 1824 to 1881, Kiowa Agency, 1879, Record Group 75, M234, roll 385; and "2015–2020 Dietary Guidelines. Appendix 2. Estimated Calorie Needs per Day, by Age, Sex, and Physical Activity Level," accessed October 24, 2016, https://health.gov/dietaryguidelines/2015/guidelines/appendix-2/.

84. McCoy, *Historic Sketches of the Cattle Trade*, 69.

85. S. A. Galpin to the Commissioner of Indian Affairs, December 8, 1876, US Department of the Interior, Bureau of Indian Affairs, Letters Received by the Office of Indian Affairs, 1824 to 1881, Kiowa Agency, 1876, Record Group 75, M234, roll 381.

86. Lieutenant Colonel John P. Hatch, 4th Cavalry to Assistant Adjutant General, Department of the Missouri, April 12, 1879, Office of Indian Affairs, Kiowa Agency, 1879, Record Group 75, M234, roll 385.

87. White Shield to Senator George Vest, December 23, 1884, Letters Received by the Office of the Adjutant General, 1881–1889, M689, roll 275.

88. Donald Berthrong, "Cattlemen on the Cheyenne–Arapaho Reservation, 1883–1885," *Arizona and the West* 13 (Spring 1971): 16.

89. General J. H. Potter to C. C. Augur, January 26, 1883, Letters Received by the Office of the Adjutant General, 1881–1889, M689, roll 275.

90. *Report of the Secretary of the Interior*, November 1, 1885, H. Ex. Doc. 1, 49th Cong., 1st sess., 1885, 18.

## CHAPTER 9

1. Eliott Lucas to James Mead, July 20, 1874, James R. Mead Papers, MS 91–03, Box 3, FF17, Special Collections, Wichita State University, Kansas.

2. "Texas Cattle," *Leavenworth* (KS) *Times*, August 8, 1869.

3. "Railroads," *Leavenworth* (KS) *Times*, October 18, 1870.

4. Ibid.

5. "The Cattle Trade," *Leavenworth* (KS) *Times*, June 5, 1869; Joshua Specht, "'For the Future in the Distance': Cattle Trailing, Social Conflict, and the Development of Ellsworth, Kansas," *Kansas History: A Journal of the Central Plains* 40 (Summer 2017), 104–19.

6. H. Craig Miner, *Wichita: The Early Years, 1865–80* (Lincoln: University of Nebraska Press, 1982), 31–49.

7. "Sedgewick County," *Leavenworth* (KS) *Times*, October 8, 1869.

8. "Atchison, Topeka & Santa Fe," *Wichita Eagle*, April 19, 1872.

9. "The Texas Cattle Trade: Wichita the Great Shipping Point," *Wichita Eagle*, May 24, 1872.

10. *Wichita Eagle*, June 14, 1872.

11. "Arrival of Texas Cattle in Kansas," *Wichita Eagle*, August 2, 1872.

12. "A Card," *Wichita Eagle*, August 2, 1872.

13. "City of Wichita," *Wichita Eagle*, December 12, 1872.

14. "Cattle Trade—Agreement," *Abilene* (KS) *Chronicle*, May 25, 1871.

15. "The Texas Cattle Question," *Ellsworth* (KS) *Reporter*, March 14, 1872.

16. "Kansas State Board of Agriculture First Biennial Report: Sumner County, 1878," transcribed from *First Biennial Report of the State Board of Agriculture to the Legislature of the State of Kansas, for the Years 1877–8* (Chicago: Rand McNally, 1878), at KSGenWeb, accessed October 1, 2017, http://www.ksgenweb.org/archives/1878/sumner.html.

17. *Sumner County* (KS) *Press*, June 18, 1874.

18. *Wichita Eagle*, August 9, 1872.

19. *Wichita Eagle*, September 6, 1872.

20. *Wichita Eagle*, April 17, 1873.

21. *Wichita Eagle*, May 21, 1874.

22. "Wichita Cattle Trade for 1874," *Wichita Eagle*, December 3, 1874.

23. "Resolutions Passed at Ninnescah Grange," *Wichita Eagle*, January 7, 1875.

24. Ibid.; C. F. W. Dassler, comp., *The General Statutes of Kansas: Being a Compilation of All the Laws of a General Nature Based upon the General Statutes of 1868 Together with Subsequent Enactments, Including the Session Laws of 1876*, vol. 2 (St. Louis: W. J. Gilbert, 1876), 996–1000.

25. "Railroad Business at Wichita," *Wichita Eagle*, January 10, 1878. In this issue of the newspaper, wheat, depending upon its quality, ranged in price from 65 to 85 cents per bushel depending upon quality, and beef prices for one-thousand-pound steers stood at $3.25 per one hundred pounds gross, or $32.50 per head. I calculated wheat values at 70 cents per bushel. I did not factor "rejected" wheat, which sold for 50 to 60 cents per bushel.

26. "Warning to Texas Cattle Drovers," *Wichita Eagle*, August 9, 1872.

27. "The Texas Cattle Drive," *Sumner County* (KS) *Press*, March 23, 1876.

28. *First Biennial Report of the State Board of Agriculture to the Legislature of the State of Kansas for the Years 1877-8*, 2nd ed. (Topeka: Kansas State Board of Agriculture, 1878), 214–15.

29. "The Cattle Trade: Its Rise and Progress on the Great Southwestern Range," *San Marcos* (TX) *Free Press*, August 10, 1882.

30. The "natural ice" trade was a massive industry prior to artificial ice making. The trade began in Boston in the early 1800s, and began shipping to southern ports such as Charleston, Savannah, and New Orleans. In the winter, ice was sawed out of rivers and lakes, stored, and then shipped. The Civil War resulted in the halt of this trade to southern cities, but it resumed after the war. By the late 1880s, the Wisconsin natural ice industry gained prominence as it supplied the beer brewing industry in Milwaukee and the refrigerated beef industry centered in Chicago. A good look at the trade is Lee E. Lawrence, "The Wisconsin Ice Trade," *Wisconsin Magazine of History* 48 (Summer 1965): 257–67.

31. Willis R. Woolrich and Charles T. Clark, "Refrigeration," *Handbook of Texas Online*, accessed November 11, 2016, http://www.tshaonline.org/handbook/online/articles/dqr01.

32. *Galveston Daily News*, May 8, 1866; and American Society of Heating, Refrigerating and Air-Conditioning Engineers, "Andrew Muhl Nominated 2014 ASHRAE Pioneer of Refrigeration Equipment 1831 to 1892," accessed November 11, 2016, http://ashraehouston.org/downloads/Historian/pioneers_of_ashrae_refrigeration_equipment_1865_through_1892_10_26_13.pdf.

33. *Galveston Daily News*, August 18, 1865.

34. "From Eastern Texas," *New Orleans Times-Picayune*, December 14, 1866.

35. "Affairs in Texas: Registration—Ice Machines and Beef-Packing—The Military," *New York Times*, July 25, 1867.

36. "A Grand Enterprise: The Markets of the World Thrown Open to the Stock Raisers of Texas," *New Orleans Times-Picayune*, July 13, 1869.

37. Ibid.; and "Refrigerating Beef," *Galveston Daily News*, June 29, 1869.

38. "Meat for the Millions," in *The Texas Almanac for 1871, and Emigrant's Guide to Texas*, 174, accessed March 1, 2017, http://texashistory.unt.edu/ark:/67531/metapth123776/m1/176/.

39. Ibid.

40. "A Grand Enterprise," *New Orleans Times-Picayune*, July 13, 1869.

41. "Manufacturing Ice," *New York Times*, March 19, 1869.

42. "Beef Transportation—Bray's Refrigerators," *Galveston Daily News*, May 17, 1870. For further insights on the rather fantastic career of Lowe, see Stephen Poleskie, *The Balloonist: The Story of T. S. C. Lowe—Inventor, Scientist, Magician, and Father of the U.S. Air Force* (Savannah, GA: Frederic C. Beil, 2007).

43. "Prof. Lowe's Refrigerating Invention," *Galveston Daily News*, August 11, 1869.

44. "The Cattle Trade," *New York Tribune*, June 25, 1868.

45. "The Refrigerated Texas Beef," *Galveston Daily News*, June 23, 1870.

46. "The Refrigerator Car Company," *Galveston Daily News*, December 23, 1873; *Denison (TX) Daily News*, February 21, 1874.

47. "From New York," *Galveston Daily News*, December 11, 1873; "Refrigerator Cars," December 14, 1873; and "Refrigerated Beef," December 20, 1873.

48. *Galveston Daily News*, November 25, 1873.

49. "The Refrigerator Car Company," *Galveston Daily News*, December 23, 1873.

50. Ibid.

51. "Cheaper Beef for the East," *New York Times*, December 8, 1873.

52. Ibid.

53. "Fresh Texas Beef in New York," *Galveston Daily News*, March 1, 1874.

54. *Austin Weekly Statesman*, November 2, 1882.

55. *New York Times*, February 2, 1869.

56. Morris, "Statement in Regard to the Early Shipments of Cattle and Dressed Beef to Europe," in Nimmo, *Report*, 198; "Chicago Grain and Cattle Markets," 702; "Chicago Market," *Buffalo* (NY) *Commercial*, September 24, 1868; and "The Cattle Trade," *The Times* (London, England), September 25, 1868. Transatlantic shipping firms charged around $13 per head to transport cattle from a US port to England.

57. "Texas Beef—Its Transportation," *Galveston Daily News*, November 19, 1869; and *New Orleans Picayune*, November 10, 1869.

58. "American Beef for Old England," 277–79.

59. Nimmo, *Report*, 68–71, 190–94.

60. "Spring Cattle Driving: Extent of the Western Trade," *New York Times*, April 14, 1876, 2.

61. Nimmo, *Report*, 28.

62. *Proceedings of the First National Convention of Cattle Growers of the United States, Held in St. Louis, Mo., November 17th to 22d, 1884* (St. Louis: R. P. Studley, 1884), 1.

63. Ibid., 15.

64. Ibid., 41, 44.

65. Ibid., 50.

66. Ibid., 51.

67. "An Act for the Protection of Cattle against Contagious Diseases," in *Compiled Laws of Kansas, 1885* (Topeka: Geo. W. Crane, 1885), 930–34.

68. *Dodge City Times*, March 12, 1885; and "Like Wichita," *Dodge City Times*, October 15, 1885.

69. *Proceedings of the First National Convention of Cattle Growers*, 82–83.

70. Paradoxically, Dodge City would regain both its "wild west, cattle-town" persona and the Texas cattle trade. After World War II, with the popularity of such television shows as *Gunsmoke*, the city created and marketed a tourist destination based on a re-creation of Front Street with its saloons and retail shops. The highlight, of course, was the re-creation of "Boot Hill Cemetery."

As the great slaughterhouses and stockyards of Kansas City and Chicago became less desirable in a modern urban setting, the industry started moving its operations to giant feedlot facilities and meat-packing factories in the Great Plains. Today, Dodge City supports two of these meat-processing megaplants, National Beef and Farmland Industries, and Cargill Meat Solutions, Excel. Together, these two plants employ over five thousand workers and process eleven thousand beeves daily.

71. *Wichita Daily Eagle*, October 23, 1915.

## CONCLUSION

1. "Joseph G. McCoy," *Wichita Daily Eagle*, October 20, 1915.

2. Ibid.

3. Ibid.

4. The Ecological Society of America defines an ecotone as "the edges and physical boundaries" where one ecosystem meets another. "The term refers to the transition from one ecosystem to another." See "Ecotone Explained," Ecological Society of America, accessed March 19, 2017, http://www.esa.org/esablog/about/ecotone-explained.

5. *Wichita Eagle*, April 26, 1872.

6. James Mead to his sister, February 7, 1875, James R. Mead Paper, MS 91–03, Box 7, FF25, Special Collections, Wichita State University, Kansas.

7. Ibid.

8. Colonel John P. Hatch, "Condition of the 'Indian Pony Fund,' and the Practical Working of the Experiment of Making the Indians at the Reservation a Pastoral People," March 31, 1877, US Department of the Interior, Bureau of Indian Affairs, Letters Received by the Office of Indian Affairs, 1824 to 1881, Kiowa Agency, 1877, Record Group 75, M234, roll 382.

9. Kurt Jax, "Thresholds, Tipping Points and Limits," updated 2016, www.openness-project.eu/library/reference-book/sp-thresholds.

10. D. D. Briske, S. D. Fuhlendorf, and F. E. Smeins, "State-and-Transition Models, Thresholds, and Rangeland Health: A Synthesis of Ecological Concepts and Perspectives," *Rangeland Ecology & Management* 58 (January 2005): 5. Also see Zak Ratajczak, Jesse B. Nippert, and Troy W. Ocheltree, "Abrupt Transition of Mesic Grassland to Shrubland: Evidence for Thresholds, Alternative Attractors, and Regime Shifts," *Ecology* 95 (September 2014): 2633–45.

11. Zak Ratajczak, John M. Briggs, Doug G. Goodin, et al., "Assessing the Potential for Transitions from Tallgrass Prairie to Woodlands: Are We Operating Beyond Critical Fire Thresholds?" *Rangeland Ecology & Management* 69 (July 2016): 280–87.

12. Colonel John Hatch to Assistant Adjutant General, Department of the Missouri, March 31, 1877, US Department of the Interior, Bureau of Indian Affairs, Letters Received by the Office of Indian Affairs, 1824 to 1881, Kiowa Agency, 1864–80 M234, roll 382.

13. O'Neill, "Is It Time to Bury the Ecosystem Concept?," 3280–82. O'Neill's thinking is akin to the concept of the Anthropocene. An excellent look at the some of the most recent views of the Anthropocene is W. John Kress and Jeffrey K. Stine's edited volume, *Living in the Anthropocene: Earth in the Age of Humans* (Washington, DC: Smithsonian Institution, 2017).

14. Ibid., 3280.

15. Ibid.

16. Jim Hoy, "Joseph McCoy and the Creation of the Mythic American West," in *John Brown to Bob Dole: Movers and Shakers in Kansas History*, ed. Virgil Dean (Lawrence: University Press of Kansas, 2006), 80.

17. McCoy, *Historic Sketches of the Cattle Trade*, 54.

18. "William K. McCoy (1829–1898) Find A Grave Memorial," accessed April 15, 2016, http://www.findagrave.com/cgi-bin/fg.cgi?page=gr&GRid=74790741; "Local Boy Loses Legs in Accident," *East Oregonian* (Pendleton), June 22, 1910; "Death Claims Aged Woman," *East Oregonian* (Pendleton), March 8, 1912.

19. *Daily Commonwealth* (Topeka), January 11, 1881; *Topeka Daily Capital*, October 15, 1882; "Death of James P. McCoy," *Daily Commonwealth* (Topeka), June 22, 1886; and "Funeral Notice," *Topeka Daily Capital*, April 18, 1911.

20. *Wichita Eagle*, December 19, 1884.

21. J. E. Pettus, "Had Less Trouble with Indians than with the Grangers on the Trail," in *Trail Drivers of Texas*, 526.

# Selected Sources

The story of Texas cattle trail driving is rooted in the mythic West. It's a powerful story of rugged individualism, as portrayed in classic Hollywood movies such as *Red River* (1948), which starred the film screen legends John Wayne, Montgomery Clift, and Joanne Dru, or in books and television miniseries such as Larry McMurtry's *Lonesome Dove* (1985). But no historian has produced a book-length study of this industry for several decades.

Scholars of the American West are quite familiar with two of the core texts on the Texas cattle trade: Joseph McCoy's *Historic Sketches of the Cattle Trade of the West and Southwest* (1874) and J. Marvin Hunter's compiled and edited volume, *The Trail Drivers of Texas* (1924). Both of these have been reprinted many times, and are readily available today.

Many old classics on the Chisholm Trail are still in print today. The primary histories are Sam Ridings, *The Chisholm Trail: A History of the World's Greatest Cattle Trail* (1936, reissued in 2015 by First Creative Texts); Wayne Gard, *The Chisholm Trail* (University of Oklahoma Press, 1954); Frank Dobie, *Up the Trail from Texas* (Random House, 1955); Henry Jameson, *Miracle of the Chisholm Trail* (Tri-State Chisholm Trail Centennial Commission, 1967); and Donald E. Worcester, *The Chisholm Trail: High Road of the Cattle Kingdom* (University of Nebraska Press, 1980).

A few books have been written about the cattle trade in general. Notable are Edward E. Dale, *The Range Cattle Industry* (University of Oklahoma Press, 1980); Jimmy Skaggs, *The Cattle-Trailing Industry* (1973, reissued in 1991 by University of Oklahoma Press); Betty Fussell, *Raising Steaks: The Life and Times of American Beef* (New York: Houghton Mifflin Harcourt, 2008); and Maureen Ogle, *In Meat We Trust: An Unexpected History of Carnivore America* (New York: Houghton Mifflin Harcourt, 2013). Robert Dykstra, *The Cattle Towns* (Alfred A. Knopf, 1968), and H. Craig Miner, *Wichita: The Early Years, 1865–80* (Lincoln: University of Nebraska Press, 1982) remain the best works on the nature of these cattle outlets.

Some books cover more specific topics related to the cattle trade such as race, culture, and gender. These works include Philip Durham and Everett L. Jones, *The Negro Cowboys* (University of Nebraska Press, 1965); Lewis Atherton, *The Cattle Kings* (University of Nebraska Press, 1961); David Dary, *Cowboy Culture* (Avon Books, 1982); Sara R. Massey's edited collection *Texas Women on the Cattle Trails* (Texas A&M University Press, 2006); and Jacqueline M.

Moore, *Cow Boys and Cattle Men: Class and Masculinities on the Texas Frontier, 1865–1900* (New York: New York University Press, 2010).

A few younger scholars have explored aspects of the trade, and their work has yet to reach book stage. Kristin Hoganson's "Meat in the Middle: Converging Borderlands in the U.S. Midwest, 1865–1900," *Journal of American History* (March 2012), explores the cultural intersection of the trade in Illinois. Joshua Specht's "The Rise, Fall, and Rebirth of the Texas Longhorn: An Evolutionary History," *Environmental History* (April 2016), stresses how the longhorns were "both technology and laborer . . . ideally suited to nineteenth-century ranching, largely because the animals themselves performed much of the labor involved in beef production." Specht's work is the most cutting edge to date.

My work sees the unfolding of the cattle trade differently than William Cronon's *Nature's Metropolis* (W. W. Norton, 1991). Rather than the Chisholm Trail as a form of "second nature," I argue that the trail was a transitional ecosystem bridging the wild grasslands managed and shaped by Indians, and the Euro-American farming landscape dominated by domesticated grasses such as wheat, oats, and sorghum. This work also responds to Donald Worster's contention that ranching has "had a degrading effect on the environment of the American West." Worster tends to see ecosystems as self-regulating entities that more often than not are fouled by human activities. For me, it's more telling to see humans as a keystone species whose cultures intertwined with other forces as they shaped historically dynamic ecosystems. In this light, Joseph McCoy's efforts joined with other natural forces in creating a historical grassland.

Two works are most important in influencing my take on humans as a keystone species. Ecologist Robert V. O'Neill's "Is It Time to Bury the Ecosystem Concept? (With Full Military Honors, of Course!)," *Ecology* 82 (December 2001): 3280–82, has largely formed my view of humans as a keystone species. Also, Daniel Botkin's *Discordant Harmonies: An Ecology for the Twenty-First Century* (New York: Oxford University Press, 1990) informed my early views of the integral role humans played as a contributing species shaping ecosystems.

The following works are excellent introductions to grassland ecology: Alan K. Knapp, John M. Briggs, David C. Hartnett, and Scott L. Collins's edited volume, *Grassland Dynamics: Long-Term Ecological Research in Tallgrass Prairie* (New York: Oxford University Press, 1998); Fred B. Samson and Fritz L. Knopf's edited volume, *Prairie Conservation: Preserving North America's Most Endangered Ecosystem* (Washington, DC: Island Press, 1996); and James R. Estes, Ronald J. Tyrl, and Jere N. Brunken's edited volume, *Grasses and Grasslands: Systematics and Ecology* (Norman: University of Oklahoma Press, 1982).

An important component of grassland systems is the effects of fire. Four works are an excellent start on understanding the dynamic, historic role people have played in shaping their respective ecosystems with fire: Stephen J. Pyne, *Fire in America: A Cultural History of Wildland and Rural Fire* (Princeton, NJ: Princeton University Press, 1982); Scott L. Collins and Linda L. Wallace's edited volume, *Fire in North American Tallgrass Prairies* (Norman: University of Oklahoma Press, 1990); Omer C. Stewart, *Forgotten Fires: Native Americans and the Transient Wilderness*, edited by Henry T. Lewis and M. Kat Anderson (Norman: University of Oklahoma Press, 2002); and Julie Courtwright, *Prairie Fire: A Great Plains History* (Lawrence: University Press of Kansas, 2011).

SELECTED SOURCES

## NEWSPAPERS

*Abilene* (Kansas) *Chronicle*, 1871–1875
*Arkansas City* (Kansas) *Weekly*, 1881–1885
*Atchison* (Kansas) *Daily Patriot*, 1870
*Austin Weekly Statesman*, 1871–1885
*Belvidere* (Illinois) *Standard*, 1870
*Buffalo* (New York) *Commercial*, 1868
*Cherokee Advocate* (Tahlequah, Cherokee Nation), 1880–1885
*Chicago Tribune*, 1865–1885
*Daily Commonwealth* (Topeka), 1881–1886
*Daily* (Lawrence) *Kansas Tribune*, 1867–1885
*Dallas Daily Herald*, 1880–1885
*Decatur* (Illinois) *Weekly Republican*, 1873
*Denison* (Texas) *Daily News*, 1874
*Dodge City Times*, 1880–1885
*East Oregonian* (Pendleton), 1910–1912
*Ellsworth* (Kansas) *Reporter*, 1870–1875
*Emporia* (Kansas) *Weekly News*, 1860–1870.
*Galveston Daily News*, 1865–1885
*Howard Union* (Glasgow, Missouri), 1865
*Junction City* (Kansas) *Union*, 1866–1885
*Kansas City Times*, 1924
*Kansas State Record* (Topeka), 1865–1885
*Lawrence* (KS) *Daily Journal*, 1869–1872
*Leavenworth* (Kansas) *Times*, 1867–1870
*Lincoln County Herald* (Troy, Missouri), 1866
*Macon* (Missouri) *Argus*, 1868
*New York Times*, 1865–1885
*New York Tribune*, 1865–1885
*New Orleans Picayune*, 1865–1885
*Olathe* (Kansas) *Mirror*, 1865–1870
*Saline County Journal* (Salina, Kansas), 1867–1885
*San Marcos* (Texas) *Free Press*, 1882
*Sumner County* (Kansas) *Press*, 1874–1876
*The Times* (London, England), 1868
*Topeka Daily Capital*, 1882–1911
*Walnut Valley Times* (El Dorado, Kansas), 1880–1885
*Sumner County Press* (Wellington, Kansas), 1874–1885
*Wichita Beacon*, 1903
*Wichita Daily Eagle*, 1872–1885
*Wyandotte* (Kansas) *Commercial Gazette*, 1866–1870

## PRIMARY SOURCES

"An Act for the Protection of Cattle against Contagious Diseases." In *Compiled Laws of Kansas, 1885*. Topeka: Geo. W. Crane, 1885.

Bell, William A. *New Tracks in North America: A Journal of Travel and Adventure Whilst Engaged in the Survey for a Southern Railroad to the Pacific Ocean During 1867–8*. London: Chapman and Hall, 1870. Reprint, Albuquerque: Horn and Wallace, 1965.

Copley, Josiah. *Kansas and the Country Beyond on the Line of the Union Pacific Railway, Eastern Division, From the Missouri to the Pacific Ocean*. Philadelphia: J. B. Lippincott, 1867.

Crawford, Governor Samuel. Letters Received. Archives Division. Kansas State Historical Society.

De Voe, Thomas F. *The Market Assistant: Containing a Brief Description of Every Article of Human Food Sold in the Public Markets of the Cities of New York, Boston, Philadelphia, and Brooklyn; Including the Various Domestic and Wild Animals, Poultry, Game, Fish, Vegetables, Fruits*. New York: Hurd and Houghton, 1867.

———. *The Market Book: Containing a Historical Account of the Public Markets in the Cities of New York, Boston, Philadelphia, and Brooklyn with a Brief Description of Every Article of Human Food Sold Therein*. Vol. 1. New York: printed for the author, 1862.

Hunter, J. Marvin, ed. *The Trail Drivers of Texas: Interesting Sketches of Early Cowboys and Their Experiences on the Range and on the Trail during the Days That Tried Men's Souls—True Narratives Related by Real Cowpunchers and Men Who Fathered the Cattle Industry in Texas*. Austin: University of Texas Press, 1924, 2006.

Kansas Pacific Railway Company, *Guide Map of the Great Texas Cattle Trail from the Red River Crossing to the Old Reliable Kansas Pacific Railway*. Kansas Pacific Railway, 1874.

*The Kansas Pacific Railway Company v. Joseph G. McCoy*, transcript. Manuscript Division. Kansas State Historical Society, Topeka.

Leland, Charles Godfrey. *The Union Pacific Railway, Eastern Division, or, Three Thousand Miles in a Railway Car*. Philadelphia: Ringwalt & Brown, 1867.

McCoy, Joseph G. *Historic Sketches of the Cattle Trade of the West and Southwest*. Kansas City, MO: Ramsey, Millett & Hudson, 1874. Reprint, Columbus, OH: Long's College Book, 1951.

McCoy, Joseph Geating. Diary, 1880–81, MS 406, Kansas Historical Society, Topeka.

McCoy, Joseph vs. the Kansas Pacific. J. G. McCoy Collection, Archive Division, Kansas Historical Society, Topeka.

Mead, James R. Papers. MS 91–03. Special Collections. Wichita State University, Kansas.

Monthly England and Wales Precipitation, 1766–2014, accessed February 5, 2015, https://www.metoffice.gov.uk/hadobs/hadukp/data/monthly/HadEWP_monthly_qc.txt.

Nimmo, Joseph, Jr. *Report in Regard to the Range and Ranch Cattle Business of the United States*. Washington, DC: Government Printing Office, 1885.

Patrick, M. R., Lewis F. Allen, and Jonathan Stanton Gould. *Report of the New York State Cattle Commissioners in Connection with the Report of the Metropolitan Board of Health, in Relation to the Texas Cattle Disease*. State of New York, no. 9. In Senate. March 12, 1869.

*Proceedings and Debates of the American Convention of Cattle Commissioners, Held at Springfield, Ill., December 1st, 2nd, and 3d, 1868*. Ely, Burnham, and Bartlett, Official Reporters. Springfield: Illinois Journal Printing Office, 1869.

*Proceedings of the First National Convention of Cattle Growers of the United States, Held in St. Louis, Mo., November 17th to 22d, 1884.* St. Louis: R. P. Studley, 1884.

*Proceedings of the Second Annual Convention of the National Live Stock Association, Denver, Colorado, January 24, 25, 26 and 27.* Denver: News Job Printing, 1899.

Oakes, T. F. *Guide Map of the Great Texas Cattle Trail from the Red River Crossing to the Old Reliable Kansas Pacific Railway.* Kansas Pacific Railway, 1874.

*Report of Lieut. Col. James H. Simpson, Corps of Engineers, U.S.A., on the Union Pacific Railroad and Branches, Central Pacific Railroad of California, Northern Pacific Railroad, Wagon Roads in the Territories of Idaho, Montana, Dakota, and Nebraska, and the Washington Aqueduct. Made to Honorable James Harlan, Secretary of the Interior, November 23, 1865.* Washington, DC: Government Printing Office, 1865.

Reports of the Secretary of the Interior. 1875–1885.

*Reports on the Diseases of Cattle in the United States, Made to the Commissioner of Agriculture, with Accompanying Documents.* Washington, DC: Government Printing Office, 1869.

*Senatorial Excursion Party over the Union Pacific Railway, E. D.: Speeches of Senators Yates, Cattell, Chandler, Howe and Trumbull; Hon. J. A. J. Creswell, Hon. John Covode, M.C., and Hon. Wm. M. McPherson.* St. Louis: S. Levison, 1867.

Snow, Edwin M. *Report upon the Convention of Cattle Commissioners, Held at Springfield, Illinois, December 1, 1868, and upon the Texas Cattle Disease.* Providence, RI: Providence Press, Printers to the State, 1869.

Territorial Survey Map, Township 13 South, Range 2 East, July 1857. Kansas Historical Society, Topeka.

Territorial Survey Map, Township 32 South, Range 2 West, February and March 1871. Kansas Historical Society, Topeka.

United States Army. "Meteorological Register, Fort Arbuckle, Indian Territory," 1867–70; "Meteorological Register, Fort Duncan, Texas," 1873–79; "Meteorological Register, Fort Hays, Kansas," 1867–79; "Meteorological Register, Fort Richardson, Texas," 1868–78; "Meteorological Register, Fort Riley, Kansas," 1867–83; and "Meteorological Register, Fort Sill, Indian Territory," 1870–85. www.ncdc.noaa.gov/EdadsV2/library/FORTS.

US Congress. House. *Leasing Indian Lands to Citizens of the United States, Etc.*, H. Rep. 1345, 48th Cong., 1st Sess., 1884.

US Congress. Senate. *Letter from the Secretary of Interior, Transmitting, in Compliance with Senate resolution of December 4, 1883, Copies of Documents and Correspondence Relating to Leases of Lands in the Indian Territory to Citizens of the United States for Cattle Grazing and Other Purposes.* S. Ex. Doc. 54, 48th Cong, 1st sess., 1884.

———. "Report: The Committee on Indian Affairs." Report no. 225, 41st Cong., 2nd sess., June 22, 1870.

———. *Testimony Taken by the Committee on Indian Affairs of the Senate in Relation to Leases of Lands in the Indian Territory and other Reservations.* S. Rep. 1278, 49th cong., 1st sess., 1886.

US Department of the Interior. Bureau of Indian Affairs. Letters Received by the Office of Indian Affairs, 1824 to 1881. Cherokee Agency. Record Group 75, M234, rolls 100–103.

———. Kiowa Agency. Record Group 75, M234, rolls 375–385.

———. Neosho Agency, Record Group 75, M234, rolls 534–537.

———. Osage Agency, Record Group 75, M234, rolls 633–636.

———. "Special Files of the Office of Indian Affairs, 1807–1904," Files 134–138. Record Group 75, M574, roll 27.
US Department of the Interior. Reports of Commissioner of Indian Affairs, 1857–1885.
US Department of War. Letters Received by the Office of the Adjutant General, 1881–1889, M689, roll 88, and roll 275.
*The War of the Rebellion: A Compilation of the Official Records of the Union and Confederate Armies*. Series 1, volume 1. Washington, DC: Government Printing Office, 1880.

## SECONDARY SOURCES

Ajmone-Marsan, Paolo, José Fernando Garcia, Johannes A. Lenstra, and the Blobaldiv Consortium. "On the Origin of Cattle: How Aurochs Became Cattle and Colonized the World." *Evolutionary Anthropology* 19 (July/August 2010): 148-157.
Allred, B. W. "Bluestem on the Longhorn Trails." *Journal of Soil and Water Conservation* 5 (October 1950).
———. "Historical Highlights of Grazing in the Central and Southern Great Plains." *Journal of Range Management* 13 (May 1960): 135–138.
Adams, Ramon F. *Cowboy Lingo: A Dictionary of the Slack-Jaw Words and Whangdoodle Ways of the American West*. New York: Houghton Mifflin, 1936, 2000.
"American Beef for Old England." *Harper's Weekly* 21 (April 7, 1877): 277–79.
American Society of Heating, Refrigerating and Air-Conditioning Engineers. "Andrew Muhl Nominated 2014 ASHRAE Pioneer of Refrigeration Equipment 1831 to 1892." http://ashraehouston.org/downloads/Historian/pioneers_of_ashrae_refrigeration_equipment_1865_through_1892_1-_24_13.pdf. (accessed November 11, 2016).
Anderson, George L. "From Cattle to Wheat: The Impact of Agricultural Developments of Banking in Early Wichita." *Agricultural History* 33 (January 1959): 3–15.
Andreas, A. T. *History of the State of Kansas*. Chicago: A. T. Andreas, 1883.
Arcari, M., A. Baxendine, and C. E. Bennett. "Babesia, Trypanosomes & Leishmania." Diagnosing Medical Parasites through Coprological Techniques 11, copyright 2000, http://www.soton.ac.uk/~ceb/Diagnosis/Vol11.htm.
Bailey, Jack. *A Texas Cowboy's Journal: Up the Trail to Kansas in 1868*. Edited by David Dary. Norman: University of Oklahoma Press, 2006.
Barrell, Joseph. *The Red Hills of Kansas: Crossroads of Plant Migrations*. Rockford, IL: Natural Land Institute, 1975.
Beehrer, George, and Julie Beehrer Colyer. "Freighting across the Plains." *Montana: The Magazine of Western History* 12 (Autumn 1962): 2–17.
Bentivenga, S. P., and B. A. D. Hetrick, "Relationship Between Mycorrhizal Activity, Buring, and Plant Productivity in Tallgrass Prairie," *Canadian Journal of Botany* 69 (1991): 2597–2602.
Berthrong, Donald J. "Cattlemen on the Cheyenne–Arapaho Reservation, 1883–1885." *Arizona and the West* 13 (Spring 1971): 16.
———. *The Cheyenne and Arapaho Ordeal: Reservation and Agency Life in the Indian Territory, 1875–1907*. Norman: University of Oklahoma Press, 1976.
Briske, D. D., S. D. Fuhlendorf, and F. E. Smeins. "State-and-Transition Models, Thresholds, and Rangeland Health: A Synthesis of Ecological Concepts and Perspectives." *Rangeland Ecology & Management* 58 (January 2005): 1–10.

Burrill, Robert M. "The Establishment of Ranching on the Osage Indian Reservation." *Geographical Review* 62 (October 1972): 524–43.

Caetano-Anollés, Gustavo. "Grass Evolution Inferred from Chromosomal Rearrangements and Geometrical and Statistical Features in RNA Structure." *Journal of Molecular Evolution* 60 (2005): 635–52.

"The Cattle Plague." *Harper's Weekly*, February 17, 1866.

"The Cattle Plague." *Harper's Weekly*, August 29, 1868.

"Cattle Trade for Europe." *Harper's Weekly* 23 (September 27, 1879).

"Chicago Grain and Cattle Markets." *Harper's Weekly* 12 (October 31, 1868): 702.

Choate, Judith. *Dining at Delmonico's: The Story of America's Oldest Restaurant.* New York: Stewart, Tabori & Chang, 2008.

Clemen, Rudolf. "Cattle Trails as a Factor in the Development of Livestock Marketing." *Journal of Farm Economics* 8 (October 1926): 427–42.

———. "Waterways in Livestock and Meat Trade." *American Economic Review* 16 (December 1926): 640–52.

Cobb, Josephine. "Alexander Gardner." *Image* 7 (June 1958): 124–36.

Collins, Scott L., and Linda L. Wallace, eds. *Fire in North American Tallgrass Prairies.* Norman: University of Oklahoma Press, 1990.

Cook, C. Wayne, and Edward F. Redente. "Development of the Ranching Industry in Colorado." *Rangelands* 15 (October 1993): 204–7.

Courtwright, Julie. *Prairie Fire: A Great Plains History.* Lawrence: University Press of Kansas, 2011.

Dassler, C. F. W., comp. *The General Statutes of Kansas: Being a Compilation of All the Laws of a General Nature Based upon the General Statutes of 1868 Together with Subsequent Enactments, Including the Session Laws of 1876.* Vol. 2. St. Louis: W. J. Gilbert, 1876.

Dobie, J. Frank. *The Longhorns.* Edison, NJ: Castle Books, 1941.

Doman, Claude E., and Richard J. Wolfe. *Suppressing the Diseases of Animals and Man: Theobald Smith, Microbiologist.* Boston: Boston Medical Library, Francis A. Countway Library of Medicine. Distributed by Harvard University Press, 2003.

Doran, Michael. "Antebellum Cattle Herding in the Indian Territory." *Geographical Review* 66 (January 1976): 48–58.

Dugas, Vera Lea. "Texas Industry, 1860–1880." *Southwestern Historical Quarterly* 59 (October 1955): 151–83.

Ebert, Roger. "Red River (1948)" in *Great Movies Archive.* http://rogerebert.suntimes.com/apps/pbcs.dll/article?AID=/19980301/REVIEWS08/401010355/1023 (accessed May 14, 2012)

Emsley, Clive, Tim Hitchcock, and Robert Shoemaker. "London History: A Population History of London." Old Bailey Proceedings Online, accessed February 3, 2015, version 7.0, http://www.oldbaileyonline.org/static/Population-history-of-london.jsp.

Erlandson, Erik M. "Cattle Plague in NYC: The Untold Campaign of America's First Board of Health, 1868," https://scholarsbank.uoregon.edu/xmlui/bitstream/handle/1794/12138/Erlandson-final.pdf?sequence<1 (accessed December 27, 2016).

Fehrenbach, T. R. *Lone Star: A History of Texas and the Texans.* New York: American Legacy Press, 1983.

Fiege, Mark. *The Republic of Nature: An Environmental History of the United States*. Seattle: University of Washington Press, 2012.

Foreman, Carolyn Thomas. "Black Beaver." *Chronicles of Oklahoma* 24 (1946): 269–92.

Freedman, Paul, and James Warlick. "High-End Dining in the Nineteenth-Century United States." *Gastronomica* 11 (Spring 2011): 44–52.

Fritz, Henry E. "The Cattlemen's Frontier in the Trans-Mississippi West: An Annotated Bibliography (Part 1)." *Arizona and the West* 14 (Spring 1972): 45–70.

———. "The Cattlemen's Frontier in the Trans-Mississippi West: An Annotated Bibliography (Part 2)." *Arizona and the West* 14 (Summer 1972): 169–90.

Fussell, Betty. *Raising Steaks: The Life and Times of American Beef*. New York: Houghton Mifflin Harcourt, 2008.

Galenson, David. "Cattle Trailing in the Nineteenth Century: A Reply." *Journal of Economic History* 35 (June 1975): 461–66.

———. "The Profitability of the Long Drive." *Agricultural History* 51 (October 1977): 737–58.

Ganskopp, Dave and Dave Bohnert. "Nutritional Dynamics of 7 Northern Great Basin Grasses." *Journal of Range Management* 54 (November 2001): 640–47.

Gard, Wayne. "The Impact of the Cattle Trails." *Southwestern Historical Quarterly* 71 (July 1967): 1–6.

———. "Retracing the Chisholm Trail." *Southwestern Historical Quarterly* 60 (July 1956): 53–68.

———. "The Shawnee Trail." *Southwestern Historical Quarterly* 56 (January 1953): 359–77.

Gelo, Daniel L. and Wayne J. Pate. *Texas Indian Trails*. Dallas: Republic of Texas Press, 2003.

Gibson, Arrell Morgan. "Native Americans and the Civil War." *American Indian Quarterly* 9 (Autumn 1985): 385–410.

Glaab, Charles N. *Kansas City and the Railroads: Community Policy in the Growth of a Regional Metropolis*. Lawrence: University Press of Kansas, 1993.

Graebner, Norman Arthur. "History of Cattle Ranching in Eastern Oklahoma." *Chronicles of Oklahoma* 21, no. 3 (1943): 300–311.

Haley, J. Evetts. *Charles Goodnight: Cowman and Plainsman*. Norman: University of Oklahoma Press, 1936, 1949.

Hartnett, David and Gail W. T. Wilson. "Mycorrhizae Influence Plant Community Structure and Diversity in Tallgrass Prairie." *Ecology* 80, no. 4 (1999): 1187–95.

Havins, T. R. "Texas Fever." *Southwestern Historical Quarterly* 52 (October 1948): 147–62.

Hayden, Bruce P. "Regional Climate and the Distribution of Tallgrass Prairie." In *Grassland Dynamics: Long-Term Ecological Research in Tallgrass Prairie*, edited by Alan K. Knapp, John M. Briggs, David C. Hartnett, and Scott L. Collins. New York: Oxford University Press, 1998.

Haygood, Tamara Miner. "Cows, Ticks, and Disease: A Medical Interpretation of the Southern Cattle Industry." *Journal of Southern History* 52 (November 1986): 551–64.

"The Health of the City." *Harper's Weekly*, January 20, 1866, 35.

Heijedn, Marcel G. A. van der, Richard D. Bardgett, and Nico M. van Straalen, "The Unseen Majority: Soil Microbes as Drivers of Plant Diversity and Productivity in Terrestrial Ecosystems," *Ecology Letters* 11 (2008): 296–310.

Herrington, George Squires. "An Early Cattle Drive from Texas to Illinois." *Southwestern Historical Quarterly* 55 (October 1951): 267–69.

Hetrick, B. A. D., G. W. T. Wilson, and C. E. Owensby. "Mycorrhizal Influences on Big Bluestem Rhizome Regrowth and Clipping Tolerance." *Journal of Range Management* 43 (July 1990): 286–90.
Hoy, Jim. "Joseph McCoy and the Creation of the Mythic American West." In *John Brown to Bob Dole: Movers and Shakers in Kansas History*, edited by Virgil Dean. Lawrence: University Press of Kansas, 2006.
Igler, David. "Industrial Cowboys: Corporate Ranching in Late Nineteenth-Century California." *Agricultural History* 69 (Spring 1995): 201–15.
———. "Miller and Lux and the Transformation of the Far West, 1850–1920." *Pacific Historical Review* 69 (May 2000): 159–92.
Jager, Ronald B. "The Chisholm Trail's Mountain of Words." *Southwestern Historical Quarterly* 71 (July 1967): 61–68.
Kelly, Kevin. *What Technology Wants*. New York: Viking, 2010.
Klein, Maury. *The Life and Legend of Jay Gould*. Baltimore: Johns Hopkins University Press, 1986.
Klironomos, John N., Jenny McCune, Miranda Hart and John Neville. "The Influence of Arbuscular Mycorrhizae on the Relationship Between Plant Diversity and Productivity." *Ecology Letters* 3 (2000): 137–41.
Knapp, Joseph G. "A Review of Chicago Stock Yards History." *University Journal of Business* 2 (June 1924): 331–46.
Kress, W. John and Jeffrey K. Stine, eds. *Living in the Anthropocene: Earth in the Age of Humans*. Washington, DC: Smithsonian Institution, 2017.
Lawrence, Lee E. "The Wisconsin Ice Trade." *Wisconsin Magazine of History* 48 (Summer 1965): 257–67.
Love, Clara M. "History of the Cattle Industry in the Southwest." *Southwestern Historical Quarterly* 19 (April 1916): 370–99.
Lynn-Sherow, Bonnie. *Red Earth: Race and Agriculture in Oklahoma Territory*. Lawrence: University Press of Kansas, 2004.
Mayhall, Mildred P. *The Kiowas*. Norman: University of Oklahoma Press, 1987.
McClelland, Clarence P. "Jacob Strawn and John T. Alexander: Central Illinois Stockmen." *Journal of the Illinois State Historical Society* 34 (June 1941): 177–208.
McNeur, Catherine. *Taming Manhattan: Environment Battle in the Antebellum City*. Cambridge: Harvard University Press, 2014.
McShane, Clay, and Joel Tarr. *The Horse in the City: Living Machines in the Nineteenth Century*. Baltimore: Johns Hopkins University Press, 2007.
Miner, H. Craig. *A Most Magnificent Machine: America Adopts the Railroad, 1825–1862*. Lawrence: University Press of Kansas, 2010.
———. *Wichita: The Early Years, 1865–80*. Lincoln: University of Nebraska Press, 1982.
Ogle, Maureen. *In Meat We Trust: An Unexpected History of Carnivore America*. New York: Houghton Mifflin Harcourt, 2013.
O'Neill, Robert V. "Is It Time to Bury the Ecosystem Concept? (With Full Military Honors, of Course!)." *Ecology* 82 (December 2001): 3280–82.
Pace, Mildred Mastin. *Friend of Animals: The Story of Henry Bergh*. Ashland, KY: Jesse Stuart Foundation, 1995.

Peterson, Anne E. "Alexander Gardner in Review." *History of Photography* 34 (November 2010): 357–58.
Pollan, Michael. *The Omnivore's Dilemma: A Natural History of Four Meals*. New York: Penguin Books, 2006.
Ponting, Clive. *A Green History of the World: The Environment and the Collapse of Great Civilizations*. New York: St. Martin's Press, 1991.
Rainey, George. "Letters and Documents: The Chisholm Trail." *Southwestern Historical Quarterly* 44 (October 1940): 249–52.
Ranhofer, Charles. *The Epicurean: A Complete Treatise of Analytical and Practical Studies on the Culinary Art*. New York: Charles Ranhofer, 1894.
Ratajczak, Zak, Jesse B. Nippert, and Troy W. Ocheltree. "Abrupt Transition of Mesic Grassland to Shrubland: Evidence for Thresholds, Alternative Attractors, and Regime Shifts." *Ecology* 95 (September 2014): 2633–45.
Ratajczak, Zak, John M. Briggs, Doug G. Goodin, et al. "Assessing the Potential for Transitions from Tallgrass Prairie to Woodlands: Are We Operating beyond Critical Fire Thresholds?" *Rangeland Ecology & Management* 69 (July 2016): 280–87.
Redman, R. E., and E. G. Reekie. "Carbon Balance in Grasses." In *Grasses and Grasslands: Systematics and Ecology*, edited by James R. Estes, Ronald J. Tyrl, and Jere N. Brunken. Norman: University of Oklahoma Press, 1982.
Reichman, O. J. *Konza Prairie: A Tallgrass Natural History*. Lawrence: University Press of Kansas, 1987.
"The Relief of Broadway." *Harper's Weekly*, January 6, 1866, 3.
Renehan, Edward J., Jr. *Commodore: The Life of Cornelius Vanderbilt*. New York: Basic Books, 2009.
Reynolds, Heather L., Alissa Packer, James D. Bever, and Keith Clay. "Grassroots Ecology: Plant-Microbe-Soil Interactions as Drivers of Plant Community Structure and Dynamics." *Ecology* 84 (September 2003): 2281–91.
Rideing, William. "How New York Is Fed." *Scribner's Monthly* 14 (October 1877): 729–43.
Rollings, Willard Hughes. *Unaffected by the Gospel: Osage Resistance to the Christian Invasion 1672–1906: A Cultural Victory*. Albuquerque: University of New Mexico Press, 2004.
Ross, John. *The Papers of Chief John Ross*. Vols. 1 and 2. Edited by Gary E. Moulton. Norman: University of Oklahoma Press, 1985.
Rossel, John. "The Chisholm Trail." *Kansas Historical Quarterly* 5 (February 1936): 5–7.
Rotenstein, David S. "Hudson River Cowboys: The Origins of Modern Livestock Shipping." *Hudson Valley Regional Review* 19 (March 2002): 1–15.
Saey, Tina Hesman. "Longhorn Ancestry Traced to Asia." *Science News* 183 (May 4, 2013): 10.
Schnitzer, Stefan A., et al., "Soil Microbes Drive the Classic Plant Diversity–Productivity Pattern." *Ecology* 92 (February 2011): 296–303.
Sherow, James E. *The Grasslands of the United States: An Environmental History*. Santa Barbara, Calif.: ABC Clio, 2007.
———. "Water, Sun, and Cattle: The Chisholm Trail as an Ephemeral Ecosystem." In *Fluid Arguments: Five Centuries of Western Water Conflict*, edited by Char Miller. Tucson: University of Arizona Press, 2001.

Sherow, James E. and John Charlton. *Railroad Empire Across the Heartland: Rephotographing Alexander Gardner's Westward Journey*. Albuquerque: University of New Mexico Press, 2014.
Simard, Suzanne W. and Daniel M. Durall. "Mycorrhizal Networks: A Review of Their Extent, Fucntion, and Importance." *Canadian Journal of Botany* 82 (August 2004): 1140–65.
Sklar, Robert. "'Red River' Empire to the West." *Cinéaste* 9 (Fall 1978): 14–19.
Specht, Joshua. "'For the Future in the Distance': Cattle Trailing, Social Conflict, and the Development of Ellsworth, Kansas." *Kansas History: A Journal of the Central Plains* 40 (Summer 2017): 104–19.
Sternberg, Martha L. *George Miller Sternberg: A Biography by His Wife*. Chicago: American Medical Association, 1920.
Stromberg, Joseph. "What is the Anthropocene and Are We in It?" *Smithsonian Magazine*. (accessed June 3, 2016) http://www.smithsonian.com/science-nature/what-is-the-antropocene-and-are-we-in-it-164801414/?no-ist.
Surdam, David G. "The Antebellum Texas Cattle Trade across the Gulf of Mexico." *Southwestern Historical Quarterly* 100 (April 1997): 477–92.
Thomas, William G. *The Iron Way: Railroads, the Civil War, and the Making of Modern America*. New Haven: Yale University Press, 2011.
Traubel, Horace. *With Walt Whitman in Camden*. New York: Mitchell Kennerley, 1914.
Unrau, William E. "Joseph G. McCoy and Federal Regulation of the Cattle Trade." *Colorado Magazine* 43 (Issue 1, 1966): 32–43.
Utley, Robert M. "The Range Cattle Industry in the Big Bend of Texas." *Southwestern Historical Quarterly* 69 (April 1966): 419–41.
Valentine, K. A. "Distance from Water as a Factor in Grazing Capacity of Rangeland." *Journal of Forestry* 45 (October 1947): 749–54.
Van Patten, Edwin H. "A Brief History of David McCoy and Family." *Journal of the Illinois State Historical Society* 14 (April–July 1921): 122–27.
Vileisis, Ann. *Kitchen Literacy: How We Lost Knowledge of Where Food Comes from and Why We Need to Get It Back*. Washington, DC: Island Press, 2008.
"A Visionary on the Prairie: Joseph McCoy." *Journal of the West* 25 (January 1986): 22–27.
Wheeler, A. C. "On the Iron Trail." *Scribner's Monthly*, August 1876, 529–43.
White, Richard. *Railroaded: The Transcontinentals and the Making of Modern America*. New York: W. W. Norton, 2011.
Wilson, James A. "Cattlemen, Packers, and Government: Retreating Individualism on the Texas Range." *Southwestern Historical Quarterly* 74 (April 1971): 525–34.
Woolrich, Willis R., and Charles T. Clark. "Refrigeration." *Handbook of Texas Online*, accessed November 11, 2016, http://www.tshaonline.org/handbook/online/articles/dqr01.
Zieren, Gregory R. "A Century of Meatpacking and Packinghouse Labor in Chicago: A Review Essay." *Annals of Iowa* 49 (Spring 1989): 692.

# Index

*References to illustrations appear in italic type.*

Abilene, Kans.: beginnings of, 6, 25, 30–39, 45–47, 62–65, *78*, *83*; and cattle business, 40, 44, 107–11, 114, 134–37, 141–43, 156–59, 201–3, 225–26, 286; competition with, 153–55, 250–55, 265; economic growth of, 136–37; routes to, *116*; naming of, 30–33; and natural resources, 125–26, 128; and shift from cattle business, 113, 139, 162, 171, 255–64, 274, 284–85; and Texas fever, 151, 154–56, 165–67
accidents, 18–19, 266–67
Ackermann, C. W., 95, 134
Ainsworth, John, 220
Albany, N.Y., 107–8, 150, 152, 170
Alexander, John Tracey, 25, *74*, 142, 147, 149–50, 164, 167–68
Allen, Lewis, 163
Allen, Sam L., 52, 121
Allerton, Samuel, 19–20, 23
Allerton Stockyards, 19–25, 73, 130
allotment legislation, 216, 249
American Society for the Prevention of Cruelty to Animals (ASPCA), 26–27, 72
Anchor Line steamship company, 43, *78*, 133, 188, 270
Angus cattle, 119
animal cruelty, 26–29, 42, 72, 157–58, 165, 176
Apache Indians, 243, 281
Arapaho Indians (Southern Arapaho), 11, 104, 224, 238–40, 245–46, 249, 272
Argell, A. J., 101–2
Argell, E. L., 101–2

Aransas County, Tex., 119
Arkansas City, Kans., 252
Arkansas River, 87, 89, 127, *181*, 250, 252–53, 257–59
Armour, Philip, 12, 170, 190, 269
Arrasmith, A., 55
Atchison, Kans., 154
Atchison, Topeka, and Santa Fe Railroad (AT&SF), 31, 128, 251–55, 259–61, 271
Atlantic and Great Western Railroad (A&GW), 27, 42
Augur, C. C., 248
Austin, Tex., 113, 122

Bailey, Jack, 122, 148, 210–11
Banquete, Tex., 231
Barnes, J. J., 169
Baum, Charles N., 228–29
Baxter Springs, Kans., 57, 168–69, 236
Beede, Cyrus, 240–41
beef: chef preparation of, 130–31; high quality of, 115, 128, 131; low quality of, 28, 42, 50, 130; and refrigeration, 263–69; from sick cattle, 161
Bell, A. J., 154
Bell, William, 106, 259
Belugshe, Jane, 220
Bemis, C. C., 259
Bennett, Walter A., 262
Bennett, William J., 31, 52, 120–21
Bent, William, 241
Bergen, N. J., 27
Bergh, Henry, 26–28, 72, 157
Bethlehem, Pa., 219

329

Bexar County, Tex., 134
Big Bow, 222
Billings, Mont., 103–4
bison hunting, 221–25, 230–31
bison tour publicity stunt, 155–58, *175*
Black Beaver, *80*, 84–89
Blair, Newton, 63
Blaney, James V. Z., 160
blizzards, 10, 24, 173, 192–93, 204–7, 223, 256, 285
Board of Commissioners of Health, New York City, 16
Bogy, L. V., 229
boomers, 184, 214–16, 244, 249, 272, 285
Bosque County, Tex., 231
Boston, Mass., 26, 42, 135, 313n30
Bourbon County, Kans., 49
Brady, Mathew, 35
Brahmin cattle, 119
Brantford Township, Ontario, 165
Bray, Wilson, 262–63
Brazos River, 95, 113, 122, 164, 231
Briske, D. D., 280
Brodbent, C. S., 137, 139
Brown, Kate, 103–4
Brown, William, 61–62
Brown, Willis L., 276
Bryden, James, 254–55
Buck Creek, 223
Buffalo, N.Y., 27, 138, 150, 152, 163, 266
Buffalo State and Line Railroad, 27
Bureau of Animal Industry, 170–71, 177
Bureau of Indian Affairs, 87, 238–39, 248
Burkhart, John, 114
Burks, Amanda, *182*, 231–32
Burks, W. F., 231
Burnside, Ambrose, 151
Burrows, G. O., 135
Bushman, John, 88
Bushyhead, Dennis W., *183*, 212, 238, 240
Butler, George, 217
Butler, James, 219
Butler, Pleasant Burnell, 235
Butler County, Kans., 253

Cairo, Ill., 142, 145, 147, 160, 164–65
Caldwell, Kans., 240
Camden and Amboy Railroad (C&A), 23
Campbell, Bill, 156–57
Camp Colorado, 86
Camp Supply, 230. *See also* Fort Supply
Campville, N.Y., 146
Canada, and Texas fever, 142, 151, 153, 165

Canada Southern Railroad (CS), 266
Canadian River, 237
Capt, W. W., 123
Carré, Ferdinand, 261
Carroll, J. A., 273–74
Carroll, Jake, 156
Catharine Market, 14, 130–31, 294n2
cattle numbers: and Abilene, 107, 135–36, 141, 154; charts showing, 22, 24, 136; and Chicago, 41, 107; and Chisholm Trail, 55, 203; of deaths, 168, 207–8; and Indians, 212, 217, 220–21, 241–44; and Kansas, 135–36; and New York market, 23–25; and overseas transport, 44, 187; and Wichita, 254–55
cattle taxes, 212–15, 223, 235–39, 285
cattle trade: summary of, *172*, *174*, *190*; map of, *21*
Census Bureau, 11, 213, 285
Central Branch Union Pacific Railroad (CBUP), 154
Centralia, Ill., 145
Central Railroad of New Jersey (CNJ), 23
Champaign, Ill., 152
Champaign County, Ill., 147
Chandler, Zachariah, 244, 281
Chapman Creek, 156, 208
Chase County, Kans., 251
Chautauqua County, Kans., 55
Cherokee cattle, 11, 151, 166–67, 216–17
Cherokee Nation, 23, 57, 213–18, 220–21, 224–26, 236–40, 246, 285
Cherokee Neutral Lands, 55–56
Cherokee Outlet, 183, 212–14, 238–39, 245–46, 249, 254, 272
Cherokee Strip. *See* Cherokee Outlet
Cherokee Strip Live Stock Association (CSLSA), 240, 272
Chetopa, Kans., 236, 268
Cheyenne Indians (Southern Cheyenne), 11, 104, 224, 238–40, 245–49, 272
Chicago, Burlington, and Quincy Railroad (CB&Q), 157
Chicago, Ill., 19–20, 25–27, 40–43, 107–8, 129, 154–60, 268–70
Chicago Union Stockyards, 20, 27, 41–42, *73*, 149–51, 166, *190*, 269
Chickasaw Nation, 212, 217, 219–20, 234, 236, 244, 268
Chisholm, Jesse, *81*, 84, 87–89, 217
Chisholm Trail: beginnings of, 3, 80–81; and calendar, 112–15; ecosystem of, 44–45,

90–106, 113–15, 122–24, 282; and Indians, 11, 122–24, 236; maps of, *116*, *215*; and railroad, 32; route of, 82, 90, 101–3, 112–16, 236, 239–40, 294n1; and shift from cattle business, 11–12, 257, 268, 284; and Wichita, 31, 250–54
Choctaw Indians, 212, 217–21, 235
cholera, 16, 26
Chouteau, A. P., 88
Christian County, Ill., 58
Christie, David, 165–66
Chugwater, Wyo., 273
Cincinnati, Ohio, 151
Civil War, 7, 41, 49–53, 86–89, 129, 218–21, 228, 261
Clermont (Osage chief), 224
Cleveland, Grover, 249
climate, 10, 90–94, 97, 114, 117–19, 124–27, 132–33. *See also* temperatures; *specific weather events*
Coffman, Lot, 33
Colley, D. W., 241–42
Colorado, and cattle trade, 271–72
Colorado County, Tex., 145
Colorado River, 113
Comanche Indians, 11, 87–89, 212, 221–24, 229–30, 235–46, 280–82
Communipaw Abattoirs, 20, 23, 43, *73*, 149–52, *174*
Concordia, Kans., 206
Connors, John, 266–67
Convention of Cattle Commissioners, 1868, Springfield, Ill., 133–34, 142–43, 153, 159, 162–67
Convention of Cattlemen, St. Louis (1884), *189*, 272–76, 286
Convention of the National Live Stock Association, 1899, 3–6
Copley, Joseph, 106
Cornell University, 171
Corpus Christi, Tex., 119, 122, 231
Cottonwood Falls, Kans., 139, 251–52
Cottonwood River, 48
Courtright, H. H., 41
cowboys: definition of, 5, 283–84; lingo of, 293nn1–9; wages of, 135–36
Craig, James, 236
Crawford, Samuel J., 53–54, 63, 252–53
Creek Indians, 212, 216–17, 220, 236
Crittenden, Thomas, 273
Cude, W. F., 124
Cureton, W. E., 131

Daggett, E. M., 51
Dallas, Tex., 234
Danville, Ill., 229
Daugherty, James M., 56–57, 79
Daugherty, M. A., 5
Davidson, J., 222
Davis, John, 197–99
Davis, Martha Ann Powell, 197
Dawes Act of 1887, 249
Decatur, Ill., 197
Decatur County, Ill., 197
Delaware Indians, 80, 85–89, 240
Delmonico, Charles, 15
Delmonico, John, 15
Delmonico, Peter, 15
Delmonico's Restaurant, 15, 40, 71, 130–31, 247
Del Rio, Tex., 121
Denison, Tex., 265–68, 284
Denver, Colo., 3, 12, 25, 92,
Department of the Missouri, 245–46, 248
De Voe, Thomas F., 17
Devon cattle, 119, 217
Dickinson County, Kans., 36, 63, 107, 142, 255–56
dishonesty in cattle business, 137–39, 167
Dodge, J. R., 159–60
Dodge City, Kans., 122, 259–61, 268, 271–72, 315n70; and shift from cattle town, 261, 275–76
Douglas County, Kans., 55
Dow Creek, 48
Downton, W. J., 97–98
Drake, Ben, 123
Drew, Daniel, 137
drover, definition of, 284
Drovers Cottage, 38–39, *76*, 77, *83*, 110–11, 163
Durham cattle, 110, 119–20, 217, 240–41, 254, 283

Eagle Creek, 48
Eagle Pass, Tex., 117
Earle, A., 167
Earp, Wyatt, 260
East Liberty stockyards, 19–20, 147
Eaton, M., 164–65
ecotone, 278–79, 315n4
Edwards, Elisha, 148
Edwards, Harvey, 152
Edwards County, Kans., 260
Ehrlich, Paul, 171
Ellis, Kans., 256, 260

Ellis County, Kans., 260
Ellison, J. F., 134
Ellsworth, Kans., 113, 128, 192–94, 200, 207, 250–53, 256, 268
Ellsworth, William, 54, 57
Ellsworth County, Kans., 204, 208
El Niño, 93
El Reno, Okla., 89
Elwood, James, 220
Emerson, D. C., 145
Emory, William, 86–87
Emporia, Kans., 49, 61, 253, 265
England: demand for beef in, 8, 43, 115, 132–33, 160, 187–88, 269–71; and Texas fever, 9, 168
En-sa-te-her, 220
Erie Railroad, 137–38, 146, 266
Eureka, Kans., 57
Eureka Valley (Kans.), 110

Fant, Dillard R., 119–20
Farmer, W. H., 57
Farragut, David, 49
Fenton, Reuben, 16, 149–50, 152–53, 155
Few, Louisa, 220
Fiege, Mark, 284
Fisk, James, 137–38
Fitch, William, 149–50
"Five Civilized Nations," 11, 122, 212, 216–18, 220–21, 226, 244
Flint Hills, 109
Flowerpot Mound, 101
Ford County, Kans., 260
Fort Arbuckle, 85–87, 100
Fort Chadbourne, Tex. 86
Fort Cobb, 86–87
Fort Duncan, Tex. 117–19, 127
Fort Gibson, 88, 219
Fort Harker, Kans., 106
Fort Hays, Kans., 126–27, *173*, 204–7
Fort Larned, Kans., 11, 226–27
Fort Leavenworth, Kans., 48, 86–87, 248
Fort Lyon, Colo., 271
Fort Reno, 245
Fort Richardson, Tex., 117–19, 126–27, 229, 287–91
Fort Riley, Kans., 47, 100, 126–27, 195, 202, 205–7
Fort Scott, Kans., 57, 148, 219
Fort Sill, 11, 193, 223, 230, 243–44, 247, 279
Fort Supply, 248. *See also* Camp Supply
Fort Towson, 48
Fort Washita, 86

Fort Worth, Tex., 51, 113, 119, 231
Fort Zarah, Kans., 128
Forwood, William, 118–19, 287–88
Fossil Creek, 156
Franklin Market, 14
Frio County, Tex., 117
Fulton Market, 14, 262
Furlendorf, S. D., 280

Galloway cattle, 119
Galveston, Tex., 44, 146, 261–62, 264
gambling as metaphor, 6–7, 46, 111, 137, 140, 142–43, 286
Gamgee, John, 158, 160–61
Gardner, Alexander, 32–39, 76–78, 103
Gardner, James, 35
Geary, John W., 149
Gibson, Isaac, 224–25
Glasgow, Scotland, 43, 133, 269–70
Goliad, Tex., 50
Goliad County, Tex., 119, 233, 286
Gonzales, Tex., 119
Goodlet, John A., 33
Goodnight, Charles, 273
Gore, James W., 38, 76, 111
Gore, Louise "Lou," 38, 76, *77*, 111
Gould, Jay, 137–38
Gould, John, 163–64
Graham, S. F., 48
Grant, Ulysses S., 236
grass: and cattle health, 98–102, 109; as resource, 95–102, 112–17, 123–24, 128, 228, 233; types of, 92, 96–100, 126
grassland ecosystems, 10, 44, 85, 90–106, 125–26, 203, 227, 278–82. *See also* prairie fires
Gray, C. C., 119
Great Bend, Kans., 103, 127–28, 241, 259
Great Western Stock Yards, 39, *78*, 107, 111, 114, 125, 138–39, 141–42, 151, 284. *See also under* Abilene, Kans.
Great Western Trail, 239–40
Greenwood County, Kans., 56, 57
Gregory, John F., 4
Gregory, Lillian, 4
Grierson, Benjamin H., 11, 230–31
Griffith, A. G., 220
Guadalupe River, 113
Gypsum Creek, 202

Hackensack River, 146
Hancock, John L., 160
Hankins, J. M., 101

Hannibal, Mo., 266
Hannibal and St. Joseph Railroad (H&StJ), 41, 48, 54, 154
Hargus, J., 56–57
Harper, G. R., 48
Harris, Cyrus, 220
Harris, Elisha, 146, 149–50
Hatch, John P., 244–45, 247–48, 279–82
Havana, Cuba, 44, 263
Hawes, Arthur, 266–67
Hawn, Frederick, 33
Haworth, James M., 221–22, 243, 247
Hayes, Rutherford B., 151
Hays, Kans., 109, 126, 128
health inspectors, 146, 149–52, 160, 190, 267
Healy, Patrick, 221
Henry, T. C., 142, 256
Hereford cattle, 119, 283
Hersey, Eliza, 33, *75*
Hersey, Mariah, 33, 75
Hersey, Sylvia, 33
Hersey, Timothy F., 33, *75*, 142
Hickok, S. A., 121
Hidalgo County, Tex., 119
Hoboken, N.J., 18
Hoffman, John, 16
hogs, 14–15, 20, 23, 25, 85
Holliday, Cyrus K., 253
Holstein cattle, 119
Homestead Acts, 275
Horsford, Eban Norton, 42
Houston, Samuel Dunn, 194–95, 226
Houston, Tex., 52
Howard, H. P., 262
Hoy, Jim, 283
Hudson City, N.J., 146
Hudson River, 14, 20, 68
Hudson River Railroad (HR), 23, 138
Hughes, William, 273
Hugo, Kans., 208
Hunt, Philemon B., 222, 244–46
Hunter, R. D., 273
Hutchinson, Kans., 128

ice making, 261–63, 313n30. *See also* refrigeration
Illinois cattle market, 22–26, 129–30; and Texas fever, 147–52, 160–67
Illinois Central Railroad (IC), 27, 145, 164
Indianola, Tex., 263–64
Indians: and allotment legislation, 216, 249; and bison hunting, 221–25, 230–31; and cattle, 11, 122, 212, 213–18, 220–21, 226–31, 240–49, 272; and cattle taxes, 212–15, 223, 235–39, 285; and land, 214–16, 224–25, 228–31, 233–34; and pastoralism, 11, 240–49, 280–82; and rations, 44, 223, 226, 245–48; and tolls, 11, 233, 235–38. *See also names of specific tribe*
Indian Territory: leasing of land in, 183, 224, 238–41, 246–49, 272; map of cattle trade in, 215; traveling through, 232–37
Ingalls, John James, 97
interbreeding, 29, 119–20, 216–17, 283
Iroquois County, Ill., 145
Ithaca, N.Y., 171

Jackman, Bill, 234
Jackson, J. D., 232
Jackson County, Tex., 134, 192
Jacobs, Celia, 220
James, Martin, 220
Janeway, John, 204, 206
Jersey City, N.J., 18, 20, 24, 68, 72, 138, 174, 266–67
Jewett, W. T., 258
Johnson, Andrew, 15, 34
Johnson, Tom, 156
Johnson County, Kans., 55
Jones, Josiah, 38, 142
Joplin, Mo., 57
Junction City, Kans., 59, 62, 108, 153, 194–95, 197, 202, 206–7, 226, 264

Kansas City, Kans., 34, 62, 162
Kansas City, Mo., 239–40, 251, 262, 264, 268–69, 276–77, 285, 315n70
Kansas Pacific Railway (KP), 31, 39, 112–13, 128, 132, 138–39, 256, 264
Kansas River, 47–48
Kansas Stock Yards, 252
Kansas Supreme Court, 139
Kelly, Kevin, 103, 105
Kennedy, M., 122
Kicking Bird (Kiowa), 222, 230
King, Henry, 131–32
King, Richard, 122, 301n
Kinnaman, Josiah, 57
Kiowa Indians, 11, 87–89, 212, 221–24, 229–30, 240–48, 272, 280–82
Knight, Den, 232
Koch, Robert, 171
Kregan, Matilda, 18–19
Kutz, Elias, 18–19

Lamb, William, 63
La Niña, 93
Larkin, Arthur, 128
Las Animas, Colo., 271–72
Lauderdale, Jasper, 94
Lavaca County, Tex., 192, 193
Lawhon, Luther, 122
Lawrence, Kans., 87, 157, 208
Lawson, Thomas, 287
leasing of public land, 189, 273–76
Leavenworth, Henry, 85
Leavenworth, Jesse, 241–43
Leavenworth, Kans., 40–41, 55, 89, 135, 162, 264
Leedy, John, 285
Leland, Charles, 103
Leona River, 120
Lincoln, Abraham, 15, 25, 35, 284
Lincoln, George B., 149
Linn County, Kans., 56
Lipe, D. W., 212
Little Arkansas River, 253
Little Bear (Osage chief), 224
Little Ice Age, 91
Little Robe (Cheyenne), 248
Liverpool, England, 270
livestock inspection, 125, 143, 166, 190
Loch, Abraham, 18
Lockhart, Tex., 59, 156, 210, 225
Locust Grove, Okla., 218
London, England, 8–9, 28, 43, 115, 132, 269–70. *See also* England
Long, D. B., 208, 256
Loring, L. V., 207
Love, Bob, 235
Lowe, Thaddeus S. C., 263–64
Lucas, E., 250–51
Lyon County, Kans., 47, 48, 49, 148
Lyon Creek Valley, 148

Macon County, Ill., 152
Madison, Thomas C., 47
Madison County, Kans., 48
Majors, Alexander, 5
Maltby, Frank, 247
Manhattan, Kans., 93–94, 100, 110, 194
Mann, M., 169
Marcy, Randolph, 85
Marfa, Tex., 232
Marshall, Tex., 51
Martin, George, 195, 197
Martindale, Tex., 56
Matamoros, Mexico, 261

Mathis, T. H., 119
Maunder, Edward Walter, 90–91
McCann, Adam, 220
McClung, Zarah, 258–59
McCoy, Caroline "Carrie," 285
McCoy, Florence, 4, 276–77
McCoy, James, 6, 13, 25, 39, 60, 64–65, 70, 78, 84, 110–11, 138–39, 154, 157, 286
McCoy, Jane, 286
McCoy, Joseph, 66, 70, 78; career summary of, 3–10, 284–86; death of, 277–78; family of, 4, 67, 276–77, 285–86; on livestock industry, 3–6; as livestock inspector, 285; as tax collector, 238–39, 285
McCoy, Mary "Mamie," 4, 159, 276
McCoy, Sarah Epler, 4, 67, 159, 285
McCoy, Virgil, 285
McCoy, William, 6, 13–14, 23–25, 60, 70, 134, 138, 156, 285
McCrary, George, 244
McCulley, J. S., 257
McCulloch, Henry E., 86
McCusker, Philip, 229
McPherson, Joseph, 20
Mead, Agnes, 89
Mead, James R., 89, 250–54, 279, 282
meat-packing companies, 11–12, 170, 190, 264, 269–72, 284–85, 315n70
Medicine Lodge, Kans., 87
Medicine Lodge Creek, 84
Medicine Lodge Treaty (1867), 221–22, 243
Metropolitan Board of Health, New York City, 14–20, 26, 42–43, 146, 149–51, 155, 163
Meyer, Matthew, 18–19
Miles, John D., 245–46
Miller, Benjamin, 240
Miller, James F., 119
Miller, Joaquin, 199
Mills, G. W., 124, 210
Mississippi River, 50–51, 145–47, 160
Missouri, Kansas, and Texas Railroad (MK&T or Katy), 236, 265–66
Missouri Pacific Railroad (MoPac), 41, 56, 141
Missouri River, 41, 48, 54
Missouri River, Fort Scott, and Gulf Railroad, 169, 236
Mitchell, W. G., 230
Mobeetie, Tex., 201
Mobile, Ala., 50, 263
Morgan County, Ill., 25
Morris, G., 86
Morris, Moreau, 146, 151–52, 163

Morris, Nelson, 269–71
Morris County, Kans., 251
Morse, R. S., 265
Mound City, Kans., 148, 304n21
Mud Creek, 33, 37, 62, 235
Muhl, Andrew, 261
Murdock, Marshall, 286
Murdock, Victor, 278, 286
mycorrhizae, 98–99
Myers, John Jacob, 59–60, 225

National Stockyards, New York City, 43
national trail, hope for, 273–75
Nave, Andrew, 218–19
Nave, Jane Ross, 218–20
Neosho River, 48
New Braunfels, Tex., 113
New Jersey Stock Yard and Market Company, 20, 23
New Orleans, La., 49–52, 142, 146, 263–65
Newton, Kans., 253–54
New York and Erie Railroad (Erie), 23
New York and Harlem Railroad (NY&H), 23
New York and New Haven Railroad (NY&NH), 23
New York Central Railroad (NYC), 138
New York City: and cattle market, 8, 13–19, 22–26, *68–69*, 134–35, 163; charts showing cattle market of, 22, 24; and demand for beef, 129–30; and refrigeration, 263–70; and Texas fever, 150–51, 154, 163
Niagara Falls, 138
Nicholson, William, 227
Nimmo, Joseph, 121
Ninnescah River, 172
Nolan, Nicholas, 223
Northern Pacific Railway Company (NP), 104
North River (now Hudson River), 14, 18
Nueces County, Tex., 231
Nueces River, 122

Oakes, T. F., 112–13, 128
Ogallala, Nebr., 226–27
Oglesby, Richard J., 25, 152–53, 163
Oklahoma City, Okla., 123
O'Neill, Robert V., 104, 282
Ontario Board of Agriculture, 151
Orvis, Joseph U., 25
Osage Indians, 11, 88, 212, 224–25, 228–29, 235–41, 252–53
overseas shipping. *See* ships and cattle transport

overwintering, 103, *179*, 203–4; and Texas fever, 10, 109–10, 114–15, 118, 127, 144, 166–67, 191–92
Owl Creek, 56

panic of 1873, 74, 267–68, 285
Parker, Isaac C., 214
Parker, Quanah, 222
Park Hill, Okla., 218–19
pastoralism, 11, 240–49, 280–82
Patton, Robert, 220
Patton, William, 220
Pawnee County, Kans., 260
Paw-nee-no-pashe, Joseph, 235–36
Payne, David, *184*, 214–16, 249, 272, 285
Payson, Henry, 150
Pease River, 223
Pendleton, Ore., 285
Pennsylvania Railroad (PRR), 20, 147
Perry, John D., 34–35, 40, 64–65, 104–6, 138–39
Peters, Thomas, 253
Pettus, J. E., 233, 286
Philadelphia, Pa., 20, 262, 270
photography, 32–39
Pierce, W. H., 226
Piper, Edward, 152
Pitt, Samuel, 56
Pittsburgh, Pa., 19–20, 147–49, 155
Pleasant Hill, Kans., 56
Polk, F. M., 123, 237
Pond Creek, 235
Poole, Joseph, 166
Pope, John, 223, 245–46
Potter, J. H., 248
Powder Horn, Tex., 52, 121
Powell, John Wesley, 197, 276
prairie fires, 10, 58, 96, 99–101, 109, *178*, 191–204, 230, 280–81
Prairie Lea, Tex., 101
Preemption Act, 275
Presidio County, Tex., 232
Price, Hiram, 239, 245–46
Price, Sterling, 220
prices of beef and cattle, 8, 50–52, 60, 108, 111, 131, 134–36, 156, 217, 227, 255, 267, 313n25
profitability, 3, 8, 107–11, 129, 134–37, 263; and annual returns, 15, 25, 136, 163; and exports, 270–71; and income, 137; and losses, 114, 142, 168, 192–94, 203–4; and profit margins, 135–36; and railroads, 138–39, 259; and sales, 135, 156, 217, 227, 267; table showing, 136. *See also* prices of beef and cattle

Pryor, Ike T., 234
Pumpkin Creek, 228

Quapaw Nation, 236
quarantines, 9, 146, 155; and laws for, 61–63, 113, 147–48, 250–52, 259, 271, 275–76. *See also* Texas fever
Quincy, Ill., 41

railroads: and Chisholm Trail, 103–6; rise of, 31–35, 40–42; and stockyards, 19–20, 23, *72*, *83*
rainfall, 47, 53, 93–94, 125–27, 133, 196, 302; and cattle health, 99–101
ranchman, definition of, 284
Randall, George M., 245–46
Ranhofer, Charles, 15, 71, 130–31
Rankin, T. S., 265–68, 284
Rauch, John, 163

rations, 44, 223, 226, 245–48
Red Cloud Agency, Dakota Territory, 226–27
Red River, 112–13, 122–23, 192, 221–23, 233, 237, 245, 273
Red River Crossing, 231, 235
Red River Station, 112–13
Red River War, 221–22
refrigeration, 43–44, 133, 170, *188*, 261–69. *See also* ice making
Remington, Frederic, 178
Reno County, Kans., 259
Renwick, Seymour G., 216
Republican River, 47, 197
restaurants. *See* Delmonico's Restaurant
Rice, E. W., 220
Richardson, M. E., 160
Rideing, William, 130
Ridley, Nimrod, 148
Riley County, Kans., 202
rinderpest, 28–29, 149, 160
Rio Grande, 117, 120
river crossings, 53, 113, *181*
Roaring Creek, 193
Robinson, Charles, 49
Robuck, E. A. "Berry," 209
Rock Creek, 55
Rockport, Tex., 119
Rogers, C. M., 119
Rogers, Dud, 210
Ross, Daniel, 218
Ross, Edmund, 224
Ross, Elizabeth, 218

Ross, James, 219
Ross, John, 218–19
Rush County, Kans., 260
Rush Creek, 192
Russell, Ed, 274–75
Rust, C. H., 113

Salamanca, N.Y., 150
Salina, Kans., 62, 151, 153–54, 199
Saline County, Kans., 202
Saline River, 156, 202
Salt Creek, 201
Salt Lake City, Utah, 135
San Antonio, Tex., 52, 86, 95, 113, 120–21, 134, 261
San Bernardino, Calif., 131
San Francisco, Calif., 131
Sangamon County, Ill., 152
San Marcos, Tex., 113
San Marcos River, 134
Santa Fe depot, Wichita, Kans., *186*
Santa Fe Trail, 31, 33, 87
Satanta, 11, 230–31
Saunders, George O., 214, 237–38
Saunders, W. D., 50–51
Scammon, J. G., 25
Schmitt, Philipp, 170
Schmitt, Theresia, 170
Schultz, Jackson, 16–17, 20, 23
Scott, G. W., 209
Sedalia, Mo., 48, 55–59, 228
Sedgwick County, Kans., 252–53, 257–58, 279; surveying of, *185*
Seminole Indians, 212, 217
Se-no-wa, 220
Settle, Willie, 220
Shawnee County, Kans., 48
Shawnee Indians, 85, 88, 240
Shawnee Trail, 48
sheep, 14–15, 20, 23, 50, 121, 270
Sheridan, Philip, 244, 246, 249
Sherman, John Brill, 20, 42
Sherman, William Tecumseh, 242, 273, 281
ships and cattle transport, 43–44, 78, 133, 187–88, 270–71. *See also* steamboats and cattle transport
Shockly, William, 48
Shouse, Jouett, 276
Shreveport, La., 51–52
Sigerson, William, 252–53
Simpson, John, 273
Sioux Indians, 242

Slaughter, C. C., 273
slaughterhouse steam treatment, 17–18
Smeins, F. E., 280
Smith, Edmund Kirby, 86
Smith, E. P., 221
Smith, John Q., 227
Smith, Stephen, 146
Smith, Theobald, 10, 170–71, *177*
Smoky Hill, 197
Smoky Hill River, 33, 37, 47, 128, 155
Smoky Hill Trail, 33, 37
Society for the Prevention of Cruelty to Animals (SPCA). *See* American Society for the Prevention of Cruelty to Animals (ASPCA)
Solomon City, Kans., 62
Solomon River, 201
Solomon Valley, 207–8
South Canadian River, 124
Spanish fever. *See* Texas fever
Spotted Horse (Cheyenne), 248
Sprague, Elizabeth, 241
Springer, John W., 5
Springfield, Ill., 6, 13, 25, 60, 67, 142, 152–53, 159, 162–63
Springfield, Mass., 266
stampedes, 95, 123–24, *180*, 209–10
Stapler, Mary, 218
Starr, George, 16, 18–19
steamboats and cattle transport, 31–32, 51, 145, 165, *176*, *188*. *See also* ships and cattle transport
Sternberg, George, 195–97, 200
Sternberg, Levi, 200–204, 256
Sternberg, Margaret, 200
Stiles, Henry Reed, 164
St. Joseph, Mo., 48, 54–55, 57
St. Louis, Mo., 31, 38, 40–41, 64, 138, 154, 157, 162, 189, 273
stockman, definition of, 5, 283–84
stockyards and slaughterhouses, conditions in and near, 13–19, 26–27, 42–43, *69*
Stone Calf (Cheyenne), 248
Stover, Charles, 39
Stover, Janet, 39
Suggs, W. W., 58–59, 246
Sumner County, Kans., 101, 257–58; surveying of, 82
Sun Boy, 223
sunspots, 90–91, 94
surveying land, 33, *82*, 88, *185*
Swan, Alexander, 273

Swift, Gustavus, 12, 170, 190, 269

Tahlequah, Okla., 218
Tall Chief (Osage), 224
Tarrant County, Tex., 119
Taylor, Jim, 193
Taylor, L. D., 234–35
Taylor Grazing Act (1934), 276
Teller, Henry, 239
temperatures, 47, 117–19, 127, 196, 204–7, 287–91, 302n45. *See also* climate
Texas cattle, northern vs. southern, 115, 117, 120–22
Texas fever, 29, *174*; beginnings of, 29, 47–49, 53; cause of, 118, 143–45, 171, 177; and cautiousness of residents, 48–49, 55–58, 62–63, 148, 168; conjectures about, 9, 159–70; and epidemic of 1868, 9, 142–71, *174*, 191; investigation of, 160–61, 167, 170–71, 177; and laws, 49, 57–58, 152–53, 166–69; prevention of, 10, 109–10, 115, 118, 127, 147–50, 171; settlements for losses from, 107, 110–11, 255–56; skepticism about, 142, 147, 169–70
Texas Livestock Association, 119
Thomas, J. M., 145–46
Thompson, Charles, 33, 62–63
Thompson, J. C., 210
Thompson, William H., 276
thunderstorms, 100, 192, 209–11
ticks, 9–10, 118, 144–45, 159–61, 164–65, 283; life cycle of, 143–44; removal of, 171
Toledo, Ohio, 266
Toledo, Wabash, and Western Railroad (TW&W), 146, 266
tolls, 11, 233, 235–38
Tolono, Ill., 145, 160, 164–68
Topeka, Kans., 253, 286
Towanda, Kans., 89, 253
Transcontinental Railway Act, 34
Travis County, 52
Trego County, Kans., 260
Tregunna, E., 97–98
Trinity River, 113, 231
Tufts, John, 239
Tupper, Tullius C., 229
Turkey Creek, 55
Turner, Frederick Jackson, 91
Twiggs, D. E., 86
Tyler, George, 41
Tyndale, Simon, 25

Union Pacific Railroad (UP), 61–62, 94, 111, 132, 202
Union Pacific Railway, Eastern Division (UPED), 25, 32–40, 44–46, 58–64, 103–6, 110–11, 153–58
union stockyards, rise of, 19–20, 23
United States and West India Meat and Fruit Company, 262–63
University of Illinois, 198
urban demand for beef, 8, 15, 19, 22–26, 115, 128–33, 135, 153, 161–62, 267
US Department of Agriculture, 10, 159, 167, 170–71, 177
US Department of the Interior, 238–41
Uvalde, Tex., 117, 121

Valentine, K. A., 95
Vandalia, Ill., 145
Vanderbilt, Cornelius, 137–38
Van Horn, R. T., 239
VanSickle, W. H., 259
Verdigris River, 48, 228

Walls, Ben, 220
Ward, Marcus Lawrence, 149
War Department, 167
Warren County, Ind., 145–46
Washington Market, New York City, 13–17, *68*, 138, 267–68
Washita River, 124, 192, 248
water sources, 8, 88, 94–96, 102, 124
Waterville, Kans., 154
Watie, Stand, 218
Waverly, Mo., 148
Weehawken, N.J., 138
Welch, S. Morgan, 148
Wentworth, John, 118

West, George, 194
West, Sol, 134, 192–94
West Lebanon, Ind., 146
wheat farming, 256–60
Wheeler, Andrew Carpenter, 30–31
Whipple, A. W., 88–89
White Cowbird, 223
White Hair (Osage chief), 224
White Lake, N.Mex., 209
White Shield (Southern Cheyenne chief), 248
Whitman, Walt, 35
Wichita, Kans.: and cattle trade, 31, 103, 121, 127, 134, 169, *186*, 250–55, 279, 284–86; land before settlement of, 81, 87, *181*, *185*; and shift from cattle town, 257–60, 268, 274–75
Wichita and Southwestern Railway Company (W&SW), 253
Wichita Indians, 221–22, 249
Wichita Town Company, 253
Wier, Christopher, 17
Wildcat Creek, 202
Wilkison, Samuel, 60–61, 110, 217
Williams, John, 152
wintering. *See* overwintering
Wirz, Henry, 35
Withers, Mark A., 156–57, 210, 236–37
Withers, Richard, 94
Wolf Creek, 124
Wolff, Simon, 220
Wood, Sam, 251–52
Woodville, Miss., 50
Worrall, Henry, 83, 179
Wortham, James, 87
Wright, Robert, 271, 275

Yates, Richard, 106

www.ingramcontent.com/pod-product-compliance
Lightning Source LLC
Chambersburg PA
CBHW051942200225
**22283CB00001B/1**